OVERDETERMINED

Overdetermined

HOW INDIAN ENGLISH LITERATURE
BECOMES ETHNIC, POSTCOLONIAL,
AND ANGLOPHONE

Ragini Tharoor Srinivasan

Columbia University Press
New York

Columbia University Press
Publishers Since 1893
New York   Chichester, West Sussex

Copyright © 2025 Columbia University Press
All rights reserved

Library of Congress Cataloging-in-Publication Data
Names: Srinivasan, Ragini Tharoor, author.
Title: Overdetermined : how Indian English literature becomes ethnic, postcolonial, and anglophone / Ragini Tharoor Srinivasan.
Description: New York : Columbia University Press, 2025. | Includes bibliographical references and index.
Identifiers: LCCN 2024050778 (print) | LCCN 2024050779 (ebook) | ISBN 9780231218856 (hardback) | ISBN 9780231218863 (trade paperback) | ISBN 9780231562461 (ebook)
Subjects: LCSH: Mukherjee, Bharati—Criticism and interpretation. | Bhagat, Chetan—Criticism and interpretation. | Chaudhuri, Amit, 1962- —Criticism and interpretation. | Lahiri, Jhumpa—Criticism and interpretation. | Identity (Psychology) in literature. | Group identity in literature. | East Indians in literature. | East Indian Americans in literature. | LCGFT: Literary criticism.
Classification: LCC PR9499.3.M77 Z94 2025 (print) | LCC PR9499.3.M77 (ebook) | DDC 820.9/954—dc23/eng/20250108

Cover design: Julia Kushnirsky
Cover image: Shutterstock

GPSR Authorized Representative: Easy Access System Europe, Mustamäe tee 50, 10621 Tallinn, Estonia, gpsr.requests@easproject.com

One of the things . . . I believe one must do is the persistent critique of what one cannot not want.

GAYATRI CHAKRAVORTY SPIVAK

Disavowal is not merely a principle of negation or elision; it is a strategy for articulating contradictory and coeval statements of belief.

HOMI BHABHA

For what is crucial to humanistic thought . . . is that it is a gesture of resistance and critique.

EDWARD SAID

Contents

Preface   ix

Introduction: Identity and Other Open Secrets   1

CHAPTER 1
What Was Multiethnic Literature?
Or, Bharati Mukherjee Doesn't Have an Indian Accent   37
[My Institutional Position]   37
[Syllabus] English Literature with an Accent: ENGL 347   39
[Accented Reading]   43

CHAPTER 2/RECESS 1
You Wouldn't Say That to Gayatri Spivak   71
[My Institutional Position]   71
[Recess]   73

CHAPTER 3
When the Anglophone Reads "Like Hindi":
Or, On Not Teaching Chetan Bhagat   84
[My Institutional Position]   84
[Syllabus] Against English, or, The Anglophone and Its Critics: ENGL 788   85
[Accented Reading]   89

CHAPTER 4/RECESS 2

The Ambivalence of Homi Bhabha's Discourse   119

[My Institutional Position]   119

[Recess]   120

CHAPTER 5

Fictions of Divergence:
Or, Amit Chaudhuri Doesn't Write the Postcolonial   131

[My Institutional Position]   131

[Syllabus] Literatures of Return: ENGL 396A   133

[Accented Reading]   137

CHAPTER 6/RECESS 3

The Idea of Edward Said   166

[My Institutional Position]   166

[Recess]   167

CHAPTER 7

A Desire Called the Post-Anglophone:
Or, On Not Being Jhumpa Lahiri   179

[My Institutional Position]   179

[Syllabus] The World and South Asia: ENGL 222   182

[Accented Reading]   186

Afterword   215
Acknowledgments   223
Notes   227
Bibliography   275
Index   301

Preface

Before I wrote this book, I was determined not to.

I was an undergraduate student of critical theory and cultural studies in a US university in the first decade of the 2000s. I was a "literature" major, and I was trained by a generation of poststructuralists working after what Christopher Lee has called the "post-identity" turn.[1] I thought that an Indian American who chose to work on Indian English literature would be capitulating to the imperative to "know and write the self" that haunts scholars of non-Western cultural production, especially diasporic subjects and women of color. I wrote a self-reflexive, embattled undergraduate thesis on Rey Chow's seminal 2002 book, *The Protestant Ethnic and the Spirit of Capitalism*, in which Chow elaborates the "process (identitarian, existential, cultural, or textual) in which those who are marginal to mainstream Western culture are expected . . . to resemble and replicate the very banal preconceptions that have been appended to them."[2] I had already given in many times to this self-objectifying process of "coercive mimeticism." Beginning in the 1990s, I had been a regular columnist for a Bay Area–based Indian American magazine called *India Currents*. After college, I became its chief editor.

By the time I started working on a PhD in the interdisciplinary humanities, I believed I had learned the lessons I set out to unlearn when I moved, about-face, from the theoretical critique of ethnic representation I had undertaken as an undergraduate to its community-focused praxis and production in my work as a magazine editor. There was a vast discursive terrain that was neither strictly complicit in liberal and neoliberal multiculturalist diversity politics nor consistently producing antiracist solidarities and progressive coalitions across caste and class lines. Our magazine's content was messy, contradictory, and shot through with the competing desires of writers, readers, and editors. It was variously "Indian," "Indian American," "South Asian," "diasporic," and "ethnic"—and it put pressure on each of those terms.

I wanted to move on from Indian texts; at the same time, I could no longer comfortably level the same critiques of ethnic cultural production. On top of that, graduate school presented me with a new set of texts and demands to resist: those of postcolonial literature. I knew that if I became yet another Indian postcolonialist, I risked being read as a "wannabe Spivak." I risked it anyway—for the same reasons that black feminist scholars in US academe variously accept, revise, and resist the demand that, in Jennifer Nash's words, they "embody the analytic" of intersectionality.[3]

I wrote a dissertation titled "After New India," which charted my pursuit of New India's Anglophone literature as object, as well as generic transformations in contemporary Indian English literature that were responsive to the New India discourse. Each sentence of the dissertation was ambivalent. "This is not the dissertation I intended to write," I began. "In fact, I tried hard not to write this dissertation, even while I was writing it." It was a version of a sentence I'd written two years earlier in a review of Jhumpa Lahiri's *The Lowland*: "Before beginning graduate school, I promised myself that I would never write about Jhumpa Lahiri."[4]

So how did I end up writing about Lahiri and, for that matter, Chetan Bhagat, Amit Chaudhuri, and Bharati Mukherjee, to name the writers of Indian English literature whose work is centrally addressed in this book? Over the past decade, I have assumed precisely the position that I have also continually tried to repudiate. I have been hailed as a subject who has to deal with a certain kind of object: an object I resemble in identitarian terms. I was never able to say no to this hailing, to ignore the interpellation, to keep walking down the street away from Althusser's finger-pointing policeman.[5]

Just as Chow predicted.

And even though I knew better.

This book is about what happened after.

In 2016, the dissertation that I tried not to write became my entrance ticket into the US professoriate. I was a finalist for three assistant professorships in English, advertised as jobs in Global Anglophone Literature, Literature and Media of the Anglophone Global South, and Twentieth- and Twenty-First-Century Anglophone World Literature. Taken together, all but one finalist for these positions was of Indian origin. None of the jobs had been advertised as intended for an Indian working on Indian literature, but each was ultimately filled by a candidate who fit that bill.[6] They knew. We candidates knew. What did we know? That the Anglophone is a strategic, market-driven renomination of the postcolonial, for one.[7] That the South Asian example generally and Indian example specifically play an outsized role in postcolonial studies, for another.[8] And perhaps also a version of what Tilottama Rajan wrote in the early 2000s: "Indians, we can assume, will work on Indian writing, generally in English. Of course, they are not forbidden to work on Shelley or Dickinson, but they stand little chance of being hired, whereas if they work in the right areas they can become like Spivak or Bhabha."[9]

In 2016, I was hired as an English department's "global Anglophonist."

In 2017, I joined another English department, where I was legible as a "postcolonialist."

I had become an Indian American English professor, whose writing and teaching participate in the construction of ethnographic images of India, South Asia, and Asia from within the English literary studies classroom in US academe.

Then, COVID. This is not a pandemic book, but it would not have been written in quite this way if not for the occasion of the coronavirus pandemic. This book centers a classroom that I did not actually enter for many of the semesters during which I was writing and revising it. Some sections of this book imagine my standing in the flesh before students whom in fact I saw only virtually in two-by-two-inch squares onscreen from a bedroom closet of my house in Tucson, Arizona, where, in March 2020, I set up what would be my primary workspace until May 2022.

I admit that I did not miss the in-person classroom during those months. I was disillusioned with my job and ashamed of my disillusionment. Even before the pandemic, I felt distanced from my students and colleagues. I was anxious for undergraduate students who were taking on tremendous debt and trying to balance weighty, competing responsibilities to work and school. I was worried for graduate students who were underprepared for graduate-level work yet tasked with teaching multiple undergraduate classes each semester—all while absorbing and deflecting delegitimating discourses about the value of the humanities, with dismal job prospects to boot. I was frustrated, too, with my then-department's conservative English literature program, which was primarily organized around the teaching of American and British literatures, with scant attention, I felt, being given to non-Western texts.

In fall 2020, I was eligible for "junior research leave": one semester without teaching to focus on the book I would need to satisfy the requirements for tenure. Finally, I thought with relief, I could put classroom concerns aside. I looked afresh at my dissertation on the literature of New India and to my abortive attempts at refashioning that work into a book. The joke was on me. Each attempt at knowing something about the Indian English literary objects in question was clearly anchored in my experiences of having tried to teach that literature, by my expectations of and aspirations for teaching, by my specific institutional positions, and by my pedagogical experiments, misfires, desires, and fears.

I hadn't researched literature in order to then teach it, I realized. I had been teaching literature as a proxy for researching it.

To put that realization in different terms, I began my professional training as a graduate student with the same questions about structures of ethnic protest, native informancy, and identity that I now pursue in this book. These questions had their genesis in my undergraduate education and work as editor of an ethnic magazine. But I did not have satisfactory material with which to pursue them until I became a professor. Teaching Asian American and South Asian Anglophone literatures as a member of the English faculty at three US universities raised and answered questions for me that reading and analyzing the same literatures—however closely, however critically—never did. This, I suggest, is because it is in the teaching and the writing, in the address to the student and to the reader, that literature becomes intelligible as an object of study in the first place.

Accordingly, the geographic and institutional contexts of this book's writing and its embeddedness in US academe cannot be overstated.

Growing up in Calcutta, India, in the 1970s, my mother and her peers at an English-medium convent school read "from Beowulf to Virginia Woolf" in classrooms of Indian students led by Indian teachers.[10] The institution of English literary studies in the former Commonwealth was well established, and my mother's teachers taught with an army behind them.[11] They didn't need to negotiate their identitarian resemblance to or interpellation by the texts they taught, because they were teaching the Canon (through syllabi "so canonical as to warm the hearts of conservative culture warriors in the USA").[12] They were also pointedly inducting Indian students into a tradition of knowledge adjacent to the technocratic Nehruvian project of scientific advancement and modernization via English.

By the early 2000s, this state of affairs in Indian education had shifted. As Akshya Saxena recounts, English departments in Indian universities began to revamp their curricula, hoping to "undo the damage of colonial education practices and make English literary studies more relevant—less alienating—to the postcolonial Indian student." The addition of empire-writing-back-type fare (read: Salman Rushdie and co.) diversified what Saxena and her classmates at the University of Delhi were reading but not how they were reading it: as a "colonial compulsion" expressed in the work of "upper-caste writers." English was made newly distant from India as students returned "anxiously" to "the colonial origin story."[13]

The story I'm telling in this book about Indian English literature's itineraries in contemporary US academe runs in parallel to Saxena's. The same "empire-writing-back" fare reads differently in the United States than it does in India, as it emerges into a different history of reading and reception. My American university students, unlike students at the University of Delhi, do not only or primarily read a writer like Rushdie as a subverter of imperial codes but also inevitably as a medium through which to access India, Indian subjects, Indian experiences, and Indian lifeworlds. Moreover, ethnic and postcolonial literary studies in US academe remain unevenly institutionalized and reliant upon having teachers in the classroom who, to cite Nash again, embody the analytics on offer.

In the 2010s, I found myself teaching Lahiri and Rushdie in Reno, Nevada, and Tucson, Arizona, because ethnic and postcolonial literatures are my chosen research fields. But it is also true that I chose to work in these fields because they are marginal in English, marginal like me, which is another way of saying that I was "not in a position of choice in this dilemma."[14]

The "I" who speaks in this book is thus a contemporary variant of a familiar, historically specific figure. The familiar figure is the Indian teacher from Calcutta who doesn't stay in India to teach English but rather moves to the United States in the decades after the Immigration and

Nationality Act of 1965, where she is not expected to work on Woolf anymore but instead becomes a purveyor of postcolonialism. To recall R. Radhakrishnan's "Aha!" moment from the mid-1990s: "The same scholars and intellectuals who were teaching Keats and Shelley back home are the ones who are teaching postcoloniality away from home. It is the same interpellation working in both cases: the one the flip side of the other."[15] The contemporary variant is the "I" who was born in the United States in the mid-1980s and who has never taught Keats or Shelley. The interpellation this "I" experienced was that of an American ethnic subject compelled to perform her investment in an inherited archive by reckoning with the postcolonial text.

The chapters to follow address this inherited archive and its cast of overdetermined characters: a group of writers and theorists who, as Gautam Premnath once told me, "furnish the rooms" I move through. Mukherjee, Bhagat, Chaudhuri, Lahiri. Said-Bhabha-Spivak: "the Holy Trinity of colonial-discourse analysis."[16] These are writers by whom I've been hailed in particular institutional contexts, who have variously written about people like me (nominally, Indians) or the place I come from (nominally, India) and whose texts I have taught or refused to teach, which means that I have already enlisted them in acts of pedagogical and critical informancy.

In a way, I don't really want to write about them. Yet that is precisely why I have been moved to undertake close consideration of the critical discourse on their texts. As Chaudhuri observes, aversion can turn into devotion; dismissal of a text might well be followed by one's becoming consumed by it. "What's bored us might begin to obsess us," he writes. "What seemed important might, one day, lose its interest."[17]

I started writing this book in the spring of my sophomore year at Duke University, when I took a class on South Asian women's diasporic literature. I started writing it again in my senior year of college when I read *The Protestant Ethnic* and responded with my own ethnic protest. I started writing it anew in graduate school at UC Berkeley when I attempted to quit literary studies for the anthropology of India. I continued writing this book when I was hired as a Global Anglophonist at the University of Nevada, Reno, and then again at the University of Arizona, where I taught postcolonial theory, and most recently at Rice University, where I am affiliated with transnational Asian studies. It is also true that I started writing this book when my mother encouraged me to pen a personal essay for a contest called "Growing Up Asian in America." I was ten years old, and my essay was titled "Why I Never Became a Girl Scout."

What I'm trying to say is that it's resistance and disavowal and informancy and protest all the way down for me. And that while this is not the book I once intended to write, I've been writing it ever since I started writing, and I've structured it this way, with these particular literary examples contextualized within these particular institutional scenes and in relation to these particular syllabi so that it's entirely clear why I couldn't have written anything else.

OVERDETERMINED

Introduction

Identity and Other Open Secrets

This book takes as provocation an open secret, a phenomenon in English literary studies that is both widely observed and taken for granted, as well as strenuously undertheorized and understudied: the pervasive identitarian correspondence of scholar-subject and studied object in minority literary fields in US academe.

It is also a book about bad politics, in two senses. It's about the supposedly bad—but fundamentally inescapable—politics of identity. And it's about books with bad politics: books that commit the sins of liberal feminism, reactionary antielitism, classism, casteism, and apoliticism. But I have—many of us have—taught them anyway.

Formally, this book enacts what I will call *accented reading*: a method of literary reading and discourse analysis that stages and assesses the relationship between the burden of representation experienced by ethnic, postcolonial, and non-Western writers of Anglophone literature, on the one hand, and the overdetermining interpellation experienced by the ethnic, postcolonial, and non-Western critics and scholars who study them, on the other hand.

Finally, this is a book about scenes of instruction and disciplining. It's about what happens to twentieth- and twenty-first-century Indian English literature when it is listed on syllabi and enlisted in debates in Asian American and South Asian literary studies in US academe: how it becomes legible as ethnic, postcolonial, and Anglophone. To put that differently, this is a book about how contemporary Indian English literature becomes

American, through a process of reterritorialization that is historically and institutionally specific, with implications for our reading, writing, teaching, and critical practice.

The Identities of Indian English Literature

My primary textual object in this book is "Indian English literature" as I have studied and taught it in US academe. I enlist the scare quotes because I want to flag at the outset that I do not take the identity of this object for granted. Indian literature in English is sometimes Asian American, but also not quite. It is key to the pedagogy of South Asia in the United States, yet marginal in South Asian studies. The study of Indian English literature is embattled by concerns about the inauthenticity of nonresident, expatriate writers and English's remove from the "real" India. At the same time, the study of Indian English literature in US academe is dominated by diasporic Indian scholars who have been hailed as informants by the identitarian imperatives of English. Indian English literatures must therefore meet the simultaneous demands of representing ethnic subjects, correcting for colonial histories of asymmetrical knowledge-power relations, and accounting for the vernacularization of English as a social and cultural system.

Not all ethnic literatures are Indian English, of course. Not all postcolonial literatures are Indian English. Not all Anglophone literatures are Indian English. But all Indian literatures in English—when they appear on syllabi and in scholarship in Asian American studies, comparative literature, English, and South Asian studies—become ethnic, postcolonial, or Anglophone. What, then, is Indian English literature, this object that does at least triple-duty and typically appears in the drag of other objects?

It is commonplace to observe that the discipline of English is conventionally organized into subfields corresponding to national imaginaries ("American"; "British") and periods ("Medieval"; "Victorian"). By that same token, efforts to expand curriculum and canon, ongoing since the mid-twentieth century, have led to a proliferation of fields that complicate these modes of organization. I am not only referring to subcategories of the national like "Asian American" and "Chicanx," which participate in the logic of the national even as they pluralize it. Rather, I am referring to the phenomenon in which extranational categories are conjoined with regionally specified rubrics for the study of temporally unspecified non-Western literatures, like "Global Anglophone," "African Diaspora," and "Transnational Asian."

There are, of course, cynical ways to describe these particular field formations. They are refashioned hiring categories aimed at diversifying the professoriate. Opportunistic attempts to piggyback on social movements, from #BlackLivesMatter to #StopAAPIHate. Pragmatic bids to win increasingly rare tenure-lines from university administrators under pressure from austerity-enacting state governments. Efforts to depoliticize the ethnic and postcolonial.[1]

All arguably true. But what interests me about these rubrics is that their emergence was predicated on the existence of hitherto-unnamed fields of English literary study in which many scholars have been working all along: fields in which we were already studying literary objects bound not by fidelity to frames like "Nineteenth Century American" or "Early Modern," but rather by the way they stick to us students, readers, and writers, and are interpellated alongside us and in our names.

In this book, "Indian English literature" is one such object that is not named, in a field that is not one: national, transnational, and extranational; historically emergent yet transhistorical; not a hiring field, but a field carried in the body of some hires. It is produced through the object-oriented call and response of writers and teachers, critics and scholars, whose charge is to work across and against the various other fields to which their texts might provisionally belong. In the chapters that follow, Indian English literature emerges as a mutant, plural and many-faced: American, Ethnic, Postcolonial, Modernist, Global, Anglophone, and Post-Anglophone. This is not because Indian English literature is sometimes ethnic and sometimes postcolonial, sometimes American and sometimes Anglophone. It is, I propose, because what we call "Indian English literature" emerges through the dynamic interplay between literature writers' and literature scholars' attempts to conform to, accommodate, and, most crucially, resist these very rubrics.

Native Informants and Protesting Ethnics, Again

The preface that opens this book is ostensibly about my own experience. But the "I" that speaks in those pages is not special. What it describes is the widely shared position of Gayatri Chakravorty Spivak's "Native Informant" and Rey Chow's "protesting ethnic subject," under the conditions of liberal and neoliberal multiculturalism and the diversity politics of US academe.[2] My inhabitance of the position of protesting-proxy-native-informant (proxy: because as an Indian American, I am an "impure native")[3] is neither new, nor mine, and there are already many persuasive accounts of *how* someone like me ends up writing something "overdetermined" like this book, Spivak's and Chow's accounts chief among them.[4]

"Overdetermined" is the description Spivak used in 1981 to describe her own academic trajectory as "an upper-class young woman in the Calcutta of the fifties."[5] It is how Chow defines "marginalized ethnicity in cross-ethnic representation": as "an ideologically overdetermined position in modernity."[6] Overdetermination speaks to what Stephen Greenblatt, writing in 2001, observed as a "risk of enforced performativity" in English literary studies: the "disturbing tendency in literature departments to expect that graduate students with Hispanic surnames will work on Hispanic subjects, that gay and lesbian students will naturally be directly engaged with queer theory, that Asian Americans will inevitably write dissertations on Asian American literature."[7] Equally, it captures what Tilottama Rajan, writing in 2006, called the "pressure to work on one's roots": a form of "compulsory ethnicity" particular to contemporary departments of literature and culture in which the demands of diversification and globalization run together.[8]

These tendencies and pressures are still very much with us. To give one example, in fall 2022, a Vietnamese American graduate student in one of my classes decided to change her dissertation topic from an ecocritical examination of Asian Anglophone literature to a study of diasporic Vietnamese literature. "I've long resisted doing 'mesearch,'" she wrote to me by email. When she shared her decision to focus on Vietnamese literature with her peers in our seminar, she narrated it as a form of failure.[9]

This book is a response to and an act of fellowship with that student, and so many others hailed into the subject position of native informant or trapped in coercive mimetic performances of their ethnic selves. In using overdetermination to speak to those experiences, I mean to activate its colloquial senses of interdependent, multiple causality, on the one hand, and plural, even contradictory expressions of necessity and desire, on the other. While the term "overdetermination" is often invoked in either an Althusserian or Freudian sense, my usage is neither Marxist nor psychoanalytic, but rather textual, institutional, and disciplinary.[10]

At the same time, I use the Althusserian language of interpellation to describe the identitarian demands of texts and disciplines, in contradistinction to the language of enforcement (Greenblatt), compulsion (Rajan), or coercion (Chow). I do this in order to affirm the complex agencies of the ethnic, postcolonial, and non-Western writers and scholars (and teachers and students) in question. They are not—*we* are not—dupes. There are mechanisms and structures operative in the scenes of native informancy and coercive mimeticism that exceed the pragmatic, the cynical, and the weak. We are navigating burdens of representation that precede and will succeed us, and we may offer performances of "native intelligence" that we do in fact have and from which our students and readers will indeed learn.[11] We are all overdetermined by our "historical positioning"[12] in the space of the classroom and on each page of the text. We are never just playing parts scripted by capitalist forces; neither are we in any simple sense resisting them.

This is a taboo topic, for multiple reasons. I will flag two here. For one, as per the preceding paragraph, it necessitates the provisional articulation of a "we" that inevitably excludes some readers.[13] Also, it requires acknowledging and confronting the fact that even the savviest critical assessments of the trap of identity have not secured our release.

Chow's "coercive mimeticism" is just one name for this trap and the process by which the fields of ethnic and postcolonial studies hail student-scholars of color. Curiously, the introduction to *The Protestant Ethnic* closes with a story about the inverse process of "antimiscegenation" by which white scholars are supposedly expelled from those same fields. A white graduate student, Chow recounts, was discouraged by a white advisor from "pursuing postcolonial studies" because they were not a person of color. She writes: "In representing—or constructing a discourse about—a field such as postcolonial studies as the exclusive domain of peoples of color, what this adviser accomplished was not merely racism *tout court* (in the naked form of a white flight from a colored neighborhood) but rather a racism that was sophisticatedly couched in an enlightened discourse of respect for other peoples' cultural or ethnic differences."[14] Chow offers this story in the singular, but the general conclusion is that fields like ethnic and postcolonial studies—that are in fact sustained by the labor of scholars of color—are being ghettoized.[15] The processes of "antimiscegenation" and "coercive mimeticism" are twinned; both are "plantational in effect."[16]

This story is deeply provocative; at the same time, it begs scrutiny. Even as the white student in this example is discouraged from pursuing postcolonial studies, white students and scholars have always had more latitude than scholars of color in terms of their objects and methods of study. Who, we might ask, is encouraged to write globe-trotting dissertations that survey the contemporary and worldly by sampling literatures from across nations, languages, and ethnic groups in service of synthetic readings? Who, meanwhile, is accused of doing "mesearch"?

It should not be controversial to observe that scholars of color are often subtly pressed to stick to their corners of the map and at the same time criticized for failing to address universal concerns. This, too, is an open secret.[17] Many are subject to structural inequalities during their academic journeys, but may then be gaslit with the erroneous idea that their ethnicity or race is what has enabled their professional advancement.[18] The morning I typed the first version of this sentence, Lorgia García Peña, who was denied tenure at Harvard in 2019, tweeted in solidarity with a graduate-student-led call for the hiring of ethnic studies faculty at Harvard who are not, as recent job candidates had apparently been, white Latin Americanists. "So let me get this straight," García Peña tweeted, "the work of ethnic studies scholars is too narrow, it is navel gazing when faculty of color perform it, but if I white professor does it, it is totally cool?"[19]

As a doctoral student at UC Berkeley in the early 1990s, Viet Thanh Nguyen was discouraged from writing a dissertation on Vietnamese and Vietnamese American literature:

> [I] told the English department chair that I wanted to write a dissertation on Vietnamese and Vietnamese American literature and he said that I could not do that. I would not get a job. He was not wrong in 1992, but his message was that English—my language, my literature, my profession—would not acknowledge the fate of the bodies that had shaped me. As an English scholar, I would have to wait over twenty years to complete the project that I thought I would work on in graduate school.[20]

In 2020, Nguyen, who was by then a Pulitzer-winning novelist and fully promoted scholar, was invited to offer a Presidential Plenary address on Vietnamese American literature at the Modern Language Association's annual convention. This trajectory is evidence not of progress, Nguyen noted, but of the importance of the student of color's commitment to their object of study, however delegitimated it may be. To borrow Keguro Macharia's words, the student-scholar must try, against all odds, not to be conscripted into the pursuit of their "own negation."[21]

What follows in this book is similarly uninterested in pursuing the negation of the postcolonial or ethnic scholar, in that I reject the assumption that such a figure's informancy or protest is ever exclusively abject. We should recall that for Spivak the position of the "native informant" is suspect and dangerous, yes, but also fundamentally unavoidable. It is a position she herself always risks occupying as a metropolitan migrant intellectual. For Spivak, attending closely to and remaining critical of the position of the native informant is a crucial way to ward against essentialist readings of the postcolonial text, as if its only function were to deliver up the truth of the periphery and its subaltern subjects. Informancy, like strategic essentialism, is a contingent method to be employed provisionally and self-consciously. But it is not, in my reading, a reference to a subject position to be obliterated.

For Chow, the "protesting ethnic subject" internalizes the imperative of appearing as ethnic, which is to say appearing as a nonsubject who is inferior to the nonethnic—who is, by contrast, a subject. The ethnic American is "future-oriented, always looking ahead to the time when the United States will have fully realized its universal ideals—that is, when ethnic particulars . . . no long really matter."[22] In Chow's treatment, ethnic subjectivity is a form of interpellation articulated as an impossible and ultimately self-defeating demand for recognition and redress. But Chow leaves open the possibility of generating a critical method of reading out of what she describes as abjection. Might we not look ahead to a time when ethnic or postcolonial particulars matter *differently*, specifically because we have developed a self-reflexive methodology by which to harness the intellectual labor and critical practice of the protesting writers and scholars in question?

Two things can be true at once, I want to insist, circling back to the story recounted in *The Protestant Ethnic*. The white advisor's advice to the white student may be racist. At the same time, the scholars of color occupying the minority field, whether ethnic, postcolonial, or Anglophone literature, might be doing something there that only they can do—not by virtue of who they are or what they know, but by virtue of how they got there, and the account they've had to give along the way.

The Miseducation of the Overdetermined

To be clear: students and faculty of color are of course instrumentalized in US academe. The figures who Nancy Leong terms "identity capitalists" routinely extract surplus value from our ethnic protest and performances of informancy, even as we are also rewarded for giving legible accounts of our selves.[23] Numerous scholars in the emerging critical university studies have produced unflinching, incisive analyses of this circuit of extraction, reward, and disciplining, through their work on the outcomes of diversity hiring and firing, the neoliberal politics of inclusion, and the relationship between institutionalized racism, tenure denials, and the collapsing academic job market.[24]

But what happens *after* we metabolize the critiques of antimiscegenation, coercive mimeticism, and identity capitalism? What if we ethnic, postcolonial, and non-Western scholars know very well that our assumption of identity is meant "to satisfy someone else's need for it," but we assume it anyway?[25]

To begin to answer these questions, I believe we need a better, more honest account of the reasons why so many minority scholars in US academe respond to identity's call and, even more importantly, of what the implications are for our teaching and critical practice. Each chapter of this book therefore begins after the so-called diversity hiring is over, after the scholar has failed to outrun the interpellation, and after they have assumed their portfolio of classes, as they stand at the front of a classroom and do the identity work that teaching literature always requires of us, even when—perhaps especially when—our project is the critique of "Diversity University" and its cooptation of ethnic, postcolonial, or non-Western "difference."[26]

In a sharp essay on political whiteness in academe, Mohan Ambikaipaker tells a revealing story that further illuminates the need for this kind of inquiry. It starts like this: "Let us say that there is a faculty job search about to be commenced at Diversity University. The job search has arisen because an associate professor who was the only faculty member teaching African American studies recently left her post for another job. She was also the only professor of African American descent teaching at the department."[27] The circumstances of the faculty member's departure are highly contentious; so, too, is the search to replace her. An African

American candidate at first prevails but is not made a competitive offer by the dean. The second-choice Asian candidate is deemed unacceptable for specious reasons by some number of the faculty. The third-ranked candidate, a white lesbian who works on "environmental issues and race," gets the job, and a senior member of the department notes with pride that the department has managed to preserve and ensure "diversity" after all.

This story, even oversimplified as presented here, dramatizes one of the problems to which this book responds. The main reason Diversity University can replace an African American who works on African American Studies with a white lesbian who works on the environment and race is because we have not yet given, or have not yet acknowledged, a rigorous, cleareyed, and unapologetic account of what the identitarian correspondence of subject (scholar) and object (studies) affords, specifically as a method of knowledge production, in the fields in question.[28] By "we" I mean those of us who both respond to and resist interpellation by Diversity University, who hope not to be coopted, who seek to do our academic jobs on our own terms even as we are conscripted into the conversion of identity into capital, and who are working to give more incisive accounts of why our fields are constituted as they are, so that we might both sustain and transform them. We: the overdetermined.

In a contrarian, self-reflexive spirit, this book offers an affirmative case for the work of the protesting-proxy-native-informant whose reading, writing, and teaching are overdetermined by the call of identity. The operative word here is affirmative. This book's focus is not the trap of identity, identity's "discursive instability"[29] and imaginary status, or the violence of identitarian interpellation, broadly defined—although I will be attuned to all of these dynamics. Rather, I am interested in what the overdetermined scholar *does* with identity within the field of English literature, a field in which identities like Asian American, South Asian, Indian, ethnic, postcolonial, and Anglophone exist, as Colleen Lye has argued, "largely at the level of the course syllabus, scholarly research monograph, or publisher's catalogues, rather than at the level of an individual text."[30]

For the overdetermined, identity is always anchored in processes and relations. It is a rhetorical strategy through which we readers negotiate our responses to texts and through which we as teachers present them to our students. It is a principle through which to apprehend the literary object—not on the basis of authorship, content, form, or time period, but rather through the affective intimacies of reading and in classroom transactions of identity knowledges. It is a method of textual approach. More than a category of individual assignment, identity for the overdetermined is a disciplinary assignment. In specifying identity thus, I take up Robyn Wiegman's insight that "within the disciplinary apparatus of knowledge production, one does not simply study literature, politics, or social organization. One is constituted as belonging on an identitarian basis, where the imperative to *be* a biologist, philosopher, political scientist, even a critical theorist is to partake in an identitarian project."[31]

Two further clarifications are in order. First, this book forwards no normative judgment about who should teach what, or where they should teach it, or to whom. I will not be criticizing Indian scholars "for working on Hegel instead of the *Upanishads*," a reproach Rajan reports having received more than once.[32] To the extent that this book offers arguments against the teaching of specific texts in specific ways, or for the affordances of particular student-text relations in the classroom, it does so in order to open up the range of questions we might ask about the presence of certain texts and certain bodies in certain classrooms. Please do not "[mistake] critical response for prohibition."[33]

Also, I am not arguing that identity *should* determine what anyone studies, teaches, reads, or writes. I'm observing that it often *does*. Something called identity—whether we claim it, or whether it claims us, "fiction"[34] though it may also be—inflects our scholarly itineraries, even when we least expect it, even when we are trying to avoid it, and even if we are not sure what identity even *is*. I'm arguing that when it does—when in fact something identitarian overdetermines the literature scholar's chosen objects and fields—it does so with implications for our teaching and writing that demand critical consideration.

In making this argument, I am putting pressure on claims like Spivak's that the only reason a scholar studies an object they resemble on an identitarian basis is an "accident-of-birth."[35] I am building on Christopher Lee's insight that postidentitarian readings are also always profoundly identitarian and that "identity remains generative and productive even when placed under erasure."[36] I am also extending questions that Macharia asked about his own experience of the "diasporic reterritorialization"[37] of postcolonial Anglophone subjectivity into American ethnicity, after he, a Kenyan, was interpellated as his US university's "safe" and "post-black"[38] emblem of racial diversity: "*What am I doing here, and what is it doing to me?*"[39]

In this book, I ask not only "what am I doing here?" but *what is my being and doing here*—as an Indian American scholar assembling Indian English texts "to teach, interpret, or purvey"[40] as ethnic, postcolonial, and Anglophone in US academe—*doing for my students, colleagues, and readers?* Not just "what is it doing to me?" but *what is it doing to my object of study?*

To rephrase and extend these questions more polemically: What difference does it make if Indian scholars study and teach Indian literature (or, ethnics the ethnic, postcolonials the postcolonial, Asians the Asian, and so on)? What transformations does the object itself—here, Indian English literature—undergo because of the dynamic circuit of resistance and affiliation, repudiation and desire, that characterizes the overdetermined scholar's relationship to their object of study? How does Indian English literature become ethnic, postcolonial, and Anglophone in US academe?

This book makes two arguments in response to these questions. I will present the first in general terms and the second in terms particular to Indian English literature, though, as the coming sections discuss, it too is generalizable beyond this case.

First, all literary objects are constructed as objects of scholarly inquiry *in the process of address*. This is an argument for the significance of *accent*. Building on my work as a coeditor of a field-announcing book in interdisciplinary accent studies, I offer accent as a comparative and dialogical term that focuses our attention on relations between speakers and listeners, teachers and students, writers and readers.[41] Accent teasingly promises to reveal the identity of the speaker, writer, or text in question, at the same time as it doubles back into and emerges from the ears and eyes of the listener or reader. In this way, accent produces a relation of proximity between scholars and the writers from whom they might otherwise stand at a distance. I will further elaborate on accent and the literary-critical method I call *accented reading* later in this introduction.

Second, Indian English literature becomes ethnic, postcolonial, and Anglophone by and through *resistance to being Indian*—through a deeply felt, variously articulated, widely shared yet underexamined disavowal of India and Indianness. This resistance is expressed rhetorically by writers, scholars, students, and teachers. It is literary, critical, and pedagogical. It is amplified by failures to be Indian, attachments to being Indian, disaffiliation from Indianness, and desires for Indianness. To borrow language from feminist theorists of disidentification, what is resisted is not only Indianness but "having to *be*" Indian.[42] For instance, Amit Chaudhuri, discussed in chapter 5, resists writing about India even as he acknowledges the impossibility of complete disidentification: "I'm an Indian, so of course I write about India . . . But then again, I don't write about India. I'm not interested in writing about India."[43] In this book, I examine such disavowals as a specific manifestation of a broader resistance to the disciplinary categories of the ethnic, postcolonial, and Anglophone that is constitutive of each field's imaginary.

Together, these two stories of Indian English literature's becoming—through address and through resistance—serve this book's larger effort to clarify the case for the affordances of identity in English literary studies. Both stories center the relations through which the literary object accrues value and meaning, in contradistinction to approaches that center the value or meaning of the literary object in itself. My readings lay bare the overdetermination of the scholar-teacher's choice of literary object, their critical apprehension of that object, and the pedagogical uses to which it might be put. I show that resistance to identity is at the heart of both the literature writer's navigation of the burden of representation and the literature scholar's negotiation of a corresponding demand.

With this approach, I offer a complement to market-focused accounts of the production of minority and non-Western literary canons in US academe. To date, many scholars have examined the overdetermining forces of the international literary marketplace and prestige cultures on ethnic, postcolonial, and Anglophone literatures.[44] In what has been described as the sociological turn in literary studies, scholars have focused on literary institutions and the formal transformations wrought within Anglophone literature in the context of the American and global program eras.[45] Our collective attention to topics like the prizewinning novel, the literary festival circuit, and the diversity politics of the publishing industry has been incredibly revealing. At the same time, it has led in my view to a one-sided conception of canon formation, and we have missed the equally fundamental significance of teachers' and students' embodied performances of informancy and transactions of identity knowledges within the literature classroom. Rather than automatically attribute the canonicity of well-known Indian English writers to their market success or Pulitzer or Booker prizes, I seek to illuminate other interpersonal, institutional, and pedagogical dynamics that return certain texts and debates to our syllabi, anthologies, and classrooms, semester after semester, year after year.

English Literary Studies as Identity Studies

One of the first lessons one learns as a student of feminist, postcolonial, and cultural studies is the importance of situating oneself and one's knowledges, and of producing scholarship that responsibly and self-reflexively travels from the *where* from which one strives to know, to the *what* one strives to know about, and *why*. There are no "god tricks" in this book.[46] I advance my readings from my vantage as a second-generation Indian American of caste and class privilege, a non-Black person of color, a brown woman professor, a cisgender woman married to a cisgender man, a parent of young children, the beneficiary of the resources of a tenure-track job, and a teacher of contemporary literature in the United States. I proceed with a self-consciously raised eyebrow in full awareness of the routinization and even banalization of such identitarian self-positioning, as well as through my commitment to its integrity and force—just so long as the work of situating knowledges does not stop at rhetorical self-positioning.

So, let me not stop there. This is a book about the critical afterlife of postcolonial studies in US academe. It is primarily focused on Indian English literature and scholarship written by Anglophone elites. I myself am a version of an Anglophone elite: specifically, an American college professor. What I discuss is neither comprehensive nor representative of Indian English literature writ large. My chapters are interested in Bharati Mukherjee, Chetan Bhagat, Amit Chaudhuri, and Jhumpa Lahiri because of their distinct identities as ethnic, Anglophone, postcolonial, and post-Anglophone writers. My recesses address the iconicity of Gayatri Chakravorty Spivak, Homi Bhabha, and Edward Said because critical assessments of the postcolonial have always included scrutiny of their particular legacies. I read texts and icons in order to explore how they implicate and hail readers, not in order to perform my own detached or superior analysis.

I proceed with what Spivak has described as "an acknowledgment of complicity (being folded together with what I critique)": an acknowledgment that does not "excuse" or "accuse" but requires me to "enter that social formation that [I] am criticizing as thoroughly as [I] can . . . to turn the whole thing around to serve purposes other than its original self-comprehension."[47] I seek what Spivak terms "critical intimacy" with each text, at the place where it will allow me "to turn it around and use it—to use its best energies for the project at hand."[48] This book therefore focuses on the ways in which I have actually—in real time, in real life, in past semesters—enlisted these writers and texts in my efforts to present Indian English literature in US academe. This, I propose, is what it means to do identity studies: not only to account honestly for identity's call, but to then be responsible to one's own pedagogical and critical desires, choices, and missteps made in light of that call.

My use of the term "identity studies" follows Wiegman's usage in *Object Lessons*, in which she argues that fields like women's studies, queer studies, American studies, and whiteness studies are all bound by having "identity objects of study," even if and when the objects of study themselves are in question.[49] For example, Wiegman shows how women's studies has been animated by resistance to its seemingly readymade object—*women*—and consequent efforts at expansion and clarification of the discipline's brief through repeated renomination (e.g., "gender and women's studies" or "women's, gender and sexuality studies").[50] Wiegman also argues that identity studies fields are bound by their practitioners' commitments to and aspirations for deriving social justice through and from their identity objects.

Notably, the discipline of English, in which Wiegman herself was trained, is not theorized under the identity studies umbrella, neither by Wiegman nor by those writing after her. There are many reasons why this may be. Some literature scholars may be wary of identity because the dominant modes of instruction in our discipline involve training students not to engage with texts in ways that risk partaking in the intentional fallacy (what did the author mean?) or affective fallacy (how did it make you feel?). Also, identification—whether with characters or authors—is often construed as a suspect response of naïve readers. More specifically and ironically, identity is a third rail in ethnic and postcolonial literary studies, and anything that smells of essentialism or nativism is routinely rejected by scholars of non-Western Anglophone literatures. If at all one is to be an essentialist, it must be as an anti-anti-essentialist; it must be strategic, pragmatic, apologetic, and qualified.

Take the Asian American example. As Lee has shown, the critique of identity politics in the 1990s led to a broadly shared critical consensus on the "fictional," "imaginary," even "amnesiac" quality of the "Asian American" identity that nevertheless occasions the field.[51] As a result, practitioners of Asian American literary studies are in the ambivalent and contradictory position of having to automatically critique identity even as we continue to work with it. "Post-identity . . . unfolds as an inherent and integral dimension of identitarian thinking," Lee writes, which is why "despite frequent declarations about the constructedness and/or incoherence of identities, aspects of identitarian thinking continue to persist as affective investments, means of knowledge production, and modes of ethico-political engagement and imagination."[52]

The same post-identity turn happened in postcolonial studies in the 1990s. "Identity as such is about as boring a subject as one can imagine," Edward Said wrote. "Nothing seems less interesting than the narcissistic self-study that today passes in many places for identity politics."[53] "I am not an identitarian," Spivak has declared more than once.[54] She additionally stresses: "[I] am not a South Asianist. I turn to Indian material because I have some accident-of-birth facility there."[55] Such disavowals remain common among postcolonialists. "I do not think of myself as a South Asianist or an Indianist or an Indologist or an expert in Indian literature," writes Sangeeta Ray.[56] "I guess I am a South Asian by provenance," R. Radhakrishnan admits, before adding: "Am I condemned to be a South Asian so long as I live and breathe?"[57]

To be clear, what is being rejected in each of these instances is not exactly identity, but rather rank identitarianism and identitarian assignment—which of course require rejection. We must absolutely be vigilant about what Olúfẹ́mi Táíwò describes as "deference politics": the practice of passing the mic instead of redistributing resources; of assuming that a brown or black body in the room can sufficiently represent all the other brown and black bodies barred entry into it.[58] We must attend to what Keeanga-Yamahtta Taylor rightly describes as the failure of identity politics: that is, when identity functions as a substitute for actual politics.[59] As Jodi Melamed argues, the canon wars of the 1980s and 1990s in effect served as a "counterinsurgency against the robustly materialist antiracisms of the 1960s' and 1970s' new social movements." Debates over the canon both "overvalorized and undertheorized literature," with the effect that "multicultural literature [became] a metaphor for a just America" that would, ultimately, remain metaphoric.[60]

Resisting the metaphorization of antiracism by the multiculturalist project of inclusion is still a vital task. By that same token, it is also the case that scholars of ethnic and postcolonial literatures have risked revoicing a more general critique of identity and caricature of identity politics that is now, in the 2020s, being weaponized by right-wing culture warriors, critics of higher education, and pundits participating more generally in the discrediting of the academic humanities.[61] In doing this, we not only participate in our own delegitimization, but also risk throwing the proverbial baby of identity, with all its complex affordances, out with the bathwater of bad identity politics.

By situating this book's inquiry within US university classrooms in which Indian English literatures are really—and not just metaphorically—put to work, I seek to tell a more nuanced story about identity than the story of liberal multiculturalism's failed politics of representation or the story of minority students' quests for recognition. The story I want to tell begins by acknowledging that the identitarian correspondence of scholar-subject and literary-object does not produce better knowing. The overdetermined scholar does not have special expertise on Indian texts by virtue of being Indian, just as the metropolitan native informant does not "speak for" the Indian subaltern just by virtue of having "India" as a shared term. As Spivak writes, "It is a very dubious assumption that people in English departments will know academically and intellectually about 'Indian Reality' because they are Indians."[62] Likewise, the postidentity turn in Asian American studies was a vital attempt to correct for the discursive and political homogenization of a community that is, crucially, not *one*.

At the same time, I want to insist that taking identity seriously in literary studies does not mean that we have to instruct our students into a mode of reading that solipsistically and naively centers the self or the politics of recognition. It does not mean that we have to instruct our students into a mode of writing that violates vital principles of aesthetic autonomy and freedom. It does not mean that we forbid white students from studying ethnic or postcolonial literature, and it does not mean that we disqualify the work of those who do. What it means is that we cannot dismiss as essentialist those modes of identity-inflected reading and invocations of experience, biography, and history that are in fact essential to the critical apprehension of the literatures in question.

What I've been describing as "overdetermined interpellation" is not actually a problem to be fixed, then, as much as it is a problem that has been misdiagnosed. Chow's early 2000s worry about the racist advisor, for example, was not simply about the ghettoization of ethnic and postcolonial studies. Gentrification, after all, is not a desirable corrective to an earlier moment of white flight from a colored neighborhood. Rather, Chow was anticipating reactionary gatekeeping. If ethnic and postcolonial literary studies were genuinely to become the exclusive domain of scholars of color, then what would be considered the proper domain of the white scholar? If "they" can't teach Gloria Anzaldúa or Salman Rushdie, then how can "we" teach Charles Dickens or Virginia Woolf? Said voiced this anxiety as well: "To say that women should read mainly women's literature, that blacks should study and perfect only black techniques of understanding and interpretation . . . is the inverse of saying along with Carlyle and Gobineau that all the lesser races must retain their inferior status in the world."[63]

Of course, we should not accept the "inferior status" of the ethnic and postcolonial. But what I find profoundly dissatisfying about this line of critique is that the assessment of what is very clearly a coercive situation ("to say that women *should* read women's literature") forecloses the critical assessment of the inevitable one (when women *do* read women's literature).

Because, inevitably, we do.

It should be clear by now that my primary interest in this book is not actually identity but rather *resistance* to identity, or identification with disidentification, which appears in two coarticulated forms: the literature writer's resistance to the burden of representation, on one hand, and the literature scholar's resistance to overdetermining interpellation, on the other. Each of my chapters examines this resistance in the Indian English context, but the dynamic that I am identifying extends far beyond that, with wider implications.

In fact, I would go so far as to say that resistance to the burden of representation is the signal issue taught in classes on ethnic, postcolonial, and non-Western Anglophone literatures in US academe. This resistance is what we introduce through the Frank Chin versus Maxine Hong Kingston debate on "real" and "fake" Asias.[64] This resistance is what Mark Chiang identifies when he observes that Asian American literature inevitably " 'fails to stand for' Asian Americans," because it is always judged in terms of its referential relation to an Asian American collectivity it can never totally represent.[65] Equally, this resistance is at the heart of Vikram Chandra's polemical critique of "the cult of authenticity" that deems both the English language and diasporic distance as disqualifying vantages from which to attempt the representation of India and Indians.[66]

We teach the writer's resistance to the burden of representation through Timothy Yu's *100 Chinese Silences*: "To make an American poem in English / We must level the mountains of language with dynamite / and in the rubble build an ethnic theme park / of charming accents and seething quiet."[67] It's there in Ada Limón's poem "The Contract Says: We'd Like the Conversation to Be Bilingual": "bring your brown- / ness so we can be sure to please / the funders."[68] And in Kiese Laymon's poignant revision of "what real Black writers do."[69]

As Mrinalini Chakravorty and Swati Rana have explored in the postcolonial and ethnic literary contexts, respectively, contemporary writers are quite plainly aware of and self-reflexive about their conscription into predictable performances of race and legible resemblance to stereotypes.[70] In fact, writers and artists in the United States are increasingly being rewarded by the market for knowingly satirizing this conscription, as in Paul Beatty's 2015 Booker-winning *The Sellout*, Charles Yu's 2020 National Book Award–winning *Interior Chinatown*, and Cord Jefferson's 2023 film, *American Fiction*, based on Percival Everett's 2001 novel *Erasure*. Every one of these writers and culture-producers has read their Chow, so to speak. Now, rather than seek rewards for performing the ethnic self, they are rewarded for narrating resistance to the coercive mimetic imperative of performing as the ethnic self.

By contrast, contemporary scholar-critics of the ethnic and postcolonial have generally erred on the side of disavowing identity and identity politics, while staying relatively silent about their—*our*—own overdetermination by identity's call. This silence plays into the hands of our detractors, who willfully misunderstand our disidentifications and critiques. Here, then, are three more examples from writers of literary nonfiction and fiction, from which we scholar-critics stand to learn.

Growing up in the 1990s, the writer Jay Caspian Kang despaired that the only Asian American novelist anyone had ever heard of was Amy Tan. "I, of course, hated Amy Tan," he writes. "If I had been asked back then what I planned to write about . . . the only concrete pledge I could have given you was, 'I will not write *The Joy Luck Club*.'"[71]

Tommy Orange resisted reading celebrated "Native" writers like Sherman Alexie until he started his MFA because, he writes, "Sherman was very rez, and I avoided a lot of rez Indian writing, because it made me feel isolated—and like it was the only way to Indian write."[72]

In a 2014 foreword to John Okada's *No-No Boy*, Ruth Ozeki writes, "When [*No-No Boy*] was reissued in 1976, I was . . . quite a good reader, but I'm afraid I still didn't read it . . . the fact is that I wasn't very interested in the Japanese American cultural movement . . . I didn't think of myself as Japanese American."[73]

Yes, *but*: Kang by his own description now writes "almost entirely about race and identity." With the publication of Pulitzer-finalist *There There* in 2018, Orange became a celebrated "Native" writer and a mentor at the Institute of American Indian Arts. And Ozeki has now written multiple novels about the Japanese American experience.

As Kang tells it, the trouble he faced as an aspiring artist was the imperative of meeting the white gaze. No matter what he produced, he would be read as an immigrant writer. Yet, he went on to become a version of the "race writer" he did not want to be: "Today I write almost entirely about race and identity, although not exactly by choice. My job—even what you're reading now—is part of my career of explaining Asian-Americans to white people. It's fine. But even if it weren't, what am I going to do about it?"[74] Kang's protest and eventual capitulation are textbook examples of how ethnic subjects are interpellated into marketable performances of their identities for the dominant US audience-consumer. At the same time, Kang also makes an affirmative argument for his seemingly cynical embrace of a career of informancy ("explaining Asian-Americans to white people"). As a Korean immigrant, he notes, he is positioned to talk about issues pertaining to his community specifically, and Asian Americans more generally, in a "real" way. As an Asian discussing Asian issues with other Asians, he can facilitate exchanges that might even be "therapeutic."

This is exactly the kind of claim that the postidentity scholar will at first deem essentialist. But it is in fact a widely shared hope among minoritized Anglophone writers. British-Palestinian writer Isabella Hammad similarly describes taking inspiration from Yasmin El-Rifae's call for women to fight patriarchal violence by "speaking to one another ... thinking together ... supporting one another," as opposed to "appealing to or trying to educate men." Hammad writes: "Writing in English about Palestine, I often find myself asked if my aim is to educate 'Westerners,' a suggestion I always find reductive and kind of undignified. But I like this idea of breaking into the awareness of other people *by talking candidly among ourselves.*"[75] I will return to the implications of these statements later in this introduction.

Orange raises a different problem, which begs a different resolution. He avoided Indian writing that sounded a particular way ("rez") because it brought home for him his divergence and alienation from that form of writing. He was searching for another way "to Indian write." The phrasing is important: the problem is not Indian content as such (he is not searching for something else to write about), but rather the form in which he is given to write. The trouble is writing into a field that has been designated a priori as formless, because ethnic and minority literatures by definition are constituted in terms of their referentiality. In simpler terms, the problem for Orange is not the *what* of identity, but the *how*.

Ozeki is also vexed by her relationship to the literature that is given as "hers," not because of the overdetermining white gaze, or the limitations of racialized form, but because of her desire for contemporaneity. She feels disconnected from stories of the Japanese American experience, because they are primarily World War II stories of internment that seem "like ancient history." When she finally reads Okada's novel, she is stunned by "how profoundly shaped [she'd] been by the normative post-war assimilationist values that were so prevalent among people of Japanese heritage living in America."[76]

Given the hypocrisies of both American multiculturalism and the publishing industry, it makes sense that ethnic and postcolonial writers would at first reject those texts that appear readymade as their own: whether because of the outsized presence of another writer who "looks like" them or because of the market's demand that writers of color produce historical fiction.[77] For Kang, Orange, and Ozeki, encountering writers they resemble (Tan, Alexie, and Okada), or subjects about which they're expected to write (race, rez life, World War II), at first produces an alienating experience of hearing the self as other. It is the kind of alienation that Julie Beth Napolin describes as hearing a recording of your own voice played back to you on an answering machine, familiar yet distorted.[78] *Is that really what I sound like?*

Each writer resists being read in terms of what David Palumbo-Liu calls their "assumed"[79] identities and Jhumpa Lahiri terms their "imposed"[80] identities. Ultimately, however, they are compelled to address them. This belated response to the call of identity then becomes the enabling condition of their craft. Chapter 7, on Lahiri's move from writing in English to writing in Italian, offers our most extended example of this movement. At first locked in "a circuit of critical and at times painful self-hearing,"[81] Lahiri trades languages in order to hear herself anew. She subverts what is wounding about hearing her own voice (in English) by reengineering the return to herself from a (linguistic) distance.

Again, the burden of representation faced by ethnic and postcolonial writers in the United States is a familiar subject that we routinely teach to our students. What I am distinctly focused on in this book is how the operations of interpellation, informancy, and protest that inflect the writing of literature *also* underlie the critical practice of literary scholarship and the pedagogy of contemporary literature. I am sketching the shared terrain between someone like my student not wanting to do "mesearch," and Kang's not wanting to write *The Joy Luck Club*; and between my not wanting to write about Lahiri, and Ozeki's not wanting to read *No-No Boy*. In each situation, the reader-writer has to respond to the text in question by grappling with its refamiliarizing, as opposed to defamiliarizing, effects. The journey in question is one from imposition to embrace. From self-estrangement to self-avowal. In Napolin's words, "It is only through the far distance that the object comes back to itself."[82]

Ethnic, postcolonial, non-Western, and more generally minoritized scholars in US academe labor under the same structures of legibility, illegibility, and overdetermined address as writers of literature. We are also measured in terms of our referential relations to texts we inevitably fail to represent. But we have yet to adequately theorize the implications of this fact: namely, what it means for our teaching and scholarship for us to be at once embattled and enabled by our proximity to and distance from objects we resemble in identitarian terms.

The problem for literary studies is that the position of the scholar interpellated in this way destabilizes what Michael Warner describes as the conventionally "clear opposition between the text object and the reading subject." Understood in these terms, the overdetermined scholar's "freedom and agency"—expressed as products of distance from the object of critique—are by definition compromised.[83] By that same logic, the scholar's very "uncriticality"—understood as a function of proximity to the object—might well be the basis of their appeal to an academic institution, a hiring committee, a department, and their students. This uncriticality is part and parcel of how we, to borrow Radhakrishnan's elaboration of the pedagogical function, "negotiate with the text on behalf of the student who expects edification from the way we mediate ourselves with the texts."[84] Identification, after all, is not simply an obstacle to critique but also a vehicle for and modality of it.

It is time to admit that the critique of identitarianism, liberal multiculturalism, essentialism, the politics of recognition, racism, or ethnonationalism (choose your mode of bad identity politics) often follows from and is itself a form of response to identity's call—which means that those of us prepared to admit and theorize our own overdetermination might be best positioned to assess the limits and possibilities of identity itself.

To circle back to Wiegman, if we are to acknowledge the ways in which English literary studies functions as identity studies, we have to be willing to plumb the depths of our uncriticality. We have to admit that we are always already producing certain literary texts in certain contexts as identity objects of study. And we must recognize that the literature scholar overdetermined by identity also seeks a kind of justice through and from their object. The justice we seek is in part for the object, weighed down by the burden of representation. Equally, the justice we seek is for ourselves, vexed as we are by the object's failure to represent us and our corresponding failure to represent it. This is why Lee ends *The Semblance of Identity* with a call for "abandonment" in Asian American literary studies, in both senses: a call to give up the field's identity, and at the same time to give ourselves over to it.[85] We seek both to destroy the object and to free it, to remake it in its own image and, at the same time, in our own.

Toward a Method of Accented Reading

But how?

After eight years of teaching in departments of English in US universities, I've come to believe that the problem with identity is not conceptual, but actually methodological. It is not epistemological, but about "the epistemological *performance*": "how you construct yourself, or anything, as an object of knowledge."[86] The question is not what identity *is* or *knows*. The question is what identity *does*, and how we *do* with it. *To what end* do practitioners of English literary studies take up the identity object? What does identitarian interpellation do to our criticism and scholarship, especially when we think we are sloughing identity off?

In recent years, ethnic, postcolonial, and otherwise minoritized and racialized scholars of English literature have been increasingly emboldened to consider how identity interrupts our readings of texts that are not ours, and that may in fact structurally exclude us from the position of the intended reader. This is a project we have long been discouraged from pursuing. For example, consider Aniket Jaaware's caution, quoted approvingly by Spivak: "when Shakespeare wrote his works, he did not know that we

Indian students of English literature would exist [and] therefore, we should not think about our experience as the context for everything."[87]

But what about our experience as the context for *something*—namely, a particular method of reading? In an essay on encountering Orientalist tropes in the work of Dickens, Jane Hu observes that because Victorian studies has not developed the "tools" to understand how Asian readers should engage scenes of "casual racism" against Asians, readers like her have been left with "only one way" to read such scenes: "privately, personally, as a problematic that could only be about [us], and thus never sufficiently scholarly."[88] Manu Samriti Chander makes a related observation in the afterword to *Brown Romantics*, when he describes being in graduate school, assuming he was "supposed to be studying" postcolonialism, hating his dissertation on Romantic Orientalism, and ultimately searching out a new archive of brown Romantics with whose "cultural in-betweenness" he could identify.[89]

With respect to the Victorians and the Romantics, Hu and Chander both serve as versions of the figure Elaine Castillo terms the "unexpected reader": the reader "who does not read [the work of the dominant writing subject] the way they expect—often demand—to be read; often someone who has been framed in their work and in their lives as an object, not a subject."[90] Together, what they make clear is the need for an established methodology by which to conduct identity-inflected readings of texts from which one is excluded as a reader as well as texts that hail one in identitarian terms.

Here are two examples of scholars beginning to reckon with the latter. In a short reading of Ling Ma's *Severance*, Eugenia Zuroski writes through her identification with protagonist Candace Chen: "I know what it feels like to cry on a Manhattan fire escape; I did it several times while in college in the 90s." She continues: "I too have been a twenty-something Chinese American weed, proving hardy enough in the inhospitable landscape of New York under neoliberalism."[91] Similarly, Sarah Chihaya describes being hailed by a particular passage in Viet Thanh Nguyen's *Nothing Ever Dies*: "I felt as though Nguyen, who'd been keeping a low profile under the brim of his critical hat for a while, unexpectedly looked up and fixed me with his eyes. . . . [T]he passage felt like a chute that opened beneath my feet and sent me plummeting to another level of readerly identity—certainly not the part of me reading Nguyen's work for

PMLA, nor any analytically reading part at all, but a personal and vulnerable part."[92]

These moments lay bare both what drives identitarian investment ("I too have been") and how it feels ("like a chute that . . . sent me plummeting"), and they powerfully inflect the readings they anticipate.[93] To date, however, such accounts of identitarian interpellation exist primarily in fugitive form: in disclaimers, parentheticals, asides, prefaces, and afterwords like Chander's, or in two thousand words tucked into a special forum, like Zuroski's piece. They are often bracketed off from the work of professional analytical criticism, as Chihaya's partitioning of "levels of readerly identity" makes clear.

In an even more striking act of partitioning, the introduction and chapters of Min Hyoung Song's *The Children of 1965* are all written in "a third-person critical voice" so that he can highlight the question of "what might be lost" if we "collapse distinctions between autobiography and the critical essay." A first-person conclusion then offers "autobiographical rumination" on topics like Song's own experience as a student of Asian American literature, but he "leaves discussion about its significance for elsewhere."[94] The personal and vulnerable, it is implied, is a risky point of entry into the text.

The idea that scholarly criticism can or should be free of identity (here couched in terms of "autobiography") is analogous to the idea that art can or should transcend race. As Beth Loffreda and Claudia Rankine observe, debates on "craft" in the creative writing community often assume that "the imagination is or can be somehow free of race . . . as if the imagination is not part of me, is not created by the same web of history and culture that made 'me.'" But neither art nor scholarship is "some special, uninfiltrated realm that transcends the messy realities of our lives and minds," and criticism and scholarship can no more be postidentitarian than creative writing can be "postracial . . . posthistorical [or] postpolitical."[95]

In the following chapters, I strive to perform readings that refuse to turn away from the writer's eyes fixed on mine, and I stay at the level of vulnerable readerly identity where Chihaya's chute leads. In this effort, I join all those scholars who also reject the ideological construction of a neutral position of reading and reception in American literary studies. For example, writing on *American Dirt*'s racist representation of Mexico and Mexicans, Ignacio Sánchez Prado performs what he terms "invested" criticism that makes space for the articulation of relations that are experiential, embodied, historical, and biographical.[96] This mode of criticism is not fettered by these relations, but enabled by them. Similarly, Napolin develops "acoustic" criticism as a mode of reading and writing in which the critic takes seriously "the conditions of resonance" and "repetitions of echo" that inhere both within the literary text itself and in the reader's response to it.[97] For Anita Starosta, "accented criticism" inaugurates the project of returning the subject "to the critic's otherwise subjectless speech"; it "names the desire for a permanent disruption in the tendency toward monologic, neutral speech."[98] Jess Shollenberger identifies an ongoing movement of "personalization" among minority, queer, and nondominant scholars, in which "the window of an individual life and its relation to social structures might [finally] be offered—if not accepted—as a gesture of resistance and a *source* of critical authority."[99]

In concert with these efforts, this book develops a method of reading and metacritical discourse analysis that is interested in both writers' and readers' embodied and affective responses to literary texts—but not ultimately reducible to them. This method seeks out *how* ideas about a text's identity are produced by acts of reading and criticism, as opposed to adjudicating the identity of the text itself. It requires foregrounding the constructedness of our reading positions as critics, both by dominant ideologies of the ethnic, postcolonial, and Anglophone, and by writers of literature themselves. I call this method *accented reading*, because reading is fundamental to the practices of criticism and pedagogy, and because of the specific affordances of the concept of accent for the study of texts at the ethnic-postcolonial-Anglophone intersection.

So, what is accent? Accent may be minimally defined as a style of pronunciation, a tone of voice, or a way of speaking.[100] Everyone has an accent, but only some subjects are perceived as accented. Linguists distinguish between L1 and L2 accents, depending on whether they indicate the contexts of first-language learning (e.g., a Southern accent; a prep school accent) or the trace of a first language within a second (e.g., Hindi-accented English; a French accent). Colloquially, an accent indexes difference. It is an excess, trace, or residue that affixes to an individual or group. This is why accent is conventionally understood to signify identity: it seems to indicate facts like where someone is from, their level of education, and what languages they speak.

Only, that's not all that accent is or does, and not all that accent has to teach us. In this book, I leave aside the colloquial significations and begin instead with the concept of accent developed in the critical introduction to *Thinking with an Accent*, by Pooja Rangan, Akshya Saxena, Pavitra Sundar, and myself. In our cowritten work, drawing on scholarship across the humanistic disciplines, we demonstrate that accent is relational and comparative; it is a mode of perception inherent in exchange. Accent does not betray origins or identities. Rather, it lays bare logics of representation, interpretation, and identification, and catalyzes processes of authentication through which ideas of authenticity are produced. The event of accent resides in the interstices of reception and production, just as any text's meaning emerges at the nexus of reading and writing. Accent can therefore be used to theorize discourses and modes of critical accommodation beyond voice and language.

In her memoir, *In Other Words,* Lahiri tells a story about accent that illustrates its operation in these very terms. She is in a shop in Rome, where she speaks "for quite a long time with [a] saleswoman, in an Italian that is fluent but not completely natural." Her Greek-Guatemalan-American husband, who looks Italian, enters the store speaking comparatively monosyllabic Italian with "a Spanish accent." And yet, at the end of the encounter, the Italian saleswoman remarks to Lahiri that her husband "must be Italian" because, "he speaks perfectly, without any accent."[101]

The saleswoman is listening to both Lahiri and her husband with what the poet Li-Young Lee calls "a coloring ear, which [bends] the listener's eye and, consequently, the speaker's countenance; it [is] a kind of narrowing, and unconscious on the part of the listener, who listens in judgment, judging the speaker even before the meaning or its soundness [are] attended to."[102] Lee's description, inverting as it does conventional understandings of the functions of ear and eye, captures the workings of accent not only across senses but as that which crosses senses and gives the skin "tones," to use Chow's term.[103] The ear does not simply receive sound; it is a "coloring ear," which shades the voice. Accent inflects encounters "even before" meaning, irrespective of the speaker's identity, and prior to the act of interpretation. To borrow from linguistic anthropologist Jonathan Rosa, both Lahiri and her husband *look like a language* and *sound like a race*—just not the same ones.[104]

Lahiri's shop scene demonstrates that accent happens between people. In this exchange, accent at first seems to signify identitarian difference—that is, the difference between the clearly not-Italian Lahiri and the "must be Italian" husband. In fact, however, accent is in the ear of the saleswoman-receiver, who deems the semantic content of Lahiri's speech (*what* she said) less important than its sonic envelope (*how* it was said, and by *whom*). For Lahiri, this experience of accent is strained, deuniversalizing, and wounding. For her part, the saleswoman thinks she is using accent to locate her customers, when in fact accent is locating her.

But there's more. While accent is in the ear of the receiver, it is also produced by the speaker: performatively, strategically, unintentionally, or deliberately. In "Cicadas in the Mouth," Divya Victor relates a scene of intimate exchange between two diasporic Indian poets: one Singaporean, one American, both Gujarati. They are in a hallway, talking about art. In service of a joke, one poet puts on an Indian accent. The accent, Victor writes, lands like "heavy bronze bangles around a slim wrist" which curve "to the familiar body," and, at the same time, like a "giant space helmet while we're still on land." What is key here is that the too big helmet fits just like the bangles do: fits the scene, fits the poets. "The accent is exaggerated," Victor writes, "it is a costume that makes us look like each other to each other—fellow aliens. This is a warm parody of belonging and a kind of love between migrants. We laugh; we lean in."[105]

We have become accustomed to conceptualizing ethnic and postcolonial scenes of languaging as violent experiences of "self-alienation in self-hearing."[106] Recall, for example, Maxine Hong Kingston's description of the narrator's cut frenum in *The Woman Warrior*, and Gloria Anzaldúa's account of the taming of her wild tongue in *Borderlands/La Frontera*.[107] But it is also the case that hearing a version of the self—hearing a voice that sounds familiar, hearing an accent that you recognize, or hearing yourself pronounce words that you share with others—can be pleasurable, joyful, and affirming. In Victor's scene, accent does not wound. Accent is style, knowledge, and affiliation. It is an invitation to talk "candidly among ourselves," in Isabella Hammad's words. One that might even be "therapeutic," to return to Jay Caspian Kang.

Accent is history: it is how we have learned to speak and sound; it is Lahiri's twenty years of Italian-language study; it is her husband's Spanish; it is love between two Gujaratis in diaspora. It is what Lawrence Abu Hamdan calls a "biography of migration."[108] It is expertise and skill. Equally, accent is the future: it is how we wish to speak and be heard; it is affinity, aspiration, attunement to, and accommodation of the other. It is what Lahiri calls her "desperate love" for Italian. It is the reason Victor's poet leans in.

What I've just offered are two short readings via Lahiri and Victor that illustrate how accent happens and what accent *is*: both the affordance of identity and the event of its unmaking. I want to turn back now to *accented reading*, which is not just a means of locating accent in the text, but rather a method of reading with the knowledge of accent. This is a project distinctly inaugurated by Saxena and myself in our respective single-authored chapters for *Thinking with an Accent*. For Saxena, what makes a reading "accented" is that accent is construed not "as a relation of knowing but the moment before it, the moment of unknowing difference."[109] In my treatment, accent is a metacritical and metalinguistic "form of approach" to an object.[110] What Saxena and I share is the sense that, as she puts it, "what readers hear" is also always "their own voice."[111] And, as I have written, that accented reading names the limits and possibilities of the reader's own critical position, over and above those of the writer.[112]

In redescribing invested, acoustic, accented, and personal *criticism* in terms of *reading method*, I seek to situate this book's intervention in an ongoing debate in English literary studies about the status of close reading as the discipline's dominant mode of textual engagement.[113] Some of the current conversation has to do with the advent of new technologies, of course. (How are we to read now that computers, broadly defined, can read so much more and so much faster than humans?) But it is also about decentering the ways in which many of us were taught to read—and what. As Juliana Spahr puts it, reading has always been "a learned and regulated act . . . taught in school so as to walk hand in hand with assimilation [and] at its most oppressive when taught through principles of absolute meaning."[114]

Accented reading is a method of analyzing how a text's "identity" is simultaneously produced and dismantled through a critic's efforts to identify it—as they, as we, also inevitably identify with or against it. Accented reading means reading with the knowledge that what I read might not sound the same to another reader, and that I may not be a text's intended addressee. As a method, it requires two co-constitutive critical operations: the first attends to the position of reception and the critic's own reading practice; the second to the identitarian avowals and disavowals of the writer of the text. In this way, accented reading is a form of rereading. In the words of Barbara Johnson, on our initial reading of a text "we can see in it only what we have already learned to see before."[115] On rereading, we come to understand how and why we learned to read that way in the first place.

Let me now put it as simply as I can. An accented reading is not a reading of a text. An accented reading is a reading of a *relation* to a text and an account of a *journey* with a text—a journey toward the text or away from it, alongside, against, and back again.

Accented reading is what I, as a scholar overdetermined by identity's call, strive to perform in this book. It is not a retrospective description of how I have taught. Also, once more, I am not using accented reading to make an argument for privileged identity-based knowing. The identitarian correspondence of critical-subject and literary-object does not even produce *better* knowing. What I suggest is that it produces better *not* knowing.

We the overdetermined arrive at the scene of reading, writing, or instruction having already had to confront our own hard-earned failure to insert a gap between subject and object, a failure registered as resistance to the imperative of representing the authors, texts, or communities in question. That's where we distinctly begin: not through efforts to produce our proximity to the object (whether through language study or participant observation), but through efforts to produce our distance from it. We don't just have to find our way *to* the object as accented readers; rather we have to find our way *back* to the object after we have already been repelled.

I begin each chapter from the premise that it is not "easy to write what is nearest to me" and that "[it] should be difficult to write what one 'knows.' "[116] Accented reading thus also advances the project of unlearning the ways in which many of us in US schools and universities have been taught to write.

The Sociality of Criticism and the Hermeneutic Circle: A Chapter Breakdown

With these dynamics at the forefront of my inquiry, I present a cultural study of literary studies that is metacritical, institutionally situated, and true to my experience as a student and professor in US academe. In addition to the texts I read, the scenes, conversations, asides, espousals of communal affects, and even tweets that I discuss in this book show us the unspoken rules of our fields. I seek to understand the sociality of criticism that underlies interpretation and analysis, and that develops through the cross-cultural encounters and pedagogical exchanges that we have in the course of our professional engagement with literature.

My approach to literary studies involves tracing the complete hermeneutic circle enclosing critics, writers, readers, teachers, and students. In the process, I show that these are all subject positions as well as textual categories, along with author, character, and narrator. Each chapter and recess therefore begin with a contextualizing scene of institutional positioning. What I offer as "my institutional positions" unfold between 2003 and 2022, and are intended to touch on different stages of an academic life and career, even as I recognize that no scene recounted here is universal.[117] Every author-focused chapter is additionally framed by a syllabus for a class I have taught. I am including the syllabi in their original forms as faithful representations of the curricular conversations into which the chapters enter.

The author-focused chapter is a conventional feature of the literary studies monograph, but my distinct take on this form aims to defamiliarize and renew it. For one, I strive for modularity and utility; each chapter therefore engages distinct arguments and can stand alone. By that same token, they all rotate around shared pedagogical and methodological axes. Each chapter mines the critical discourse around an author of twentieth- or twenty-first-century Indian literature in English, asking not just what their texts say or do in theory but what they have said or done in practice, in specific curricular contexts, and in particular classrooms. I attend differently to how each author theorizes their own literary project, and I consider the implications of taking contemporary writers at their word. Throughout, I am interested in how the critic's reading position is anticipated, produced, solicited, and thwarted by writers who are deeply attuned to how they are being read. I identify a cross-pollinating dynamic between writers of literature and literature scholars who all risk being misrepresented by one another, and whose worries to that end crucially overdetermine the positions they take in their respective fields.

Each chapter is also written about or against a prior disavowal. My approach is rhetorical, not psychoanalytic, which means I am interested in literary projects that explicitly emerge through some version of the locution: "I am not ___."[118]

Bharati Mukherjee (chapter 1) disavows Indian American authorship and ethnic subjectivity—but writes her way into the American multiethnic sphere. "I am not an Indian writer," she says. This disavowal powerfully inflects the "American accents" on offer in her fiction, on the basis of which she became an Asian American ethnic literary pioneer and curricular mainstay. The case of Mukherjee shows us that being multiethnic is not about the coercive mimetic performance of ethnic subjectivity as such; the author disclaims her Indian accent. Ironically, Mukherjee becomes multiethnic through her attempts to ventriloquize the American voice.

Chetan Bhagat (chapter 3) repudiates literary Anglophonism—but fetishizes English. "I am not an intellectual," he says. This disavowal motivates Bhagat's calculated, accented presentation of his "bad English" as a conduit to the Indian vernacular sphere and the life-worlds of "real" New Indians. Ironically, Bhagat's "more Indian than the Indians" English shows us how the Anglophone functions as a repudiation of both literary English and postcolonial criticism, while unsettling the premises of both the postcritical and the post-postcolonial.

Amit Chaudhuri (chapter 5) writes against hegemonic postcolonialism's investment in the nation in a self-consciously "literary" accent. "I am not interested in writing about India," he says. This disavowal underlies his work in relatively minor genres, like the novella and autofiction, as well as his counterwriting of the domestic, even as it produces another India as the referent of his texts. Chaudhuri's simultaneously self-effacing and self-obsessed mobilizations of the first person, and his canny refusal to speak for the subaltern, lay bare the ways in which fields are constructed at their margins.

Jhumpa Lahiri (chapter 7) disowns the English language—but it underpins her Italian work. "I am not rooted in this language," she says. This disavowal reveals the continuities between the ethnic American and post-Anglophone literary projects, which both enact a politics of identitarian refusal in order to shore up a reparative form of identitarian assignment. Lahiri began her career as an exemplary Indian American writer, turned to postcolonial India in her second novel, and then moved into the writing and translation of Italian, opening up a new vantage from which to query what it means to be Indian, what it means to be an American, what it means to be Anglophone, and what it means to have an English accent.

These four writers share "India" and "English"—but different Indias and different Englishes. Two, Bhagat and Chaudhuri, are Anglophone returnees to India whose books give American readers provisional purchase on the global and neoliberal transformations of New India. Two, Mukherjee and Lahiri, are US-based writers whose books give global readers provisional purchase on the seductions and frustrations of American ethnic subjectivity. Two, Mukherjee and Bhagat, are invested in the production of *proximity*: to America and India, respectively. Two, Chaudhuri and Lahiri, are concerned with the enactment of *distance*: narrative and linguistic, respectively. As for their English accents, Bhagat's is "bad," Mukherjee's is "American," Chaudhuri's is "literary," and Lahiri's is "Italian." But none of these writers is defensive about their use of English. Writers of caste, class, and canon-privilege, they nevertheless use English with "little nostalgia, guilt, denial, or qualification," not unlike those Dalit Anglophone writers for whom English holds out the promise of "casteless modernity." I mention this not to flatten differences between the subject positions in question, but as further evidence of the heterogeneity within the field construed as postcolonial and "caricatured as global."[119] Even elite Anglophonism is not *one*.

In between the main chapters are three interchapters styled as "recesses" offering short meditations on the iconicity of postcolonial theorists Gayatri Chakravorty Spivak, Homi Bhabha, and Edward Said. The key word here is iconicity. Spivak, Bhabha, and Said are the central figures of postcolonial studies in its US dispensation, and each represents a specific mode of working through identity, language, or politics. Spivak—the "academostar"—challenges the discipline of English with her multilingual pedagogy and translational ethic. Bhabha—the "bad writer"—models commitment to the unfinished work of Theory. Said—"the public intellectual"—is a lodestar for the historical elaboration of the worldliness of the text. Each of these postcolonialists resisted the "postcolonial" moniker. All three were critics of the canonization machine who have seen their work canonized.

Like the other chapters, each recess emerges out of an institutionally grounded scene: a chance meeting in the lobby of a conference hotel (chapter 2/recess 1, after Spivak); a revealing exchange on academic Twitter (chapter 4/recess 2, after Bhabha); and a memorial service for a departed scholar (chapter 6/recess 3, after Said). Through readings of interviews, reviews, and paratextual notes, I ask how the personas of Spivak-Bhabha-Said have been constructed—not what they argued or theorized. I take this approach because, as Hamid Dabashi writes, it is important to produce "a record of our own location next to towering figures who have bracketed our intellectual life."[120] Dabashi's own such record is one of intimacy with his friend Said. In my case, I don't personally know any of these towering figures and do not imagine myself as intimate with them. What I do know is that each of them represents a form of anxiety that inflects knowledge production in the contemporary humanities. So as not to overgeneralize, I will admit specifically to the worries that underlie my own work and that I have heard expressed by some of my students: that we haven't read enough; that we don't know enough languages; that we might not understand the text; that our prose is not sufficiently theoretical; or that our theory is not adequately political.

Where is the space, and when is the time, to examine such concerns? I have styled these interchapters as recesses in order to distinguish the discussions they offer from the more formal academic criticism in the other chapters. My wager is that if we are to reflect honestly on what it means to read literature and theorize the postcolonial in the twenty-first century, we have to consider how, why, and to what end the work of certain thinkers has become "adjectified" (e.g., Saidian). We have to examine how subject positions like "academostar," "bad writer," and "public intellectual" inflect ongoing debates on the crisis of the humanities, the decline of language study, the end of theory, and the casualization of academic labor.

I argue that ideas about Spivak, Bhabha, and Said, and their own paratextual framings of their work, have overdetermined the questions it is now possible to ask within English, generally, and postcolonial studies, specifically. Can the subaltern speak, and if so, with what accent? Can performative, creative texts disrupt or subvert official discourses and ideologies? Should we be training our students to be exilic and critically amateur public writers? Each recess contextualizes the emergence of such questions. Each is a space-time for thinking frankly about the culture of academic celebrity and its relationship to the canonization machine; a space-time to acknowledge the challenge of writing about hallowed figures in the field, and the problematic combination of deference and frustration that they inspire. Each, finally, poses the big picture questions submerged within our close readings: Who are we? What should we read? How should we write? What should we teach? And to whom should we be speaking?

Teaching the Research Machine

This book is not about pedagogical methods or philosophies, but it is a book about teaching—at least to the extent that I could not have written about any of these authors, theorists, or texts without having taught or considered teaching them first. Perhaps, then, it is more accurate to say that this is a book that takes teaching seriously. This is a book that considers teaching not only *in* relation to research, but *as* a relation to research, as a venue not for the deliverance of knowledge but for its cultivation. My focus is on understanding what some of us contemporary literature professors are doing with literature, what we think we can or should do with it, and what we want to do with it—over and above what literature does in and of itself.

In the following pages, I look backward from the perspective of the student, and I look forward from the perspective of the professor on whom the student might look back. I am concerned with how I and others have been "recruited" by the demands of classroom, curriculum, and canon, and the opportunity of interlocution with students, into a relation to literary studies that both secures and obscures understanding of its "critical motives, historical conditions [and] ways of knowing."[121]

Not just any classroom, of course. This book develops insights gleaned from my years studying and teaching at five specific US research universities: three public, land-grant universities in the American West and Southwest, and two private research universities in the American South.[122] Each chapter draws on my work in specific departments of literature, rhetoric, and English.

Equally, not just any students, but primarily Anglophones, and primarily students born, raised, and educated in the United States, like myself. That said, in narrating scenes from my classroom, my point of departure is generally the *idea* of the student as a potential recipient of a particular argument or field-specific curricular intervention, as opposed to specific students I have taught, none of whom is named in this book. While I do not seek to flatten or massify my students, and while my chapters variously account for students as agents of their own education, this is not an ethnographic study.

Finally, it must be stressed, I am not writing about just any kind of teaching. I have had the increasingly rare opportunity of holding what some readers will recognize as a series of "40-40-20" tenure-track academic positions: a job that is officially described as 40 percent research, 40 percent teaching, and 20 percent service to department, college, university, and profession. These kinds of positions have been in short supply for years. They were further reduced during the COVID pandemic when many universities instituted a hiring freeze and paused graduate admissions. The vast majority of faculty hired in recent decades have been off the tenure track. At the time of this writing, at least 75 percent of those teaching in US colleges and universities are graduate students or non-tenure-track and contingent faculty on temporary contracts.[123]

Although this book is not centrally about the adjunctification of higher education, it aims to affirm the value of the humanities and the importance of tenure, unionization efforts, and solidarity across ranks through its sustained elaboration of the "hyphen" that connects the 40 percent teaching to the 40 percent scholarship in the theoretical tenure-track role statement. Much obfuscation of our disappearing jobs is happening at the site of this hyphen. The swelling of the ranks of contingent labor in the university is not only of the underpaid and precarious, but also of one side of the hyphen on an institutional scale. It's commonplace for faculty in positions like mine to lament that the 40 percent of our job descriptions that encompasses "research" is being cannibalized by the remaining 60 percent. This cannibalization is now happening at the scale of the profession, as far more than 60 percent of new faculty are hired into jobs with little or nothing on the "research" side of the breakdown. The overdrawn division between teaching and research eclipses this situation and undermines efforts toward our collective mobilization.

What, really, is the relationship between teaching and research—not in the abstract, but as it is daily negotiated in our jobs and lives? It is not just that the former can be made "to feed" the latter, which is what many of us are trying to do: to make the teaching serve the research. The teaching *is* the research, and vice versa. That is one of the arguments at the heart of this book, and it is one of the reasons why more faculty must continue to have resourced research programs with the protections of academic freedom and time, healthcare, and (more than) a living wage. Any hiring plan or vision for a humanities faculty that does not take as axiomatic the cross-pollination of teaching and research is grossly underestimating the capacities of both.[124] To borrow the title of a recent *Post45* dossier, it is time to theorize "contemporary literature from the classroom."[125]

Developing new critical methods for writing about teaching might prove to elongate the lifespan of the academic humanities in another important way: it will highlight what is distinct about literary scholarship. Journalists, freelancers, essayists, professional non-academic critics: they all can and do write what is legible and widely circulated as literary criticism. The distinction of the literary criticism produced by the scholar-teacher inheres in the fact that we also teach in field- and discipline-specific contexts. Moreover, writing about teaching is something that we can do that the distant-reading computers and algorithmically writing AI bots cannot. As Rachel Sagner Buurma and Laura Heffernan write in *The Teaching Archive*, "Perhaps singularly among the disciplines, literary study is enacted rather than rehearsed in classrooms; the answer to the question 'Did I miss anything last week?' is truly 'Yes—and you missed it forever.'"[126]

DEVONthink can scan the archives faster than we can, and ChatGPT can instantly imitate how we write, but they both missed class last week and the week before and the week before that. The record we have to offer of what we've been doing in our classrooms—and how and why—will be missed forever if we don't learn how to write it.

What follows is one sincere and considered attempt.

CHAPTER 1

What Was Multiethnic Literature?

Or, Bharati Mukherjee Doesn't Have an Indian Accent

[My Institutional Position]

In spring 2018, I began an interinstitutional collaboration with fellow academics Pooja Rangan, Akshya Saxena, and Pavitra Sundar. We were working to develop "accent" as a keyword for new research in the interdisciplinary humanities.[1] In the process of coediting the book that would announce our intervention, we decided to codesign a course. The idea was that we would each teach a version of the class in our home institution, with adjustments to the syllabi befitting our particular departments and students. One of our classes could foreground film; another would emphasize sound; the third might center the politics of translation.

My version was an undergraduate course in contemporary American literature. I called it "English Literature with an Accent." The title was a spin on Rosina Lippi-Green's canonical linguistics textbook.[2] The course synopsis—which appears in the syllabus that follows—opened with two questions: "Do literary texts have accents, the way people do?"; "How do we read the accented voices of English?"

I sought to produce an alternative, if not a corrective, to what my colleague Scott Selisker had described to me as the phenomenon of the "American Voices" course, in which students are invited to "hear the voice of the other" while also hearing America's voice as "harmonious and polyphonic." At their best, such classes advance a pluralistic vision of a country that is not *one*. At their worst, such classes coopt linguistic, vocal, and textual difference in the ideological production of American unisonance.

I had a hunch: that reading multiethnic American texts through the rubric of *accent*, which is at once indexical and nonindexical, might give us a fresh point of entry into debates on the literary representation of both American ethnic subjects and the American voice. Via accent, we would hear and see anew nonstandard American Englishes. We would reconsider the project of articulating the voice-consciousness of the United States. And we would put pressure on the ambivalent claims that the national makes on the ethnic, and vice versa.

The form of the class I designed was simple: We were to read interdisciplinary accent theory, broadly defined, each Tuesday, and read literary texts with the knowledge of accent on Thursdays. We would attend to pace and rhythm, syntax and spelling. We would consider bilingual asides and narrative description, alongside questions of semantics, typographical conventions, and the relationship between geography and voice. These were the kinds of data points and textual evidence that I thought we would have access to as close readers, and that, in other literature classes, I'd been trained to consider as features of style, tone, mood, perspective, and point of view. These terms are conventional in literary studies and proximate to accent. My aim was to bring them into productive tension, occasioned by the tensions of the multiethnic archive itself.

We needed a work of literature to which to return throughout the semester, one that could serve as a thread throughout our inquiry. Should I include the motley plurilingual stylings of G. V. Desani? Or the famously "chutnified" work of Salman Rushdie? No, I needed an ethnic American text, not a postcolonial one—a text invested, however problematically, in sounding the American voice.

A chance conversation with another colleague, Stephanie Brown, presented a solution. Brown had recently taught Bharati Mukherjee's 1989 novel *Jasmine*, and her students completely rejected its protonationalism and retrograde liberal feminism. Mukherjee's work, Brown told me wryly, "has aged very poorly."

This immediately struck me as true. Despite her canonical status in Asian American literature, I myself had never taught Mukherjee. Like many scholars, I was wary of her staunch rejection of Indian American identity and the outmoded celebration of assimilation on display in so many of her texts.

It also struck me as an opportunity. If I taught Mukherjee's work, I would be giving my students the chance to grapple with texts that are from our present vantage anachronistic, even obsolete—texts we already know how to critique, which meant we would be free to do other work with them. I decide to teach selections from her 1988 collection *The Middleman and Other Stories*.

Mukherjee tried to write her way into the American literary canon by repudiating ethnic hyphenation and extranational qualification. Was her entrance into the Asian American canon a mark of her project's failure or success? What might reading Mukherjee in the 2020s reveal about the mid- to late twentieth-century project of American multiethnic literature? Through the accents of the outmoded Mukherjee, could we read and hear the ethnic anew?

[Syllabus]

English Literature with an Accent
English 347 | University of Arizona
Spring 2020

Do literary texts have accents, the way people do? How do we read the accented voices of English? This class explores voice and accent in English literature and cultural production, including podcasts, audiobooks, film, and television. Everyone has an accent, but not all accents are created equal. Some are heard as "neutral" and others as markers of difference. This has serious implications in the real world: accent discrimination costs jobs, housing applications, and asylum claims. What are the implications in the field of multiethnic literature? Students will examine ethnic American literatures alongside interdisciplinary scholarship on topics including race and voice (e.g. brown voice, white voice, "Mock Asian," Black English), the cybernetic voices of virtual assistants like Siri, forensic listening, and call centers. Students will gain broad understanding of the politics of literary voice and accent, while learning to use their own accented voices to produce close, critical readings and informed social interventions.

COURSE SCHEDULE

Thu., Jan. 16:   Introductions

UNIT 1: Accent and Ideology

Tue., Jan. 21:   Rosina Lippi-Green, "Introduction" and "The Myth of Non-Accent," *English with an Accent: Language, Ideology, and Discrimination in the United States* (1997)

Bharati Mukherjee, "A Wife's Story," *The Middleman and Other Stories* (1988)

Thu., Jan. 23:   Angela Reyes, "The Voicing of Asian American Figures: Korean Linguistic Styles at an Asian American Cram School" (2016)

Tue., Jan. 28:   Screening Session: *Do I Sound Gay?*, dir. David Thorpe (2014)

Thu., Jan. 30:   Mary Bucholtz, *White Kids: Language, Race, and Styles of Youth Identity*, "I'm like yeah but she's all no: innovative quotative markers and preppy whiteness" (2010)

UNIT 2: Voice and Listening

Tue., Feb. 4:   Anne Karpf, *The Human Voice*, "How We Color Our Voices with Pitch, Volume, and Tempo" (2006)

Amanda Weidman, "Voice," *Keywords in Sound* (2015)

Tue., Feb. 11:   Gloria Anzaldúa, "How to Tame a Wild Tongue" (1987)

Thu., Feb. 13:   Sujata Bhatt, "Search for My Tongue" (1986)

Dominic Pettman, *Sonic Intimacy: Voice, Species, Technics (or, How to Listen to the World)*, "The Aural Phase" (2017)

Tue., Feb. 18:   Bharati Mukherjee, "Jasmine," *The Middleman and Other Stories* (1988)

"The Speech Accent Archive": http://accent.gmu.edu/index.php

Thu., Feb. 20: Tom Rice, "Listening," *Keywords in Sound* (2015)

Nabeel Zuberi, "Listening While Muslim" (2017)

UNIT 3: The Sonic Color Line, or Hearing Difference

Tue., Feb. 25: Jennifer Lynn Stoever, *The Sonic Color Line: Race and the Cultural Politics of Listening*, "The Sonic Color Line and the Listening Ear" (2016)

Thu., Feb. 27: James Baldwin, "If Black English Isn't a Language, Then Tell Me, What Is?" (1979)

Zora Neale Hurston, "Story in Harlem Slang" (1942)

Tue., Mar. 3: H. Samy Alim, *Articulate While Black: Barack Obama, Language, and Race in the U.S.*, "A.W.B. (Articulate While Black)" (2012)

Thu., Mar. 5: Zadie Smith, "Speaking in Tongues" (2009)

Tue., Mar. 17: Bharati Mukherjee, "Danny's Girls," *The Middleman and Other Stories* (1988)

Thu., Mar. 19: Bharati Mukherjee, "The Tenant," *The Middleman and Other Stories* (1988)

UNIT 4: Sounding Identity, or Performing Accent

Tue., Mar. 24: Micah Stack, "The G.R.I.E.F." (2015)

Thu., Mar. 26: Screening Session: *Waiting for Guffman*, dir. Christopher Guest (1996)

Tue., Mar. 31: Sarah Kessler, "The Voice of Mockumentary" (2018)

"Yard Sale," *Modern Family* (2012)

Thu., Apr. 2: Dolores Inés Casillas, Sebastian Ferrada, and Sara Veronica Hinojos, "The Accent on *Modern Family*: Listening to Representations of the Latina Vocal Body" (2018)

Tue., Apr. 7:   Shilpa S. Davé, *Indian Accents: Brown Voice and Racial Performance in American Television and Film*, "Apu's Brown Voice: *The Simpsons* and Indian American Accents" (2013)

"Much Apu About Nothing" (*The Simpsons*, Season 7, Episode 23)

The Problem with Apu, dir. Hari Kondabolu (2017)

Thu., Apr. 9:   V. S. Naipaul, "His Chosen Calling," *Miguel Street* (1959)

UNIT 5: The Cybernetic Voice

Tue., Apr. 14: Dominic Pettman, *Sonic Intimacy: Voice, Species, Technics (or, How to Listen to the World)*, "The Cybernetic Voice" (2017)

Thu., Apr. 16: Ted Chiang, from *Exhalation* (2019)

UNIT 6: Forensic Listening, or Adjudicating Accent

Tue., Apr. 21: Rosina Lippi-Green, "Real People with a Real Language: The Workplace and the Judicial System" (1997)

Thu., Apr. 23: Lawrence Abu Hamdan, "Aural Contract" (2014)

Naomi Waltham-Smith, "Excursus2: L. A. Hamdan's Border Crossings" (pre-print)

"Aural Contract Audio Archive"

UNIT 7: Mimeticism, the Call Center, and the Neutral Accent

Tue., Apr. 28: Bharati Mukherjee, "Loose Ends," *The Middleman and Other Stories* (1988)

Shehzad Nadeem, "Accent Neutralisation and a Crisis of Identity in India's Call Centers" (2011)

Dan Sinykin, "White Voice" (2019)

Thu., Apr. 30: *Nalini By Day, Nancy By Night*, dir. Sonali Gulati (2005)

[Accented Reading]

> I am not an Indian writer, not an exile, not an expatriate.
> —BHARATI MUKHERJEE

By her own description, Bharati Mukherjee was not an "Indian" writer. But she was born in pre-Partition India in 1940 and much of her work explored the twentieth-century Indian experience in a transnational or global frame. She earned an MFA and PhD at the University of Iowa in the 1960s, during the early years of "the program era,"[3] and from 1989 onward, she worked as a professor of English at the University of California, Berkeley. Over the course of four decades, beginning with *The Tiger's Daughter* in 1971, Mukherjee published eight novels and seven books of short fiction and nonfiction. Her final novel, *Miss New India*, released in 2011, consummated the diasporic narrative of departure, arrival, and return that she both charted and chafed against in each of her books.

Mukherjee's total oeuvre pursues what she called "the epic narrative" of immigration. In her work, migration emerges as a narrative form, registered in her novels' plots, character development, and temporal structures. Obituaries written upon her death in 2017 celebrate her specifically as a "writer of immigrant life."[4] Although she always denied writing versions of her own story—"I am not at all an autobiographical writer"[5]—her work is especially attuned to the transformations undergone by Indian and South Asian women migrants to North America, like herself.

In a much-cited 1993 essay, "The Anxiety of Indianness," the India-based literary scholar Meenakshi Mukherjee (no relation to Bharati) clubbed Bharati Mukherjee along with a number of "cosmopolitan" writers like Chinua Achebe, Gabriel García Márquez, and Salman Rushdie who were, she wrote, preoccupied with rootlessness, displacement, and hybridity.[6] Meenakshi Mukherjee cited a notorious remark of Bharati Mukherjee's as justification: "I have joined imaginative forces with an anonymous driven underclass of semi-assimilated Indians with sentimental attachments to a distant homeland, but no real desire for permanent return. . . . Indianness is now a metaphor, a particular way of comprehending the world."[7]

Much has been written about Meenakshi Mukherjee's response to this line—in particular her counterassertion of the "non-metaphorical" (read:

real) India to which the India-based Indian writer must attend. What I want to flag here is that, in 1985, Bharati Mukherjee (hereafter "Mukherjee" again) considered herself "semi-assimilated" with "sentimental attachments" to India. Less than a decade later, her self-description had changed. By the early 1990s, Mukherjee had declared herself to be fully assimilated; her primary attachment was now indisputably to the United States. "I am an American writer," Mukherjee wrote, "in the American mainstream, trying to extend it. . . . I am not an Indian writer, not an exile, not an expatriate. I am an immigrant."[8]

Mukherjee didn't want to be read as an ethnic writer. Like other "accommodationist, apologist, and assimilationist" American writers of the twentieth century identified by Swati Rana, she claimed "unhyphenated American identity."[9] To that end, she didn't want to be read as postcolonial, either. In a 1997 essay, Mukherjee explicitly narrated her divergence from the dominant trends in "expatriate" Indian English writing. The problem, she wrote, is that the expatriate construes migration as "loss" instead of "gain": "By becoming a US citizen and exercising my voting rights, I have invested in the present and not the past. . . . I celebrate racial and cultural mongrelization."[10] As an immigrant, Mukherjee prided herself on having willingly undergone the "the trauma of self-transformation" in order to "belong" in America. The same is true of many of her characters and almost all of her heroines.

In embracing an immigrant as opposed to expatriate identity, Mukherjee rejected the preoccupations of postcolonial studies: "We need to apply globalization discourse, diasporic discourse, and theories of transnational [and] national identity-formation, not postcolonial theory, to better understand the negotiations necessary in the contemporary era of globalized economies."[11] In fact, Mukherjee rejected exactly those postcolonial concerns that Meenakshi Mukherjee had attributed to her work when she noted that Indian English writers were in thrall to the fads of "progressive American universities" that were privileging "colonialism as the framework for the major cultural experience of the century" (fiction writers in the "Indian languages," by contrast, Meenakshi Mukherjee argued, were not concerned with colonialism at all).[12]

Such is the challenge of writing about Indian English writers who have been assimilated into the pedagogical and research rubrics of both the ethnic and the postcolonial: often, we cannot distinguish our immigrants from our expatriates, or our patriots from our cosmopolitans. And neither, for that matter, can they—which, as the following pages explore, is maybe also the point.[13]

The Multiethnic "Was" and "Is"

The title of this chapter—"What Was Multiethnic Literature?"—draws inspiration from Kenneth Warren's 2011 "What Was African American Literature?" in which he argues that the social, political, and juridical conditions under which African American literature emerged and to which it critically responded, namely Jim Crow, "no longer obtain." African American literature was, but is no longer, a coherent project, Warren posits, because the condition it was "fighting to overcome was the very condition that gave [its] existence meaning." It was a "prospective" project looking toward a future in which it would no longer have to exist. By contrast, Warren charges, African American literature is now a retrospective and classist project that remains cathected to the solidarities forged in the era of de jure segregation. These solidarities can no longer be assumed, nor do "claiming to be *different from* and claiming to be *the same as* the dominant society" have the same "critical force" that they once did.[14]

Different from, and same as. "Almost the same, but not quite."[15] Versions of these refrains are familiar in the study of ethnic and postcolonial literature and cultural production. The legibility of the particular has always hinged on the simultaneity of its partial insertion into the universal, on the one hand, and its necessary resistance to incorporation, on the other. Cue Mukherjee's obstinate self-descriptions. Marginality, to quote Gayatri Chakravorty Spivak, is "an economic principle of identification through separation."[16] To be a qualified human, which is also to say, to be an ethnic or postcolonial subject, is to be recognizable as human and, at the same time, incontrovertibly other. This is also true of any literature that emerges as a response to dominant preconceptions of its constitutive "inferiority,"[17] which must then be signaled and nullified in the same textual breath. What Warren terms the "critical force" of African American literature emerges from the dialectical relation between these seemingly opposed imperatives.

Or rather, *emerged*, with emphasis on the past tense. In today's literary landscape (I use the word "today" advisedly; I revised this parenthetical in 2023), Warren observes the exhaustion of this force and the evacuation of its critical impetus, not only in African American literature, but in ethnic literatures more generally. He sets up this extension, noting that for American writers in the 1980s and 1990s, the "pressing problem" became "making sure that people have the proper identities."[18] It isn't praise.

This chapter follows Warren in attempting to elaborate the *was*-ness and *is*-ness of the multiethnic American literary project. Let's begin with a "before" and "after" that map closely onto Warren's: Multiethnic literature *was* (or wanted to be) a literature of identity that posed a rebuttal to the identity of American literature; it looked toward a future in which it—the qualification "multiethnic"—would not have to be expressed. Now, however, multiethnic literature *is* (or has proven to be) an alibi in service of the fictions of American multiculturalism.[19]

We've heard versions of this critique before: for example, in Rey Chow's account of ethnic subjectivity as a form of epistemic interpellation that is articulated as an impossible and ultimately self-defeating demand for recognition and redress. As discussed in the introduction, Chow's "protesting ethnic" internalizes the imperative of appearing as ethnic, a form of nonsubjectivity that is abjectly inferior to the nonethnic. Warren doesn't refer to Chow, but their arguments dovetail in important ways. Already in Chow's text the "hyphenated American" is theorized as "future-oriented, always looking ahead to the time when the United States will have fully realized its universal ideals—that is, when ethnic particulars, while continuing to exist, no long really matter (because they have been reduced to the merely picturesque)." In other words, multiethnic literature, like the African American literature it followed in time and impetus, was premised on the expectation of its own dissolution in the realization of an alternatively national—which is also to say, universal—American literary project. That we still teach these literatures as African American, Asian American, and ethnic is proof, according to Chow and Warren, that what appeared to be a horizon was an enclosure, or a form of "existential entrapment."[20]

Was it? Is it? Must it be? In addition to a gambit for inclusion, an avowal of difference, a performance of singularity, and a form of protest, what was multiethnic literature? What purpose does it serve in—or how might it be made to serve—an undergraduate literature course in US academe today?

To be clear, "multiethnic" is not a disciplinary identity. We are not "Multiethnicists." We are African Americanists and Asian Americanists.

Yet, "multiethnic" persists as a qualification used by some professional societies and journals.[21] It is a job market category, too; positions may be advertised for US Multiethnic Literature with a specialization in Latinx or Native American literature, and so on. My use of the term—as an alternative to, as proximate to, and as juxtaposed with the more familiar term "ethnic"—is deliberate. I aim to access a field that both does and does not exist, that attempted to come into being but never did, and that persists despite uncertain origins. "Multiethnic" also speaks to Mukherjee's own chosen mode of self-identification: not as an ethnic Indian American, or as a postcolonial Indian, but as a multiethnic American.

The dictionary definition of multiethnic is "composed of or involving several ethnic groups." The category obtains because there remains an unmarked, hegemonic American literary archive that is read and taught as a national literature, and because the ethnic particularity of an Emerson, Whitman, or Faulkner has been invisibilized. By that same token, the multiethnic is an aspiration, variously stated and unstated, of American literary studies. The field itself strives to posit the multiethnic qualification as redundant; any Americanist worth their salt would claim an engagement with multiethnic literatures, at the very least in the minimal terms of authorship or characterization.

This is where the stakes of the ethnic-multiethnic distinction come sharply into relief: The card-carrying Americanist does not seek to become an "Asian Americanist" or a "Chicano/a Studies" scholar; such specialization would amount to an identitarian reduction, from the national to the ethnic, from the unmarked to the marked. But the desire to be multiethnic, to claim as immanent the multiethnic identity of America, is characteristic of both the field of American literary studies and many of its practitioners. Caroline Rody's argument that there is "a rich ethnic heterogeneity at the heart of Americanness itself" that must nevertheless be respecified in terms of the "interethnic" exemplifies this trend.[22] The multiethnic, then, is not a category that collates distinct ethnic literatures (each of which accents the central archive, thereby producing difference within the American corpus), but rather one that metabolizes the ethnic in the name of American plurality.

The multiethnic is central to the field imaginary of American literary studies.[23] Following Warren, I offer "multiethnic" as a periodizing term, as opposed to a transhistorical category, that tells us what an incipient American literary project thought it was and wanted to be, and how we might from our present vantage apprehend its pyrrhic success. Warren's "was" is not my "was," however. My "was" might more aptly match his "is." His "is" perhaps already "was." Warren's "was" terminates in the civil rights legislation of the mid-1960s and the formal end of Jim Crow (not to be mistaken, he stresses, for the end of racism and inequality). His "is" gathers steam in the 1970s and 1980s. My "was" refers to the institutional consolidation of a multiethnic archive that was indebted to the foundational work of African American studies and ethnic studies scholars, students, and activists whose "separatist" demands in the mid-1960s set the terms for both the "canon wars" and our present rethinking of what it means to be "included."[24] My "is" is the moving horizon of the classroom as time machine.

It is tempting to date the multiethnic in terms of the "post-65." This is a conventional periodizing marker in Asian American literary studies, referring to the 1965 Immigration and Nationality Act, which opened the United States to non-European immigrants in general and professional-class Asians in particular. Within the field, "post-65" is used interchangeably to signify two different populations of writers: immigrants and children of immigrants. Rody's post-65, multiethnic archive includes the work of first-generation "newcomers" like Mukherjee, who sought to "admit differences into the center of [America's] imaginative life."[25] Mukherjee was born in 1940 and immigrated to the United States in 1961; her first book was published in 1971.[26] By contrast, Min Hyoung Song's "children of 1965" are second-generation writers like Jhumpa Lahiri (born in 1967; her first book, *Interpreter of Maladies*, was published in 1999), Susan Choi (born 1969, published *The Foreign Student* in 1998), and Adrian Tomine (born 1974, literary debut in 1998).[27]

Periodization is a tricky business. Take Mukherjee and Lahiri. Born on either side of 1965, they seem to neatly represent the break between the "first" and "second" generations of Indian American writers. But when Rody argues that "the classic Americanization novel has become a novel of initiation into interethnicity," she's not talking about the difference between a Mukherjee and a Lahiri. She's distinguishing between the "Americanization" novels of John Okada and Maxine Hong Kingston, on the one hand, and the "intercultural" fictions of writers like Mukherjee and Chang-rae Lee, on the other.[28] Yet Kingston and Mukherjee are technically contemporaries, both born in 1940; the difference is that the former is US-born, and the latter an immigrant. Likewise, Lahiri and Lee are contemporaries—born in London and South Korea in 1967 and 1965, respectively—and both moved to the United States at age three. In terms of sensibility, however, Lee shares Mukherjee's "interethnic imagination," while Lahiri's Pulitzer-winning debut offers an ethnographic account of diasporic inheritance.

I won't belabor these examples. The point is not that any particular writer was before their time or, conversely, retrograde, but rather that a periodizing marker like "post-65" primarily serves to alert readers to the binaries that are going to structure our readings: here, first and second generation; expatriate and immigrant; immigrant and American. Warren's periodization, which registers his suspicion of the postracial discourse on offer during Barack Obama's first term as president (2009–2012), is also fundamentally heuristic. When I began writing this chapter in summer 2020, during the first year of the COVID pandemic and the global Black Lives Matter protests, African American literature and books by Black authors generally were experiencing a market renaissance in the United States, cueing some indignant critics to counter Warren's argument that "African American literature is over" and scoff at his title's premise: "*Was?*"

I am not a scholar of African American literature, and this chapter does not presume to answer Warren's question. But I am thinking alongside Warren here because we have what I take to be a common concern: specifically, a concern with elaborating the identity of a literature that aims to be both reflective and productive of a community with tenuously shared commitments; a literature that aims to give voice to a people for whom it ultimately cannot speak; a literature that then aims to make audible this people through the impossible sounding of their voice—a voice, singular, that cannot possibly be theirs, plural, and yet also is.

In the following pages, I approach this tangle through the epistemology of accent, which I offer as the critical node at which the text, author, and reader are co-constituted. As discussed in the introduction, accent colloquially indexes difference. By contrast, I elaborate accent as the sticky tissue between what we say and how we sound, between subjects and ideas of subjects. Accent does not sound authenticity; it sets into motion processes of "authentication" through which the regime of authenticity is produced.[29] Accent does not betray identities; it lays bare logics of identification. In this way, I use accent to reroute questions of identity and voice, so that we might ask not only what multiethnic literature was and is, but *how* it is, how it sounds to whom, and how it resounds in and beyond the classroom.

Warren's argument about the "was-ness" of African American literature was never about the number of books sold, after all, and his critique of the politics of representation stands more powerfully than ever. Class fractures between racialized Americans cannot be overcome by "the romance of racial solidarity"; nor can we "assume that shared identity means a shared commitment to the strategies"[30] that would materially improve people's lives. This is precisely why I am interested in the course contexts in which ethnic and postcolonial texts (read: minority literatures in US academe) are put to work. I aim to subject the theoretical critique of literature to the sobering test of the pedagogical scene and the heterogeneous temporality of the classroom.[31] Because, while readers may have "rushed to buy books about race and racism" in 2020, it isn't at all clear that they actually read them.[32] In our class, we did.

An Immigrant's Romance with America

The syllabus for English Literature with an Accent was structured around repeat returns to Mukherjee's *The Middleman and Other Stories*. Here's why. *Middleman* was the first collection by a naturalized American citizen to win the National Book Critics Circle Award. When it was published, a glowing *New York Times* review by Jonathan Raban called it "a consummated romance with the American language" and "a romance with America itself."[33] Rody describes the book as "a pioneering venture into the multicultural American sublime" and "perhaps the clearest case in which multiethnic encounter becomes in itself the occasion for fiction."[34] Ruth Maxey finds in the collection "polyphonic energy and multiethnic scope" that reflects Mukherjee's "exhilaration" at having become a US citizen.[35]

Indeed, Mukherjee's "exuberance about assimilation" into the United States has always played a significant role in her public and academic reception.[36] Throughout her writing, Mukherjee holds up the United States as her "object of desire."[37] This is one way to read *Middleman*, which assembles a motley cast of "American" characters, including a Vietnam War veteran, an Iraqi Jewish guerrilla, an Atlanta investment banker, a motel owner named Patel, and recent immigrants with wives back in the Hungarian countryside, uncles in Chengdu, and lonely husbands in Ahmedabad. These characters do not just sit side by side in the table of contents. They intersect and interact, as in the story "Orbiting" about a relationship between Italian American Rindy and her Afghani American boyfriend, who she'd like to teach to "walk like an American . . . how to fill up a room as Dad does." Mukherjee writes America as multiethnic and New York as South Asian, "with Nepalis, Ugandan Indians, Punjabis, and Gujaratis all taking their place within its rich immigrant diversity."[38] Most of her characters express disappointment with their lives after having landed stateside. By that same token, their "romances with America"—offered primarily through dramatic monologues in the present tense—are continually affirmed.

"A Wife's Story," first published in *Mother Jones* in 1986, follows Panna, a graduate student in New York, as she reflects on the India she has left behind and the America into which she has arrived, an America that renders immigrants "funny" and "disgusting" in turn as a kind of acceptance-trial-by-fire. The story begins with a textbook scene of constrained ethnic protest, as Panna contemplates sending angry letters to David Mamet, for his insulting references to the Patel community in *Glengarry Glen Ross*, and Steven Spielberg, for his depiction of Indians eating monkey brains in *Indiana Jones: Temple of Doom*. "It's the tyranny of the American dream that scares me," Panna reflects. "First, you don't exist. Then you're invisible. Then you're funny. Then you're disgusting. Insult, my American friends will tell me, is a kind of acceptance. No instant dignity here." Panna never actually writes the letters to Mamet or Spielberg; moreover, she internalizes the negative, stereotypical representations as a sign that "We've made it." Although she recognizes "the tyranny of the American dream," Panna cathects to it nevertheless. "I've made it," she thinks to herself. "I'm making something of my life."[39]

Because critiques of America like Panna's are typically neutralized in the action of her stories, Mukherjee has long "satisfied the demand for . . . multiculturalism" in US academe.[40] American readers—including professors, critics, and anthologists—can take heart that the nation, no matter its betrayal of immigrants, remains Mukherjee's and her characters' desired home. The novel *Jasmine*, and the short story "Jasmine" from which it emerged, are cases in point: both depict young women whose dream of arrival in the United States (in the novel, from Punjab to Iowa; in the story, from Trinidad to Detroit) is tested and betrayed, but then also ultimately consummated in sexual relationships with white American men.[41]

In the story "Jasmine," which is collected in *Middleman*, the title character is employed as a domestic worker in Ann Arbor. She is seduced by her married employer, Bill, who hails her as a "flower of Trinidad." A self-described "girl with ambition," Jasmine overlooks the exoticization, infidelity, and asymmetrical nature of their intercourse and "[gives] herself up to it."[42] The well-known passage from the story's final page is worth quoting at length:

> [Jasmine] felt so good she was dizzy. She'd never felt so good on the island where men did this all the time, and girls went along with it always for favors. You couldn't feel really good in a nothing place. She was thinking this as they made love on the Turkish carpet in front of the fire: she was a bright, pretty girl with no visa, no papers, and no birth certificate. No nothing other than what she wanted to invent and tell. She was a girl rushing wildly into the future.[43]

If Trinidad is a "nothing place," then Ann Arbor is a something place, somewhere. Being undocumented ("no papers") becomes in Mukherjee's telling a condition of possibility, where otherwise it would signal precarity. Jasmine has successfully rid herself of her history. The future is hers to invent. Most of the stories in *Middleman* also end like this, in the middle of the action, with Mukherjee's characters in the process of wild "arrival" into Americanness. As Maxey observes, Mukherjee's ambiguous endings are "a technique by which to emphasize the pressures, excitements and uncertainties of the present moment."[44] Her immigrants are desiring subjects, even when they seem to be, in Lauren Berlant's terms, desiring against their own interests.[45]

The most anthologized stories by Mukherjee are precisely those that "reproduce a particular gendered and racialized dynamic: the Indian woman apparently freed by North America from patriarchal traditions in the ancestral homeland." By that same token, Mukherjee's work does not feature in many of the major anthologies of South Asian American fiction published in the late twentieth century, including *Our Feet Walk the Sky: Women of the South Asian Diaspora* (1993) and *Contours of the Heart: South Asians Map North America* (1996). Maxey speculates that this is because Mukherjee's fiction is "not sufficiently innovative or politically oppositional vis-à-vis US identity politics. . . . [She is] too fervent in her devotion to America and too dismissive of India."[46]

Indeed, many feminist literary and cultural theorists have identified the ways that Mukherjee's work, exemplified by "Jasmine," holds out "the dominant scripts of exotic otherness as an avenue to the American Dream."[47] As erin Khuê Ninh puts it, *Jasmine* in particular "makes itself convenient to both patriarchal and Western anxieties."[48] Inderpal Grewal argues that Mukherjee is best understood as a "nationalist," whose rejection of ethnic hyphenation entails the articulation of both US American and Bengali forms of neoliberal, national identification.[49] Mukherjee's own pronouncements ("I became a citizen by choice")[50] confirm her metabolism of a voluntaristic ethic of American national identification. Grewal further argues that Mukherjee's commercial success and incorporation into the Asian American canon were premised on her ability "to articulate the trope of the Asian woman within the context of a liberal idea of America" in which Asia, and India specifically, represents tradition, repression, and stagnation, while the United States represents modernity, freedom, and choice.[51] In Susan Koshy's estimation, Mukherjee produces "strategic affirmations of the dominant fiction of the immigrant's desire for America, itself an ideological construct for the reproduction of nationalism."[52]

These were the kinds of critiques of Mukherjee that I'd read and internalized before I decided to try to teach her work anyway. I intended to make space for such readings in my class. In fact, I sought to create the conditions in which these kinds of critical responses might emerge through our class's real-time discussions. We would contest xenophobic nationalisms and historicize the emergence of assimilationist imperatives.

But I also sought to open up the terms of the conversation, from consideration of Mukherjee's romance with *America*, and here I'm returning to Raban's review, to the question of her "romance with the *American language.*" I hoped that assessing Mukherjee's manipulation of accented language, over and above her characterization and plots, would allow us to advance our critique through consideration of her work's acousticality, a property of narrative form that Julie Beth Napolin describes as "neither showing nor telling but sounding."[53] This would allow us to emphasize formal considerations in the treatment of multiethnic literatures, which have long been overdetermined by questions of recognition and representation, while also putting pressure on the form-content distinction.

How does Mukherjee construct her characters' voices as foreign, nonnative, nonstandard, other, minor, and minority? What is an American accent in *Middleman*? Is it a property of a "white" voice?[54] Who has one, and who doesn't? Is Mukherjee's accent audibly and legibly American or Indian—or neither? What does an Indian sound like? And whose is the voice of America?[55]

Teaching English Literature with an Accent

I wanted to ask my students these questions. But I realized in our initial class sessions that we would first have to disentangle "accent" from that debased term "dialect," which my students were accustomed to using to describe nondominant varieties of English. As Jennifer Lynn Stoever argues, all readers tune into texts with "the listening ear," which produces as derivative and deficient that which is different from the ideologically produced norm.[56] Scholarship on Black English would be our class's guide through this tangle, from James Baldwin's powerful elaboration of language as a political instrument,[57] to John Baugh's foundational theorization of "linguistic profiling" in *Black Linguistics*,[58] to H. Samy Alim and Geneva Smitherman's astute diagnosis of the trap of "articulate blackness."[59]

Zora Neale Hurston's 1942 "Story in Harlem Slang" was our literary accompaniment to these texts, and it lay bare the profound challenge of unhearing what the listening ear thinks it hears.[60] As we read Hurston, it was difficult for my students and me to identify what was accent and what was "slang," what was English, what was dialect, and what was another language entirely. "Wait till I light up my coal-pot and I'll tell you about this Zigaboo called Jelly," Hurston's story begins. Jelly wears a "zoot suit with the reet pleats." He tells his friend, Sweet Back, that he's "too blamed astorperious." He comes on to a woman on the street, saying, "I'd walk clear to Diddy-Wah-Diddy to get a chance to speak to a pretty lil' ground-angel like that."

Is this English, my students asked? Do we know, I countered, what English is? I pointed out that Hurston's representation of African American men and Black English in 1940s Harlem hinges on the linguistic performance approaching—but never crossing—the horizon of unintelligibility. "We" in our class might not know the slang on offer, but we can still understand the story of Jelly and Sweet Back, infer the historical context of the Great Migration, and hear equal parts predation and desperation in Jelly's catcall. Each vernacular utterance cues the outsider reader's apprehension of racialized difference. By that same token, the story is written in such a way as to (provisionally, seductively, perhaps misleadingly) let that outsider in.

At the close of the story, Hurston offers a three-page glossary. A number of the entries are short. A "Zigaboo" is "a Negro." "Solid" means "perfect." Other entries are poetic and comprise what some scholars have read as "a modernist textual apparatus, analogous to footnotes, guides, and glossaries commonly associated with high modernist texts."[61] A "zoot suit with the reet pleats" is a "Harlem style suit, padded shoulders, 43-inch trousers at the knee with cuff so small it needs a zipper, to get into, high waistline, fancy lapels, bushels of buttons, etc." "Diddy-Wah-Diddy" is "a far place, a measure of distance," but it is also, and here the entry slips into another register, "another suburb of Hell, built since way before Hell wasn't no bigger than Baltimore. The folks in Hell go there for a big time."

Hurston's glossary is an illuminating paratext. It translates and defines in conventional terms, serving to inform the outsider reader and, in so doing, to produce that reader as an intended addressee of the text. It also, however, disrupts the authority of the writer-translator and the centrality of the outsider-reader by mixing standard and nonstandard Englishes within the glossary entries themselves. Consider again the definition of "Diddy-Wah-Diddy"; to understand the term, one should already be versed in what Hurston calls "slang." What appears as a translation from one linguistic register to another is instead an extension of the defamiliarization of the main body of the text into the glossary, which both promises explanation and confounds the reader's expectations of it. At the same time, the insider-reader who does not need the glossary is produced through this displacement as the ethnographic subject and an object of anthropological interest.

What did this have to do with accent? We have all been trained into particular modes of listening and reading, speaking and writing, to and toward objects that are variously proximate to and distant from us. I wanted Hurston's story to alert our class to the workings of the listening ear, to the production of the nondominant or vernacular as "slang," and to the vexed promises of translation and intelligibility. I wanted us to keep Hurston's story in mind as an example of how our ways of reading others' "ways of speaking" are themselves already racialized, because, as readers, we "accent [our] readings."[62] I wanted us to understand through Hurston how accented language produces the speaker-writer and listener-reader, as well as the text in question, whether as "multiethnic," "African American," or "American." Only then could we ask ourselves who, ultimately, was speaking in "Story in Harlem Slang." To whom were we listening? Whose voice was on offer?

We then had to disentangle "accent" from "voice": that sonic, material, embodied, powerfully metaphoric figure for the subject, agency, and autonomy. One's voice is one's self; yet, the paradox of the voice is that it takes "leave" of the one from whom it issues: "What I say *goes*."[63] We watched David Thorpe's 2015 documentary film, *Do I Sound Gay?*, which recounts Thorpe's efforts to modify, via speech therapy, his "gay-sounding" voice. In the process, he investigates its origins (female company?) and the origins of his dislike (internalized homophobia?). The film is powerfully ambivalent: Thorpe concludes that he can and cannot change his voice; the voice does and does not speak him; he performs the voice and it performs him in turn. Accent is not Thorpe's key term, but I enlisted the film to help our class locate accent in the interstices of being and sounding, and as a modality through which voice both produces and deconstructs the self.

Focusing on voice, however, risked relegating accent to the status of "paralanguage"[64] or "sonic envelope."[65] Voice appeared as primary, and accent as secondary, as if the former was vested with the imprimatur of authentic identity, and the latter merely a technology of affectation or advertisement. Seeking to foreground accent qua accent, I introduced a series of televisual case studies on the phenomenon of what Shilpa Davé terms "brown voice."[66]

We began with critiques of the heavily accented character Apu Nahasapeemapetilon on *The Simpsons*. Apu is voiced by the white actor Hank Azaria, who modeled Apu's accent on 7/11 clerks he heard in Los Angeles and Peter Sellers's brownface performance in *The Party*.[67] After years of ignoring protests from South Asian Americans, which received an overdue airing in Hari Kondabolu's 2017 documentary film, *The Problem with Apu*, Azaria announced in 2020 that he would no longer give voice to Apu. This move was criticized by another Indian American comic, Aakash Singh, whose 2022 comedy special *Bring Back Apu* protested that the canceling of Apu was an "overcorrection" by Indian Americans playing the victim card.[68] The "Apu debate" hinges on whether Apu's accent is, as Kondabolu argues, "a white guy doing an impression of a white guy making fun of my father"; or, in Singh's account, a "beautiful" accent that "your parents have."

From this ambivalent knot on the politics of authentic voicing, our class compared Apu's accent, voiced by a white actor, with that of the character Gloria on *Modern Family*, who is played by Sofia Vergara. Both Vergara (the actress) and Gloria (the character) are of Columbian origin; yet the former's performance of the latter's exaggerated Spanish accent, malapropisms, and "vocal body" are, as many critics have argued, no more "authentic" than Azaria's performance of Apu.[69] Vergara's performance turns the show's single Latina character into a punch line; in so doing, it contributes to the establishment of "racial and gendered hierarchies" that privilege Standard American English.

As with the discussion of Thorpe, our televisual case studies opened onto slippery-slope territory. Is the "voicing of a figure"[70] to whom one has a close, identitarian relation less objectionable than the performance of an accent that isn't "yours"? What about comedian Margaret Cho's mimicry of her mother's Korean accent? If Azaria's performance of Apu was a species of brown voice, then what did that mean for any author who tries to write in the accented voice of the other?

I assigned a short story "The G.R.I.E.F.," published in 2015 in *Oxford American* and written by a straight, cisgender white college professor, Micah Stack, in the charismatic voice of a gay, Black, hip hop fan.[71] This is how the story begins:

> Full disclosure up front: I am a gay black man, a proud New Orleanian, thirty years old, five out of the closet, a decade on the down-low before that; bi-dialectal as every educated brother in this city must be, a code-switcher as needed; a poet in my spare time, in my unspare time a poetry teacher devoted to dead French guys and live black ones. Like most black men of my generation, I belong to the hip-hop nation, and like any sensible gay man, I'm ashamed at times to say I'm a fan.

"The G.R.I.E.F." follows its narrator, Charles D'Ambreaux, following the career arc of his favorite hip-hop artist, Mr. Stillz, and the story is fundamentally about the leaps of faith and imagination required to sustain fandom and fiction. It is about the kinds of identification, transference, and investment that drive both the writer's development of characters, and the fan's development of an admired subject as character. The story is also about secrets and disclosures. It's about D'Ambreaux being ashamed to say, and Mr. Stillz being ashamed to admit, and Stack being mistaken for both of them, as the history that drove him to this particular accented performance is eclipsed by the seemingly obvious, and stunningly inadequate, fact of his non-Black identity.

At first, I didn't tell the students anything about Stack's identity, but it wasn't a setup. I offered the story as a virtuosic "attempt at compassion" as opposed to "an act of containment," to use the binary Zadie Smith sets up in her defense of a fiction that is "suspicious of any theory of the self that appear[s] to be largely founded on what can be seen with the human eye."[72] The last thing I wanted was for my students to read Stack's representations of his Black characters as cultural appropriation. As if literature is not by definition performative. As if our task as students and scholars of literature is to adjudicate fidelity to the real. Rather, via Stack, I sought for us to generate a theory of multiethnic literature as an aural-textual performance of accents that cannot be made to fit neatly within an authentic-inauthentic or pure-impure binary.

This was the challenge I posed to my class: to read Stack without crying "appropriation," while considering carefully the formal mechanisms by which Stack's narrator was addressing us as readers and cueing our responses. This narrator had "no existence 'outside' the text yet [brought] the text into existence."[73] Literary voice thus had to be understood as an element of narrative infrastructure, and as a "mode of action"[74] fundamental to the constitution of the narrated world.

Without Stack, there would be no D'Ambreaux, no Stillz. Could Stack be charged with failing to give Stillz an authentic voice, if the voice on offer was his in the first place?

The Question of Ventriloquism

Our class had arrived at "ventriloquism": the art of throwing one's voice so that it sounds like it's coming from another speaking subject. It is a concept central to ethnic and postcolonial studies. Spivak memorably asked whether the subaltern "can speak," not only for herself, but at all, saying, "The ventriloquism of the speaking subaltern is the left intellectual's stock-in-trade."[75] For Trinh T. Minh-ha, the problem was how to speak without "point[ing] to an object as if it [were] distant from the speaking subject or absent from the speaking place."[76] Multiple generations of scholars have since "made their task the study of the politics of representing the Other. . . . There is now no escaping the questions 'who is speaking here, and who is being silenced?' "[77] Who can speak, and in whose voice?

I had chosen to teach Mukherjee's *Middleman* for its iconic "multiethnicity," but also because critics have consistently characterized her writing as a species of *ventriloquism*. Maxey writes that "Mukherjee ventriloquizes an impressive array of subject positions across gender, nationality, and ethnicity."[78] McGurl refers to her "authorial skills in ventriloquism."[79] Arguing that immigrant writers give the American South its "cosmopolitan" credentials, Leslie Bow focuses on how, in "Fighting for the Rebound," Mukherjee "ventriloquizes a white, southern yuppie."[80] "Mukherjee's cross-ethnic narration seems the work of a master ventriloquist," Rody notes, "one who can do anybody's voice, and anybody's voice in dialogue with anybody else."[81]

In American literary studies, "ventriloquism" is often leveled as an accusation against white writers stereotypically depicting nonwhite characters (Jeanine Cummins's widely criticized 2019 *American Dirt* comes to mind), though occasionally it is lauded as a formal strategy (as in the case of Dave Eggers's 2006 *What Is the What*).[82] A 2014 edited volume on "white-authored narratives of Black life" critiques the dominant narrative lens on race in the United States as a white-authored one, produced through decades of cultural appropriation, verbal mimicry, and "racial ventriloquism."[83] In Mukherjee's case, however, scholars and critics unanimously call her ventriloquism of characters across racial lines the most creditable feature of her work. As Rody writes, Mukherjee's ventriloquial performance is "designed to dazzle and, by dazzling, to jar readers into a sense of the momentousness of the societal shifts wrought by global migration."[84]

Let us be performatively dense for a moment. If the ventriloquism of non-white characters by white authors risks appropriation, then why is Mukherjee's assumption of "an impressive array of subject positions" uniformly deemed "dazzling" and worthy of praise? Is it because the Indian

American woman-writer is not expected to write about or from the perspective of anyone but herself? Because she seems to flout the imperatives of coercive mimeticism? Rody's claim, like Raban's apprehension of Mukherjee's "romance with the American language," is premised on the idea that the American language is *other* to Mukherjee. It is a language she can pursue, covet, love, and perform—but not originate. And yet, if we are to read her as a ventriloquist, then Mukherjee is by definition the originator of each voice on offer in her text.

The challenge of theorizing ventriloquism is precisely that it can serve as accusation and commendation at the same time. Is ventriloquism "the power to speak through others" or "the experience of being spoken through by others"?[85] Michael Denning's distinction between "ventriloquism" ("throwing one's voice into the form of another") and "impersonation" ("assuming the voice of another in one's own form") is instructive here. Every sign, every word, every character in a text, Denning writes, is "fought over."[86] It matters who is writing and who is being written; it matters who is reading and who is being read. By that same token, mere facts of biography do not wholly determine the ideological struggle that subtends the acts of literary production and reception. Following Denning, if Mukherjee is enacting ventriloquism, it is a practice whereby the author's voice and perspective are invested in characters who do not share the author's "form." By contrast, a writer who is guilty of impersonation, like Cummins, is attempting to transmit the voice of a community of readers through characters who more properly share her form. In short, Mukherjee is speaking *as* (ventriloquism) and a writer like Cummins is speaking *for* (impersonation).[87]

Helen Davies's work further underscores the importance of distinguishing between skillful ventriloquism, on the one hand, and the kinds of impersonation we might also term "blackface" and "brownface" (or "blackvoice" and "brownvoice"), on the other hand. There are always two subjects in any ventriloquial relation, Davies notes: the ventriloquist and the dummy. By focusing on their relation, we can understand ventriloquism as a canny performance of authority and control, consolidated through the orchestration of the opposite: namely, a lack of control. Technically a process of self-estrangement, in which one's voice is taken from the self and given over to the other, ventriloquism enlists the audience-listener-reader in the apprehension of a performance that ultimately shores up the ventriloquist's skill and mastery. Thus, even when the dummy-character appears to be talking back to (or telling off) the performer-actor-writer, fundamentally "we know that the dialogue between ventriloquist and dummy is entirely orchestrated by the performer."[88] Understood thus, ventriloquism, or speaking as, is a performance that foregrounds its performativity. Impersonation, by contrast, is a performance that attempts to elide the gap between the speaker and the one for whom they speak.

Here's an example of what ventriloquism looks like when specified in these terms—but also how easily it slips into impersonation. In 2016, *The Simpsons* aired a nominally self-critical episode that anticipated the Apu debate. In it, the character Apu's nephew, Jay, gave voice to his critics, saying: "You're my uncle and I love you, but you're a stereotype, man. *Take a penny, leave a penny. I'm Indian, I do yoga.* Why don't you go back to the Temple of Doom, Dr. Jones!" The scripted performance offered, following Davies, an "illusion of abnegated autonomy on the part of the ventriloquist as s/he orchestrates her/his own lack of control."[89] Here was Jay (*The Simpsons*) telling off Apu (*The Simpsons*). But there was no contrition. The episode displayed the show's mastery of the codes of ethnic protest by ventriloquizing critics like Kondabolu. At the same time, by enlisting Indian American actor Utkarsh Ambudkar to voice Jay, *The Simpsons* sought to authenticate the character's voice, and in so doing to align the show's interests with that of the impersonated Indian American community.

Back to *Middleman*. Our class had to take seriously the proposition that Mukherjee's "ventriloquism" had given the short story collection its imprimatur as a multiethnic American classic. We also had to remain vigilant about the distinction between ventriloquism and impersonation, while attending to the calculated performances of authority, control, and mastery on offer in each story. And we had to do this while bearing in mind that Mukherjee, in her own description, was "not striving after some sort of realistic, mimetic voice." "I leave that to tape recorders," she said.[90]

We turned next to her story "Loose Ends," which follows a white Vietnam War veteran named Jeb who is working in Miami as a hired killer. It's a story about sexual violence and violence against immigrants, as well as interethnic hostilities. Restless and bored with his job, Jeb oversteps his charge and kills a young girl while on a hit. He then makes a run for it, sexually assaulting and possibly killing an Indian American woman in the process. The story includes numerous scenes in which an Indian American woman writer may be said to be, as per the above discussion, ventriloquizing a white American man as he abuses and assaults brown women.

Here's how the story sounds: Jeb, the white veteran, speaks colloquial Americanisms—"You want to blow sixty bucks?"—that shift seamlessly into first-person narration directed at a cosmopolitan readership—"You can smell the fecund rot of the jungle . . . while gull guano drops on your car with the soothing steadiness of rain." Contractions ("Jeb m'boy") communicate social relations. Idioms ("at loose ends") signal disposition. Deliberate Anglicizations like "Haysoos" enact microaggressive racist violence at the level of orthography. Syntactical rearrangements like "Are you wanting a room?" carry forward another language's phonology into English. Describing a matron as "British" accents an otherwise unremarkable line of dialogue.[91]

More is going on in these lines than at first meets the eye. For one, the dialogue includes both L1 (geographic, regional) and L2 (second-language) accents, but never marks them as distinct. "You want to blow sixty bucks?" (L1) and "Are you wanting a room?" (L2) appear to analogously situate individual characters in the text through their linguistic idiosyncrasies and nonstandard speech. The former, however, is meant to signal Jeb's origins in terms of geography and class. The latter is meant to signal the ethno-racial difference and "forever foreignness" of motel-owner Patel through "the breakthrough of native language phonology into the target language."[92]

Jeb's insulting rendering of Jesús ("Mr. Vee") Velásquez's name as "Haysoos" transliterates an exaggerated, Anglicized pronunciation in order to show how a white American subordinate can use language to position himself as superior to his boss. Jeb technically works for Velásquez, but he wields those seven letters—"Haysoos"—over him as a threat, as in these passages:

> "You look like hell, Marshall," is the first thing he says.
> "I could say the same to you, Haysoos," I say.
> His face turns mean. I scoop up a mint and flip it like a quarter.[93]

> "What did you do that for?" he shrieks.
> "I could get you deported real easy." I smile. I want him to know that for all his flash and jangle and elocution lessons so he won't go around like an underworld Ricky Ricardo, to me he's just another boat person.[94]

In the first exchange, "Haysoos" can be read as a species of "eye dialect," insofar as "the convention violated is one of the eyes, and not of the ear."[95] The idiosyncratic orthography of "eye dialect" typically signals something about the identity of the speaker, like their class position or level of education. The violated convention serves as "a knowing look which establishes a sympathetic sense of superiority between the author and reader."[96] "Haysoos" does establish sympathy between author and reader; however, the sense of superiority being communicated is Jeb's. "Haysoos" tells the reader not how Jeb would spell Mr. Vee's name (as if he doesn't know better), but rather that he spits it out with undisguised animus. The second passage further indicates the powerful "skin tones"[97] of Jeb's whiteness by explicitly noting that, no matter how hard Jesús Velásquez works to change his accent via elocution lessons, he will still be "just another boat person" to men like Jeb in the United States.

Through these economical forms of accented writing and reading, Mukherjee and her reader together produce the character of Jeb as an impediment to the multiethnic: as one who resists, and sometimes violently extinguishes, those who embody its promise. Jeb's exchanges with the Indian immigrants who run the motel further indicate the extent to which "language possession is translated into and receives its value as skin color."[98] "Are you wanting a room?" Patel asks. Jeb reflects and responds: "I've never liked the high, whiny Asian male voice. 'Let's put it this way. Are you running a motel or what?'" The profession of dislike sets up Jeb's later reactions to the Patels. Jeb knows perfectly well that the immigrants can speak English ("The women jabber, but not in English"; "'Who'll marry her?' [one of the Indians] says in English to one of his buddies."). What offends Jeb, and where he strives to police them, is *how* they speak it: "'Hey,' I yell. 'I need a room for the night. Don't any of you dummies speak American?'" The source of conflict here is not the language the immigrants speak but rather their voices and accents. They all share "English," but only Jeb speaks "American."[99]

Jeb is not a unique character in Mukherjee's oeuvre. In *Jasmine* (the novel) a white American veteran called Half-Face refers to Asia as "the armpit of the universe,"[100] shortly before raping the title character. Another story in *Middleman*, "Fathering," features a white American veteran, Jason, who refers to his Vietnamese daughter, Eng, as his "Saigon kid"; he wonders if her "Asian skin bruises differently from ours."[101] These characters don't tell us how a certain stratum of white American men see nonwhite Americans and Asian women specifically. They don't even tell us how *Mukherjee* thinks white American men see nonwhite Americans and women. What the reader "hears" as and through the voices of these characters is what Mukherjee wants the reader to confront through her ventriloquial performance. In other words, Mukherjee is inviting the reader to authenticate or resist her orchestration of the characters' contested conceptions of "us" and "ours" in relation to an immigrant-"them" to which she and hers (and maybe "we" as readers) provisionally belong.[102]

Mukherjee gives voice to Jeb, Jason, and Half-Face; she speaks *as* them. She has each man perform various forms of violence—both rhetorical and physical—in an attempt to "reestablish [his] control of a 'lost' America."[103] In the process, she, Mukherjee, establishes her control over these men. To return to "Loose Ends," when Jeb asks if any of the Indian American "dummies" speak "American," what is communicated is actually that *Mukherjee* speaks American. Mukherjee is the ventriloquist. *Jeb* is the dummy. Writing Jeb as a character obsessed with dominating ethnic subjects, Mukherjee performs her mastery of Jeb's white voice.[104] Writing Jeb's American accent, Mukherjee credentials her own.

Mukherjee's American Accent

Who can speak in whose voice? Can an immigrant writer voice the nation? What was multiethnic literature?

One aim of English Literature with an Accent was that my students and I would learn how to specify "accent" as our primary object of study—without conflating it with dialect, collapsing it into voice, or capitulating to the cult of authenticity. I also aimed to provide, via accent, a fresh point of entry into the discussion of outmoded texts like Mukherjee's *Middleman*, which appear on the surface to be capitulating to the failed project of multiculturalism. On the one hand, Mukherjee's work advances an ideological fantasy of a "fully realized" America that the writer of ethnic literature was conscripted to advance. On the other hand, Mukherjee slyly uses accent to comment on what American literary studies wanted to sound like at the end of the twentieth century: namely, multiethnic.

The stories of *Middleman* depict a range of accented voices; in so doing, they problematize the "American" ideal of immigrants speaking one language in many voices, or many languages in one voice. "A Wife's Story" and "Jasmine" turn on immigrant characters divesting themselves of their histories and "rushing wildly into the future."[105] By contrast, "Loose Ends" alerts readers to the ways in which history lives on as linguistic residue, or accent. Native, foreign, nonstandard, minority, citizen: all appear together on the page of *Middleman*, contesting one another's belonging and, in their spatial coincidence, performing belonging at the same time. Mukherjee's characters might all be "new Americans," as critics have noted, but none of them is assimilated into the nation's normative and dehistoricizing sonic project. Each character speaks in such a way as to explicitly register their histories and itineraries; each accent is a "biography of migration."[106]

Rather than communicate stable origins, the American accent emerges in *Middleman* as an unstable register of "borrowed and hybridized phonetic form":[107] it lays bare each character's routes, not roots, to use the classic homonymic distinction from diaspora studies. And, as a consequence of each narrator's multiaccented performance, the white American voice reads as just one of many ethnic voices on offer in both nation and text. In this way, *Middleman* doesn't hold up the corporate interest of multiculturalism as the loss or unlearning of accent. Rather, it lays bare the construction of the American accent through the simultaneous containment and celebration of motley voices as both outside the national linguistic norm and constitutive of it.

By definition comparative, accent is in the ear of the listener and the eye of the reader. Accent is not, in the final instance, on the page. What Mukherjee's accents teach us about multiethnic literature, then, is not how difference is figured in the text, but rather how we as readers receive and perceive difference. Accent reorients our study toward the question of the literary mediation of difference, as distinct from its representation. It doesn't deliver identity; instead, it lays bare technologies of apprehension of aural otherness. The menace of accent is its capacity to challenge our closely held mythologies about the "unchanging and singular" nature of the voice and about ourselves as selfsame.[108] This is also accent's condition of possibility. It is a mode of producing and contesting intelligibility: specifically, the intelligibility of the multiethnic as an aspiration and horizon for American literature. In this light, what's generative about *Middleman* is that few of its characters sound like Americans according to the dictates of the listening ear—yet all of them are. That's the whole point of the text.

Mukherjee did not want her Indian roots to overdetermine her American reception, or for an Indian accent to sound in her text. She wanted to be a multiethnic American, not an ethnic subject. Yet she had to authorize her fictions through a performance of ethnic distinction that would be audible and legible as such—by which I mean, that would authorize her entrance into the American literature classroom. With English Literature with an Accent, I sought to demonstrate for my students how the literary politics of ethnic demarcation in Mukherjee takes the form of a performance of mastery of American accents (plural) and white voice in particular. Contra the thesis of coercive mimeticism, hers was not an abject performance of marketable Indianness. To this end, even her problematic nationalism and compromised liberal feminism might be read as a species of the ventriloquial orchestration of a loss of control in the face of dominant narratives.

Multiethnic literature, and here I'm circling back to Warren's "What Was African American Literature?," was a "prospective" project. It sought to erase the conditions that necessitated its existence, which also meant that it looked forward to the day it would no longer be marked and marketed as such. Mukherjee played this game, and remade it. After all, what could any contemporary reader seek from literature *less* than the neutralization of origins, the erasure of ethnicity, and the representation of American accents as unmarked voice?

Coda: A Return to India

That's where the story might have ended—with Mukherjee having rejected hyphenated ethnic identity and written herself into the multiethnic canon through her canny ventriloquial performance of American accents—if her final work had not enacted a surprising, yet telling, return to India and effort to produce an "Indian" voice.

Here's what happened. In the early 2000s, Mukherjee had a telephonic encounter with a call center agent that inspired her to reterritorialize what had become a primarily textual, imaginative, and distant relation to India. As recounted in the opening pages of this chapter, India had for years been for Mukherjee "a metaphor, a particular way of comprehending the world."[109] And now here was the voice of New India, sounding oddly familiar. Mukherjee described this experience to an interviewer some years later:

> As we got talking, [the agent] seemed to take me into her confidence and said yes, I'm speaking to you from Bangalore. And I was touched by this confession, or should I call it revelation, and at the same time intrigued by the phenomenon of a whole group of Bangalore-based employees assuming American identities during their work shift to earn their livelihood, then presumably reverting to their customary languages and personalities during their off-the-job hours. I didn't know ... that the call center customer service personnel were young men and women, mostly women, who had migrated to call center "hub" towns, such as Bangalore, from all over India.[110]

Mukherjee experienced a moment of identification ("I was touched") with a woman she recognized as a fellow Indian, fellow woman, fellow migrant, and, most significantly, fellow inhabitant of an "American" identity, if only for the space-time of a work shift.[111] Moved by the virtual encounter, she undertook a series of research trips to India, studied "the history and architecture of Bangalore," and interviewed numerous call center agents for what would become her last book, the 2011 novel *Miss New India*.[112]

Miss New India tells the story of aspiring call center agent Anjali Bose, who migrates from small-town Bihar to urban Bangalore, a city that "will accommodate any story line." The first part of the book describes Anjali's life in Gauripur, where she is emotionally manipulated by Peter Champion, a former Peace Corps volunteer. She is also sexually assaulted by her would-be arranged marriage match, Subodh Mitra. This violation has stultifying effects later in the novel. In return for a new cell phone, Anjali allows herself to be initiated into an exploitive sexual relationship with an older journalist. She describes herself as "terrified, tempted, and corrupted by the infusion of vast sums of new capital" in the New India but does not know what to do as a result. When Anjali meets Monish Lahiri, a Wharton MBA who returns to India "because this is where the money is, money and opportunity," she is envious and enraged that her country has been "overrun with repatriates and immigrants."[113]

In Bangalore, Anjali is inducted into the world of fast-talking "customer-support service specialists" who brandish their call center English as "a sign of competence." She is fascinated by the way the Young Indians speak: "Landlords are crooks"; "She's a real cutie. Hot and going fast"; "Dudes, dudes, what is this, a bitch session?"; "They got 'tudes . . . but we got game." In a move reminiscent of *Jasmine*'s Jasmine-alias-Jane-Ripplemeyer, Anjali refashions herself as "Angie." She tries to get a call center job, but then discovers that she does not have the malleable disposition required for customer-support labor. "I think," a call center trainer notes, "you have a great deal of difficulty erasing yourself from the call. . . . Being a call agent requires modesty. It requires submission. We teach you to serve. That's not in your makeup."[114] The trainer's critique is a sign of Mukherjee's identification with Anjali, who is a lot like Jasmine and Mukherjee's other favorite protagonists: all "pioneers" who privilege "rebellion against age-old traditions and [the] headstrong quest for personal happiness."[115]

Why, after four decades of preferring not to, did Mukherjee say "yes" to being interpellated by Indians and India in this way? If, in her earlier fictions, India had been a place where "identities [remain] frozen,"[116] lacking the dynamism of the United States, then *Miss New India* was an attempt to reckon with an India that was thawing out, at least in its urban centers. On the one hand, the novel marked a departure from Mukherjee's long-standing concern with assimilation within the territorial bounds of the United States. On the other hand, it continued her project of detailing the transnational processes of migratory "unhousement" and "rehousement" by translating the story of international migration into one of in-country migration within India itself.[117] Mukherjee was still pursuing dynamics of assimilation, but this time with respect to the call center agent's accented accommodation of dominant ideologies around globally intelligible, accented English.

As I have argued elsewhere, the call center agent's emergence as the iconic subject of New India in the twenty-first century was deeply ironic, for two reasons that I'll review here.[118] First, it was ironic because the New India discourse was invested in the idea of India speaking in its own voice, and the call center was best known for the practices of accent modification and neutralization that would make its agents' voices sound placeless. The idea was that agents located in cities like Bangalore and Manila should be intelligible everywhere: i.e., *global*.[119] However, when Indian agents spoke the neutral, placeless call center English, they were actually speaking a form of *Indian* English. Neutralization was thus both about eliminating the difference of "Mother Tongue Influence" and about cultivating very specific, acceptable, profitable forms of difference. The idea was never simply that Indian call center agents should imitate American or British speakers, but rather that they had to "refashion themselves into ideal Indian workers." The Indian agent had to become the best version of herself by "emulating, through accented voice, an ideal transnational call center worker."[120] As A. Aneesh writes, "cultural simulation [became] the basis of authentic performance."[121] Coercive mimeticism, redux.

A second irony. The call center agent most significantly resembled the figure she was supposedly superseding as a global Indian icon: the expatriate writer in diaspora. Mukherjee returned to India because she recognized in the neutral accent of the Indian agent something akin to her own American voice. The call center agents were pioneers like her, ventriloquists like her, and migrants like her. She was drawn to them on account of their familiarity as much as their distinctiveness, because of the critical resemblance between virtual migration and immigration, and because even privileged fictionists and scholars are subject to dominant ideologies underlying the social, cultural, and economic complex of global Anglophonism.[122] Both call center agents and expatriate writers are Indian subjects whose voices travel the world in technologically mediated forms, whether phone calls or books. Both are ideologically constructed "third-world" subjects who seem to promise the Anglophone listener and reader direct access to India.

On the one hand, then, *Miss New India* was a product of the expatriate writer's desire for direct access to the real New India. This desire was shared by numerous other writers and scholars who undertook versions of the same journey, like Chetan Bhagat, who returned to India from Hong Kong in the early 2000s in order to talk directly to Young Indians. I will examine this premise closely in chapter 3's discussion of how Bhagat's linguistic accessibility and politics of vernacularity come to be read as purchase on the nation. On the other hand, Mukherjee's desire was not just for direct access to the other (e.g., the New Indian), but for renewed access and return to the *self* through an encounter with an intimate other, someone between kith and kin—or both and neither.

When I taught *Middleman* in spring 2020, it was the only text of Mukherjee's that we read. But what might have happened if I had asked our class to also read *Miss New India*? Would we have found that *Middleman* offers *ventriloquial* performances of the white American male voice, while *Miss New India* is an ironically compromised attempt at *impersonating* a young Indian woman? What would it reveal about the project of multiethnic literature if we were to decide that Mukherjee's Jeb is a more fully realized and robustly voiced character than her Anjali Bose? If her American accent is more convincing than her Indian one? Reading *Middleman* in light of *Miss New India* would call into question anew what it means to read any accented voice as American or Indian in the first place—or as almost the same, but not quite.

In seeking to identify Mukherjee's accents, we most powerfully name the desires with which we tune in to her texts.

CHAPTER 2/RECESS 1

You Wouldn't Say That to Gayatri Spivak

[My Institutional Position]

In March 2019, during the annual meeting of the American Comparative Literature Association, I met Gayatri Chakravorty Spivak. It was 6:45 in the morning, and I was in the lobby café of a Georgetown hotel, intending to grab a coffee before quickly retreating to my room. A fire alarm went off, and an announcement came over the loudspeaker: we must stay where we were; no movement was permitted via stairs or elevators. I was in line behind a well-known Stanford professor and an editorial collective member from *boundary 2*. Many of us were in pajamas and winter coats. Spivak was nearby having a chat with Amitav Ghosh.

I should say something, shouldn't I? Before I could lose my nerve, I introduced myself to Spivak as a student of one of her former students. Searching for the right words, I told her the most memorable critique my advisor had written in the margins of my dissertation: "You wouldn't say that to Gayatri Spivak." Spivak smiled.

I offer this anecdote because of its punch line. Spivak is a theorist of representation and aesthetics, of the politics of "strategic essentialism" and native informancy, of language and translation, of pedagogy, of "unlearning one's privilege as loss," and of the (im)possibility of subaltern speech and agency, theorized most famously in "Can the Subaltern Speak?" "Above all," Sangeeta Ray observes, "and in everything she writes, Spivak continues to take to task modes of critical self-representation."[1] So it makes a perverse kind of sense that I would introduce myself to Spivak by shamelessly activating my elite academic lineage ("a student of your student") and admitting that all throughout graduate school I struggled and failed to say something worthy of her.

In fact, I had met Spivak once before, in spring 2010 at an event at UC Berkeley. What I remember most is the effect of her accented self-presentation. Nervous graduate student that I was, I said a timid hello to Spivak in a crowded room where she sat thronged by admirers. Afterward, we all filed into a small theater-sized classroom for her lecture. It was so crowded that some attendees (even Judith Butler, I recall) had to sit cross-legged on the side of the stage behind the podium.

Thanks to the archival function of email, I know that we students were very much abuzz about Spivak's talk. I received this email from a classmate afterward:

> Did you see Spivak speak? How was it?—I wasn't there. I saw her speak once; it was quite a tour de force performance talking about an artist who works with elephant dung while she (Spivak) simultaneously juggled cell phone calls from a cousin and consumed a McDonald's fish fillet.

I replied:

> Yes, I saw GCS and what a performance it was! She sang "Love is a many-splendored thing," called "Can the Subaltern Speak?" the work of an ignorant person, took NGOs and middle-class philanthropic pretensions to task, and was generally so present, vivacious, charismatic, and funny that the sizeable audience was floored. I had also seen her earlier in the day at a lunch, during which she was juggling phone calls and talking about how she works out at the gym and has manly shoulders to show for it. What a woman!

I didn't know it then, but my email-correspondent and I had each witnessed a performance of a performance—or, to put that differently, an ironic and knowing restaging of the disruptive event of Theory, and in particular its embodiment by postcolonial, feminist, and queer theorists, in US universities in the 1980s and early 1990s.

This recess is about that disruptive event and the idea of Spivak that emerged in its wake. It's about how, why, and what the name "Spivak" continues to signify, powerfully. Writing in 2003, Rey Chow worried that the "theoretical critical language" of scholars like Spivak had begun "to assume a new mythical life—as a trendy global commodity whose market appeal lies precisely in its near inaccessibility." Two decades later, did that commoditization come to pass? Is it possible to speak the name "Spivak" and signify something other than English's desire for "theoryness"?[2] What does Spivak represent today to scholars of the postcolonial, literary comparatists, and departments of English in US academe?

[Recess]

To state briefly what some future reader might not immediately know: Gayatri Chakravorty Spivak was—*is*—among a handful of twentieth- and twenty-first-century academics with celebrity bona fides, in and beyond the United States, and in and beyond academe.[3] She is known primarily as a postcolonial theorist, although she has preferred variants of "Marxist-feminist-deconstructionist" or "British literature modernist and French and German comparativist."[4] After her 1967 translation of and introduction to Jacques Derrida's *Of Grammatology,* Spivak wrote over a dozen books, published numerous translations, and wrote multiple versions of and reflections on her signature essay on the subaltern.[5] Many monographs and edited volumes have been published about Spivak's oeuvre. Indeed, there is more than one book devoted entirely to the exegesis of "Can the Subaltern Speak?," which, according to Google Scholar, has been cited over thirty-nine thousand times (surely an undercount).[6] If the currency of academic stardom is citation, Spivak is a supernova. Her name has been "adjectified": one might produce a "Spivakian" reading of a text, not unlike a "Saidian" or "Foucaultian" one, or one that is "Butlerian, Derridean, Bhabhaesque."[7]

All of this might sound terribly vulgar to Spivak ("I would not say this to Gayatri Spivak"). Or perhaps just overly obvious. But it is not beside the point.

The careers of the academic celebrity, or "academostar," prompted much discussion in the late 1990s and early 2000s.[8] In numerous special issues, scholars debated the relationship between the star system and the neoliberal university, the demands of professionalization and the academic jobs crisis. They asked whether or not humanists, in the grips of deconstruction, had given up on all evaluative consensus categories other than status. In Jeffrey J. Williams's assessment, the star system had become "central to the current construction of professionalism. . . . It is not a corruption but represents a different historical model of career, and code of academic evaluation, negotiating among incommensurate practices in the research university. . . . To put this another way, it forms a kind of professional imaginary, of present-day academic career, expectations, and rewards, which hails and incorporates us."[9]

Following Williams, I am using this recess to pay attention to Spivak's star status in our shared professional imaginary and to ask how the name "Spivak" hails and incorporates some scholars.[10] I take this approach not to impugn the seriousness of Spivak's work, but rather to take seriously her symbolic power, the disciplinary and interdisciplinary significations of her name, and the implications of her material, corporeal, sari-clad person having been attached to a particular field—a field from which, at the same time, she also distanced herself.

The field in question is of course postcolonial studies. Since the 1978 publication of Edward Said's *Orientalism*, postcolonial theory and interventions have been widely taken up across the humanities and interpretive social sciences. However, in US academe, unlike in Europe, the field largely does not have the institutional imprimatur of department status. In recent years, numerous scholars have observed that the postcolonial also seems to be disappearing as a hiring category. In departments of English, the postcolonial is being supplanted by the Anglophone, which now serves as a third term alongside American and British literatures.[11] By that same token, faculty continue to be legible as postcolonialists, and we still teach classes in postcolonial literature.

I propose that the persistence of the postcolonial might have something to do with the stardom of figures like Spivak, Homi Bhabha, and Edward Said, whose writings are secured in the Theory canon, and whose faces appear, figuratively and literally, quite prominently in English's family photographs and marketing brochures. I offer the phrase "family photographs" advisedly. Academic hiring is driven by certain pragmatic, insidious, and overobvious resemblances—especially now in the postpatronage era, in which the old boys' network has been replaced with the star system. South Asian women scholars thus learn early on in graduate school that they—*we*—might have "some accident-of-birth facility," to borrow Spivak's phrase, in auditioning for Spivak's role in English.[12] As I riff elsewhere, "every English department needs a little Spivak."[13] Or, as Tilottama Rajan wryly observed in the early 2000s, if the right scholars "work in the right areas they can become like Spivak or Bhabha, the only Indians to achieve stardom."[14]

But what kind of aspiration is this: to try to become "like Spivak"? To ask the question differently, what is the nature of the comparative operation—this likening—that English departments make between South Asian women scholars in general and the doyen of comparative literature specifically, whose ethics, politics, and aesthetics of literary scholarship pose a fundamental challenge to the field?

In the opening pages of her 2009 book on Spivak, Ray tells a story about how Spivak knowingly plays the identity game. Spivak sees how she is seen; she hears how she is heard; she speaks herself seeing, and she hears herself speaking. After all, even Spivak is hailed; even Spivak informs and protests.[15] Ray writes:

> Interestingly, it is accent, an English accent, which is used to displace anxiety and lack of control over being read by others. In India, despite her tremendous fluency in Bengali, she can use her accent to help produce herself as an eccentric if she so desires. In the US, enraged by a screaming white guy who did not realize that she lived and owned a home in the same street, she can roll down her car window and scold him in a very English accent, "*Stop muttering.*" "And he was so amazed, that someone dressed like me had said [that] to him."[16]

Accent is doing significant work here. It is not just the fact that Spivak speaks English that conditions her reception in India and the United States. It is *how* she speaks it: in both cases, by activating the listener's imaginings of her itinerary from and through elsewhere. Spivak has always been vigilant about the signifying power of her name, body, dress, work, and words—and about what mobilizing each enables and forecloses. As a teenager in the late 1950s, she learned to speak with an "'English' accent" to turn herself into a "marketable commodity": a teacher of English conversation.[17] Now, she knows exactly how she is going to be read, and where: in India, as an eccentric with short, masculine hair; in the United States, as a foreigner. So, she cues and displaces the reading before it even begins, transmuting the listener's perception of her identity before they themselves have registered it. More than the fact of speaking a language that the listener does not expect to hear coming out of her mouth, it is the accent in which Spivak speaks that has the effect of disciplining the listener.

Sometimes, of course, the accented exchange misfires, and didactic disciplining is received as casteist bullying. This is what happened in May 2024, in a widely reported incident at Jawaharlal Nehru University (JNU) in Delhi in which Spivak corrected an Indian scholar's mispronunciation of W. E. B. DuBois's last name, asking, "Would you please learn his name? . . . This is supposed to be an elite university." Spivak had just given a lecture on DuBois, in which she reportedly stressed the importance of pronouncing the African American sociologist's name the way he himself insisted it be pronounced: that is, with an American, not French, accent. During the Q&A, a questioner who identified himself as a founding professor of the Center for Brahmin Studies, but was later also identified as a Dalit sociology graduate student, posed a question to Spivak in which he "insistent[ly]" mispronounced "DuBois."[18] A testy exchange followed; the student never got to ask his question, and Spivak never answered it.

The ensuing brouhaha (after a video of the exchange went viral) exposed various contours of the linguistic color line in India, including the continued use of English-pronunciation as a tool to discipline unfluent-English speakers, from the colonial educational apparatus to call center accent modification. It was deeply ironic to see Spivak advocating the subaltern's (DuBois's) pronunciation of his own name while a questioner claiming the position of the subaltern (the Dalit student) refused to play along. Spivak was caricatured as an elitist bully and ultimately pressured to offer a quasi-apology: "As an old female teacher confronting a male student, and especially since I had not been given the information that he was Dalit, my wounded remark that I did not want to hear his question was a gesture of protest."[19]

Is it possible to read the JNU incident as one in which Spivak's correction is an act of fellowship, not condescension? A subtle pointer from one Indian to another, two fellow members of the transnational academic elite seeking to dismantle caste, class, and linguistic hierarchies that have been variously imposed on them both? After all, Spivak has always understood the lecture hall as "a text."[20] She knows very well that in India she risks being overdetermined by her location in diaspora and the Ivy League. As she said to students at the University of Pune in 2012, "I am trying to understand the difficulty of myself as an other for my subaltern clientele, myself a gentlewoman from the capital, class and caste enemy from abroad."[21]

Entirely missing from the online discourse following the JNU exchange was any acknowledgment of how, in the years since Spivak entered US academe, unsympathetic listeners and suspicious readers have variously attempted to discipline *her*. Writing in 1993, Martin Jay described Spivak as an "academic woman as performance artist." In an almost humorously censorious article, he named Spivak, along with Butler, Jane Gallop, Avital Ronnell, and Eve Kosofsky Sedgwick, as a species of theorist-artist who was blurring the line between substantive scholarship and public persona. On the one hand, Jay grudgingly conceded, these marginalized academic women were subverting white, masculinist, heteronormative codes of critical civility: "Now not only can the subaltern speak, but she does so on her own terms and in her own idiom." On the other hand, he wrote in finger-wagging terms, their "academic performance artistry" undermined "the assumptions of the culture of critical discourse too thoroughly."[22]

Jay continued in defense of this culture: "The neutral culture of critical discourse in which persuasive ideas come before personal authority and disembodied minds argue without reference to their corporeal ground may be a utopian fantasy in its purest form, but it still provides a regulative ideal, which we abandon at our jeopardy." Jay's dated and gendered polemic—he calls Spivak a "Third World Woman (via Paris) with a score to settle"[23]—has been roundly critiqued: for example, by Ann Pellegrini, who notes that "performance can actually be a means of producing and re-generating community in the face of material deprivations and cultural dismissals."[24] Those who are not heir to institutional, historical, and structural privilege might at first have no method of claiming authority other than charismatic seizure. My interest in revisiting Jay's essay here is both to underscore Pellegrini's point and to make two others. The first has to do the ideology of neutrality espoused by Jay; the second, with the ongoing implications of Spivak's (disruptive, threatening, enabling, disciplining) academic stardom. I will take each in turn.

First, let us consider Jay's defense of the dominant ideology of *neutrality* as a value for critical discourse and his claim about the importance of upholding "a neutral culture" of "critical persuasion" (in contradistinction to "personal authority") as a "regulative ideal." The preceding chapter closed with a discussion of the twenty-first-century call center, where the regulative ideal of neutrality is in full swing and a new linguistic politics of accessibility serves as its own form of global currency. The call center agent and Spivak occupy different worlds, of course; yet vexed questions of locution and location have been as pertinent to the reception of the latter's work as they are to that of the former. Like call center agents, postcolonial theorists are charged with giving an account of the global South in its radical particularity. At the same time, they are asked to do so in universal terms.

By Spivak's own account, she, Bhabha, and other scholars of South Asian origin accidentally gained prominence as the vanguard of "postcolonialism" in the 1980s and 1990s, securing South Asia's centrality to that now-international discourse in the process.[25] All the while, the reception of their work was inflected by expectations of native informancy and ethnographic accuracy. This was always a deeply ironic state of affairs, given that Spivak is a powerful critic of the fantasy of direct access to the global South. In "Can the Subaltern Speak?", she lays bare how Michel Foucault, Gilles Deleuze, and early practitioners of Subaltern studies valorize the subaltern as subject and fetishize the empirical reality of oppressed others *over there*. They want their marginalized, hitherto silenced others to know themselves and to desire in accordance with their interests. They fantasize that just there—behind the curtain, backstage, in the factory, or in the cubicle—the subaltern are speaking for themselves.

Meanwhile, the postcolonial theorist is expected to be both behind the curtain and in front of it, pulling it back to the make the subaltern speak. Not just in any voice, though—but in a voice that is particular and global, Indian and intelligible, native and neutral *at the same time*. Just like, as I discussed at the close of the last chapter, the voice of the call center agent.[26]

From the vantage afforded by three decades, it is clear that what Jay called "neutrality" is a nightmare for many, a real regime to which they are daily subject, and not a utopian fantasy. It is clear, too, that his ungenerous screed was part of a broader paranoid response to Theory with a capital-T. It's now impossible to read the charge of nonneutrality without recalling criticisms of Spivak's writing as dense, impenetrable, inscrutable, and "obscurantist."[27] "They have read Gayatri's paper," Spivak herself ventriloquized critics, "And they said they couldn't understand it."[28] Like other feminist and postcolonial theorists of her generation, including Butler and Bhabha, Spivak was accused more than once of "bad" writing (the subject of the next recess).[29] Many critics couched this accusation as a concern about political efficacy: Can a text change the world, if only the elite can read it?[30] Should this essay stay on our syllabi, if our students won't fully understand it?[31]

Flippant critiques of Spivak after the JNU incident ("'Can the subaltern speak' without Spivak correcting his pronunciation?" online commentators howled) ignored her decades of work in subaltern schools in India and efforts to dismantle caste hierarchies. Likewise, the familiar line of questioning about Spivak's inaccessibility is premised on forgetting the actual circulation and popularity of Spivak's work outside academe. In 1991, Spivak gave a talk in Detroit that was so successful it merited mention in the introduction to *The Spivak Reader*. She received a standing ovation from an audience including numerous nonacademics, particularly from the African American community. The editors recall: "One woman carried a much-read copy of Spivak's translation of Derrida's *Of Grammatology*. Her daughter . . . was reading *In Other Worlds* for a course at her inner-city high school. For these women, Spivak's feminist critique of the links between racism and capitalism had been crucial for their intellectual development. They embraced her as a profoundly political sister, not as an inaccessible academic."[32]

Defending Spivak against Terry Eagleton's criticism of her "inaccessible style," Butler makes a similar observation. Spivak's "critical interrogation of the political status quo in its global dimensions has reached tens of thousands of activists and scholars. So perhaps it is precisely her well-earned popularity, her ability to reach so many people, and change their thinking so profoundly, that forms the basis of Eagleton's *ressentiment*."[33]

Inaccessible to whom?

Let us turn back to the question of Spivak's stardom. Jay's "theorist-artist" was clearly a gendered instantiation of the "academostar." In his view the rise of Spivak was a threat to the status quo. From the present vantage, Spivak's example is less a threat than a challenge—or rather, challenges, plural, to more than one constituency. This recess will close with two.

To begin with, Spivak poses a profound challenge to South Asian student-scholar-writers who either seek to become "like" her or are hailed despite themselves into the position of South Asian postcolonialist. The challenge is to resist the demand that "we"—here, we critics and scholars, but also novelists like Bharati Mukherjee, Chetan Bhagat, Amit Chaudhuri, and Jhumpa Lahiri; all of us "upwardly mobile metropolitan migrant[s]" wearing the garb of "the postcolonial"[34]—become native informants who can pull back the curtain and make the subaltern speak. Instead, Spivak advocates rigorous multilingualism, robust reading, and aesthetic imagination as resistance to informancy and interpellation. She writes:

> So therefore my biggest undertaking, my biggest task, is actively to dramatize the imagination as an instrument of othering. In other words, to teach how to read in the most robust sense, that is to say, suspending oneself and entering the text and the other. If indeed we are thinking about othering as a good thing, it is a kind of chosen othering, as it were, the chosen othering through the imagination. Strictly speaking, nothing is more conducive to this than working on a cultural script that is not supposedly yours.[35]

This is the nonidentitarian's mantra: to suspend oneself; to enter the text of the other; to pronounce the other's name in their accent, not yours; to undertake "a painstaking learning of the language of the other."[36] The implication here is that when we pursue literatures and cultural scripts that are, by contrast, *ours*, we are foregrounding, rather than suspending, ourselves—and that this is a comparatively unrobust, or even uncritical position to adopt.

But what if the cultural scripts that are not obviously yours seductively invite you into identification with them? And what if the scripts that *are* "supposedly yours" most profoundly serve as instruments of othering? "Why might I assume it is easy to write what is nearest to me?"[37] These, of course, are questions at the heart of this book.

Second, Spivak poses a specific challenge to English literary studies in the age of the Anglophone: namely, the challenge of comparative literature as a discipline characterized by "a care for language and idiom" and "the skill of reading closely in the original."[38] Spivak's example has always been one of strenuous, global pedagogy and commitment to multilingual literary scholarship. She is particularly known for her militance against the decline of language study in the academic humanities. At a time when fewer students are reading Antonio Gramsci, Spivak demands that her students learn Italian in order to read him in the original. She herself learned German to read Marx and Mandarin to read Mao Tse Tung.[39] She taught Aristotle in Hong Kong with her "miserable classical Greek."[40] When she translated Derrida, she was learning French. "Learn French, the French book says."[41] At Columbia, where she holds the university's highest rank of University Professor, Spivak routinely takes undergraduate classes to learn new languages, including Arabic and Cantonese.[42] "If you want to learn languages, you can learn languages," she says. "Stay with it."[43]

Some of these stories may be apocryphal. But they are consistent with Spivak's advocacy of language learning as activism and key to her iconicity. In the multilingual Indian context, Spivak has long urged students of English to harness the language's and literature's possibilities: "You can absolutely utilize the excellence of English studies: make it your own, sabotage it, turn it round"; use it "to go towards a comparative literature of Indian literatures."[44] In US academe, Spivak counters the regime of Global English with the challenge of planetarity. "We must . . . learn to think of ourselves as the custodians of the world's wealth of languages, not as impresarios of a multicultural circus in English," Spivak addressed the 2009 MLA convention, adding, "the learning of languages is the first imperative . . . [we must not give in] to the demand for convenience in a country where multiculturalism goes hand in hand with monolingualism."[45]

Given increased attacks on public education broadly, the humanities generally, and language learning and pedagogy more specifically, Spivak's decades-long call for the reinvigoration of comparative literature merits particular attention in the 2020s. Her vision was of a discipline that could marry the theoretical sophistication and "metropolitan enthusiasm" of ethnic and cultural studies with "the linguistic rigor" of area studies. At stake was never just language study qua language study, but a critical disposition and epistemological ethic that would be "capable of keeping the academy internally practicing learning rather than simply acquiring and producing knowledge, and externally learning to learn from below."[46]

The irony is that it has often been departments of English in US academe that serve as host and home to faculty and students working on minority archives, oppositional knowledge projects, and underfunded languages, literatures, and subjects. In part, this is because English has been relatively inoculated from the kinds of austerity-driven cuts being made to area, ethnic, and identity studies departments (emphasis on "relatively"). But also, it's part of our history.

Beginning in the 1980s, English departments in US academe "played host to the imagination of literature as a privileged medium for the working out and possible resolution [of] (subaltern) 'experience' and (French) 'theory.'"[47] English has since enlisted Theory in order to make certain worlds and certain modes of thought accessible to Anglophone readers—certain "unknowns known," in Frederic Jameson's words.[48]

On the one hand, this has always been a pernicious intellectual division of labor, in which some are known as objects, by others who are knowing subjects—and all of us know very well just who will be playing which part. English is an imperial knowledge project and global translational apparatus where the archive of world literature is interpreted through a limited, Eurocentric archive of Theory and continental philosophy. By way of a familiar example from a course that might be called Introduction to Literary Theory, English is where the interpretation of Mahasweta Devi's Bengali fictions (in translation, of course) requires the deconstructive theory of Derrida, and the critique of Asian American literature requires the psychoanalytic insights of Jacques Lacan—but not necessarily the other way around.

On the other hand, English is also where the colonial history of the British abolition of sati in India prepares the ground for the critique of Foucault and Deleuze, where "an Asian [can] take Europe as the object of investigation,"[49] and where the reading of Devi becomes essential to the reinvigoration of comparative literature, a field long stuck on "Europe and the extracurricular Orient."[50]

Or at least, that is English—the language, translational apparatus, and critical project—as inhabited, utilized, and disciplined by Spivak. The kind of English literary studies that Spivak's "nonneutral" work and accent make possible.

If we are to make an affirmative case for the study of English in the contemporary conjuncture, it really must be a case for an English like that.

(I might even say so to Gayatri Spivak.)

CHAPTER 3

When the Anglophone Reads "Like Hindi"

Or, On Not Teaching Chetan Bhagat

[My Institutional Position]

It was 2016, and I was on the job market for the first time, applying for assistant professorships in English. I was about to go on a campus visit. I wrote a job talk that was trying to do double duty as an account of my doctoral research on the New India discourse's registration in contemporary Indian English literature, and as an account of the Anglophone as an emerging area of study and hiring field. In the talk, I discussed the popular fictionist Chetan Bhagat as the "global" inheritor of the formerly central position of "postcolonial" expatriate writers like Salman Rushdie.

I knew that my audience of English faculty and graduate students would know Rushdie well. But Bhagat? The right-wing, defiantly nonintellectual investment banker who became India's best-selling writer in the early 2000s? I worried that few would have heard of him. By making a case for Bhagat's centrality to cultures of New Indian Anglophonism, I could perform my field-specific expertise and trade in the currency of the "new" while, crucially, couching both in terms of an analogy to Rushdie that would be legible to those I hoped would be my future colleagues.

Midway through my presentation, while discussing "the larger discursive machinery of the Bhagat phenomenon," I mused out loud that Bhagat's books are rather bad, and that I frankly didn't like reading him, nor would I ever teach his work.

It became apparent during the Q&A that this comment had raised alarms in the audience. "If you won't teach Bhagat in a college classroom, why are you discussing his books in a research talk?"

I demurred, without explicitly articulating the anxieties underlying my aside. To what India would Bhagat give my students access? Would they assume that Bhagat makes the subaltern speak? What kind of Indian does Bhagat sound like, and what if my students came away thinking all Indians sound like Bhagat?

In the years since, I have taught graduate classes in South Asian Anglophone literature at the University of Nevada, Reno, and at the University of Arizona. A syllabus for the former, titled "The Anglophone and Its Critics," appears below. I have thrice taught an undergraduate class in South Asian Anglophone literature at Rice University. But I still haven't taught a novel or even an essay by Chetan Bhagat.

Why not? And if I were, finally, to change my mind, how would I teach him?

[Syllabus]

Against English, or, The Anglophone and Its Critics
English 788 | University of Nevada, Reno
Fall 2016

This English graduate seminar pursues the problem of English as a literary and cultural system. How has the spread of global Anglophonism complicated the way we understand and undertake the study of contemporary English literature? When Aamir Mufti urges us to *Forget English!* (2016), which Englishes are to be forgotten and by whom? When Minae Mizumura conjures a dystopic *Fall of Language in the Age of English* (2015), how is the Anglophonist to carry on?

In order to pursue these questions, we will examine twentieth- and twenty-first-century Anglophone postcolonial literature and criticism, primarily but not exclusively routed through the South Asian subcontinent and its diasporas. In the South Asian context, English is both psychically alienating, on the one hand, and socioeconomically enabling, on the other.

We will consider first how the critique of colonial Anglophonism attempted to reconcile the epistemic violences of English with its evident relations to political power and class mobility. Then, we will pursue the self-critiques and disavowals that have followed the postcolonial and ethnic metabolism of the imperial language—how, for example, the embrace of the vernacular has served as a rhetorical foil for the Anglophonist, and how the critique of English has ironically served to shore up the language's dominance in the South Asian world of letters and the Asian American ethnic canon.

While South Asian literatures will serve as our primary case study, these issues are relevant to all scholars who consider themselves Anglophonists, all creatives writers who traffic in accented voices, and all those who have picked up the phone and heard an inscrutable global English. We will develop strategies for the study of plural, vernacular, and demotic Englishes as well as a framework for comparative literary study, while engaging critically with the problems and possibilities of translation and mistranslation. Finally, whether you work *on* English or simply *in* English, this course will provide students with a lens for responsibly engaging literatures outside Western European and Anglo-American traditions.

COURSE SCHEDULE

W, Jan 9: Introductions

UNIT 1: English Studies and Literature in Colonial India

W, Jan 16: Gauri Viswanathan, from *Masks of Conquest: Literary Study and British Rule in India* (1989): Preface to the Twenty-Fifth Anniversary Edition; Introduction; Chapter 1; Chapter 6; Conclusion

Sanjay Seth, from *Subject Lessons: The Western Education of Colonial India* (2007): Introduction; Chapter 1; Chapter 6; Epilogue

W, Jan 23: Homi Bhabha, "Of Mimicry and Man: The Ambivalence of Colonial Discourse" (1990); "Signs Taken for Wonders: Questions of Ambivalence and Authority Under a Tree Outside Delhi, May 1817"(1990)

Dipesh Chakrabarty, "Postcoloniality and the Artifice of History: Who Speaks for 'Indian' Pasts?" (1992)

UNIT 2: The Postcolonial Language Debate

W, Jan 30:   G. V. Desani, *All About H. Hatterr* (1948)

Secondary: Andrew Goldstone, "Hatterr Abroad: G. V. Desani on the Stage of World Literature" (2014)

W, Feb 6:   Frantz Fanon, from *Black Skins, White Masks* (1952)

Chinua Achebe, "English and the African Writer" (1965)

Ngũgĩ wa Thiong'o, from *Decolonising the Mind: The Politics of Language in African Literature* (1986)

Salman Rushdie, "Damme, This is the Oriental Scene for you!" (1997)

Vikram Chandra, "The Cult of Authenticity" (2000)

UNIT 3: From Postcolonial to World Anglophone

W, Feb 13:   "From Postcolonial to World Anglophone: South Asia as Test Case," Special Issue of *Interventions: International Journal of Postcolonial Studies*, Volume 20, Number 3 (2018); introduced and edited by Ragini Tharoor Srinivasan; essays by Nasia Anam, Monika Bhagat-Kennedy, Roanne Kantor, and Akshya Saxena; responses by Gaurav Desai and Rebecca Walkowitz

UNIT 4: From Postcolonialism to Global Modernism

W, Feb 20:   Mulk Raj Anand, *Untouchable* (1935)

B. R. Ambedkar, "Gandhism" (1945)

Secondary: Jessica Berman, "Neither Mirror nor Mimic: Transnational Reading and Indian Narratives in English" (2012)

	Daniel Morse, "An 'Impatient Modernist': Mulk Raj Anand at the BBC" (2015)
W, Feb 27:	Salman Rushdie, *Midnight's Children* (1981)
W, Mar 13:	Rebecca Walkowitz, from *Cosmopolitan Style: Modernism Beyond the Nation* (2007); from *Born Translated: The Contemporary Novel in an Age of World Literature* (2015)

UNIT 5: Lost and Found in Translation

W, Mar 20: Rashmi Sadana, "A Suitable Text for a Vegetarian Audience: Questions of Authenticity and the Politics of Translation" (2007); "Managing Hindi: How We Live Multilingually" (2012); "Found in Translation: Self, Caste, and Other in Three Modern Texts" (2015)

Emily Apter, "Untranslatables: A World System" (2008)

UNIT 6: English Accents

W, Mar 27: Rosina Lippi-Green, from *English with an Accent: Language, Ideology, and Discrimination in the United States* (1997)

Rey Chow, from *Not Like a Native Speaker: On Languaging as a Postcolonial Experience* (2014)

Lawrence Abu Hamdan, from *Inaudible: A Politics of Listening in Four Acts* (2016)

UNIT 7: Forgetting English

W, Apr 10: Aamir Mufti, *Forget English! Orientalisms and World Literature* (2016)

W, Apr 17: Jhumpa Lahiri, *In Other Words* (2015)

Secondary: Minae Mizumura, from *The Fall of Language in the Age of English* (2015)

UNIT 8: The Anglophone and the Anthropocene

W, Apr 24:   Amitav Ghosh, *The Great Derangement: Climate Change and the Unthinkable* (2016)

Kanishk Tharoor, "Swimmer Among the Stars"(2017)

UNIT 9: Indian Anglophone Experiments

W, May 1:   Short Prose Selections from Nirad Chaudhuri, R. K. Narayan, Raja Rao, Upamanyu Chatterjee, and Sunetra Gupta, from *The Vintage Book of Modern Indian Literature*, ed. Amit Chaudhuri

Poetry selections from Meena Alexander, Agha Shahid Ali, Sujata Bhatt, Namdeo Dhasal, Bhanu Kapil, Meena Kandasamy, Kersey Katrak, A. K. Ramanujan, and Vijay Seshadri

---

[Accented Reading]

> I am not an intellectual. Abuse me, but don't call me that sir.
>
> I don't come from that "English literature honors" kind of background.
> —CHETAN BHAGAT

Chetan Bhagat was born in New Delhi in 1974. He published his first novel, *Five Point Someone: What Not to Do at IIT*, in 2004, transforming the sphere of Indian English writing with his demotic prose and direct address to India's youth. *Five Point Someone* spoke to the university-bound demographic whose experiences most closely matched those of the author, who grew up in a middle-class family and was educated at the elite Indian Institute of Technology (IIT)–Delhi and the Indian Institute of Management (IIM)–Ahmedabad. Bhagat's next novel, *One Night @ the Call Center* (ON@CC), expanded his subject and audience to a different socioeconomic group: call center workers. Together, the two books secured Bhagat's status as India's "paperback king"¹ and the first author of "truly popular" Indian English books.² In the 2000s, he was considered "a national youth icon" and "harbinger of a new India."³

What was the New India? The conventional story goes something like this: New India emerged after the liberalization of the nation's financial markets, starting with the International Monetary Fund–led economic reforms in 1991. In the first decade of the twenty-first century, the term gained traction as a descriptor of India's economic "dream run" between 2003 and 2008, its neoliberal enterprise culture, its global ambitions, and the confluence of its "hard" economic and "soft" cultural power. New India named a nation that had become a central node of the world economy and would rival Rising China in the Asian Twenty-First Century. New India's entrepreneurs, outsourcing companies, and call centers could, as Aravind Adiga wrote in *The White Tiger*, "virtually run America now."⁴

New India emerged as a market-driven discourse of aspiration. It also served as an ideological smokescreen for the self-aggrandizing, communalist, anti-Muslim politics motoring the Hindu-nationalist Bharatiya Janata Party's "India Shining" campaign in 2004, unsuccessful though it was.⁵ New India was thus a highly contradictory, Janus-faced discourse that valorized both future-oriented economic globalization and historically revisionist fantasies of indigeneity and nativity. A reanimated New India discourse led to the BJP's electoral triumph in 2014 and the appointment of Rashtriya Swayamsevak Sangh member and former Gujarat chief minister Narendra Modi as India's fifteenth prime minister. Modi was then reelected as leader of the BJP's winning coalitions in 2019 and 2024, and he remains prime minister at the time of this writing.

Even as India's economic growth foundered in the 2010s, and despite Modi's authoritarian enactments of disastrous policies like the 2016 demonetization, the rhetorical power of New India obtained. In August 2017, Modi spoke of a "New India" of "equal opportunity for all; where modern science and technology play an important role in bringing glory for the nation in the global arena."⁶ Launching a five-year plan called "Sankalp Se Siddhi," the prime minister exhorted his "countrymen" to take a "New India pledge" toward a corruption-free, poverty-free, terrorism-free, casteism-free, communalism-free, clean nation. It was a deeply cynical repurposing of what was already an ideologically fraught term.⁷

In short, New India was "global" as opposed to postcolonial, "young" as opposed to old, and "modern" as opposed to traditional. It was a Hindu "Naya Bharat" as opposed to a secular republic, and a "Hindi-speaking" India as opposed to an English-speaking one.[8]

The New India no longer required—indeed, it rejected—representation by its Anglophone diasporas in the West. Put simply, it was an India that could finally speak *in its own voice*. (Thus, again, the irony of the call center's emergence as a symbol of New India and Bharati Mukherjee's late-life efforts to give New India voice, discussed in chapter 1.) Moreover, New India would speak *Indian* languages that would have greater purchase on the nation than English ever could. Down with Cambridge-educated prime ministers like Jawaharlal Nehru and Manmohan Singh; up with the Hindi- and Gujarati-speaking Modi. Down with self-appointed nonresident Indian ambassadors of the nation; up with "new, more independent voices that [could] talk more authoritatively about a changing India."[9] Prominent among these new, authoritative voices was that of Bhagat, who belonged to a crop of popular writers who could "talk directly of, and to New India."[10] Ironically, Bhagat talked directly to and about what Samanth Subramanian called an "India after English" *in English*.[11]

This chapter's inquiry begins from this simple, counterintuitive fact: Bhagat became an icon of the post-Anglophone New India by writing best-selling English-language pulp fictions. His oeuvre came to signify a new phase in the indigenization of English in India and fresh possibilities for English's purchase on Indian life-worlds, even as the cultural and symbolic capital of English in India was being challenged significantly and arguably even waning for the first time since independence. How, and why? The critical consensus is that Bhagat came to prominence by writing in an English that is accessible, provincial, and global, and yet also undeniably *Indian*—a tangle of contradictory descriptions of a piece with the New India discourse. As Ulka Anjaria argues, Bhagat writes into "a new space where English and the *bhashas* can meet again"[12] and where "everyday lives speak for themselves."[13] His simple English, one reader reflects, is "like Hindi. It doesn't tax my brain."[14] Bhagat has taken this description to heart, as per the account he gives in his motivational speeches: "Koi baar log kehthe hein ki aapka Angrezi Hindi ki tharah hein. [Sometimes people say that 'your English is like Hindi.'] That's a good compliment for me, because I am able to communicate."[15]

But if Bhagat's English is like Hindi, what relationship does it have to Hindi itself, and for that matter to any other Indian language it "meets" in the Indian and global literary spheres? What does the case of Bhagat, and in particular his emergence as an object of critical consideration in Anglo-American literary studies, tell us about English, the fate of comparative literature, the challenges of reading New India and teaching the global contemporary, and—contra longstanding efforts in postcolonial theory—the persistence of the fantasy of accessing India's unmediated, authentic voice?

Bhagat's iconicity exposes a problem endemic to English literary studies in US academe: namely, the problem of enacting comparative literary analysis within English itself.[16] It is increasingly evident, even within departments dominated by the teaching of American and British literatures, that the discipline of English has a pedagogical responsibility to literatures of the non-West. The question is: How should English literatures of South Asia or East Africa, for example, be contextualized in terms of the relevant subcontinental and regional literatures in other languages? Should texts originally written in Urdu, Swahili, or Arabic, and then translated into English, be taught in English departments, by faculty who may not work in the languages in which the texts were first written? Proponents of the pedagogy of world literature in translation—offered in this chapter as a successor to comparative literature—might answer in the affirmative. Proponents of the global Anglophone—offered as a renomination of the postcolonial—might respond in the negative.

World literature and the global Anglophone are rival theories of how to enact literary comparison through English, given the decline of (by which I also mean, cuts in funding for) language study in US academe. Bhagat's popular fiction at first presents an enticing solution to the seeming impasse between these contested pedagogies: between the limits of translation and the inevitability of untranslatability that haunt world literature, on the one hand, and the global Anglophone's depoliticizing reappropriation of the formerly colonized world, on the other hand. Bhagat writes in English, so he need not be translated for Anglophone audiences, who are able to travel the world via his English. To this end, the Bhagat novel presents a curious instance of Rebecca Walkowitz's "born translated" text: it focuses on a non-Anglophone geography, contains the world without circulating through the world, and reminds us that "readers do not own the language they read."[17] By that same token, Bhagat's English does not read "like" English: neither like the "good" English that critics usually analyze, nor like the "hard" English with which Bhagat's intended readers, who are typically not fluent in the language, often struggle. His English is so accessible that it reads "like" a vernacular despite being devoid of vernaculars. As a consequence, it seems to afford a comparative vantage on other Indian languages from within English itself.

Additional enticement: Bhagat's rise in India was cotemporaneous with the postcritical turn in the Anglo-American humanities toward less suspicious moods, less paranoid dispositions, and less symptomatic reading methods.[18] This turn involved a consequential reconsideration of the lay reader, as well as ambivalent efforts by scholars to unlearn our "academic habits of reading."[19] Less observed, but also symptomatic of postcritique, was the turn from the postcolonial to the Anglophone, which may be described in two ways: first, as a turn away from supposedly exhausted postcolonial shibboleths regarding the primacy of the nation, linguistic innovation, hybridity, and diaspora; and second, a turn away from postcolonial theory à la "Said-Bhabha-Spivak" and toward the "earthy pragmatism [of] Global English."[20] Bhagat came onto the Indian popular and Anglo-American critical scenes just as literature scholars across fields were turning away from the hermeneutics of doubt, elitism, and expertise, and as scholars of Indian English more specifically were moving away from the postcolonial. We encountered Bhagat's intimate address to his readers just as we were in the process of repudiating our own conventional critical operations.

This chapter proposes that Bhagat's anointment as an Anglophone literary icon with purchase on the "everyday" New India lays bare the ongoing challenges of teaching non-Western Anglophone literatures in US academe. If the challenge of teaching Mukherjee is negotiating her desired Americanness, the challenge of teaching Bhagat is mediating his declared Indianness. In order to distinguish Bhagat's "global" writing, language, and voice from that of his "postcolonial" predecessors, critics have read Bhagat as a kind of vernacular Indian writer (read: "vernacular" as code for "authentic," "native," and "real"). But when we grant Bhagat's popular fiction vernacular credentials, we risk undermining the case for reading Indian literatures in translation in the English literature classroom and reauthorize the suspect position of the Anglophone reader seeking access to India's "real" voice. At the same time, we participate in the long-time devaluation of regional languages in postcolonial India and of

"Southern Hemisphere languages" in post–Cold War US academe—both couched in rhetorics of inevitability, pragmatism, and efficiency.[21]

I acknowledge that I am in practice producing my own paranoid discourse about what some "we" risks participating in in theory. But I offer this line of inquiry as part of an effort to understand how "the sanctioned ignorance of the metropolitan migrant" diagnosed by Gayatri Chakravorty Spivak comes to be sanctioned—even when scholars and critics are working to produce the opposite outcome.[22]

On the one hand, we have to contend with a pernicious politics of differentiation between Western and non-Western languages in the wake of poststructuralism. As Rey Chow has argued, for the contemporary Anglophone literary theorist, the English language is in no way transparent; we are reading and writing after the separation of words and things; signifiers are not sutured to signifieds. And yet non-Western languages (the ones anthropologists learn before going into the field) are still assumed to signify unambiguously and reveal the truth of the Other. In this way, the vernacular remains shorthand for "a privileged—because nativist—way into a culture, a key that opens all doors."[23]

On the other hand, we have to contend with the linguistic and literary situation in India specifically, where, as Mrinal Pande argues, the vernacular does in fact signify a realm that is "unknown in the West," the majority of Indian Anglophone elites have themselves "never actually read a vernacular daily," and "access to India's largest markets is currently available only to the vernacular communicators."[24] We have to contend with the hierarchies exposed in the JNU incident discussed in the last chapter/recess, which inspired an MPhil student at Oxford to recount how Spivak's pronunciation-policing forced him to relive the "embarrassment and humiliation" of speaking bad English in his school days.[25] We have to acknowledge that Indian writing in English "assumes an 'India' in a way that no regional literature can."[26]

For all of these reasons, Bhagat's "English like Hindi" puts us in a bind.

In what follows, I try to disarticulate Bhagat's claim on English from his claim on India, in order to understand what critical assessments of his work both afford and foreclose for literary comparatists generally, and postcritical post-postcolonialists, specifically. I ask: How does Bhagat's English travel, sound, and resound outside India? How do we read Bhagat's accent, and with what sorts of desires do we tune into his texts?

The Bhagat Phenomenon

By some metrics, Bhagat is bigger than Rushdie. Bigger than Arundhati Roy, Amitav Ghosh, or any other internationally known writer. By 2008, Bhagat's first two novels had sold over a million copies and he was officially India's "biggest-selling English-language novelist."[27] His 2014 novel, *Half Girlfriend*, had an initial print run of two million.[28] His ten novels (to date) have done so well that India-based publishers of English-language books divide the market into "pre- and post-Chetan Bhagat periods."[29] Five of Bhagat's books have been adapted into popular Bollywood films, including *3 Idiots* in 2009, the second-highest grossing Bollywood film of all time in the overseas markets and the highest grossing Indian film of the 2000s.[30] He has written four essay collections; the first three are nonironically titled *What Young India Wants*, *Making India Awesome*, and *India Positive*.

Bhagat also writes journalism in both English and Hindi. In 2008, he began an opinion column in the Hindi-language newspaper *Dainik Bhaskar*. He described this as "a chance to reach the majority, the real India" while flouting expectations that "an English language author in India . . . had to be elitist."[31] An early adopter and enthusiast of social media, Bhagat is a screenwriter, YouTuber, motivational speaker, reality-TV judge, podcaster, and prolific tweeter whose aim is to spread his "ideas" by any and all available means. He is not invested in the bookness of books, he says: "Book is what? Paper, bound together. . . . I'm not in the paper business."[32] A staunch supporter of the BJP at the time of the 2014 elections, Bhagat has been called "the cultural logic of Narendra Modi."[33] Bhagat denies partisanship, however. Consistent with his carefully curated image as relatable pundit of the everyman, he describes himself as "neutral" and "not aligned to any political party."[34]

As this chapter continues, I will primarily write about Bhagat in the past tense, with reference to the decade and a half after the 2004 publication of *Five Point Someone*. However, Bhagat continues to write best-sellers. He remains a prominent, voluble member of New India's club of "self-styled public intellectuals" and right-wing "raconteurs."[35] If I do not strive to keep up to date with Bhagat here, it is because my aim is to retrospectively assess his emergence as an object of criticism in Anglo-American literary studies. In the first decade of the 2000s, India-based reviewers largely pooh-poohed Bhagat's "paperback atrocities."³⁶ Meanwhile, critics outside India were not yet aware of him. Writing in *The Guardian* in 2008, Randeep Ramesh called Bhagat "the biggest-selling writer in English you have never heard of"—*you* being the average reader in the West. I started graduate school stateside in 2009. In 2010, Bhagat made *Time*'s "100 Most Influential People in the World." By the time of my doctoral candidacy, between 2012 and 2016, Bhagat's work had become a key signifier of the transition from the postcolonial India to the global New India.

Rashmi Sadana's *English Heart, Hindi Heartland* was published in 2012; Bhagat surfaced in her brief conclusion as representing a new Anglophone "phenomenon."³⁷ In 2014, Mrinalini Chakravorty read Bhagat's *One Night @ the Call Center* as signifying a new "speculative, uncertain orientation in depicting the postcolonial" in the last chapter of her book on South Asia in the global literary imaginary.³⁸ The Bhagat phenomenon was the subject of two 2015 essays: Ulka Anjaria's "Chetan Bhagat and the New Provincialism" and Priya Joshi's "Chetan Bhagat: Remaking the Novel in India." Joshi's essay is the twentieth of twenty-five roughly chronological chapters in a field-surveying volume on the Indian novel in English (the first examines Bankim's 1864 *Rajmohan's Wife*); it is clubbed with entries on contemporary popular culture, including chick lit, graphic novels, fantasy fiction, and film adaptations. Manisha Basu's 2017 *The Rhetoric of Hindu India* examined Bhagat as a "mediocre" but ubiquitous writer who cannily indigenized English in the process of becoming "the millennial *avatar* of Hindutva."³⁹

Sadana, Chakravorty, Anjaria, Joshi, and Basu belong to a generation of literature scholars working in US academe who are advancing the study of contemporary Indian literature in and beyond English. In each of their texts, Bhagat represents a key inflection point—from postcolonial to global—in India's self-conception and representation. This point is marked rhetorically with a claim to Bhagat's former invisibility to critics. Sadana notes that "the fact that [Bhagat's] novels are not literary makes most critics dismiss them."⁴⁰ Anjaria's essay opens by stating that Bhagat is "virtually unheard of abroad."⁴¹ Joshi writes that Bhagat's "novels have mostly been ignored in the culture of reviews, prizes, and metropolitan bookstores and most markedly by literary critics."⁴² Basu begins by saying that Bhagat "has so far not received a great deal of scholarly-critical attention from the Anglo-American academy."⁴³

Given the vagaries of publishing timelines, it is of course possible that all of these scholars were working on Bhagat at the same time, and that each had to draw on journalistic sources to make up for the lack of critical treatment, as Joshi notes. I am not suggesting that the later critics did not read those who came first. What I am observing is that the Bhagat phenomenon in India was followed by a distinct, microphenomenon of critical attention in US-based studies of Indian English literature. For a few years, everyone was reading and writing about Bhagat, while noting that nobody was reading and writing about Bhagat. The fact of writing about Bhagat as a scholar situated outside India was consistently presented as an authorizing condition of discussing his work. "Firstness" was more than a claim to having identified a formerly unidentified object. It established that critique itself had until now been withheld from this object, as if Bhagat had been denied certain readers and forms of readings—that is, critical readers and critical readings; "good" readers, for his "bad" writing.

As for the scholar of Indian English literature, the affordances of the emerging Bhagat oeuvre were multiple. A prize-winning fictionist like Aravind Adiga might have greater claim on the contemporary. A newspaperman-turned-novelist like Raj Kamal Jha might have greater claim, via his journalistic depictions of the New Indian city, on the real. A graphic novelist like Sarnath Banerjee, who shares a visual idiom with comics and fantasy fiction, might have greater claim on the popular. But Bhagat could be used to annex all three: present concerns, authentic narratives, and mass appeal.

If initial evaluations of the Bhagat phenomenon were that he had "something to do with middle class youth . . . and something to do with India's growing affluence and presence in a globalised world," it was clear by 2012 just what that "something" was.[44] Bhagat was writing English-language books for nonelite, lower- and middle-class Indians with "weak English" whose relationship to the language had changed dramatically in postliberalization India.[45] Bhagat called them "E2" Indians, who went to vernacular-medium schools, whose parents don't speak English, and who "have not been taught in an environment that facilitates . . . continuous improvement through the consumption of English language products."[46] Bhagat offered these E2 Indians an accessible, neutral language that most closely resembled the "modular" and "serviceable"[47] English of the call center and would seed "a new consciousness about their own social mobility."[48] In the process, he became the "voice of the new [Indian] middle class."[49]

As Bhagat's star rose, he explicitly dismissed other Indians writing in English, especially postcolonial expatriates and elites, whom he called "EIs." "What is the point of writers who call themselves Indian authors," he asked, "but who have no Indian readers?"[50] Unlike "Rushdie and friends,"[51] who Bhagat claimed pandered to Western audiences, he held a mirror and microphone up to the "real" India. He also professed to be writing toward a "change in the mindset of Indian society.... I want to reach as many people as I can."[52] At a book reading in Dehradun, a young woman reportedly asked Bhagat a "silly question" about his hairstyle. "She would never have asked that question to Salman Rushdie," he proudly said, affirming his relatability to average Indians. "She would not even have raised her hand."[53]

In fact, numerous readers approached Rushdie in the 1980s and 1990s with similarly intimate questions and gratitude for his having "told their stories."[54] Rushdie became Rushdie precisely because he reached readers—not because he alienated them. But the strategic forgetting of a writer like Rushdie's Indian audience enabled Bhagat's identification of his own intended readership. "I want my books next to jeans and bread," Bhagat said. "I want my country to read me."[55] In service of this goal, publisher Rupa Publications complied with Bhagat's requests to keep his books at unusually low prices: initially an average of about 95 rupees each, or $1.13 at the present exchange rate.[56] As a result, Bhagat's books reached "constables, drivers, low-brow security personnel at airports, even tribals in the Indian hinterlands" who used his novels to "learn the English language, and implicitly therefore, to make themselves in the image of a new, youthful, middle-class India."[57] Many of these readers had never read a book in English before reading Bhagat. For them, Bhagat's fiction served as the uncanny, belated occasion for what Homi Bhabha once called "the discovery of the English book."[58]

Bhagat's novels were marketed and read almost exclusively within India. They were an exemplary instance of novels that "stay home," in contradistinction to "world literature" that travels.[59] This antiworldliness, ironically consummated by the figure of the global Indian, was the substance of Bhagat's appeal in US academe. Here was a writer with a finger on the pulse of the New India who was expressly *not* cosmopolitan in sensibility or trafficking in the "the postcolonial exotic."[60] Here was someone writing for an exclusively Indian audience, who was not going to win any literary prizes, whose novels were not meant to be translated, and who wrote in an anodyne call center English. "[Bhagat's books] represent the actuality of what many people in the world are reading today," Anjaria wrote. "International readers will likely find little exciting in Chetan Bhagat. But that, it seems, is precisely the point."[61]

Bhagat achieved the symbolic heft in conversations on global Anglophone Indian literature that only Rushdie had in the postcolonial context. He was described as having renewed the relationship "between English and the vernaculars"[62] and as representing "a new kind of genre and . . . a new readership."[63] He was credited with using English as if it were "'native' to the Indian habitus"[64] and with "inspiring a vast readership within India"[65] that had never before been reached "by India's literary fiction in *any* language."[66]

Let me emphasize that striking final point. Bhagat's books did what the literary qua the literary had never been able to do: they made readers out of nonreaders. At the same time, as discussed in the next section, they called into question the reading habits of certain other readers: namely, academic critics. Bhagat became a compelling object in US literary studies not because he won any international awards—which is how Booker-winners Rushdie, Roy, Kiran Desai, and Adiga came to prominence—but because he didn't. Not because his books were widely circulated in the West, but because they weren't.

Bhagat emerged as the iconic Anglophone writer of New India specifically because *we* were not supposed to read him. What would happen if we did?

On Reading Chetan Bhagat

The trouble for literary critics is that Bhagat's novels are not literary. They're "anti-literary"[67] self-help manuals and English primers that seek to provide his Indian readers with a mirror of their lives and the tools and inspiration to transform those lives. The novels map what we might call the New Indian universe of social positions, and each of Bhagat's characters is legible as a stock New Indian type. In addition to IIT students and call center workers, Bhagat has depicted aspiring businessmen, cricket players, Hindu priests, medical entrance exam takers, corrupt politicians, activists, students on athletic scholarship, rural schoolmasters, and young Indians bound for the United States and the United Kingdom. Many of these figures embody a form of entrepreneurial personhood associated with New Indian neoliberalism.[68]

We (over here) read Bhagat because we want to know the characters of New India (over there). Bhagat knows this. His books have the requisite "aspirational" and "authenticating" components of middlebrow cultural production, and in public appearances, journalism, and interviews, he advertises his work's credentials on precisely these fronts.[69] In his novels, he positions himself as both a member of and an ambassador for his addressed readership, while soliciting a reading of his novels as species of native intelligence. His authorial persona is consolidated through strategic identification with his fictive protagonists and through his own metafictional appearance in his novels' frame stories and primary diegesis. He makes himself a character in order to authenticate the rest of his cast of characters and to provide for his readers a model of character to which they might aspire.

Bhagat's first novel, *Five Point Someone*, begins with a prologue in which the writer, present as a character, vows to write a book about the unfolding events. His second novel, *ON@CC*, tells the story of a failing call center in Gurgaon, where agents fabricate an e-terrorism threat to save their jobs. In the novel's frame story, a passenger on a train incites the narrator, introduced as Chetan Bhagat, to tell the story of India's youth. She critiques the classism of his IIT novel, which depicts elites who do not face "real challenges." She then offers Bhagat the call center story, on the condition that he make it his second book: "If I tell you, you have to use it . . . as if it's your own story."[70] This demand is significant: Bhagat, the IIT-educated banker-author, is asked to give voice to young Indians with real challenges. Or, more precisely, Bhagat the author writes himself into the narrative as a character called to offer this ventriloquial performance.

The prologue to Bhagat's 2008 *The 3 Mistakes of My Life* begins with an emailed suicide note addressed to info@chetanbhagat.com from a self-described "ordinary boy in Ahmedabad," a city less "hip" than "Delhi, Bombay, or Bangalore" but part of "the real India."[71] The boy, a twenty-five-year-old businessman, writes that he has "no reason to live" and is taking sleeping pills. "Somehow I felt I could write to you," he tells Bhagat, who then resolves to find him and tell his tale: "I couldn't help but get involved."[72]

Bhagat's 2014 novel *Half Girlfriend* also begins with a frame story in which "a writer on a book tour" named "Chetan Bhagat" is accosted by a young man, Madhav Jha, at the hotel in which he's staying. Madhav, who comes from "the back of beyond"[73] in Dumraon, thrusts on him some journals written by a woman he calls his "half girlfriend" Riya, who is supposedly dead. Bhagat reads the journals; he then asks Madhav to tell him his abortive love story, which comprises the substance of the novel.

These frame stories position Bhagat not just as a vocal medium for New India's youth, but as their chosen representative. His self-reflexively unadorned English completes the project of anointment. In *ON@CC*, Shyam introduces himself in Bhagat's voice, saying, "My English is not that great. . . . So, if you're looking for something sophisticated and highbrow, then I suggest you read another book with plenty of long words."[74] *Half Girlfriend* begins with Madhav's similar profession that, despite his having attended the elite St. Stephen's University through the athlete's quota, "My English is still bad." The novel is explicitly concerned with the changing status of English as a "global language" in the New India. At the start of the action, Madhav speaks "90 per cent Bihari Hindi mixed with 10 per cent really bad English." "My English *was* Bihari," he says.[75]

The final plot twist in *Half Girlfriend* centers on Madhav having an opportunity to give a speech in English in front of Bill Gates, which, if successful, will result in his mother's rural Patna school winning a grant from the Gates Foundation. In pursuit of this goal, Madhav enrolls in Patna's Pride English Learning Centre, where the instructor tells him, "Don't be scared of people who use big words. These are elitists. They want to scare you with their big words and deny you an entry into the world of English. Don't fall into their trap." Riya gives Madhav a ten-step plan to learn English, including watching YouTube videos, "calling call centres and choosing the English option," and "reading simple English novels, like, the one by that writer, what's his name, Chetan Bhagat."[76]

I noted earlier that Bhagat's novels are primers for those who want to learn English. This is not an accidental by-product of their style, but Bhagat's express intention: "We have to give students . . . simple, relevant and fun English course materials that they enjoy reading, watching or learning from, so that they get into the self-driven virtuous cycle of consuming English language products. Forcing them to read antiquated or convoluted books, because some PhD in literature classifies them as good, is the same as giving a primary school student a Nobel thesis in the name of science. It will scare the child and kill any curiosity for further exploration."[77]

Rather than require English fluency, the Bhagat novel cultivates the English-language proficiency of its reader. "Bay-gulls. That's how you pronounce them, spelt b-a-g-e-l-s," a seasoned Goldman Sachs employee tells newbie Radhika in *One Indian Girl*.[78] In *ON@CC*, Shyam explains the versatility of the "T" spoken by those with American accents: "T can be silent, so 'internet' becomes 'innernet.' . . . Another way is when T and N merge—'written' becomes 'writn.' . . . when T falls in the middle [it] sounds like a D—'daughter' is 'daughder' . . . The last category, if you still care, is when Americans say T like a T . . . when T is at the beginning of a word like 'table.'"[79]

These passages are didactic. They also neatly capture the "humor and humiliation" of accent in a country that is "richly diverse and vastly unequal."[80] Overall, Bhagat's style is "laddish"[81] with short sentences, stripped-down dialogue, and little narrative description. He writes syntactically simple, unadorned, and transparent prose, like, "I think Indian mothers have two tasks—to tell children to eat more or study more."[82] As a result, Bhagat's readers are "inspired" by his novels and made to feel that they are "better at English" than they are.[83] It is as if his prose reads itself to them, not the other way around. Not knowing English well thus becomes a sign of belonging for the Bhagat reader, who joins characters like Shyam and Madhav in the fellowship of newly valorized nonknowledge and whose belonging to this fraternity of proxy-Anglophones is predicated on the strategic maintenance of partial nonfluency.

This is why some critics professed that they at first did not know how to read Bhagat. He didn't appear to be using "bad English" artistically or poetically the way a literary writer uses "rotten" or "weird" Englishes for effect.[84] He was just sort of *bad*. "We are schooled in old English," Urvashi Butalia reflected, "and suddenly people are writing in what appears to be 'bad' English. . . . They are defeating our old, elite notions of what good writing is."[85] Bhagat's arrival led to the renewed consolidation of the group Butalia terms "we" and to which I have been referring: "we" scholars and critics; "we" English professors; "we" postcolonials and diasporans. What were "we" supposed to do with Bhagat? What does the popular evidence, generally, and what could the Bhagat novel be taken as evidence for, specifically?

A consensus developed that our default, deconstructive modes of reading were not going to be adequate to this object. Bhagat wasn't writing for a reader we knew, or in a language we were used to reading. His arrival meant elite comeuppance: we would have to pay heed to Raymond William's "ordinary" culture without impugning the tastes of "ordinary" people, while also recognizing new aesthetic forms and literacies. The critical embrace of Bhagat entailed a return to the 1950s mass culture debates in Anglo-American literary studies: a return to the question of what was to be done with lay readers, to the literature of what Michael Denning called "mechanic accents," and to working-class cultural production with purchase on the zeitgeist. Reading Bhagat was plainly "a form of behavior"; "the event of reading" a Bhagat text itself merited consideration.[86]

Of course, not all critical readers were interested in updating their notions of "good writing." For Aatish Taseer, Bhagat was a sign of India's perpetual subalternity and defeat. Bhagat produces books of "such poor literary quality that no one outside India can be expected to read them," Taseer observed. "Some justly speculate that perhaps this is the authentic voice of modern India. But this is not the voice of a confident country. It sounds rather like a country whose painful relationship with language has left it voiceless."[87] Taseer's 2015 essay on the poverty of "homegrown" Indian English literature was a textbook example of what Vikram Chandra once termed the "complicated ritual war-dance against the West."[88] By calling Bhagat and his ilk "voiceless" Indians, Taseer impugned demotic forms of Indian English. At the same time, his note about Bhagat's lack of appeal outside India reasserted the value of Western-sanctioned literary bona fides. Finally, in an ironic twist, Taseer lamented that writers like Rushdie and Roy (standing in for the postcolonial canon) "came to India via the West, via its publishing deals and prizes."

This is the familiar, zero-sum game of evaluating Indian literature in English, given the dominant ideology of Anglophone nativity. The writer is either too literary, or not literary enough; either capitulating to the West, or leaving India "voiceless." Critics who sought to reject this zero-sum game read Bhagat as deliberately antiliterary, not accidentally deficient, and as voicing something so genuinely fresh that the likes of Taseer could not hear it at all. Some performed close readings of Bhagat's books in relation to books like Mohsin Hamid's *The Reluctant Fundamentalist* and Hari Kunzru's *Transmission*.[89] At the same time, in order to establish popular fiction as an object of scholarly interest, many continued to fetishize Bhagat's readership. Just *who* in India was reading Bhagat, and what "life" did they "imagine" his English would make "possible"?[90]

Bhagat's novels displayed English in action; they were examples of English's use-value in opening professional doors. Critical attention thus confirmed the Bhagat novel's primary interest as a species of literary sociology: as an artifact that would give critics insight into India's changing youth and business culture. "It does not really matter to us what Bhagat writes," Gupta noted tongue-in-cheek. "What matters is that they read him prolifically—those Bhagat readers in India."[91]

On the one hand, we critics knew better than to reduce Bhagat's texts to species of "native intelligence."[92] On the other hand, we needed access to New India. We wanted to know about "New Indians," and we could not write about them if we did not read about them and certainly not if we didn't know what they were reading. The trouble was, Bhagat's novels weren't just received as examples of "what Young India wants to read" (to adapt the title of his first nonfiction collection). They were read as representations of who Young Indians *are*.

That the Indian English text circulating outside India would be read as representing India is not a surprise. This is the burden of representation assumed by all non-Western Anglophone literatures, postcolonial writers, and scholars of Indian English literature: all are dogged by their (by our) inevitable interpellation as informants. But, in reading Rushdie or Roy, postcolonial critics in US academe at least had to be critically self-reflexive about their resemblance to the object that circulated in their name, threatening to represent them, along with India. The Bhagat text, by contrast, was an object that the US-based scholar could hold at a distance as emphatically other, because it informed on someone else.

Scholar-critics read Bhagat because he did not seem to be writing for us and because of the promise of being escorted to the New Indian backstage. We read him because he said he did not care if we read him—*except, of course, that he did*.

Bhagat's disavowals of "people who use big words" and "PhDs in literature" are perpetual provocations in his books. His "bad writing" is calculated, too. Consider this September 2020 podcast exchange with Cyrus Broacha. After teasing Bhagat about his bad spelling, Broacha asks him to respond to critics in "the literati." Bhagat replies, annoyed: "I have seven editors, all top editors. My books in Rupa, when I was there, David Davidar used to read and check my books. He discovered Vikram Seth; what are even people talking? I sometimes use certain spellings which are used—[*Broacha interrupts: colloquially*]—yah, people don't understand; that's even a harder book to edit. Very easy to do a correct English. But correct English is not how people talk."[93]

Bhagat's response to Broacha admits two things I want to underline. First, his writing is carefully crafted and vetted, even at the level of orthography. Second, in name-dropping Davidar, cofounder of Aleph Book Company and former CEO of Penguin International, Bhagat acknowledges his own place within the literary-critical establishment, which in public he continues to assail. Online, Bhagat frequently attacks the demographic to which Davidar and Seth belong, as in this November 2021 tweet: "The battle in India's opinion space is between these English-upbringing losers who think they know better and real Indians who know have [*sic*] a stronger and more real voice, even if not as polished. The losers are losing, but one must ensure such elitism is stamped out today."[94]

Bhagat's bad faith performances of antielitism are well documented.[95] But we have been so taken in by the character of Bhagat as the ambassador of the everyman, and of Bhagat as the "real voice" of Young India, that we risk removing "all the signs of that which is not consistent with it" and have generated the "object even in its failure to be realized as object."[96] To borrow the terms of Kinohi Nishikawa's work on urban street fiction, Bhagat's emergence as New Indian icon is what happens when we allow the "crudeness" of a text to become the condition of its "credibility."[97] We ignore the fact that Bhagat is himself an elite repatriated expatriate: a foreign-returned Indian who grew up in a middle-class Delhi family, was educated at IIT and IIM, and worked in Hong Kong for the investment banks Peregrine and Goldman Sachs. We have to suppress hard-won evaluative criteria regarding the literary. And we sideline the postcolonial in the moment of its eclipse and renomination as Anglophone.

Two decades after Bhagat's debut, it is clear that his privileged position of enunciation as the voice of New India has been jointly authorized by his readers and his critics. Bhagat's readers recognize themselves as his characters and in so doing cathect to him, the author. It's equally significant that he asks them to repudiate a certain other set of characters: namely, Anglophone elites, postcolonials, expatriates, and critics; in other words, readers like *us*, who have been educated into the position from which we launch our readings and, ironically, authenticate his project. Bhagat's real readers engage fictional characters whose commentary serves as ammunition against his real critics, through his writing of fictional readers, like Madhav, who encounter real characters, like Gates and Bhagat himself, who empower him to take on his fictional critics. In this way, Bhagat is not just a popular writer; he is a populist writer weaponizing distinction and producing a spectral enemy. He mobilizes the affect and imagination that makes possible Hindu nationalism, specifically, and antielite, anticosmopolitan, antisecular, and anti-Western politics, generally.

All of which is to say something that may be uncomfortable for critics to hear: We have already been written into this script. When we encounter lines like "don't be scared of [elitists] who use big words" or "one must ensure such elitism is stamped out," we have to recognize that we are being inducted into a particular hermeneutic circle with and by Bhagat. We know how we are supposed to read him, and he knows how we're going to read him, so reading him otherwise might not be the salutary, reparative critical operation we think it is. If we're going to read Bhagat, we need to be vigilant about both the massifying, quantitative operations of the global, and postcritical desires to supersede the postcolonial highbrow. In this way, reading Bhagat's fictions "might help us to reveal the fiction of character"[98]—in particular the fictions of Bhagat as the voice of New India and of a scholarly social position that could ever remain unimplicated in its object of critique.

On Not Reading Chetan Bhagat

We could also *not* read Bhagat.

If the re-valuation of the popular text is symptomatic of current dispensations against the literary and critical reading itself, then perhaps not reading Bhagat is the most appropriate way for critics to read him. In not being read, Bhagat would be in good company, joining Harold Bloom in not being read by Alejandro Zambra, and David Foster Wallace in not being read by Amy Hungerford.[99] There is not world enough and time to read everything, after all. Instead of reading Bhagat, we could enlist various methods of historical and social scientific analysis to study him: from the interviews, polls, questionnaires, and surveys of reader-response criticism, to distant reading, to the algorithmic projects of the digital humanities.[100]

"Not reading" would be the least technical method and one that enacts maximal distance from the text. That said, as Sheila Liming observes, it ironically requires "quite a lot of reading."[101] In order to justify not reading Wallace, Hungerford reads around and about Wallace. What she learns raises her hackles about the connection between Wallace's misogyny and his writing, and Hungerford refuses to play along. Liming reads this refusal as "more enticing—and easier—than genuine involvement." Not having read X is of course the perfect pretext for not having to say anything about X. But Hungerford doesn't not read Wallace because she doesn't want to say anything about him; indeed, she has plenty to say about Wallace, specifically *because* she hasn't read him. Hungerford's not reading is a political and ethical stance, as well as a critique of the "self-replicating" canonization machine.[102]

I have read half a dozen of Bhagat's books. I have also *not read* half a dozen of his books, deliberately, and I have been working on Bhagat for over a decade. My not reading Bhagat, from where I sit in an English department in US academe, doesn't have quite the same charge as Hungerford's not reading Wallace, perhaps. But I propose that it is a calculated mode of accented reading that is simultaneously attuned to the overdetermination of my position of reception and the burden of representation faced by Bhagat. To return to the scene of institutional positioning that begins this chapter, my comment that "I wouldn't teach Chetan Bhagat" was a spontaneous act of disavowal that sought to neutralize the risk of my being seen as a particular kind of reader. Equally, I said "I wouldn't teach Chetan Bhagat" because the India I want to present to my students doesn't *sound* like that—which means that Bhagat's text powerfully exposes my own "thinking with an American accent."[103]

Many years ago, when I first started writing about Bhagat, I planned to spend two focused weeks reading all his books. One a day. I would pay as much attention to a popular writer who directs the decisions of his Indian publisher as critics have always paid to writers of literature championed by the Western market. I'd then write metacritically about the experience, enacting a form of what Lucas Thompson calls "method reading": "Reading as a form of spontaneous method acting . . . that takes literary texts as invitations to engage in a particular kind of activity, wherein the reader does not merely identify with, develop sympathies for, or even recognize herself in a fictional character, but actually *performs* as someone else."[104] For Thompson, method reading is a mode of inhabiting character.[105] In a twist, I would performatively inhabit the extratextual position of the Bhagat reader. Instead of imagining how Bhagat's characters' imaginations operate, I would imagine how the Bhagat reader projects herself into the imagination of the Bhagat character.

Swiftly, I recognized that the undertaking was bound to fail. I could not perform my (method) reading of Bhagat without highlighting the act as one of my reading books not intended for me, popular books that I, no matter my critical appreciation of "ordinary" culture, wouldn't read "for pleasure"—although I grant that there are critics who do. For me, it would be like a week reading children's books. However meaningful, radical, or crassly ideological the book might be, I'd either be attempting to perform a reading from a position from which I'm structurally excluded, or offering a reading from my own reading position, which is by definition outside the text's intended address—and I'd need to mark that position. To return to the lessons of the mass culture debate, if Bhagat's popular fiction demands an "ethnography of reading,"[106] and since even ethnographic representation is fundamentally an act of interpretation, what are the stakes of writing about the Bhagat text if you are not and cannot become a Bhagat reader?

Writing "My Two Weeks Reading Bhagat," I would swiftly hit the limit of possible critical responses. Would I enjoy Bhagat's books, and if not, could I perform enjoyment anyway? I could try to put the *"mazaa"* back into my reading, but whose mazaa would it be?[107] Could I read with someone else's accent? I didn't want to voyeuristically slum like an American tourist-reader in the narrative universe of young India. Neither did it make sense to claim that I was licensing my professional reading self to read like an amateur.

I would probably conclude that Bhagat is a bad writer. But I would need to find something new to say about his badness. Would I discover that he is bad in a good way? That his books are more sophisticated than they appear? This case has already been made in persuasive terms: that despite the seeming artlessness of his texts, Bhagat's work is attuned to the contradictions of New India and offers a "subtle framing of the political ethics of enterprise, beyond either celebratory acceptance or straightforward critique."[108]

Anjaria credits even Bhagat's "formulaic characterization" with formal experimentation, arguing that Bhagat turns the "present into an aesthetic possibility" by moving away from the familiar concerns of the postcolonial, like the fetishization of the nation, depictions of diasporic hybridity, and Rushdiean wordplay.[109] She writes: "While Bhagat's might be bad writing, it is bad writing with a purpose: by taking English away from the elitist sphere of art and into the populist domain of economics and self-help, Bhagat produces a popular, indigenized English that is not only a counterpart to Rushdie's esoteric 'chutnification' but language that reflects how many Indians actually speak."[110]

To the extent that we accept this characterization of the postcolonial—certainly these are the familiar concerns of academic postcolonialism in its US dispensation—Anjaria's estimation of Bhagat is right on point: the classic concerns of postcolonial literature are emphatically not Bhagat's concerns. By that same token, this argument risks reproducing one of many "ritual gestures" of the critical reader, who, when confronted with an uncritical text or practice of uncritical reading, must argue that the uncritical text or reading "really was critical in some sense or another."[111]

There are two aspects of the argument for the criticality of Bhagat's badness that need to be disentangled. First, there is the question of the scholarly-professional critic's reading of Bhagat versus the lay-amateur reader's reading. To read as a critic is to surrender to the "ongoing [romance] of the empirical *availability* of other people's reading practices."[112] The scholarly reader might discern in Bhagat's work greater critical potential ("aesthetic possibility") than we expect to find in his work on the basis of our assumptions about his texts' aims and audience. But what this means is that the excavation of the text's formal possibility depends upon the affirmation of the critic's essential difference from the Bhagat reader, and vice versa.

Then, there is the matter of the position of the scholarly-professional critic of the New India, who in this case views their postcolonial predecessor as temporally, ethically, and aesthetically out of step with the present. The perspective of the postcolonial critic must be transcended for the post-postcolonial critic to read and understand the contemporary India represented by Bhagat. But the postcolonial focus on the past was never simply about withdrawal from the contemporary; it was also a perspective on it. If the contemporary is "collagist," to borrow Toral Gajarawala's term, why should the postcolonial be excised from its frame?[113] Can we perform what Anjaria terms "reading alongside the grain" and "with a loving eye" without dispensing with the postcolonial? Can a new reading position be installed that is postcritical but not post-postcolonial?

Whether our readings are paranoid, suspicious, reparative, loving, against the grain, or alongside the grain, Bhagat's critic cannot, by virtue of being a critic, universalize her reading position; she can neither read nor write as "the reader." Even those who enjoy Bhagat must hold themselves at a remove from his intended audience in order to assess his politics of address. Put simply, Bhagat's bad writing demands a kind of bad reading, which the good critical reader is professionally obligated to withhold.

This is why I abandoned my method reading plans, even though professional reading often involves wading through undesirable texts. Reading Bhagat, I would have had to offer a performance of post-critical amateurism, which would have entailed constructing an unknowing, uncritical reader's response to the text. In the process, I would have had to forward certain assumptions about the India and Indians he represents—about their voices, interests, aspirations, and dreams—that I feared risked condescension and cynicism. Rather than display my reading of Bhagat, I needed to further interrogate my assumptions about what knowledge that reading would yield.

On Not Teaching Chetan Bhagat

The preceding sections have focused on how literature scholars navigate the trap of reading (or not reading) Bhagat. The Bhagat text makes a different set of demands on the pedagogue, and in what remains of this chapter, I consider those demands from the vantage of the classroom. To date, my undergraduate and graduate students have primarily been Anglophones of mixed socioeconomic backgrounds at a land-grant, research university in the US Southwest. The following discussion centers but does not stop with these students. As I consider Bhagat's place in my classroom, I seek to expose assumptions underlying decisions to teach or not teach Bhagat in other institutions and to other kinds of students: assumptions about what kinds of readers our students are; assumptions about Bhagat's relationship to other Indian writers; assumptions about what English literature is, and whose work should represent it, in what contexts, and to whom.

If university teaching always involves inhabiting an institutional situation in which one risks canonizing the texts taught, what are the stakes of teaching Bhagat? How do we instruct students in the reading of "bad" English that purports to sound "like Hindi"? In what curricular contexts might teaching Bhagat be warranted? What are we teaching our students about literature, India, the contemporary, and English when we assign a Bhagat text?

Let's begin in India. In April 2017, Delhi University (DU) proposed adding Bhagat's *Five Point Someone* to the reading list in Popular Fiction for the BA in Honors English, alongside work by Louisa May Alcott, Agatha Christie, and J. K. Rowling.[114] Many India-based commentators and DU professors who hadn't been consulted balked. An English major worried that nonmajors already "know very little" about the BA in English: "And now, if they start teaching Chetan Bhagat, students will think that this is literature. Log value nahi karenge [They won't value it]."[115] English professor Gorvika Rao worried about legitimizing "trash." Distinguishing between pulp fiction and fiction meriting instruction, Rao stressed: "students are not masses."[116] How would faculty deal with Bhagat's "political leanings"?[117] Bhagat's own, giddy response didn't help: "It is obviously a huge honor, and validates my work's value even in academia, something elitists have tried to deny me for long. . . . It also shows that many who claim to be experts in literature have no idea about what literature is meant to be. If you are teaching popular fiction in India, wouldn't you talk about the most popular books?"[118] By September, DU had pulled the plug on Bhagat's inclusion in the Popular Fiction list, pledging to revisit the issue in future.

In US academe, the stakes of teaching Bhagat are both similar and different. For all the reasons explored in the preceding pages, you would not teach a Bhagat novel as a representative "Indian" text in a world literature class, following the likes of *The Odyssey*, *The Epic of Gilgamesh*, Shakespeare, and Proust. You wouldn't, for the same reason that the DU faculty balked at including Bhagat alongside Alcott, Christie, and Rowling: every syllabus enacts an analogical operation that flattens key differences between each text's audience, reception, and circulation. Which popular? Whose world?

By that same token, you might enlist a Bhagat novel as a representative "Indian" text in a class on Contemporary Pulp Fictions or the Global

Popular in US academe—for the same reason that his inclusion was challenged at DU. In most English literature classrooms in the United States, there is no broad-base of knowledge about the Indian popular sphere that would contest his inclusion; in India, there is. In a US university, you might teach Bhagat, whose novels have been adapted into many popular films, in a class on Bollywood cinema and film adaptation. Equally, Bhagat might serve as a representative pulp fictionist in a class on the Indian novel in English, in the context of plural linguistic and literary Indian Englishes developed over the course of the long twentieth and twenty-first centuries.

Versions of this last class are taught, I suspect, in many English departments that employ a scholar of the South Asian Anglophone. I have taught a basic seminar in this vein; its syllabus precedes this discussion. The course begins with the colonial institution of English literary studies, via Gauri Viswanathan; then elaborates English as a "literary and cultural system" and not just a language or literature, via Aamir Mufti; then asks, after Raja Rao and Mulk Raj Anand (and, equally, Chinua Achebe and Ngũgĩ wa Thiong'o), what can be said about India in English, and whether English has in fact become an Indian language. The course's primary aim is to defamiliarize the study of English for English students.

Another version of the class might begin with Bankim's *Rajmohan's Wife* (1864), considering its serial publication and relationship to its vernacular contemporaries. After reading the 1930s modernist fictions of Anand and Rao, the class might turn to G. V. Desani's *All About H. Hatterr* (1948), which destabilizes English with its unruly, plurilingual polyphony. Questions about linguistic and cultural impurity, standardization, and syncretism might lead to Rushdie's *Midnight's Children* (1981). Rushdie would motivate a turn to postcolonial theories of mimicry and hybridity, while raising questions about the narration of the nation and the textual representation of oral storytelling traditions.

Bhagat's novels might be an appropriate next stop when constructing a narrative about the itineraries of English in India: from colonial, to postcolonial, to post-postcolonial; from realist, to modernist, to postmodernist, to pulp. The challenge is that Bhagat's very contemporaneity lends itself to his presentation as the telos of Indian English literature. The question, fundamentally, is what story we want to tell. If one teaches chronologically, the risk is seeming to move progressively toward Bhagat as if he resolves the problem of English as a colonial bequest or completes a trajectory of indigenization. Of course, chronology need not be the determining factor of a class syllabus: one might begin with Bhagat's stripped-down English and continue on to Desani's music and Rushdie's puns, in service of a story about Indian English that is not developmental, but rather exhumes a rich body from seemingly spare bones. Do rhythmic, accented textual innovations or reader demographics determine the Indianness of English? It might be easier to teach Bhagat if he didn't have the final say.

Questions of contemporaneity may be resolved by time. My more acute concern is how to stage the encounter between the Anglophone and the vernacular in contemporary India: that is, how to teach the question of whether Bhagat's English is in any way "like Hindi." Bhagat's novels produce the impression that simple, unadorned English can access India more directly than does the English of Desani, the cosmopolitan philosophy professor, or Rushdie, the globe-trotting expatriate, or Roy, the florid wordsmith, or Adiga, the ventriloquist of the Indian subaltern. Bhagat's novels explicitly tout their purchase on the "real" India and, as I have been arguing, the extant criticism amplifies his self-representation.

To be clear, none of the scholars and critics I've discussed in this chapter argues that demotic Englishes and Indian vernaculars are equivalent; nobody is claiming that call center English and Agyeya's Hindi poetry, or *2 States* and U. R. Ananthamurthy's *Samskara*, exist on the same linguistic and literary plane. And yet, my concern is that this is exactly how both the Bhagat novel and the postcritical, post-postcolonial Bhagat discourse position student-readers to understand his English: as if it gives them access to an Indian vernacular sphere that would otherwise only be accessible via the "vernacular languages" themselves. No matter how savvy our students might be, every time we make the argument that Bhagat's English allows everyday Indians to speak for themselves, we participate in the ideological production of the popular as authentic, and the nonelite as the real, of Joe the Plumber's voice as more "American" than Barack Obama's, and the chai-wallah Modi's voice more "Indian" than the economist Singh's.

The Bhagat text is "postexotic"—to borrow Ravinder Kaur's term for the visual iconography of New India. It therefore presents a different challenge in the US university classroom than the more strictly "literary" postcolonial archive ever did. It also distinctly complicates the argument made by proponents of world literature for teaching Indian literatures in English translation after the decline of comparative literature. Works like

Midnight's Children and *The God of Small Things* (to stick with the heuristic example of "Rushdie and Roy") may have been commodified by the Western publishing industry and canonized in Western classrooms. Or, as Graham Huggan charges, their success may have been partially owed to "the skill with which they manipulate[d] commercially viable metropolitan codes."[119] But what was striking about their efforts at chutnification and "aesthetic play" was how explicitly they acknowledged the limits of their own referentiality. Chutnification meant that the absence of the vernacular was always keenly felt, through its shadow presence at the level of word, syntax, rhythm, and metaphor. Reading Rushdie and Roy, it is impossible not to recognize the constructed, contingent, provisional nature of their claims—of any claim—on Indian life-worlds. As even Huggan acknowledges, "They are conscious that their writing, ostensibly oppositional, is vulnerable to recuperation. . . . they know that their work might still be used as a means of reconfirming an exoticising imperial gaze."[120]

Moreover, the disproportionate attention paid to Anglophone literature in postcolonial literary studies—if only as "a tool to force English departments to make space for the rest of the world"[121]—itself made the case for curricular reinvestment in vernacular literatures, as did Rushdie's notorious 1997 argument for "Indo-Anglian" literature as "the most valuable contribution India has yet made to the world of books."[122] By some accounts, Rushdie's essay directly inspired Amit Chaudhuri's edited volume *The Vintage/Picador Book of Modern Indian Literature* and the polemical case for vernacular literatures he offers in its introduction.

By contrast, Bhagat's transparent, hyperaccessible English explicitly solicits an analogical comparison with the vernacular, as opposed to placing itself hierarchically above it. "English is not competing with the vernacular," he writes. "Hindi is your mother, English is your wife and it is possible to love both at the same time."[123] In this way, he obviates reparations for the vernacular's absence in the English literature classroom and ensures that we become only further "out of touch with the idiomaticity of nonhegemonic languages."[124]

Bhagat's goal is to induct his readers into a pragmatic relationship to English as a tool for professional advancement; he seeks to manipulate readers via English, not to manipulate English—what Achebe famously described as fashioning a new English—for the benefit of readers. If we leave aside the by now overfamiliar smattering of words like *yaar*, *bhai*, and *haan* that accent Bhagat's text to signal a Hinglish-speaking milieu, his novels are strikingly spare in their incorporation of any vernacular. Instead, they masquerade *as* vernacular.

Is Bhagat's English (a) "vernacular"? The answer to this question again hinges on what story we are telling about the relationship between the postcolonial and the Anglophone. Bhagat is read as a post-postcolonial writer of a global Indian English that has been divested of colonial baggage and has merged with the people it speaks. The Bhagat reader is similarly understood to have emerged through decisively global social forces: i.e., in the contexts of expanding access to English and India's increasing prominence in the world economy, as opposed to in the midst of debates about the politics of English as a colonial bequest and broader crises of Indian national imagining wrought by the experiences of 1947, 1971, and Emergency. But postcolonial language politics, broadly defined, continue to fundamentally shape the landscape in which Bhagat is writing and the critical context in which he is read—calling into question just what we mean by "global" in the first place.[125]

In *Vernacular English*, Akshya Saxena points out that scholars of postcolonial literature have for too long pitted English and the vernacular against each other, as if they have a strictly antonymic relation in which the vernacular is immediate and local, and English is distant and global. Contra conventional accounts, Saxena argues that English is a political and popular vernacular in India that touches those who can neither read nor speak it and who are not "comfortably bilingual," but for whom it has an embodied, sonic, and visual—if not linguistic or literary—life.[126] English is not strictly global, she insists; it is also familiar, ordinary, and exists for most Indians beyond "conditions of formal literacy."[127] Despite the rhetorical promise of a New India "after" English, English in India remains a vital tool of advancement and a powerful medium of middle-class aspiration.

Curiously, Saxena never once mentions Bhagat in her 2022 book, despite the fact that, at first blush, he is an almost too obvious purveyor of "vernacular English." Perhaps this is because Bhagat—with his constant, explicit repudiations of Anglophone elitism and literary culture—still seems lodged in the quagmire of the postcolonial language debate, while she seeks a way beyond its binarism. For Saxena, reading English "as a vernacular" is meant to "deprive it of its singularity."[128] But English is absolutely singular for Bhagat. He describes knowing English as one of the "most important skills to succeed in a global world" and attributes his own fame to the language: "Think about this: if Chetan Bhagat did not write in English, would he still be Chetan Bhagat—as famous?"[129]

By that same token, Bhagat also fundamentally rejects the key premise of the postcolonial language debate, which is that living between languages necessarily poses a kind of existential crisis. He effectively denudes English of its symbolic power while refashioning it as an expressly non-identitarian tool for the non-Anglophone Indian. To borrow Sadana's description of the young Indians she meets while teaching in India, Bhagat tells his readers that "English vocabulary is their right and provenance even as they are told they can't speak it."[130]

This important contradiction in Bhagat's attitude toward English (he upholds its value, while neutralizing its identitarian force) suggests again that the Anglophone does not signify the transcendence of the postcolonial; it instantiates a new orientation toward it. Put simply: English remains singular in India, but differently singular than it once was. In this light, Saxena's omission of Bhagat is a revealing tell about the distance between "vernacular English" and English that is "like" a vernacular. Vernacular English "lives in other Indian languages and media such as Hindi literature, bureaucratic documents, language legislation, Bollywood and international films, and public protests."[131] Rather than carry English into Bollywood film, Bhagat has been smuggling Bollywood plots and characterization into his English novels (e.g., his 2020 *One Arranged Murder* Indianizes the Agatha Christie novel with a Punjabi wedding-plot). His demotic English can then travel between vernacular Indian and Anglophone Indian spaces—as in the circuit from the English novel *Five Point Someone* to the Hindi film *Three Idiots*, or Nikhil Sachan's intertextual references to Bhagat in the 2017 Hindi-language campus novel *UP 65*. If what Saxena calls vernacular English is English that lives (sonically, textually, visually) in non-Anglophone Indian spaces, then Bhagat's English may not be "vernacular English" at all. It may, however, be a consequential component of its prehistory.

On Teaching Chetan Bhagat

I have been developing an argument that teaching Bhagat in US academe is an inherently risky endeavor given the assumptions about authenticity that subtend the reading of demotic non-Western Englishes. If the Bhagat novel encourages its target Indian readers to think they know English better than they do, then it might also encourage readers outside India to think we know New India better than we do—and on Bhagat's terms. We might be wary of teaching Bhagat, then, because of the kinds of arguments we have to make about the postcolonial in order to stage his legibility to our students. We might be wary because of the kinds of claims we have to make about the literary in order to justify his place on a syllabus. We might be wary because of Bhagat's politics of soft Hindutva in the age of Modi, and because of the burden of representation his novels bear as hyperaccessible works of Indian English literature. We might be wary because of the exaggerated operations of close, distant, critical, and uncritical reading we have to perform in order to stage our relationship to the object itself.

At the same time, I have been developing a counterargument: a case for teaching Bhagat, in the form of a series of questions we must ask if and when we do decide to introduce his texts into the English literature classroom in US academe. What is the value of Bhagat as a critical object, and how does that value change depending on what we desire from Bhagat as object? If we wanted to understand the "real" India, would we read Bhagat, when and why, and what would that indicate about our assumptions about the real? To whom or what does Bhagat give voice? To read New India, must we read like New Indians? What does New India sound like?

Teaching Bhagat, who is explicitly addressing Indian readers, is an opportunity to unschool students in the United States who have been habituated into the assumption that every text is addressed to them.[132] A chance to problematize the ideological construction of the "real" by deconstructing Bhagat's claims to represent it. An occasion to point out that the critical frame for the postcolonial has hitherto excluded the popular, and to insist, at the same time, that we remain critical of the supposedly reparative operations of the Anglophone. Teaching Bhagat might force us to make a clear distinction between English that is accessible to non-Anglophone Indians, on the one hand, and English that makes their lives accessible, on the other. It opens up an investigation of the premise of "English like Hindi" and the comparative project such a claim inaugurates between English and the vernacular.

Our students don't need to be taught how to read Bhagat. They need to be taught how *not* to read Bhagat: as if he is the translational medium of India's authentic voice, or as if his accessibility is compensatory for a reader's not knowing Hindi (or Tamil or Bengali or Malayalam). They need to be taught what not to read for; what readerly positions not to inhabit; what modes of criticism not to perform. The Bhagat text demands neither an uncritical response, nor a postcritical response. It demands a pedagogical response. It demands an accented reading attuned to the construction of the object as an artifact of the real. It demands grappling with the consequences of the leveling of the field between popular forms of global English and the vernaculars with which they vie in the New Indian and international literary spheres.

CHAPTER 4/RECESS 2

The Ambivalence of Homi Bhabha's Discourse

[My Institutional Position]

In 2020, J. Daniel Elam and I coedited a special issue of *Post45: Contemporaries* called "1990 at 30." Our aim was to think about what it means to be professing literature and reading Theory after the supposed end of both. In our cowritten introduction, we offered this rationale:

> By conjoining 1990 and 2020, we juxtapose two moments of world-historical reckoning: the optimism at the end of the Cold War and the pessimism at the beginning of a pandemic. We ... offer a critical time-warp, one that encompasses the speedy "time-space compression" of postmodernism and globalization theory, as well as the slow violence revealed by postcolonialism and critical race theory.
>
> Over the past thirty years, texts in capital-T Theory ... became global classics and transcended the conditions of their emergence. We ask what it means as academic readers—to borrow Ernest Renan's memorable phrasing—to "have many things in common, and also [to] have forgotten many things." At a moment when we should renew our commitment to collaborative humanistic inquiry, are these still texts to which we might append our collective name?[1]

Each contributor to the dossier wrote about a text published in 1990, by theorists Arjun Appadurai, Judith Butler, Patricia Hill Collins, Stuart Hall, David Harvey, bell hooks, Eve Kosofsky Sedgwick, and Robert J. C. Young. I wrote an entry on Homi Bhabha's "DissemiNation," first collected in his edited volume *Nation and Narration*.

When our special issue came out, it circulated in a small corner of academic Twitter, as these things do. One response, from a fully promoted scholar of postcolonial studies, caught my eye. "I mean seriously," she tweeted, "cannot get behind ['DissemiNation'] alongside the others. Just not at par!"[2] A short tweet-discussion of the value of Bhabha's work ensued, in which the senior scholar added this note: "Bhabha was always into seeing more than what was actually there or possible in the idea of discursive ruptures."

I thought about this exchange two years later when a doctoral student asked me if he could remove Bhabha from his Qualifying Exam list in Postcolonial Theory. The essays in Bhabha's *The Location of Culture* were too difficult to read, the student said; the writing was just too bad. And couldn't Bhabha's central theoretical concepts—like mimicry and hybridity—be accessed through work written after Bhabha instead?

I didn't let the student strike Bhabha from his list, but the request gave me pause. In 1990, a "commitment to theory" meant thinking the world anew and the empire writing back, often in patently challenging prose.[3] Could I ask my students to make the same commitment to Theory and the postcolonial now: in the 2020s, in pandemic times, in an era of anthropogenic climate crisis, in conditions of precarious employment and uncertain visa status? If senior postcolonialists were over Bhabha, did our students still need to read him?

[Recess]

My title owes something to the wit and wisdom of Homi K. Bhabha—in particular his essay "Of Mimicry and Man: The Ambivalence of Colonial Discourse"—but something more to the experience of working in US academe in the 2020s, in the context of the "permanent crisis"[4] of the humanities.

As in the preceding recess, my aim here is not to analyze Bhabha's work, which is a task many others have undertaken since his first major essays were published in the early 1980s. My aim is to think about what Bhabha and his accented voice have come to represent in studies of English and the postcolonial. I am paying attention to Bhabha's iconicity in service of my larger argument that one reason we continue to read theorists like Bhabha is for the status they have accrued and the identity they have secured within a field, as opposed to what they argued as such. This is what returns texts and writers to our syllabi and classrooms semester after semester: the uses to which they can be put in the consolidation or contestation of a particular field imaginary.

Like Gayatri Chakravorty Spivak and Edward Said, the other two members of "the Holy Trinity of colonial-discourse analysis,"[5] Bhabha came to prominence during the heyday of an academic star system that is now in decline. At the time of this writing, he is an endowed professor at Harvard University. Over the years, Bhabha has published relatively little (relative to his status, that is) and his star has somewhat receded (unlike Spivak, he does not often make international headlines or go viral). And yet, Bhabha continues to hold an outsized place in the collective imagination about late twentieth-century postcolonial theory and poststructuralism.

How, in the third decade of the twenty-first century, are we to understand the discourse on Bhabha's discourse—in particular, its inscrutability? Do our students still need to read Bhabha, or is it enough to have read *about* his work? Could not reading Bhabha—like not reading Chetan Bhagat—be construed as a form of accented reading? Was he such a bad writer, after all?

Between 1995 and 1998, the journal *Philosophy and Literature* ran a "Bad Writing Contest," in bad faith. Fredric Jameson won twice. The 1998 prize went to Judith Butler. Bhabha was the runner-up that year, singled out for a single sentence from "Of Mimicry and Man."[6] The concept—or accusation—of "bad writing" returns us to the discussions of both Spivak and Bhagat, in different ways. The putative "badness" of theorists Bhabha and Spivak is a charge that their writing is inaccessible beyond an elite coterie (therefore undemocratic), overly invested in the textual and discursive (therein politically regressive), and hyperperformative (thereby easily commodified). In contrast, the "badness" of pulp fictionist Bhagat has to do with his calculated accessibility and rejection of the literary. However, it too is fundamentally performative in ways that secure its marketability.

The charge of "bad writing" in each of these cases has less to do with the quality of the writing itself than with the contexts of its circulation, assumed address, and supposed politics: which is to say, its accent. "Bad writing" is enlisted in the "assignment and disciplining of identities," whether the identity of fictionist (Bhagat) or theorist-scholar (Bhabha and Spivak), even as it primarily registers "the receiver's situated knowledges and convictions."[7] Read as accent, "bad writing" signals both an excess and a lack.

The "Bad Writing Contest" followed the theory-wars of the 1980s and coincided with the infamous 1996 Sokal Affair.[8] From the present vantage, it seems quite clear what the contest was all about and whose anxieties it exploited (recall Martin Jay's critique of Spivak). The contest "clearly targeted a certain kind of politics, a certain kind of theory, and a certain kind of guru-status," Toril Moi reflects.[9] Nevertheless, it raised lasting questions about clarity as an inconsistently heralded virtue in academic argument, the politics of symbolic, poetic, and metaphorical writing, and the efficacy of "difficult" writing as a mode of disrupting dominant ideologies.

What kinds of words do what kind of work in the world? What is the relationship between Bhagat's accessibility and his conservatism, on the one hand, and the relationship between Bhabha's supposed inscrutability and his radicality, on the other? In Spivak's words, "If you have plain prose as your slogan, then you can give yourself an alibi that you are really like a good fellow on the ground and these people are elitist."[10] By that same token, if jargon is your armor, then you can give yourself an alibi that theoretical complexity is a higher value than accessibility to a broad readership. Thinking in the long shadow of the Bad Writing Contest, Moi cautions against conflating accessibility with clarity; the latter is not just "a synonym for unthinking naivety, a sign of servitude to dominant ideology."[11] By that same token, if clarity is not necessarily conservative, complexity is not necessarily radical: "The meaning of an utterance depends on who says what to whom under what circumstances."[12]

Speaking to W. J. T. Mitchell in 1995, Bhabha described the so-called difficulty of his writing as an honest reflection of his thought process: "the more difficult bits of my work are in many cases the places where I am trying to think hardest, and in a futuristic kind of way. . . . Generally I find that the passages pointed out to me as difficult are places where I am trying to fight a battle with myself."[13] Again, this is a way to understand the event of accent: The meaning of an utterance depends on who says what to whom in what way under what circumstances and why—and who, ultimately, is primed to listen.

For some years now, Bhabha has been caught in the crosshairs of resistance to performativity and the postcolonial, on the one hand, and exhaustion with Theory and discourse analysis, on the other. He is the kind of 1990s theorist we are supposed to have gotten over by now (and not just because of our collective turn away from specialized argot and embrace of public address, discussed in the recess on Said). It's all his unruly citations (Fanon and Freud, Lyotard and Lévi-Strauss, Bakhtin and Goethe and Althusser and Foucault and Said and Kristeva...!). All that hopeful deconstruction. The promise of hybridity. The possibility of subversion. As if, for example, the "problem of knowledge"[14] that was the problem of conceiving of a nation-people could be *solved*. As if we could read or write our way out of it.

In "DissemiNation," to stay with that example, Bhabha argues that the nation is an unstable, ambivalent fiction, pedagogically consolidated and subject to performative contestation. The nation is characterized by a split between official temporality and the time of the writing-people, between hegemony and uncertainty. It is "a system of cultural signification" that must be understood "*as it is written*," "through its narrative address," as "a form of social and textual affiliation," and as "a narrative strategy."[15] Importantly, the national narrative is not singular, and key to Bhabha's account is that the nation itself "opens up the possibility of other narratives of the people and their difference."[16]

Whereas Benedict Anderson's account in his 1983 *Imagined Communities* hinges on an understanding of the national "meanwhile" that "gives the imagined world of the nation a sociological solidity," Bhabha's nation consists of unstable and competing temporalities including the colonial, postcolonial, native, and modern. Bhabha's nation-people do not emerge as a solidity out of homogenous empty time, but rather out of subaltern temporalities "in a language of incommensurable doubleness that arises from the ambivalent splitting of the pedagogical and the performative."[17] The nation is riven by the split between official discourse and that which resists it. Bhabha's performative time interrupts and subverts the pedagogy of the nation. Thus, he claims that "the margins of the nation displace the center; the peoples of the periphery return to rewrite the history and fiction of the metropolis.... The bastion of Englishness crumbles at the sight of immigrants and factory workers."[18] Or, even more triumphantly, "The people will no longer be contained in that national discourse of the teleology of progress."[19]

Bhabha's writing on the nation exemplifies the optimism that Elam and I, introducing "1990 at 30," dated to the end of the Cold War. He is a theorist of agency, not oppression; survival, not submission; and creativity, not the endless, exhausting, redundant loop. Bhabha argues that natives, not anthropologists, are the key translators of culture; that the colonized subject can menace the colonial through subversive mimicry; and that migrants act powerfully on the cultures into which they arrive, as opposed to being squashed into assimilation. In a 2017 dossier on the legacy of *Location of Culture*, Robert J. C. Young describes Bhabha's achievement as having created "a new language, a new articulation, and understanding of minority positions," specifically their capacity for resistance and agency.[20] Kavita Daiya describes Bhabha as a "strategic, activist, aspirational" humanist, bent on survival.[21]

This is how Bhabha earned the status he now enjoys. By that same token, and to return to the story that opens this recess, Bhabha's work has also frequently been criticized on the same grounds of his (unrealistic, naïve) optimism. Quote tweet: "Bhabha was always into seeing more than what was actually there or possible in the idea of discursive ruptures."

I recall teaching "DissemiNation" in Tucson, Arizona, in fall 2017, a year after the election of Donald Trump as US president, a month after the white supremacist "Unite the Right" rally in Charlottesville, Virginia, and two weeks after the pardon of Arizona's own convicted racial profiler and anti-immigrant sheriff, Joe Arpaio. Would the bastion of American exceptionalism, white supremacy, and xenophobia really crumble at the sight of performative disruption? To put it mildly, my students were not convinced.

Bhabha's politics of performativity was dissatisfying to many readers upon *Nation and Narration*'s first publication, as well. Arjun Appadurai, writing in 1993, included the volume in a list of Western academic works characterized by a "disturbing tendency ... to divorce the study of discourse forms from the study of other institutional forms."[22] Michael Sprinker lamented *Nation and Narration*'s almost total omission of Marxist debates on nationalism. In 2001, Neil Larsen read this omission as revealing a desire to cleanse "cultural nationalism of its *historical* [and] *class* determination[s]."[23]

All of this is why "DissemiNation" does not appear in the bibliographies of Lauren Berlant's *The Queen of America Goes to Washington City*, Anderson's *The Spectre of Comparisons*, Pheng Cheah's *Spectral Nationality*, or Manisha Basu's *The Rhetoric of Hindu India*, to name just a few well-known works on nationalism and literature published in the intervening years.[24] It's the omission of Marxist debates. It's Bhabha's "metropolitan" fetishization of textual discursivity.[25] It's the ambivalent politics of performativity that for all its sophistication reads as terribly naïve from the vantage of the future world it by definition could not see.

Some said it was too idealistic a politics. And others said it was not a politics at all.[26]

Let's say the quiet part out loud. One reason it has become difficult to teach work like Bhabha's, specifically, and post-structuralist theory on the subversive potential of discursive rupture, generally, is that it failed to change the world.

The stronger critique of Theory as having not lived up to its promise goes something like this: Two decades after the official-national lies that spawned the Iraq War and the rise of "truthiness," as deep fake videos circulate on TikTok, and Artificial Intelligence and ChatGPT spark new paranoia about the fate of the humanities, it seems that the primary effect of 1980s and 1990s Theory in the United States was to violently destabilize norms and bolster antielitist dismissals of science and knowledge. Fox News, Trump's lies, the panic over Critical Race Theory and DEI, Covid-denialism, the discrediting of climate science, the dramatic curtailment of reproductive rights, attacks on Black, Trans, Indigenous, and Dalit lives: all of these are the unintended spawn of humanistic challenges to scientific rationality, the idea of objectivity, structural racism, dominant conceptions of sexual difference, and teleological notions of progress and Truth.[27]

Our good, robust, theoretical readings didn't transform the world for the better. In fact, this line of critique charges, willful misreadings and perversions of our work have quite dramatically achieved the opposite. Theory was a massive own goal. Why, and how? Jeffrey J. Kripal speculates that it's because contemporary humanistic inquiry now has only one criterion for truth: "the truth must be depressing." He continues: "Why on earth should anyone support a project that basically argues that there is no truth; that all our claims to truth are nothing more than power grabs; that truth is really power (and always somehow bad power); and that the goal of the intellectual life is a kind of permanent and total depression?"[28]

What Kripal describes at first sounds like a right-wing caricature of the humanities. Poststructuralists didn't argue that there is no truth, we might respond, but that truth is plural. Situated knowledges are *knowledges*, after all, not rejections of science, data, facts, or the real.

But even caricature serves a heuristic purpose. When we read Bhabha today, it is striking how deeply he believes in the power of subaltern agency, performative disruptions of the pedagogical, and the subversive potential of repetition with a difference, in good Derridean fashion. How did we get from this kind of work, foundational as it has been, to Kripal's diagnosis of our penchant for the depressing? Might it be fair to say that we are depressed now, in the 2020s, not because of what theoretical work like Bhabha's failed to achieve, but because the rest of us have forgotten how to believe in and wield the power of the word?

In spring 2023, when I was finishing the first draft of this book, you couldn't pick up an academic or para-academic journal without encountering a take on John Guillory's 2022 *Professing Criticism*. "Departments on the Defensive" was the title of Evan Kindley's piece. "Has academia ruined literary criticism?" Merve Emre asked.[29] Sarah Brouillette wrote of reading "after the university."[30] "What is literary criticism for?"[31] "Is this the end of literary studies?" asked Nicholas Dames. The reviewers, largely English professors, generally concurred with Guillory's argument that the academic discipline of literary criticism—wrested from the hands of journalists in the late nineteenth century and institutionalized over the course of a century—has now cannibalized itself so thoroughly that the most widely read criticism is being produced outside of the university and circulated in public and semipublic fora (often staffed by graduate students, contingent faculty, and former academics). The richest conversation in the profession is happening outside of the profession, in other words. As Dames observes, "It would be hard for a member of an English department not to feel, looking back on the past few decades, like Tony Soprano telling his therapist, 'I'm getting the feeling that I came in at the end.' "[32]

"The best is over." That's what Soprano goes on to say, in words that capture the widely shared experience of professional decline that marks what it has meant to be an academic, a humanist, and an English professor in the 2020s. Tellingly, this wave of eulogies for literary studies echoes a routinized conversation within postcolonial studies about its end, and ends.

Postcolonialists have been asked many times—and within the field, we have asked ourselves—if the postcolonial is over.[33] With each query the postcolonial has been reborn: in diaspora discourse, in the rubric of the transnational, in the formations of Commonwealth and Third World literature, in the transdisciplinary study of the global, in the Anglophone, and even in the Anthropocene discourse. Postcolonial studies keeps being renominated because the field's contemporaneity must perpetually be restated. That's what declaring "the end" opens up, after all: an occasion to begin again.

Something similar is happening in literary studies as we contemplate what will remain after "the end of English."[34] For while we face a structural crisis brought about by the casualization of academic labor, along with an accelerated devaluation of the humanities in a declining United States, the current conjuncture also reveals the persistence of old, foundational anxieties regarding the relevance of literature to the fate of the world and the power of words to constitute that world, our selves, and our others. Does literature matter, and how, and why? Can literature transform the world, or does it merely represent it? If literature doesn't matter, how can literary criticism or Theory?

We in US academe are living—along with everyone else who is paying attention—in the perpetual time of what Sara Marcus calls "political disappointment," characterized by "a longing for fundamental change that outlasts a historical moment when it might have been fulfilled."[35] And so, in the post-Theory era, those age-old questions about literature have taken on new force. Would better arguments about literature have produced better arguments about the world? Would another literary studies have made another world possible?

Marcus's work invites us to approach such questions with a focus on the literary studies we wanted, as opposed to the literary studies we've had. For Marcus, the relationship between disappointment and failure is complex. Disappointment is about confronting obstacles, not ignoring them; disappointment must be understood "not merely as a reaction to failure but as a form of survival." Attending to our collective disappointment with the failures of literary criticism and Theory might therefore be a way to recenter our desires, hopes, striving, and yearning. What we hoped Theory would do—not what it didn't. What we hoped the postcolonial would be—not what it wasn't. Beginning with failure can be generative, Marcus argues. Disappointment keeps desire alive, and "to keep longing for a lost future is evidence of survival."[36]

Whether we ultimately pursue or give up the lost future of the academic humanities will depend on how we understand the value of knowledge production in our fields—or, to put a finer point on it, whether we actually believe our fields have value. Moreover, do we believe work in the humanities is productive of insights on which to build vertically, or readings, interpretations, and narratives that exist alongside one another horizontally? I use the word "vertically" advisedly, and not as a synonym for progressively or teleologically. What I mean by "vertical" is a consistent and widely shared understanding of which texts and critical paradigms underlie which others and serve as their foundation. Contemporary mathematicians don't read Euclid's geometry or Isaac Newton's calculus unless they're working on a history of mathematical discourse. They are working *after* Euclid and *after* Newton—building on their work, certainly, but without giving them a backward glance (never mind a citation).

The temporal designation of "after" doesn't signify in the same way in the humanities. There are numerous examples of contemporary scholars who are generally unconcerned with their interlocutors today, choosing instead to route their discussions—even of present-day politics—through engagement with interlocutors like Kant and Derrida. In the humanities, certain theoretical texts have accrued status as primary works, akin to the status of primary literary texts, for each scholar to interpret for themselves as part of their training and the legitimation of their own scholarly projects.

The question is: At what point should secondary discourse take precedence over these supposedly primary theoretical texts, in order for new ideas, critical paradigms, and concepts to come to the fore? Is our lack of what I'm provisionally calling "verticality" responsible for some administrators' and students' dismissive responses to the humanities in US academe—like this note from a Harvard undergraduate, from a widely circulated 2023 essay on "the end of the English major"? "I think the problem for the humanities is you can feel like you're not really going anywhere, and that's very scary.... You write one essay better than the other from one semester to the next. That's not the same as, you know, being able to solve this economics problem, or code this thing, or do policy analysis."[37] Horizontal movement between texts and classes, semesters and essays, as opposed to vertical progress. In short, the student quoted is suggesting that in the humanities and in English, we never get off the ground.

Does work like Bhabha's get us off the ground? This is a question at the heart of the canonical episteme. For any field to continue to exist, its practitioners must have primary texts, both literature and Theory, that they are committed to teaching, no matter when they were written. At the same time, some secondary works must take primacy over the texts, arguments, and readings with respect to which they were originally developed. Otherwise, the field doesn't build.

In college and graduate school, my classmates and I read Lacan through Bhabha, Deleuze through Spivak, Hegel through Butler, and Nietzsche through Foucault—and we weren't always asked to go back to the primary texts. Is something similar going to happen with theorists like Bhabha, Spivak, Butler, and Foucault: that they will, going forward, primarily be read through the secondary discourse on their works?[38] When we encounter a work of literature or theory largely through secondary critical discourse, we are being asked to engage not just with explanations or exegesis of the work, but also with a scene of prior discursive struggle. Which scenes of struggle do we and our students need to rehearse and reenact for ourselves? Is Bhabha's work secondary or primary—or something in between?

In the end, there are two reasons I didn't allow my student to strike Bhabha from his Postcolonial Theory exam list. The first is Bhabha's optimism, which was in fact deeply ambivalent and qualified: in his own words, "less than the investment of hope in total liberation, and considerably more than some beaten down, dulled existence."[39] Bhabha was working to conceptualize forms of creative agency by theorizing creativity itself—including textual production—as agential. Whatever our critiques of his readings, archive, method, and conclusions, this is a project worth recalling in the era of literary criticism's supposed demise.

(Not to mention how satisfying it would be to see postcolonial studies—one of the fields "regularly understood *as* the crisis in need of management by disciplinary authority"[40] during the culture and canon wars—come to the rescue of a depleted, exhausted, and delegitimized literary studies in US academe! To literally drag us up off the depressed ground.)

Second, and to return from a different angle to the question of "bad writing," is the fact of how Bhabha writes. Another charge leveled against Bhabha is that his key concepts like hybridity and mimicry are too easily decontextualized and transported beyond the historical, linguistic, and literary situations of their initial theorization. Their mutability and metaphoricity are part of their "badness." But that is also their strength as tools with which to think.

Bhabha's work is open, available for uptake, and generatively susceptible to dissemination. It is a form of what Andrew H. Miller describes as "implicative criticism," the success of which depends upon "the extent that it enfolds its reader."[41] Said, to whom we will turn in the final recess, put it like this: "Writers like Bhabha are looking for the occasion to work out ideas. There's something unfinished about it."[42]

So maybe we don't read Bhabha to get the job done or the world fixed or the work finished. But maybe we keep reading Bhabha anyway, as part of our ambivalent search for hope "in a minor key."[43]

We read Bhabha as a small part of a larger effort to keep going.

CHAPTER 5

Fictions of Divergence

Or, Amit Chaudhuri Doesn't Write the Postcolonial

[My Institutional Position]

It was 2017, and I was in India, about to give my first-ever invited lecture as an assistant professor. It was a version of my job talk on the respectively "postcolonial" and "global" iconicity of Salman Rushdie and Chetan Bhagat, which inspired the discussion in chapter 3. This time, however, my audience would be Indian students, not American potential colleagues, and they would have all read Bhagat. I was nervous and excited to speak to an audience in the know.

The talk was a success. I got the sense that the students didn't often attend academic lectures on the likes of Bhagat. I was chuffed that I, an Indian American, had managed to give a well-received presentation to Young Indian college students about the literature of New India. Their literature, in other words.

But a conversation that transpired immediately afterward gave me pause.

After offering kudos on the lecture, the India-based professor who had invited me to speak urged me to take on other, more worthy research topics than the overanalyzed Rushdie and the overpopular Bhagat. Somewhat deflated, I nodded knowingly. I could guess the kinds of writers he had in mind: feminist poets, Dalit fictionists, vernacular experimentalists—lesser-known writers and writers with better politics.

Then, perhaps with these more salutary objects in mind, my host mentioned that he had been asked some time ago to peer-review an article about the work of the understudied writer Amit Chaudhuri. It was a curious article, he said; he advised against publication. Its author tried to offer an allegorical reading of Chaudhuri's patently nonallegorical work and then took issue with Chaudhuri's representation of domestic servants. It was so curious, this article, that he had sent it to Chaudhuri himself.

"Amit thought that perhaps *you* wrote it," my host said to me. Had I?

The offending article was indeed mine, and I could have admitted it. It was part of a chapter that never eventuated in my dissertation, a chapter in which I'd overused terms like "focalize" and "diegesis" in a bid for legitimacy as a *real literature scholar*. I should have laughed it off as juvenilia and moved on. Instead, I squirrely replied, "I've never published an article about Amit Chaudhuri"—which, thanks to the peer-review process, was technically true.

I had gotten over that rejection. Yet now I was faced with the mortifying fact that the author himself—Amit Chaudhuri himself!—had seen my amateurish attempt at critique. I knew immediately how Chaudhuri, who doesn't really know me, might nevertheless have recognized the essay as mine. There was a give-away sentence about Chaudhuri's life being "a resource for his fiction." I had used that exact phrase in an audience Q&A after a 2015 book reading of Chaudhuri's in Chicago, and it had piqued his interest.

The exchange felt surreal, like my host and I were acting out a scene from one of Chaudhuri's autofictional novellas. I was the Indian American outsider who had gone back to India to perform her relationship to the country—not unlike Bharati Mukherjee, in pursuit of the call center agent. My host was the Indian insider calling into question the diasporic critic's purchase on the country's literature, politics, and voice. It was a classic postcolonial encounter, ironically centered on the work of a writer, Chaudhuri, known for having disavowed the postcolonial.

My host's amused dismissal of the critique of Chaudhuri's representation of domestic servants was ironic, too. In fact, that line of critique had emerged from my consciousness of our shared class position and my ambivalence about the project of representing New India. In other words, it wasn't really a critique of Chaudhuri at all, but rather of my own desires to read, write about, and teach his work. It stemmed from overidentification, not an attempt at moral superiority.

Finally, the shift in discussion from Bhagat to Chaudhuri was presented as a move from "bad" to "good" literary objects. My host assumed I was stuck on the former at the expense of the latter. And yet, I could barely stand to read the former and loved the latter. I recognized in Chaudhuri's literary project many of my own preoccupations—in particular, regarding diasporic return journeys and the pursuit of the real—and I had planned to teach at least one of his books that fall.

Now, I wasn't so sure that I should. If my arguments about Chaudhuri had failed on paper, could they succeed in the classroom? Was Chaudhuri in fact a better object than Bhagat? How would he write this story about my return to the New India—and was it one that my American students might learn to read?

[Syllabus]

Literatures of Return
English 396A | University of Arizona
Spring 2018

"Return" is one of the oldest narratives in the study of immigration and diaspora. For some immigrants, the pull of home is only matched by the impossibility of going back. For others, emigration away from home and immigration into a new country must eventually be consummated with a return journey. Return can be chosen or coerced. Return can be a search for roots, or a quest for routes. In all instances, return can be narrated. We might even say that return itself is a narrative form.

This seminar will immerse students in contemporary literatures of return. Over the course of the semester, we will read narratives of reverse migration, second-generation return, temporary return, postconflict return, economic and labor migration, ancestral pilgrimage, and deportation. We will analyze how the temporality of return animates the literary apprehension of the present. And we will compare narratives of return across genres, as we engage in analysis of novels, memoirs, poetry, short stories, interviews, essays, and films. Course texts may include works by Agha Shahid Ali, Amit Chaudhuri, James Clifford, Teju Cole, Edwidge Danticat,

Mohsin Hamid, Saidiya Hartman, Jhumpa Lahiri, Valeria Luiselli, Hisham Matar, Edward Said, Rebecca Solnit, and Yi-Fu Tuan. Animated participation in class discussion is expected as well as commitment to close reading and learning the methods of literary research.

COURSE SCHEDULE

Th, Jan 11:   Introductions

Seamus Murphy, "Home Is Another Place" (2013, film)

UNIT 1: What is Diaspora? What is Return?

Tu, Jan 16:   James Clifford, "Diasporas" (1994)

James Clifford, "Varieties of Indigenous Experience," from *Returns: Becoming Indigenous in the Twenty-First Century* (2013)

Th, Jan 18:   Ngũgĩ wa Thiong'o, "The Return" (1961)

Hisham Matar, "The Return" (2013)

UNIT 2: The Black Atlantic

Tu, Jan 23:   Saidiya Hartman, *Lose Your Mother: A Journey Along the Atlantic Slave Route*, Prologue and Chapters 1–2

Th, Jan 25:   Saidiya Hartman, *Lose Your Mother*, Chapters 3–6

Paul Gilroy, from *The Black Atlantic: Modernity and Double Consciousness*

Tu, Jan 30:   Saidiya Hartman, *Lose Your Mother*, Chapters 7–10

Th, Feb 1:   Saidiya Hartman, *Lose Your Mother*, Chapters 11–12

Alondra Nelson, "The Factness of Diaspora" and "Memoirs of Return: Saidiya Hartman, Eva Hoffman, and Daniel Mendelsohn in Conversation with Nancy K. Miller," from *Rites of Return: Diaspora Poetics and the Politics of Memory*

UNIT 3: India Calling

Tu, Feb 6:	Amit Chaudhuri, *A New World*, pgs. 1–64
	Anand Giridharadas, from *India Calling: An Intimate Portrait of a Nation's Remaking* (2011)
Th, Feb 8:	Amit Chaudhuri, *A New World*, pgs. 65–131
Tu, Feb 13:	Amit Chaudhuri, *A New World*, pgs. 132–200
	Amit Chaudhuri, "My New Perspective on Calcutta" (2013)
Th, Feb 15:	Suketu Mehta, "Personal Geography," from *Maximum City: Bombay Lost and Found* (2004)

UNIT 4: Imaging Return

Tu, Feb 20:	Teju Cole, *Every Day Is for the Thief*, Chapters 1–11
Th, Feb 22:	Teju Cole, *Every Day Is for the Thief*, Chapters 12–18
Tu, Feb 27:	Teju Cole, *Every Day Is for the Thief*, Chapters 19–27
Th, Mar 1:	On Nicholas Nixon's "The Brown Sisters": Susan Minot, "Forty Portraits in Forty Years," *New York Times* (2014); "Looking at Nicholas Nixon's 43rd Portrait of the Brown Sisters," *The New Yorker* (2017)
	"Return to Aleppo: The Story of My Home During the War," *The Museum of Lost Objects*, podcast episode, 24 minutes (BBC Radio 4, June 10, 2017)

UNIT 5: Travel Literature vs. Literature of Return

Tu, Mar 13:	Rebecca Solnit, from *A Book of Migrations* (1997)
	Graham Huggan, from *Extreme Pursuits: Travel Writing in an Age of Globalization* (2012)
Th, Mar 15:	Stuart Dybek, "Qué Quieres" (2003)
	Yi-Fu Tuan, from *Coming Home to China* (2007)

UNIT 6: The Temporality of the Family

Tu, Mar 20: Natasha Trethewey, "Theories of Time and Space" (2006)

Interviews with Edwidge Danticat: "An Immigrant Artist at Work," *Small Axe* (2011); "Dyasporic Appetites and Longings," *Callaloo* (2007)

Th, Mar 22: Edwidge Danticat, *Brother, I'm Dying*, pgs. 3–61

Tu, Mar 27: Edwidge Danticat, *Brother, I'm Dying*, pgs. 62–123

Th, Mar 29: Edwidge Danticat, *Brother, I'm Dying*, pgs. 127–192

Tu, Apr 3: Edwidge Danticat, *Brother, I'm Dying*, pgs. 193–269

UNIT 7: The World is Not Enough

Th, Apr 5: Mohsin Hamid, *The Reluctant Fundamentalist*, Chapters 1–5

Tu, Apr 10: Mohsin Hamid, *The Reluctant Fundamentalist*, Chapters 6–9

Leerom Medovoi, " 'Terminal Crisis?' From the Worlding of American Literature to World-System Literature" (2011)

Th, Apr 12: Mohsin Hamid, *The Reluctant Fundamentalist*, Chapters 10–12

Rebecca Walkowitz, "This is Not Your Language," from *Born Translated: The Contemporary Novel in an Age of World Literature* (2015)

UNIT 8: Deportation

Tu, Apr 17: Deborah Boehm, from *Returned: Going and Coming in an Age of Deportation* (2016)

Sarah Stillman, "When Deportation Is a Death Sentence," *New Yorker* (2018)

Th, Apr 19:   Valeria Luiselli, *Tell Me How It Ends*, Introduction, Chapters 1–2

Tu, Apr 24:   Valeria Luiselli, *Tell Me How It Ends*, Chapters 3–4, Coda

UNIT 9: The Poetics of Return

Tu, May 1:   Sujata Bhatt, "Search for My Tongue" (1988)

Agha Shahid Ali, "Above the Cities" and "New Delhi Airport" in "From Amherst to Kashmir" (2001)

Amitava Kumar, "Against Nostalgia" (2002)

[Accented Reading]

> I'm not *interested* in writing about India.
> —AMIT CHAUDHURI

Amit Chaudhuri was born in Calcutta in 1962. He grew up in Bombay, where he "thought constantly" of the city of his birth. In the early 1980s, he left India for England to study literature. While completing his dissertation on D. H. Lawrence at Oxford, Chaudhuri experienced "random and involuntary yearning[s] . . . a desire, like a muted undercurrent, to go to [Calcutta's] Park Street."[1] He satisfied these yearnings in the writing of three novellas set, to greater and lesser degrees, in Calcutta: *A Strange and Sublime Address* (1991), *Afternoon Raag* (1993), and *Freedom Song* (1998). His next three novels, *A New World* (2000), *The Immortals* (2009), and *Odysseus Abroad* (2015) were set in Calcutta (now Kolkata), Bombay (now Mumbai), and Oxford, respectively.

In the past four decades, Chaudhuri has also written and edited numerous works of literary criticism, journalism, short fiction, and poetry, including the story collection *Real Time* (2002) and the critical essays *The Origins of Dislike* (2018). His novellas *Friend of My Youth* (2017) and *Sojourn* (2022) may be read as autofiction. *Finding the Raga: An Improvisation on Indian Music* (2021) was billed by publisher New York Review Books as combining "memoir, practical and cultural criticism, and philosophical reflection."[2]

All books keep time with their authors, but Chaudhuri's have been particularly invested in tracking his movements, both affective and spatial, with respect to the city and country of his birth. *Sublime Address* follows the school-age protagonist, Sandeep, who lives in Bombay but is visiting his cousins in Calcutta; this is a journey Chaudhuri took many times throughout his childhood. In *Afternoon Raag*, the unnamed narrator recounts his returns to both Bombay and Calcutta, from Oxford in the first instance (where he, like Chaudhuri, studies Lawrence), and from Bombay and Oxford, in the second. In *A New World*, protagonist Jayojit contemplates moving back to India, which Chaudhuri himself had just done in 1999, because he, Chaudhuri, "didn't want to discover one day that [he] was old, not far from death, and still living in England . . . it didn't seem like the right ending for the story [his] imagination had constructed of [his] life."[3]

As has often been observed, Chaudhuri's novels "form a loosely knit supertext [that] enacts a curve of representational 'development,'"[4] from the child's perspective in *Sublime Address*, to the college student's in *Afternoon Raag*, to the middle-aged Jayojit's in *A New World*, to that of the character of "Amit Chaudhuri" himself in *Friend of My Youth*. Taken together, the novellas and novels trace Chaudhuri's own itineraries, and they invite inquiry into the nature of the autobiographical as a resource for the development of the fictional world.

This—the idea of the writer's life as a resource for his fiction—is the language I used in conversation with Chaudhuri after that 2015 book reading. I was trying to avoid the standard, probing question about biography and identity that authors hate so much: "Is this book about *you*?" I'd read every one of Chaudhuri's books and I knew not to ask the question like that. Chaudhuri is a postcolonial writer who has always said that he doesn't write about the postcolonial, an Indian writer who isn't "interested" in writing about India, and an autofictionist who insists that he is not writing about himself. Which is what I love about him! His intentional divergence from market-inflected trends, expected subject matter, and legible forms sheds light on the larger structures of repudiation, disavowal, and disidentification that I am tracking throughout this book.

Moreover, Chaudhuri has managed to produce writing that is at once intimate and distant, confessional and analytical. He seems to have figured out how, as Vikram Chandra once exhorted his fellow writers, to "give up nothing, and swallow everything."[5] Every moment and phase of his life. Every relation and friend of his youth and adulthood. East and West. India and the United Kingdom. Poetics and politics. Fiction and nonfiction. Poetry and prose. Every literary genre (and he's a musician, too). Chaudhuri is famous, but not too famous. Literary, but accessible. Modernist, but also mainstream. He was there alongside writers like Salman Rushdie, Arundhati Roy, and Amitav Ghosh in the infamous 1997 *New Yorker* "family photo" of Indian English writers.[6] Even then, he managed to stand apart.

Chaudhuri prizes his apartness and has written numerous essays about his self-sustained marginality from the Indian English literary field. In his much-cited editorial introduction to *The Vintage/Picador Book of Modern Indian Literature*, Chaudhuri argues that a myopic interpretive aesthetic has been applied to the Indian English novel because of the shadow cast by the "gigantic edifice" of Rushdie's *Midnight's Children*.[7] He sets his own work against the magical realism of Rushdie and Chandra, the naturalism of writers like Vikram Seth and Rohinton Mistry, and the historicism of Ghosh. He aims for beauty, he says, while others pursue history. He chooses the private, while others set eyes on the nation. He observes the mundane, not dramatic events. He writes short novellas, not epic novels (he calls the novel "a genre that's squatted on the writer's life for two decades").[8] He opts for innovation, not Indianness.

In all of these ways, Chaudhuri represents himself as the bearer of an alternative imaginary to that of the iconic Indian postcolonial writers. He points to the "alternate" strands of literary modernism that inform his own texts.[9] His stated interlocutors and influences are both *pre*-postcolonial (he is a self-described modernist who writes in the tradition of Bengali Renaissance humanism) and *post*-postcolonial. Francesca Orsini credits Chaudhuri with having produced the necessary "counter-manifesto" to the postcolonial; in his treatment, Indian vernacular literatures emerge as "modernity's offspring."[10] Chaudhuri's recent collaborations around the topic of "literary activism"—which include an edited volume, a book series, a series of "presentations and interventions," a website, a manifesto, and an online magazine—continue this work of countering hegemonic postcolonialism by emphasizing translation and by problematizing academic literary studies' relationships to the market, publishing industry, culture of literary prizes and festivals, and Anglophone canon.[11]

Here's the rub: In repeatedly situating himself as apart from or at an angle to Indian English postcolonial writing, Chaudhuri has been as responsible as any other writer or critic for producing the dominant conception of it. It's not only that Chaudhuri's work in fact actually contributes to the dominant project of postcolonial thought, which is, as Sanjay Krishnan puts it, "whether it is possible for formerly colonized or underdeveloped peoples to articulate a creative, that is, textured, response to the institutions of modernity."[12] It is also that field imaginaries are sustained by resistance from objects that have their own "ungraspable difference," and Chaudhuri's disidentification from Indian English literature has generated the externality that defines the field.[13] His investment in his pre- and post-postcolonial critical distinction relies upon his rhetorically fixing a hypostatized postcolonial center from which to diverge. And this move powerfully implicates his critics.

One of the primary ways that we license our literary scholarship is by identifying objects that have been overlooked, undervalued, or misread. The first place we look for such works is on the boundaries of an established field. Chaudhuri's claim to originality depends upon his consistent renewal (as a critic) of the dominant imaginary against which he writes (as a literary fictionist), which means he has always already overdetermined the arguments other critics can make about his texts. Writing at the outskirts of a field he has always kept in sight, Chaudhuri-as-object comes to us ready-made, "prêt à lire,"[14] and to a large extent already read.

When the Writer Is His Own Critic

In over a dozen books written since 1991, Chaudhuri has trained his attention on three primary subjects: Calcutta, literature, and writing the "encounter with life."[15] Chaudhuri is meta: he writes about his writing and he writes about his reading and he writes about those who write about his writing. He does this because he holds that the writer's main task is "to make a case for their writing . . . to argue for how it's to be read [. . . and] to fashion the terms by which they are read."[16] Even as he was writing *Friend of My Youth*, he was writing about writing it in essays for public venues, becoming in the process an autotheorist of his own autofiction. In all his work, Chaudhuri is self-reflexive about how he (as a fictionist) has used his lived life (as a real person) to generate material for his writing (as a critic). He is equally self-reflexive about how he (as a critic) has used his writing (as a fictionist) to generate his own public persona (as a real person), as well as about how he (as a real person) has reflected (as a critic) on the intersection of his lived and imagined lives in such a way as to confound the easy historicization or categorization of his writing (as a fictionist).

I am characterizing Chaudhuri and his project, but I am also describing the space into which the poor Chaudhuri critic must write: a space filled with Chaudhuri's own self-descriptions, critical preoccupations, and directives; a space in which naïve readings have always already been anticipated and foreclosed. Within this space, the critic must contend with a writer who knows exactly how he wishes to be read and in relation to whom. In an essay on *A Strange and Sublime Address*, Chaudhuri cites Jean-Paul Sartre, Albert Camus, T. S. Eliot, D. H. Lawrence, Goethe, Nietzsche, W. G. Sebald, J. M. Coetzee, Roberto Bolaño, Günter Grass, Gabriel García Márquez, Milan Kundera, Marcel Proust, and Franz Kafka, among others, as his interlocutors.[17] He describes himself as a writer who, like Karl Ove Knausgård (this is Chaudhuri's comparison), finds "deeply boring what others [find] fundamentally interesting (story) and deeply interesting what others [find] fundamentally boring (the everyday and its poetics)."[18] And that's just some of the Western writers. Chaudhuri has also written accounts of his work in relation to that of Rabindranath Tagore, V. S. Naipaul, Buddadeb Bose, Arvind Krishna Mehrotra, and Arun Kolatkar.

This is not your typical reception management or image manipulation, nor is it the form of public relations work that publishers have come to expect of contemporary authors. If, following Richard Jean So's schema, there are four primary stages of literary production—production, reception, recognition, and consecration—it is as if Chaudhuri is trying to have a say in, if not control of, all stages of this cycle as pertains to his work.[19] Or, to use John Guillory's terms, it is as if Chaudhuri, in producing so much critical reflection on his own fiction, is writing the "documents" that will retrospectively "monumentalize" his work. He produces the literary object in the real-time present, and then goes about assessing "the calling of the object to a future present, when the object in question will fully manifest its dual nature as monument and document"—as a record and response.[20] He is called to write and, at the same time, called to assess the call of his own writing. He seeks to amplify the demand his writing will make on future readers by responding to it in advance. Chaudhuri's ambition seems to be "to deliver his text as an object whose interpretation—by virtue of the exactness of its situation in the world—*has already commenced* and is therefore already constrained, and constraining, its interpretation."[21] Another way of saying this is that Chaudhuri instrumentalizes his own work, producing almost immediately after its emergence a record of what it means, as if to foreclose the possibility that it wouldn't otherwise. At the same time, he discharges the critical impetus of other readers.

For Bhagat, discussed in chapter 3, the critic is an enemy. For Chaudhuri, the critic is merely superfluous. Still, the work of criticism goes on. Among treatments of Chaudhuri's early work, then, there are both tentative departures from and striking convergences with the author's self-assessments. Chaudhuri has been read as a "realist"[22] in the traditions of everyone from Tagore to Jane Austen, as well as a "modernist"[23] in the molds of Virginia Woolf and James Joyce. He is considered the purveyor of the realist type against the reductions of the modernist allegory, as well as the modernist counter to Rushdie's postmodernist fabulism. Saikat Majumdar attempts to get around these contradictions by calling Chaudhuri a modernist who nevertheless does *not* make "a drastic break with realism."[24] All of these readings are inflected—if not constrained—by the author's own criticism.

Whether he is a realist or modernist (or both, or neither), what critics do agree on is that Chaudhuri values the inhabitance of the quotidian over the disruptive force of the event that has long been emphasized in postcolonial studies of Indian English literature. Many famous novels in the field have centered the events of Partition and Emergency, for example: including Rushdie's *Midnight's Children*, Bapsi Sidhwa's *Ice-Candy Man/Cracking India*, Mistry's *A Fine Balance*, and Aatish Taseer's *The Way Things Were*. By contrast, Chaudhuri attends to the granular textures of life; he does not fetishize "the fantastic." His books resist the collapse of private and public spheres essential to the writing of the nation and offer instead, through their exploration of the mundane everyday, "a valuable alternative tradition of contemporary postcolonial writing."[25] His fragmented and episodic novellas are weighted with minor details that do not immediately lend themselves to allegorical extension, like the landscape of a folded sari, overflowing gutters, and the violet-black necks of copulating pigeons on a humid afternoon.

Readings of Chaudhuri as a faithful observer of the ordinary accord with his own self-professed commitments. Rather than event or story, his works set out to capture "a certain meandering lifelikeness . . . this quality of constantly revisiting the present moment."[26] Chaudhuri has also specifically argued that his avowals of the ordinary are not to be read as allegories of the nation or life within it. The publication of his first book, *Sublime Address*, coincided with the liberalization of India's financial markets in 1991, and in this way, Chaudhuri's authorial debut kept time with the appearance of the "New India." "But the two births weren't coeval or connected," he writes, at once establishing and dismissing the connection: "they took place near each other without being affected by that proximity in any way."[27] This smooth denial of the enmeshment of his private story in the dominant discourse of the Indian nation is characteristic of Chaudhuri. The question for critics is, should we take him at his word?

In chapter 3 on Bhagat, I discussed the methods of reading "alongside the grain" and with "a loving eye" that Ulka Anjaria has proposed are essential to the apprehension of the literature of contemporary India.[28] For Anjaria and other postcritical, post-postcolonial scholars, reading alongside means fully inhabiting our relationship to texts, accounting for the pleasure, delight, and mazaa they afford, whatever their politics or accessibility, and not dismissing them via the stale hermeneutics of suspicion. Reading lovingly is about refusing to take a default-antagonistic approach to the work of literature, or for that matter to the arguments of other critics. Such an approach makes sense, I reasoned, when it comes to a critically maligned object, like the Bhagat novel. By that same token, I asked, what are the stakes of reading alongside Bhagat, when he has already written us scholar-critics into the script?

I want to ask a different version of that question now with respect to Chaudhuri, whose writing is also carefully crafted to hail the critic. If Chaudhuri's literary texts come to us already theorized—both intimately and nonantagonistically—then what is the point of reading them alongside the grain? What is the purpose of reading any writer in accordance with their professed project? On the one hand, reading Chaudhuri against the grain might be the only way to do justice to the work's openness to alterity and its capacity to mean otherwise. On the other hand, such an approach requires ignoring how Chaudhuri wishes to be read (a totally reasonable move for a literary critic, of course) while refuting the terms in which he (an established scholar, critic, and teacher in his own right) reads himself.

When I first attempted to write about Chaudhuri (in the abortive dissertation chapter that became the rejected article), I erred on the side of contradicting his self-assessment. Since Chaudhuri and concurring critics had argued that *Sublime Address* was a modernist departure from postmodernist national allegory, I decided that I would read its languorous story of a boy's holiday shuttle between Calcutta and Bombay as an allegory of diasporic return to the nation. I would go to the heart of Chaudhuri's protest and excavate from within it the latent seeds of self-contradiction. Given Chaudhuri's denial of *Sublime Address*'s relationship to the market reforms of 1991, I asked the following: Must the national allegory necessarily appear in the guise of the spectacular and the fantastic, narrated through the drama of the news-making event, given that the ordinary and the banal equally shape the nation in the course of its history?[29] Could it be that as opposed to an *alternative* to national allegory, Chaudhuri is offering an alternative form *of* national allegory, predicated on the priority of the private sphere and thematized through the event of diasporic return?

This was a deliberate and motivated line of inquiry. For over three decades, scholars of postcolonial literature have been arguing in response to Fredric Jameson's 1986 essay "Third-World Literature in the Era of Multinational Capitalism" that the "non-Western" text is not didactically yoked to the nation but rather transcends it, both thematically and formally.[30] Majumdar accepts Jameson's conclusions—noting that the problem with the essay is "not that Jameson is wrong but that he is right"—but only so as to bolster his argument about Chaudhuri's transcendence of the allegory form.[31] Chaudhuri's novels, Majumdar argues, are the exceptions that prove Jameson's "rule" that all *other* third-world texts are allegories of the nation.

When I set out, in contrarian fashion, to redescribe Chaudhuri as an allegorist, it may have seemed that I was attempting to perform the combative, competitive, critical one-upmanship that Pardis Dabashi identifies as the dominant culture of argument rewarded in US academe.[32] In fact, however, I intended nothing of the sort. I did not set out to adjudicate the question of whether or not Chaudhuri *really* writes allegories ("I have no *interest* in writing about allegory," to echo Chaudhuri, with a difference). Given the overdetermining presence of the form in the field, I just thought the question begged asking. If Chaudhuri is a modernist who does not make a drastic break with realism, might it not also be the case that, by deliberately not writing allegorically, he has managed to produce a new version of the allegory form? Even if Chaudhuri does not write allegorically, can he not be read allegorically?

Far from presuming that my reading of Chaudhuri might be superior to that of other critics, I sought a means of entrance into conversation with them. By taking a position in the "Third World literature" debate, I tried to establish my own legibility in the field of postcolonial literary studies. I was attempting to speak a particular language in a particular way, to fashion words that might approximate—if never reach or capture—my object. If, as I have been arguing, accent is a metalinguistic trace of a journey of thought, then I was trying on an accent. If accent is a process of accrual by which, in speaking, we attempt to know something, and in accommodating the one to whom we speak, we attempt to consummate that speaking as knowing, then I was accenting Chaudhuri. In the process, I would accent myself.

One of the first lessons that graduate students in English literature learn is that noncanonical objects have to be justified, and noncanonical objects at the margins of noncanonical fields even more so. The Faulknerians don't feel this imperative, and Rushdie doesn't require disclaimer, but Bhagat does, and vernacular writers do, and so maybe, I thought, someone like Chaudhuri at the edge of the postcolonial field would, too. To quote a widely circulated 2015 *Chronicle of Higher Education* op-ed, "When job seekers are writing about authors the search committee knows nothing about, things could be dicey."[33] Reading this caution, I thought I should enlist familiar categories in literary studies—allegory, realism—as a means through which to underscore the value of the text. The desire subtending my attempt at disciplinary pronunciation, however misplaced, was the desire to prove Chaudhuri's worth as an object of study.

Call it dialect accommodation. I sought a form of accented convergence with the scholars to whom I imagined I was speaking.

Critics like Majumdar had sought to distance Chaudhuri from the postcolonial predilection for allegory because of the presumed crassness of its political imaginary and because of Chaudhuri's own stated resistance to the imperative of being oriented to the nation. They secured for him instead the perch of high literary stylist. Ironically, I wanted Chaudhuri's texts to have a *higher* reach of meaning, to disclose *other* meanings, and so I turned to allegory to secure Chaudhuri's purchase on the literary.[34] But

I ignored one simple, crucial fact: Chaudhuri's work cannot be read allegorically, *because "not-writing-allegory" is what Chaudhuri represents*. In this way, his position countering what is legibly postcolonial has already been secured within the field of postcolonial literary studies. Consequently, his value as object does not need to be asserted.

Which brings me to the second "curiosity" observed about my rejected article: the critique of Chaudhuri's representation of domestic servants. Was that a bad argument, too? Or had I broached another settled—perhaps even verboten—topic in the field?

Complicity and Critique

There is what is euphemistically referred to as a "social contract" in India, an arrangement whereby even middle-class Indians are able to retain (and, as a consequence, rely upon the labors of) a small team of domestic help: full- or part-time cooks, sweepers and cleaners, drivers, housekeepers, and nannies, who may or may not "live-in." In addition, there are figures like the laundry man, the ironing lady, the odd jobs man, and miscellaneous "boys" who might be hired for an afternoon to procure tender coconuts by shimmying, acrobat-like, up the palm tree out back. The women may be called "Didi," "Chechi," or "Akka"—examples of terms for an older sister in Hindi, Malayalam, and Tamil—or a generic "Ma" or "Amma" for an older maidservant. These characters (I use the word advisedly) don't appear out of nowhere; they are born into a radically stratified, caste society characterized by extreme income inequality, in a predatory, Hindu majoritarian nation-state that has failed to address the legacies of colonial appropriation and extraction, ongoing postcolonial labor exploitation, and now the consequences of neoliberal financialization.

There is also a social-critical contract among Indian scholars, in and beyond India, who write about Indian English literature. Many come from middle-class and upper-middle-class and caste families whose resources, educational backgrounds, passports, and other privileges have been enabling conditions of their professorial and literary lives. Those who don't share this background nevertheless enter into a scene in which such privilege has been normalized, if not invisibilized.[35] I was born and raised in California, but my parents grew up in India in the 1960s and 1970s, in middle-class families with social, economic, linguistic, and caste privilege. They both lived in homes where they were attended by servants, sometimes misleadingly termed "staff." Traveling biannually to India growing up, I spent my summers with grandparents who, even as retirees, always retained either part-time or live-in help.

Here's how another Indian American writer of a similar background, Anand Giridharadas, describes this social structure in his memoir *India Calling*:

> To my childhood eyes, the starkest difference between America and India was always servants. In America we spent a fair amount of time rinsing our own plates and loading the dishwasher.... [In India] we encountered a new kind of human: the servant. This was not a housekeeper or cleaning lady or chauffeur. Such words belong to someone treated as a professional.... The servant, unlike [a housekeeper or chauffeur,] lived in his masters' home, usually had family far enough away as to consume little of his time, ate his masters' food, and responded to their every shout, day or night. He was trained to sublimate his own sense of time to that of his masters, to know the precise moment to bring them tea in the morning or to serve them dinner during their favorite soap opera.[36]

Like Giridharadas, I became familiar as a child with a certain code of conduct presented as "normal" in the Indian middle-class household: lifting your legs up from the floor so X can sweep under the chair; calling Y from the dinner table for a glass or your mess to be cleaned up; handing the baby over to Z while you chat with the neighbor; giving loans that keep X in debt; paying Y's children's school fees for the greater common good; switching to English so that the delivery boy can't make out that you are calculating how much to tip. I have stayed in homes where live-in servants were expected to eat and drink with separate serving ware. They were not always permitted to use the furniture. Where there were no staff quarters, live-in help slept on mats on the floor or cots in a side room off the kitchen, but only after the rest of the household had gone to bed, and they were to clear all signs of their sleep before the rest of the household would arise.

How to be anything but disturbed by this, to stay with the deliberately euphemistic language, *arrangement*? It is structural. It is feudal. It is capitalist violence laid bare. It is exploitive, inequitable, infantilizing, and sexist.

It is the suffocation and evacuation of human potential. Everyone knows all of this and knows, at the same time, the limits of acknowledging it. Even progressive Indians in US academe might have (or have grown up with) servants back home. Ask them. If you are reading this and you are one of them, one of us, you might find what I'm saying puerile, cringeworthy, vulgar, and overobvious. *Just so totally obvious.* ("You wouldn't say that to Gayatri Spivak.") But that is also my point. The ideal Indian servants, as Raka Ray and Seemin Qayum observe, are "everywhere and nowhere ... their presence ... unobtrusive"[37]—including in the criticism of Indian English literature representing middle-class domesticity.[38]

To return to the scene of institutional positioning that opens this chapter, my critique of how Chaudhuri writes his cast of minor characters of servants, laborers, and domestic workers didn't land with the peer-reviewer. "The writer took issue with Chaudhuri's representation of domestic servants," he scoffed. The implication was that I just didn't get it; I wasn't in the know. But was part of the problem that I had commented on how Chaudhuri writes about class in the first place? What does a focus on the politics of a critique, as opposed to the content of the critiqued text, tell us about the cult of authenticity in critical practice? When does professional sociality give way to academic disciplining, and when does that serve as a form of class discipline as well? (Cue Spivak: "I go to conferences all over the world and no one ever looks at who cleans the rooms.")[39]

These questions have particular force in South Asian studies, a field that has "a discernable caste-marked, classed, and regional accent"[40] and in which certain voices, nations, languages, and knowledges are routinely privileged. Writing from the position of non–South Asian scholars of color, Isabel Huacuja Alonso and Hoda Bandeh-Ahmadi ask, "Is our idea of who a South Asianist is defined more by social in-groups than scholarship?"[41] Who is allowed to speak about class in South Asia, or to critique the representation of servants in Indian English literature?

Over the years that I have been reading Chaudhuri (in contrast to my "not reading" Bhagat, I have read every book that Chaudhuri has published to date), I have revisited my critique of his classist representations many times. I am keenly aware that my discomfiture stems in large part from my recognition of and participation in the social milieu he describes. I am implicated in what Chaudhuri writes—not above, outside, or beyond it. Pace the peer-reviewer, I'm *in* the in-group and in the know. By that same token, I continue to search for a language with which to acknowledge my participation in the worlds Chaudhuri represents and at the same time advance an honest critique of his work when I present it to my students. In this, my struggle with Chaudhuri's work is not unlike the struggle of scholar-critics who have to justify their reading and teaching of V. S. Naipaul—another writer whose compromised politics poses a perpetual challenge to the reception of his work.[42]

At the risk of being overly schematic, here are three examples of the kinds of passages in Chaudhuri's novels that I have struggled with as a reader. These passages beg scrutiny of the author's class consciousness, complicities, and condescension. I wouldn't have heard them the same way if I didn't also recognize in Chaudhuri's accent something of my own.

1. In the 1991 novella, *A Strange and Sublime Address*, Chhaya, the cleaning woman, is described in detail by ten-year-old Sandeep:

> She had a serious cultured face with a serious smile. . . . It was hard to believe she lived across the railway lines, in the clump of huts called the basti, from which whiffs of excrement rose on windy days . . .
> Her odd movement forward on her haunches had an amphibian quality, half human and half of another world. It was laborious, and yet had the simplicity and poise of a tortoise's amble. . . . At last, she would unbend her body and straighten her back . . . her body was slightly bent, as if in obeisance to an invisible god.[43]

Here, Chaudhuri utilizes the seeming artlessness and innocence of his child narrator's perspective to put forth what are obviously patronizing, even dehumanizing descriptions. "Dehumanization" is a strong accusation, but is it not accurate? Sandeep goes on to reflect that he views the servants as "the furniture in the house," with no animating principle other than the desires of those who put them to use.[44] Should readers be consoled by the knowledge that Chaudhuri knows very well how this sounds, and to whom? Does exploiting the idea of a child's unknowing perspective justify this writing by an adult who knows?

2. In the 1993 novel, *Afternoon Raag*, the Oxford-based narrator thinks about two sisters, Chhaya and Maya, who used to clean the bathroom of his family's Bombay house. "I have seen the younger one, Chhaya," he recounts, "a girl with two protruding teeth . . . grow to a young woman

with kaajal around her eyes, and unexpected breasts, two small, painless swellings."[45] After offering this description, the narrator goes on to describe the bathroom; the women and the light fixtures (recall: "furniture") are given roughly equal attention in the text.

The narrator's apprehension of Chhaya's burgeoning sexuality is fundamentally about the narrator's vision; it is not at all about the woman herself. In later chapters, the narrator's speculation on Chhaya's inner life continues to be entirely self-interested. She does not exist outside of him. Worse, he projects his own prurient fascination with Chhaya and her psychic life onto her, as if *he* is the object of her interest: "Chhaya was interested neither in work, nor in studies, nor in looking pretty. The things she was interested in were my mother's singing practice in the morning, and when I would get married."[46] Should readers be satisfied that Chaudhuri is honestly representing a privileged young man's self-involvement—perhaps even relating a series of thoughts he himself might once have had?

3. The 2000 novel *A New World* tells the story of Jayojit Chatterjee, an Iowa-based economics professor on holiday at his parents' Calcutta home. Throughout, Jayojit reflects on what it would mean to return to India and, specifically, to the Indian domestic sphere. Conversations between Jayojit and his mother frequently concern the servants, or *kaajer lok* (the working people). As Maya washes dishes, Jayojit asks his mother, "Where do you get them from?" "They sit downstairs and work in the flats in the building," she responds. "They're just a bunch of shirkers who pretend to be friendly with each other."[47]

When Maya arrives tardy one day, Jayojit's mother resolves to "be rid of her at the first opportunity." Later, Jayojit's parting thought for Maya is that the next time he returns to Calcutta he'll "have a larger paunch": "And you may not be in this job any more, thought Jayojit." The narrator does not even attribute Jayojit's knowledge of Maya's name to an interaction with her. Instead, there is this parenthetical note: "(Her name was Maya—Jayojit had overheard his mother call her this.)"[48]

Jayojit is interested in his own disinterest in Maya's individual personhood: he "sense[s] that the laws governing her life were other than those that pertained to what he called 'ordinary' life."[49] This depersonalization—the rendering of Maya as one of "them"—extends throughout the novel, confirming how employers in Calcutta "enact the immutability of class through discourses and labor practices at home, ordering of space, refusal to engage in manual work, assumption of control over the labor of others, and perception of servants as being distinctive."[50] Should readers be content that Chaudhuri is self-consciously rendering Jayojit as a type: that is, as a part of the bourgeois class to which Chaudhuri himself—along with many of his readers—belongs?

In each of these novels, we find Chaudhuri writing into a long literary tradition in which servants have been represented as "mere appendages of their masters," or as "hands." As Bruce Robbins argues, the bourgeois tradition of the nineteenth-century realist novel does not fully register the working class. When the domestic servant does appear in text, she does so "by the grace of a hierarchical parallelism that brings her out of invisibility only within a frame that excludes most of her subjectivity, routine, plans, destiny."[51] By that same token, the servant serves an essential role in the realist novel by virtue of her muteness and emptiness; she enables the writer to map a sphere of relations and universe of social positions, even as those relations and positions may remain explicitly undertheorized.

Chaudhuri would not be a writer of the mundane and everyday, the routine and banal, if he did not take note of the minor figures who orbit his characters like animated furniture. These figures—the Chhayas and Mayas—play a familiar role in the economy of his writing. Their relative absence enables his storytelling. Chaudhuri's version of the novel of manners holds space for the servant class without delving deeply into their lives. They cannot intrude too far into the narrative, however, or else they risk decentering the middle-class subject at the heart of his texts.

The irony, of course, is that the author's own literary-critical output in India is enabled by the infrastructure of his domestic staff. To put that differently, if the servant's figural absence in text enables the plots of his stories to unfold, their material presence in real life enables him to write those very stories. This is true for many other writers of Indian English literature as well. As Suketu Mehta writes in *Maximum City*, reflecting on his own family's move from New York to Bombay, the return migrant has no choice but to "live rich."[52] In Majumdar's words, servants "have always done the heavy lifting in our lives."[53]

In his 2013 memoir, *Calcutta*, Chaudhuri observes that his own family's cook, Lakkhi, does work that is "not that much better than slave labour." He is forthright and unapologetic: "Our approach to Lakkhi isn't unique to Calcutta. . . . I'm complicit not in a local mode of exploitation, but in a global arrangement."[54] He also admits the aversion that characterizes the elite Indian apprehension of lower-class Indians, calling what he feels for Lakkhi "the opposite of antipathy."[55] He contextualizes his family's situation in terms of a larger, "chafing conflict" between the kaajer lok and the middle class in New India. The Indian middle class wants dependable help, but doesn't want to remunerate that help as a professional class. The kaajer lok in turn are "unreliable and deceitful", their work a "game of brinkmanship"[56] in which they strive daily to gain the upper hand, which might mean smuggling a packet of daal into the folds of a sari, or arriving, nonchalantly, hours late for work.

Once more, the question begged by such passages is whether self-reflexivity about being what Robbins calls a "beneficiary"[57] of global capitalist divisions of labor serves as a warrant for vulgar, classist descriptions, like these: "[Lakkhi's] bodily awkwardness" means "unawareness of herself as a sexual being"; the child Raja "had no understanding of prolonged deprivation or lack."[58] Is admitting to the lived contradictions of New India an essential prerequisite to the project of developing a nuanced perspective on the history of capital or proposing an alternative to the neoliberal status quo? Should readers give Chaudhuri the benefit of the doubt, and what might that entail for our critical practice?

Here's a generous reading of the scenes and descriptions I've just recounted, from both the novels and the memoir. Chaudhuri does not ventriloquize the subaltern. He does not go behind the curtain to make them speak. He does not speak for Chhaya, or speak over Maya; instead, he describes them from afar. He studiously avoids performing what Namwali Serpell has called "the banality of empathy."[59] He writes against the routinized, disingenuous practice of virtue signaling, and he makes visible that which might otherwise go unseen.

This is the kind of argument that has been made by more than one critic who is sympathetic to Chaudhuri's project. Chaudhuri does not "delve deep[ly] into the human psyche," Majumdar observes, because "the deepest wonders of life seem to lie on its very surface."[60] For Simon During, not delving deeply is related to Chaudhuri's "moral nonchalance" and tendency not to take political stands: "[F]rom where Chaudhuri sits, the affirmation of social justice seems to put the autonomy of the literary at risk. His capacity to experience the world in a precisely literary fashion hangs on resisting the temptation to tribunalize, politically or otherwise."[61] Together with his divergence from the allegory form, what During calls Chaudhuri's literary disposition and refusal to "tribunalize" serve as a justification for the political conservatism of his novels, which demonstrate "many of the social and intellectual elitisms of European modernism."[62]

So, which is it: Dehumanization enacted through classist narrative distance, or a modernist aesthetic of detachment maintained through the ethical refusal to represent the subaltern? Is Chaudhuri arrogantly uninterested in the working women he describes, or responsibly aware of the limits of his surface-level interest? Is Chaudhuri's literary depiction of everyday domesticity a rejection of an overfamiliar postcolonial politics, or a demonstration of the fact that the domestic, too, is resolutely a political sphere?

Chaudhuri's narrative treatment of the kaajer lok returns us to larger postcolonial debates on whether or not the "real" India can be represented in English, whether the subaltern can speak, and whether postcolonial literature must always be legibly political. But the answer his work offers is contradictory: "both/and" and also "neither." In refusing to offer the ventriloquial performance of Mukherjee, refusing to produce demotic English like Bhagat, and refusing to qualify the vantage from which he writes, Chaudhuri takes a position in these debates—by rejecting their very terms.

"This Is Not About Amit Chaudhuri"

At the start of this chapter, I raised the question of whether Chaudhuri's work (which I have taught but failed to write about) is a more worthy object of study than Bhagat's (which I have written about but never taught). In fact, the antiliterary, popular Bhagat is an ideal foil for the hyperliterary, elite Chaudhuri in other ways as well. If Bhagat's books are all plot and no style, then Chaudhuri's books might be said to be all style and no plot. ("Nothing happens," critics said of his first book—to the author's great satisfaction.)[63] Bhagat claims to represent the everyman from the realist trenches, whereas Chaudhuri calls into question the very premise of accessing the real. Bhagat seeks to instruct the unfluent and subaltern reader; Chaudhuri has no interest in such readers and makes no pretense of letting the subaltern speak.

Yet relations of opposition are just that—*relations*. Chaudhuri, like Bhagat, writes contra- Rushdie. Bhagat rejects elite Anglophonism; Chaudhuri resists hegemonic postcolonialism. Bhagat's and Chaudhuri's dramatically different styles and intertexts—lowbrow and highbrow, global and modernist—similarly interpellate critics into their texts. Both are distinctly self-reflexive writers who play with the conventions of the new "market metafiction."[64] "Chetan Bhagat" often appears as a character in Bhagat's work just as "Amit Chaudhuri" is a character in Chaudhuri's. Other "real" people appear in their fictional worlds, too: Bill Gates in Bhagat's *Half Girlfriend*; Amartya Sen in Chaudhuri's *A New World*. The unnamed narrator of Chaudhuri's story "Prelude to an Autobiography" wants to have her memoir published by "David Davidar," the real-life cofounder of Aleph Book Company and former CEO of Penguin India, who has also worked on Bhagat's books.[65]

The effect of these kinds of references is twofold. For one, they collapse the distance between the real-world universe of the reader (which is to say, the public sphere of literary-critical discourse all readers inhabit outside the book), and the narrative-worlds of the books themselves, which thereby appear as actors in, as opposed to representations of, the outside world. Also, these hyperreal references situate the critic within the narratives from the get-go. This makes it that much harder to produce a critical position outside the text since we, as critics, are already in it.

Here's an example of what that looks like. Chaudhuri's 2017 novella *Friend of My Youth* is about a novelist named "Amit Chaudhuri." This "Amit Chaudhuri" is on a book tour for a novel called *The Immortals*, which is also the name of a 2009 novel by Chaudhuri. *Friend* addresses head-on the "accusation" that Chaudhuri is an autobiographical writer. Early in the novella, "Chaudhuri" notes that "[his] writing is accused of coming directly from life"[66] and narrates a scene of encounter with a journalist that bears this out:

"How much of the novel is autobiographical, sir?" the journalist asks.
"I don't like the word 'autobiography.'"
"Why, sir?"

"Because I'm not really interested in telling you about my life. The term indicates that I am."[67]

Everything in the novel and about the narrator resembles the author, Amit Chaudhuri, but "Chaudhuri" rejects this as coincidental: "What marks out a novel is this: the author and the narrator are not one. Even if, by coincidence, they share the same name. The narrator's views, thoughts, observations—essentially, the narrator's life—are his or her own."[68]

How are we to read these overly didactic words that sound like something from the first day of "English 101"? Is this the author's sincere effort to educate his readers? A playful wink to critics who are in the know? Or something else entirely? Spivak's understanding of "the structuralist imperative" at work in J. M. Coetzee's fictionalized memoir *Summertime* (which features a protagonist named "John Coetzee") applies to Chaudhuri's *Friend* as well: "Every statement has its contradiction in the book . . . The 'author' says: I'm absent, I'm absent, I'm absent—but it is part of the technique. It is the textualizing of a life, the inscription of a desire to be able to access a life."[69]

The fact is, Chaudhuri has always been skeptical about the demands of "representational fidelity."[70] In the fictionalized exchange with the journalist, he dramatizes a familiar circuit of anticipation and foreclosure, while neutralizing and redirecting the questions with which critics have conventionally approached his work. No longer can we ask whether Chaudhuri is writing about India—allegorically or otherwise—or about his own life. The question we must ask is what is "India," anyway, and what is a "life"? To borrow again from Spivak's essay on *Summertime*, "Where does life begin? How textual already is 'life' as we think we know it?"[71]

Let's consider at greater length the passage quoted in the epigraph to this chapter, which appears in an essay that Chaudhuri wrote after the publication of *Friend*: "I'm an Indian, so of course I write about India. But then, again, I *don't* write about India. I'm not *interested* in writing about India. This means I'm not entirely, or comfortably, a part of the history of the Indian novel in English either. Nor can I be part of a history that has now been appropriated by literary journalism and publishing houses: of the form of the novel. It's not that I'm resistant to appropriation. I'm *unfit* for appropriation. This may be a good place to be in."[72]

"I write about India/I don't write about India/I'm not interested/I'm unfit." We can hear in this brief equivocating passage a form of protest and self-description that is not unlike that of the ethnic and postcolonial writers described in the introduction: like Jay Caspian Kang, resolved not to write *The Joy Luck Club*; like me, resolved not to write about Jhumpa Lahiri; all of us ultimately interpellated by the subjects we have disavowed and, equally, by the challenge of doing on our own terms that which we are otherwise compelled to do on someone else's or the market's. Chaudhuri may not be interested in writing about India, but he does, and he has, again and again. Which indicates that Chaudhuri is more of a fit with the rest of us—with the rest of the history of Indian writing in English—than he might like to think.

By that same token, Chaudhuri takes the rhetorical disavowal of identity one step further than other writers we have encountered in this book thus far. For example, his 2007 musical album fuses the work of artists like the Beatles with Hindustani classical ragas. Its title? *This Is Not Fusion.* In the terms that Michel Foucault offers in his reading of René Magritte's *Ceci n'est pas une pipe* (This is not a pipe), Chaudhuri defiantly names his work "in order to focus attention upon the very act of naming." Each element of his oeuvre—from his titles, to his self-criticism, to the books themselves—holds "an apparently negative discourse—because it denies, along with resemblance, the assertion of reality resemblance conveys—[that] is basically affirmative."[73]

This "apparently negative" yet "affirmative" discourse is at the heart of Chaudhuri's aesthetic project. It also distinctly informs his writing on the New India. Like Mukherjee and Bhagat, Chaudhuri returned to the New India at the turn of the twenty-first century. But unlike their attempts to produce a veridic discourse about New India, his catalogue of failed apprehension puts pressure on other writers' attempts to know India, the scholar-critic's attempts to teach India, and his own attempts *not* to write about India—even though he returned to India to do precisely that. Against claims to transparent referentiality, Chaudhuri problematizes the relationship between signifier and signified. He offers the provocations of a text "unfolding from itself and folding back upon itself" as opposed to "the finger pointing out from the [text] in order to refer to something else."[74] India appears in Chaudhuri's texts as both presence and absence: as "an identity, a trajectory, a history," on the one hand, and "an estrangement, a withdrawal, a blank space refusing to be filled," on the other.

Those descriptions of presence and absence come from Elif Shafak's definition of accent.[75] And that is precisely what Chaudhuri offers to our students, which is the subject of my next section.

Returns to India: Chaudhuri's and Mine

In 1999, Chaudhuri, who had been based in England, moved back to India with his wife and daughter and set up a joint-family home in Calcutta with his parents. Years later, he described this return as an exercise of personal volition and a rejection of the choice he had seen others make: "I didn't want to discover one day that I was old, not far from death, and still living in England.... I'd seen it happen to others ... always deferring the day of departure, always behaving as if they were temporary residents who'd been in England for only the last few months."[76] Chaudhuri had not only seen it happen to others; he'd written a version of that story in *A New World*, which is a fictional account of deferred return.

A New World is not a particularly eventful novel. The scholar-critic Rukmini Bhaya Nair describes it as emotion-less and "quietly asleep," as doing "no more than tell[ing] us truths already numbingly familiar."[77] Another reviewer notes that "nothing moves at all: not in Jayojit's summer days, not in the pages of the book."[78] Essentially, it's classic Chaudhuri: plotless, domestic, surface-level. It's also an exemplary case through which to examine how Chaudhuri conceives of the temporal and spatial dimensions of return, a subject that has always been the principal driver of reflection for his narrators across genres.

A New World tells the story of US-based economist Jayojit Chatterjee, who returns to India for a vacation and quickly realizes that he has lost the ability to make himself at home in Calcutta/Kolkata, a city that might have been his. Jayojit registers the New Indian surrounds as "louder and more real ... than normal." The real is almost too real, and in its hyperreality produces for Jayojit the feeling of living in a fiction. Walking the Kolkata streets, he feels "conspicuous," "strange and doubtful," and "assailed by traffic." From his perch in the United States, Jayojit had been able to "[keep] track of everything that happened [in India]" and "his thoughts about [India] had a completeness." Upon returning to India, however, he finds himself bewildered, unmoored. Although he has served from afar as an economic advisor to the Indian government, he now has "neither the means nor the confidence" to advise his retired father about living and investing in the New India.[79]

In 2013, at the behest of his agent, Chaudhuri published *Calcutta*, a first-person account of his own return to India that drew the concerns of *A New World* into the realm of nonfiction. Just as it is for Jayojit, return for Chaudhuri means confronting the competing reals of past and present. He, too, swiftly finds that he is unable to make himself at home in the city that he once called his. Present-day Kolkatans do not share Chaudhuri's sensibilities and interests, like his fascination with the "French windows" that have come to signify "Bengaliness." Instead, they seem to feel most at home in Kolkata's South City Mall, which Chaudhuri finds "bewildering." "This is the new breed," he marvels, adding: "this new breed (to which you yourself belong)."[80]

Or does he? Everyday encounters with working people impress on Chaudhuri the provisionality of his own belonging to the city. Even the homeless are more "intimate with the piece of pavement they [possess]." Emerging from Flurys tearoom on Park Street (as I read these words, I think of my own mother's stories of childhood afternoons at Flurys), he looks, as if for the first time, at his surrounds. On Free School Street, he muses: "I can remember a time when these businesses didn't exist in this location. Ramayan Shah and two other low-level entrepreneurs . . . have appropriated the terrain here." Approaching Shah's pavement food stall, he reflects: "Earlier, I would have denied this place its existence, would have seen it but shut it out, would have looked upon it as a stubborn aberration. . . . Now, for the first time, I studied it properly, not for the sake of ethnography, or from a sense of duty, but to experience again the ways in which people belonged to the city I lived in."[81]

As Chaudhuri continues on, recounting his "desultory" conversations with potential informants like Shah, his predilection for detached observation is challenged by his heightened proximity to his subjects, who differently inhabit and know the city of his (but not only his, he realizes) birth. He struggles to extract the "real" Calcutta from a city that is "already no longer Calcutta." He strains to inhabit both that "'real' Calcutta I'd visited as a child . . . and the city in which I found myself this afternoon."[82]

Let me be performatively dense for a moment. Why don't Jayojit and Chaudhuri recognize the India and Indian city they once knew? Is it all part of a sophisticated critical perspective on the impossibility of producing a veridic discourse about India? Or is it that they reject the reality of what Calcutta has become: namely, New India's Kolkata? Is Chaudhuri's problematization of "the real" a robust theory, or a way of rejecting an on-the-ground Indian reality (and people) he finds threatening or just doesn't like?

The New India discourse is ambivalent and contradictory, and has been weaponized by the BJP and Hindu right, as I have discussed in previous chapters. But one of its stated promises is social mobility: the promise that the servant's child will not grow up to be a servant, that he will learn English and read, if not Shakespeare, then at least the Bhagat novel. If India's cities were once the playgrounds of affluent, English-speaking elites like Chaudhuri, the same cities have now taken in millions of rural migrants, entrepreneurial young Indians, and Bhagat readers who are vying to establish *their* rights to the city.

This means that the story of New India is two. The story of call center agents, entrepreneurs, and aspirational "dreamers,"[83] on the one hand. And the story of the displaced social elite to which Chaudhuri belongs, on the other hand. The class that drinks whiskeys and fresh-lime sodas in the colonial-era clubs that serve as "old bastions" of their kind, while the nouveau riche who are supplanting them dine at trendy restaurants in five-star hotels.[84] The class of would-be employers like Jayojit's family in *A New World* and Chaudhuri's family in *Calcutta*, to whose comfortable lives the empowered kaajer lok pose an existential threat. The Anglophone class that is struggling to make sense of the New India and its own changing status within it.

In chapter 3, I argued a case for *not* teaching Bhagat's novels as representative Indian texts in transnational or global literature classes, precisely because of their polemical claim to represent the "real" India and "real" New Indians. The inverse is why I have to date been comfortable teaching Chaudhuri's writing on India: *because he does not claim to represent it*. Chaudhuri's fiction and nonfiction trouble the attempt to know what the real India is (and when, to whom), which is what makes it so generative in the US university classroom. In refusing to draw hard lines "between the imagined, the remembered, and the real,"[85] Chaudhuri invites critical suspicion of the burden of representation borne by all works of ethnic, postcolonial, and Anglophone literature. In ironizing his own attempt to know the other, he invites critical suspicion of the pursuit of sociological and anthropological truth.

For these reasons, I have taught Chaudhuri's work in a class called Literatures of Return, more than once. (The very first version of its syllabus, from 2018, appears at the start of this chapter; there have since been three others.) Literatures of Return is an undergraduate class on contemporary migration literature by ethnic, postcolonial, and Anglophone writers writing to and from their provisional "homes." In their work, return emerges as both a diasporic dream and a refugee's predicament. Return may be chosen, coerced, or barred. A search for roots, or a quest for routes. There is deep hope invested in dreams of return, we learn; equally, return is an ideological project. In every case, to return is to return to a space in time, to a space transformed by time, and as a subject in and of time.

In the class, we read transnationally and attempt to think transhistorically. In different semesters, we have read Edwidge Danticat on Haitian asylum seekers, Teju Cole on diasporic return to Nigeria, Hisham Matar on seeking his father's ghost in Libya, Saidiya Hartman on routes to and from Ghana, Valeria Luiselli on Central American deportees, Julie Otsuka on Japanese internment, Natasha Trethewey and Jesmyn Ward on returning to Mississippi, Ghassan Kanafani on the impossibility of returning to Haifa after the Nakba, and Rebecca Solnit on paths through Ireland. When Chaudhuri's work is situated among readings like these, students reasonably expect that it is going to teach them something about *India*—over and above the topic of return. After all, in this curricular context, Chaudhuri's are our class's representative Indian texts.

The last time I taught Literatures of Return, in Spring 2021, there was not a single Indian or South Asian student in my class. The first thing they wanted to know when we began our discussion of *A New World* was whether I had ever been to India. They phrased the question that way, with curiosity and interest, instead of asking any of the other questions that might have been lurking within it, like, *Are you able to instruct us on the pronunciation of these unfamiliar words? Are you going to adjudicate the fidelity of the representations on offer in the text? Do you speak as a native? Is Chaudhuri's India your India?*

Yes, I said, I've been to India many times. And then I asked them some of the questions Chaudhuri invites us to ask: What does it mean to have been to India—or, equally, not to have been? What knowledges of India are we bringing to our encounter with Chaudhuri's novel? What does the text itself know about India, and what can't it ever know?

My students were eager to share their knowledge and nervous that it would be found wanting. Slowly, they began to hit the raise-hand button at the bottom of the Zoom window. Together, we generated a list of ideas, associations, images, and stereotypes of India. *Slumdog Millionaire*. Family obligations. Hospitality ("the mother of my Indian friend, how she fed me!"). Caste. Call centers. Crowds! Chicken biryani and mango chutney, one student ventured with a smile. The concept of zero. Bollywood. Gandhi. Ajanta and Ellora. The Taj Mahal.

All of this, too, is "India," I said to the class: these fragmentary images of India that exist in our minds. This is *also* how India exists, between material reality and recalled image, between the past and the future, between dreams and myths and real-time meetings, between pictures of a place and the place itself. Between fact and fiction. Of course, this is not all that India is, has been, or will be, to all people. But at the level of discourse, it too *is*.

I felt confident offering my students this reassurance, given that we had Chaudhuri on the table. Chaudhuri had already shown us that the real has its deepest expression in the workings of memory. That the real is not limited to that which can be empirically observed; it is also that to which one is attached. In Chaudhuri's words, "'India' is text.... Only a relatively small bit of reality can be conveyed by narrating stories 'about' it, or representing it in pictures."[86] Or, as Spivak writes, "Literature authenticates nothing—it runs along, away from evidentiary authentication. A hard lesson—to be learnt over and over again."[87]

I also found, as our discussion progressed, that I did not need to tell my students that Chaudhuri is a privileged elite, unable or unwilling to apprehend the Indian working class, because he says it himself in so many words as an observer of the shifting balance of power between classes, languages, and sensibilities in the New India. On the final day of our collective reading, my students and I paused over a scene in *Calcutta* in which the elderly Anglophiles Anita and Samir Mukherjee invite Chaudhuri and his wife over for an English tea. They serve cucumber sandwiches on spotless napkins and brandish delicately accented Victorian vowels. The whole ritual has an air of decadence and anachronism.

Chaudhuri's description emphasizes the deformation of the class to which the Mukherjees belong. He doesn't mourn its decline, but he clearly marks it. He acknowledges unsentimentally that there is, finally, no going back from New India—even for writers like him who choose to return.

When Chaudhuri Reads What You've Written (About Chaudhuri)

If Chaudhuri has used fiction as a venue in which to mine his life, it is because, for him, the boundary between living and writing, experience and artifice, is porous. In all his work, he demonstrates that real life is always already literary. By that same token, he suggests that literature primarily enables us to inhabit—as opposed to close or cross—the distance between our lives and those of others.[88] In the words of the narrator of Chaudhuri's story "Beyond Translation," "Our worlds, essentially, remained locked to each other; we never read each other's stories."[89]

Except, of course, when we do. Except of course that our worlds—the world of the writer of literature resisting the burden of representation and the world of the scholar-critic overdetermined by identity—are now unlocked to each other and powerfully enmeshed.

I opened this chapter by recounting my unexpected encounter with a peer-reviewer. The most vexing part of that exchange for me was learning that Chaudhuri himself had been sent my article. Suddenly, I was not just a junior scholar making a poor argument. I had been exposed as a bad critic who didn't live up to the author's expectations and couldn't match the author's self-assessments.

If you write about contemporary literature, whether as a traditional scholar, literary critic, journalist, or freelance reviewer, it is likely that you have encountered some of the authors about whom you write. Maybe in the flesh: at literary festivals, readings, and lectures. Maybe virtually: on Twitter/X or in the Zoom room. In the late Program Era, it is additionally possible that some of the (creative) writers about whom you write (as a critic) are your colleagues or your colleagues' colleagues. In the stratified, hierarchical, and classed world of Indian English letters, you at least know someone who knows someone. The longer you do this work, the more likely you are to have made these connections, and the harder (or less tenable) it is to maintain a disinterested position toward the writer you are writing about. As the old safety warning goes, "objects in mirror are closer than they appear."

Like many scholar-critics working in the 2020s, I am perpetually aware of the contemporary writer's living presence, and of the fact that we have crossed paths or one day might. As a graduate student, I was able to ask questions of Chaudhuri after a book reading in a setting that was intimate enough that I could also introduce myself to him, and he then remembered me well enough to have guessed that I wrote that offending article. We know enough people in common that perhaps this chapter will get back to him, too. In general, I am very aware of the possibility that someone somewhere might communicate to a writer, via a friend of a friend of a friend, when I've attempted to pursue some argument in their name. I suspect that this is a widely shared experience underlying the postcritical debate. Within all the theoretical discussion of dispositions, methods, and moods, there is also something essentially pragmatic about our collectively deciding *not* to suspiciously critique the writers we know (or want to know, or want to have follow us back on social media).

Chaudhuri has frequently impugned those critics who focus more on writers than writing, those for whom the "writing is secondary." Perhaps I resemble that remark. Still, I cannot forget the fact of the writer's presence on the other side of a Gmail address. Chaudhuri, in turn, is keeping me in mind—well, not me exactly, but critics, scholars, and reviewers, especially the famous ones. I have noted more than once that Chaudhuri writes about his writing. He also writes about how he has been read (or not), who has reviewed him (and where), and with respect to what prizes and literary institutions. In *The Origins of Dislike*, he disparages literary prestige culture (in the first chapter, he mocks the fame-seeking: "I want James Wood to review me. Would Michiko Kakutani write about me in the *New York Times*?"). At the same time, he indulges openly in its modes of valuation (quoting, for instance, "James Wood's generous essay on my work in the *New Yorker*").[90]

If we contemporary critics cannot *not* be aware of the liveness of the contemporary writer, it is equally true that the contemporary writer cannot *not* be aware of his participation in the production of his own authorial iconicity. "The writer's job is not to be Jhumpa Lahiri (I use the name as a shorthand for our obsession with certain forms of acquisition: for instance, awards and column inches in the *New Yorker*)," Chaudhuri writes.[91] I will return to those provocative words in chapter 7. Here, let me simply point out that Chaudhuri explicitly resists the market into which he is conscripted, but at the same he is fundamentally enabled by it.

What I am describing can also be understood as an outcome of the rise of the "creative and critical": a late Program Era rubric that of course did not begin with Chaudhuri, but that he has played a significant role in bringing about in his own institutions.[92] After teaching for many years at the University of East Anglia, Chaudhuri assumed the directorship of the Centre for the Creative and the Critical at Ashoka University in Sonipat, India, where he has been since 2020. At Ashoka, criticism is now understood as "another genre of literary writing—the way prose, poetry and drama make up different genres" and "the work of the intellectual [is] inseparable from that of the artistic."[93] The concept of criticism as a literary genre is a historically specific outcome of creative writing's emergence as an academic discipline in which students might earn degrees (this is what I mean by late Program Era). Until the mid-twentieth century, "it was still well understood that scholars were one class and writers quite another. They did not belong to the same order of mind, they seemed quite antithetical in purpose and temperament, and at the very least, they needed different places to work in."[94] Today, scholars and writers in US and Indian academe work in the *same* place, with offices down the hall from one another, performing versions of the same job, pedagogy, and craft.

What all of this reveals is yet another form of the collapse of subject and object that I am exploring in this book in terms of identitarian correspondence: the collapse of critical-subject and literary-object that is happening because writers of literature are now teaching literature as professors of English in university departments, and because literature scholars are writing (and being incentivized to write) more like creative writers and public intellectuals, as discussed in the following chapter/recess. Academic scholarship and literary nonfiction are increasingly hybrid and sometimes even indistinguishable, as greater numbers of scholars take seriously the potential inherent in the fact that, as Hernan Diaz observes, "literary criticism shares a medium with its object."

The critic is the medium for the works of literature we are reading and writing about. And this fusion is the authorizing condition of our uses of the text, both in the classroom and on the page.

Once More with Feeling

In closing, I want to return to *Friend of My Youth*, this time with respect to how it furnishes Chaudhuri's philosophy of writing. In the novella, narrator "Amit Chaudhuri" returns to Bombay/Mumbai, a place that was "long ago my life." The city is then reconstituted as part of his "afterlife."

The experience of return enables the narrator to theorize writing, too, as an afterlife: as a mode of existence in its own right, as opposed to something that happens *after* one has lived (and then sits down to type it out). "Amit Chaudhuri" neither writes to live, nor lives to write. Instead, he reflects, "I live. Then something prompts me to write. The writing is not *about* life. It is a form of living. The two happen simultaneously."[95]

This philosophy is increasingly being articulated by literary scholars who understand themselves to be working at the creative-critical nexus and conceive of themselves as makers and artists. For example, Eric Hayot begins his book on writing in the humanities with an evocation of both creation and craft: "Writing is not the memorialization of ideas. Writing distills, crafts, and pressure-tests ideas—it *creates* ideas. . . . Writing is, therefore, a kind of learning."[96] Writing, on this account, is not a practice of transcription or dictation; it is not the textual recitation of what one knows or has experienced. Writing is future-oriented: not about recording ideas, but of creating them. To quote Chaudhuri again: "[L]ife doesn't have to *precede* writing. . . . Writing generates life."[97] It is not a reporting "after the fact" but "a bringing into being."[98]

Which returns me for the last time to the story with which I opened this chapter. *I've never published an article about Amit Chaudhuri*, I said to the peer-reviewer. Channeling Chaudhuri, truly mediating the literature about which I sought to write, and rising to the occasion of the creative-critical collapse, I should have probably said something like this: *Oh, that? You must be referring to an article by "Ragini Tharoor Srinivasan" about "Amit Chaudhuri," writer of the "New India." One day, in the critical afterlife of that writing, I'll excavate what was real about it and what it was really about and who it was really by. Here and now, it is already no longer mine.*

CHAPTER 6/RECESS 3

The Idea of Edward Said

[My Institutional Position]

I started college in Durham, North Carolina, on August 25, 2003. Edward Said died in New York City one month later. He was sixty-seven and had been battling leukemia for years. Although Said was not affiliated with our university, our faculty, like many around the country and world, immediately organized a memorial service in his honor.[1] Flyers went up around campus. Grant Farred, who had been a student of Said's, gave an interview to our university's press office to contextualize the memorial. "[Said] belongs to a remarkable generation of intellectuals that includes Fredric Jameson, Stuart Hall and Jacques Derrida," Farred said, "thinkers born in different parts of the world who influenced several generations of scholars and activists."[2]

Farred and Jameson both spoke at the memorial, as did half a dozen other professors and at least one graduate student. I hadn't yet read Said; it's possible I had only just heard of him. But I remember exactly where I was sitting in the main lecture hall of the literature department, and I remember the way Jameson stood leaning into the podium, and I remember the gravity, admiration, and devotion with which the tributes to Said were offered. Literature was sacred, those assembled were saying; cultural theory was sacred. And the death of the scholar-theorist was an event to be marked and mourned.

I use the word "sacred" deliberately. Said was above all a secular intellectual who refused political gods and pieties of all forms. Yet, I immediately got the sense from his students and fellow scholars that to be close to Said was to be close to an almost otherworldly being, someone too good for this world. As Hamid Dabashi wrote years later, "I have many dear and close friends and colleagues at Columbia [but] after Said's passing.... I have just been doing my job; the passion, the moral thrust of being at Columbia with Said, a sense of belonging that comes with a common purpose, are all gone."[3] Those who were not Said's students wish that they had been. Those of us who never heard him lecture live must be content now with grainy YouTube clips.

So many tributes, special issues, and anthologies have been published in Said's honor that even without transcripts from that memorial I can guess how he was described: as fearless defender and advocate of Palestine, postcolonial pioneer, scholar-activist, humanist, self-named "high culture guy," musician, "dazzlingly erudite," oppositional critic, migrant, traveler, exile, and public intellectual.[4] Someone would have spoken about Said's books, in particular his groundbreaking 1978 *Orientalism*, the ur-text of postcolonial studies, and how it has been taken up across academic fields: distinctly in Middle Eastern studies, for example, versus in English or comparative literature. Others would have stressed the beauty and precision of Said's prose across genres including the monograph, the memoir, and the interview, as well as the clarity of his thinking and political commitments. Another might have talked about his influence on writers of literature, like Nobel laureate Kenzaburo Oe, who once said, "If it ever looks like I'm not listening, I'm thinking about Said."[5]

That memorial service for a scholar I hadn't yet read set me on the course of becoming a literature major and eventually an English professor. My aim in the following pages is to consider why. What does Said represent to those of us working in the US university after his death, as opposed to alongside him? What does it mean to have been interpellated as a student-scholar of literature by the *idea* of Said and his truth-telling, political voice? And what, finally, might the idea of Said tell us about the value of the humanities, the postcolonial, and public address in the third decade of the twenty-first century?

[Recess]

There is a cult of personality around every public intellectual. That's part of what it means to be public. In the two decades since his passing, Edward

Said has become an almost mythical figure in some quarters: the embodiment of the dream of academic influence and stature that underlies much work in the critical humanities, generally, and postcolonial studies, specifically. If Gayatri Chakravorty Spivak is the multilingual pedagogue whose erudition most scholars struggle to match, and Homi Bhabha is the confounding wordsmith whose coinages are earworms the field can't shake loose, then Said represents rare intellectual and moral steadfastness in a gilded profession characterized too often by careerism. All three figures speak in different versions of what we have been trained to hear as the academic accent: didactic (Spivak); inscrutable (Bhabha); political (Said).

As in the preceding recesses, I am interested here in Said's iconicity, over and above how he theorized Orientalism, representation, cultural and imperialism, or literature. That doesn't mean that it doesn't matter what he wrote. So much of what is now commonplace in literary studies is indebted to Said's insights: that the novel is a cultural form without which imperialism would have been "unthinkable"; "that [p]artly because of empire, all cultures are involved in one another"; that "stories are at the heart of what explorers and novelists say about strange regions of the world"; and that "English literature is [not] mainly about England."[6] This book, too, might be redescribed in terms of Said's influence: the rapprochement of ethnic and area studies in the study of Indian English literature as both Asian American and South Asian Anglophone unfolds precisely through Said's elaboration of the Orientalist knowledge-power nexus. Said also gives us the vocabulary with which to theorize "the idea of India" and the "hyperreal" quantities of East and West.[7]

Plainly, Said is the only non-Indian writer to whom I am devoting a chapter of this book. I do this because of his centrality to postcolonial studies, of course. It is also the case that Said's example challenges us to rethink the complex affordances of identity and the politics of identitarian disavowal. Said was a secular intellectual and a powerful critic of the strictures of nationalist belonging and ethnocentrism. Like Spivak, he was vigilant about the position of informancy into which postcolonialists are hailed in US academe. He was deeply self-reflexive. For whom do I speak, Said asked, and to what extent is my speaking contingent upon license from the university? From whom do I seek approval with these words? Who is my "we"? Whose side am I on? "Who writes? For whom is the writing being done?"[8]

Yet despite Said's critical self-consciousness, his writing, reception, and legacy were overdetermined by the fact of his being an Arab Palestinian and an exile who could, by definition, never go "home." To put that differently, Said's status as a nonnativist, antiessentialist, anti-identitarian humanist intellectual was ironically secured by his identity as a Palestinian exile. Said was rooted in the experience of exile, out of which he generated his practice of secular criticism and philosophy of humanism. He is thus a critical figure to contend with in a book concerned with the writing and reading of subjects embattled by burdens of representation and identity in the afterlife of the postcolonial in US academe.

Moreover, Said's example challenges us to rethink the boundaries between academic, public, and semipublic writing in the postcritical, posttheoretical conjuncture. He offers a language for contending with the continued devaluation of literary studies and contesting the hand-wringing response of the "crisis consensus."[9] Finally, the idea of Said is key to how we critics, scholars, and teachers might continue to make a case for the academic humanities in the years to come—which is to say, a case for our own identities as professional academics.

Maybe other scholars wouldn't say it this baldly, but many of us went to graduate school in order to pursue some version of the intellectual vocation exemplified by Said. Katie Kadue puts it like this: we are driven by the fantasy that words have the power to "make a meaningful impact on the world, or—perhaps conversely—to constitute entire worlds in themselves."[10] This fantasy has been sustained by examples like that of Said's life and labor, as someone who addressed a broad public audience outside academe and unabashedly pursued "social change and transformation."[11] I am using the word "fantasy" deliberately; as John Guillory writes, "we cannot all be Edward Said."[12]

Said had his critics, of course: activists who "found his commitment to Western humanism irrelevant, even offensive," on the one hand, and "pure scholars of literary humanism [who] found his politics obstreperous and reprehensibly partisan," on the other.[13] He received multiple death threats, and his office at Columbia was attacked by an arsonist in 1985, leading Ella Shohat to call him "the bulletproof intellectual."[14] In response, Said doubled down, modeling what he called an intellectual ethic of "commitment and risk, boldness and vulnerability."[15]

Said dwelled in contradiction. In his writing, he explored a subject position both inside and outside the institution, particular and universal at the same time. His thinking was "syncretic, eclectic, non-systemic, partial, and non-totalizing, and pragmatically contingent."[16] In *Representations of the Intellectual*, he affirms both the intellectual's role in speaking "on behalf of" marginalized, subaltern, disadvantaged groups and the intellectual's idealized identity as "not of" or "beyond" this world.

It may sound quaint and quixotic now: the idea that the financialized, militarized, casualized university could be a place to wrestle with Stuart Hall's angels or speak truth to power like Said. But I would suggest that all professional academics with intellectual or public-facing critical aspirations strive to occupy a version of this contradictory position. Certainly, we do not enter fields like ethnic and postcolonial studies with the goal of becoming anonymous functionaries, mere employees, "timid and jargon-ridden university dons" or institutional mouthpieces, who display neither solidarity with others nor self-awareness of our positions.[17] We need our words to matter and find their audiences, because we need our work to matter, too. Otherwise, what separates us from the financial-managerial class doing David Graeber's psychologically damaging "bullshit jobs"?[18]

Again, Said lived within this contradiction—and flouted it. Trained in European and Anglo-American literature and philology, he wrote and spoke eloquently on freedom, liberation, coexistence, interconnectedness, hospitality, universalism, equality, and the human spirit. At the same time, he was critical of hyperspecialization, disciplinary-specific argot, and the canonical episteme, which he worried served to depoliticize the academic humanities and render them inutile for the political project of humanism.

Said appreciated the democratic, even populist aspirations of New Criticism, which was aimed at facilitating direct communion between readers and literature without relying on specialized historical or discipline-specific knowledge.[19] At the same time, Said's own literary scholarship put pressure on New Criticism's ideological production of an exclusionary, tacitly white, Anglo-American normative reading position.

Said wrote through his own postcolonial story of betweenness: of being "out of place" (the title of his memoir), of plural forms of identification and disidentification, of the generative mixing of his "Western" and "Eastern" educations, of the exilic experience of being at home everywhere and nowhere, and of the existential predicament of barred return. At the same time, he was skeptical about the institutionalized, disciplinary formation of postcolonial studies. Postcolonialism, Said wrote, "has become merely an academic specialty" that is "completely displaced from the real world."[20] For example, he worried that Bhabha's work serves "to falsify the colonial encounter" by turning from "the practical, historical, and the material to the psychological and the ambivalent, to a kind of slyness."[21]

In *The Age of the World Target*, Rey Chow discusses similar critiques of postcolonial studies, that more specifically attribute postcolonial theory's defects to scholars having failed to learn "the comparative, interdisciplinary, and multicultural" lessons of area studies (at its best) and of works like Said's *Orientalism*. The result, she glosses Harry Harootunian, is "a type of postcolonial studies that . . . tends to specialize in the deconstruction of the nature of language, in the amalgamation of poststructuralist theory largely with Anglo-American literary studies, and in the investigation mostly of former British colonial cultures rather than a substantial range of colonial and semicolonial histories from different parts of the world."[22]

How could scholars of the postcolonial have failed to learn the lessons of *Orientalism*? Here, again, Said's identity as a Palestinian exile may have had something to do with overdetermining readings (and, for that matter, misreadings) of his work. For instance, Said was always very clear that the only acceptable form of nationalism is articulated in self-defense, against extermination, and in the name of freedom, equality, and universalism. He focused on actual struggles for liberation and "the continuity of control and domination exercised on the formally colonized world."[23] And yet, given his prominence as a spokesperson for and embodiment of solidarity with Palestine, he was sometimes misrepresented as a nationalist.[24] Even a reader like Bhabha, who should have known better, questioned Said's so-called partisanship, writing: "The high Saidian style speaks with a moral passion that sometimes sacrifices analytic precision to polemical outrage, and his singular commitment to the Palestinian cause could create a severe hierarchy of historical choices."[25]

Reading Bhabha's words in the context of the genocide in Gaza at the hands of the US-backed state of Israel is deeply sobering. Official US university responses to student and faculty actions in solidarity with Palestine have been revealing as well. To give one example, in fall 2024, at Said's own Columbia University, the administration instituted a mandatory "antidiscrimination" training for all faculty, staff, and students that defines anti-Zionism as antisemitism.[26] Meanwhile, apologists for Israel continue to protest its characterization as a settler-colonial state occupying the land of Palestine—even though the establishment of the state of Israel in 1948 was not only the consummation of a Zionist project, but the extension of a European colonial one. It was—*is*—a colonial project outside of time, an anachronism, ironically founded in the historical era of anticolonialism.[27]

Despite this well-known and long-established history, many scholars in US academe have taught and debated the end(s) of the postcolonial as an issue unrelated to the ongoing colonial extraction, violence, and occupation in/of Palestine. I was trained in postcolonial and diaspora studies in the 2000s and 2010s; I did an entire Qualifying Exam field on nationalism, anticolonialism, and the transnational. I was never instructed in the history of Zionism and the case of Palestine was presented as marginal within anticolonial and postcolonial thought. This is not an indictment of my teachers. But it is an acknowledgment of an absence that has long been present in our fields and part of a larger reckoning with its consequences. Now more than ever we need to ask ourselves what it has meant to be postcolonial in US academe. Following Said, and pace Bhabha, it is high time for a reckoning with the severe hierarchy of *our* historical choices: in the profession, in our classrooms, and on the page.

I want to return now to a commonplace about Said that this recess has thus far taken for granted but that begs reconsideration. It is generally accepted that Said found a way to combine scholarship and politics, the world of academe and the "real" world out there.[28] "Politics is everywhere," Said wrote, "there can be no escape into the realms of pure art and thought or, for that matter, into the realm of disinterested objectivity or transcendental theory."[29] He lamented that "the study of literature is considered to be profoundly, even constitutively nonpolitical," and advocated that scholars establish "an interpretive *community*, in the secular and noncommercial, noncoercive sense of the word," as opposed to functioning like a "tiny fiefdom" disregarding nonexpert and nonspecialist discourse.[30]

In light of such statements, R. Radhakrishnan writes that Said was "unafraid to contaminate and politicize the hoary chambers of scholarship with the clamor and urgency of worldly, political issues."[31] Unafraid, yes. But what if Said was able to dwell in the seeming contradiction of being both inside and outside academe because he was able to *amplify* the distinction between his scholarship and his politics—not because he collapsed it?

Consider this passage from *Representations of the Intellectual*: "I do not therefore consider myself bound by my professional training in literature, consequently ruling myself out from matters of public policy just because I am only certified to teach modern European and American literature. I speak and write about broader matters because as a rank amateur I am spurred on by commitments that go well beyond my narrow professional career. *Of course I make a conscious effort to acquire a new and wider audience for these views, which I never present inside a classroom.*"[32]

As an intellectual, Said was politically committed; he confidently engaged with matters of geopolitics, policy, and statecraft irrespective of the so-called limits of his professional training. But as a professional academic and a member of the literature faculty, Said was strict about what he would and would not present in his classroom. On the one hand, Said acknowledged that the university is not "free of the encumbrances, the problems, the social dynamics of its surrounding environment." On the other hand, he maintained that the university "cannot be an immediately political arena."[33]

It is not entirely the case, in other words, that Said the literature professor politicized the profession ("contaminated the hoary chambers of scholarship"). Rather, he seems to have successfully split himself into different subjects. He became and learned to sustain more than one Said—rather like Jhumpa Lahiri, the subject of chapter 7, who could not become another writer within the bounds of the Anglosphere, and so decided to become "two."[34] He was Said, the public intellectual, but also Said, the specialist academic.

Let us take Said's idea of each in turn. First, the intellectual, who is an exile and amateur: someone independent, unattached, and unaffiliated, whose vocation requires "a state of constant alertness" in order to militate against "half-truths or received ideas."[35] He (almost always "he")[36] does not perpetuate "stereotypes and reductive categories" but breaks them down in the name of expanding "human thought and communication."[37] The intellectual's goal is to represent the truth to the best of his ability, no matter the designs of government officials or other authority figures. The intellectual does not cozy up to power but speaks truth to it. "I have never found it interesting to be close to power," Said said.[38]

In order to maintain his independence, Said's intellectual takes on the "double perspective" of the exile. He need not actually be an exile, migrant, or expatriate, but he must cultivate the habit of thinking like one. Thinking like an exile means thinking from the margins, contesting official-national discourses, and resisting "the conventional and comfortable." It also means resisting nativist and identitarian thinking. The intellectual's task is to militate against certainty: to be willing to go into the muddle, the mess, the doubt, the tangle, the third space, where all natural, traditional, orthodox, seemingly "god-given" entities can be shown as the "constructed, manufactured," and "invented" objects that they are, each "with a history of struggle and conquest behind it."[39] These are the grounds on which I argued the case for teaching Amit Chaudhuri in the last chapter: because he consistently and provocatively queries the constructedness of "India" and "Indians." To put a finer point on it, the three words at the heart of this book—"*I am not*"—are an intellectual's exilic locution.

But Said's intellectual is not just an exile. In order to be a value-driven truth-teller, he must also be an amateur. For Said, amateurism is a kind of energy, spirit, or attitude; it is a form of care that moves the intellectual to engage "as a committed and recognizable voice in language and in society with a whole slew of issues." Importantly, the opposite of the amateur for Said is not the expert, but rather the *professional*, whose primary concern is marketing himself to those with power and authority, and whose primary audience is a coterie of insiders or clients "to be satisfied" as opposed to "challenged."[40] This professional accumulates credentials and other hallmarks of specialization that remove him from the world, when he should instead be connecting to it. He needs "to be certified by powerful institutions and to speak their language"; therefore, he trades the potentially open language, vocabulary, and accent of the intellectual for the closed language of expertise.[41]

Said thoroughly rejected this careerist, self-defeating mode of professionalism, in which expertise is a tool of personal advancement, as opposed to a mode of acquiring and disseminating knowledge in the name of truth, emancipation, and freedom.[42] However, he nevertheless maintained his own identity as a specialist and credentialed academic, and the irony is that this position is what gave his public interventions the imprimatur of authority and expertise. To be clear: I am not casting aspersions on Said's maintenance of what any observer can see was a comfortable and privileged position as a tenured Ivy League faculty member. What I want to stress is that Said's public intellectualism was predicated on a separation of spheres between the public world of his amateur interventions, on the one hand, and the professional world of his literary scholarship and teaching in a private institution, on the other.

And this separation is frankly no longer tenable to maintain, given the thoroughgoing evisceration of one of the spheres: namely, that of the profession.

Without further rehearsing the academic crisis consensus, let me observe that the boundaries between the personal and the political, the public and the professional, the amateur and the expert have now substantially broken down. New information economies, media platforms, and communication apparatuses have fundamentally changed where and how we write and read. Our scholarly interventions are as likely to be presented on Twitter/X as in peer-reviewed articles, and our amateur interventions might appear in semipublic online forums hosted by formerly gate-kept academic journals. The COVID pandemic reorientated labor time and working conditions. Materially, our workplaces stretch from Zoom rooms in our living rooms to classrooms on campus. Our students sell their fan fiction on Amazon Kindle Direct, publish postcolonial criticism on Substack, and get book recommendations on BookTok, while in many universities, the humanities classroom hemorrhages students and majors are on the decline.

What then does it mean to be a public intellectual today? If Said's amateurism was a response to the hyperprofessionalization and specialization of disciplines that functioned like religious guilds, what is the function of amateurism now, in the age of postdisciplinarity and postprofessionalism?

In recent years, many departments of English, including my own, have tried to rise to the occasion of digital media, broadly defined, by encouraging our graduate students to do public writing. In practice, however, this is no simple thing, nor an obvious solution to the crises we face. Who is the public, and what form of writing is adequate to its needs? Public writing has two aspects, after all. It is an opportunity to reach a wider audience (emphasis on "public"), and it is a chance to work in differently accented prose genres (emphasis on "writing"). So, how much wider the address, and how different the form? You can't advocate public writing without addressing such questions.

For Lili Loofbourow and Phillip Maciak, the more relevant term for the humanities is "semipublic" writing, which bridges critical and scholarly genres, public and academic audiences, and the institutional contexts of journalism and the university. Stylistically, this might mean that endnotes are permissible, yet spare. References to scholarly texts abound but are explained. Professional academics are valued but not privileged addressees. Unlike writing that seeks the widest possible public address, the semipublic informs a relatively rarefied audience. By that same token, it is more collaborative than scholarly writing: multiple editors are involved, and the swift publishing pace enables timely reader feedback. Semipublic writing is like "giving a public lecture, starting a colloquium series, or organizing a conference."[43] In Sharon Marcus's words, it is "teacherly": "[it] does not avoid difficult ideas or terms; it explains them . . . adopt[ing] a pedagogical stance."[44]

Said didn't use the language of semipublicity, but what I have just described carries forward the spirit and aims of his intellectual, who conceives of the self as "endlessly learning, trying always to keep one's mind open to more and more, to work on that learning, and finally to *present* it in some way."[45] Semipublic writing is a form of critical amateurism; it is what I have elsewhere termed suggestive, not definitive.[46] Its aim is to open up something in the reader, who can then take the inquiry forward on their own terms. It does not close down possibilities for further reading and writing with an authoritative or deadening performance of expertise. It is a practice of ongoing and endless learning, driven by an ethic of emancipation for all.

In US academe, contributing to semipublic outlets has become the norm, and there are many venues devoted to channeling academic writers into the public sphere. At the time of this writing, these include The OpEd Project, The Conversation, The Immanent Frame, and Arcade. Numerous peer-reviewed journals publish editorially reviewed content online: for example, *boundary2* has *b2o*, *Social Text* has *Periscope*, *Critical Inquiry* has *In the Moment*, *Post45* has *Contemporaries*, and *Public Books* is affiliated with *Public Culture*. Outside these outlets, there are hybrid "little magazines" that are welcoming to academic writers "hungry for new audiences and broader forms of intellectual exchange,"[47] like the *Los Angeles Review of Books*, *n+1*, *The Drift*, and *The Point*, not to mention all the major literary book reviews and the increasingly diverse online platforms of venues like the *New Yorker*.

As a result, in two clicks online, you can find a wealth of beautifully written, academically inflected, critical, and committed yet accessible and clear writing for audiences both within and beyond academe. Political manifestos. Incisive analyses of contemporary cultural production. Rigorous research on history and its afterlives. Experiments in collective criticism. In the face of profoundly delegitimating discourses and unprecedented forms of information-overload and distraction, countless graduate students and faculty are working to "present" the work they are doing to keep learning "endlessly," to renew themselves and their commitments, in the name of a greater collective good. In the process, they have radically transformed the genres of literary criticism and cultural critique.

We are living in a golden age of semipublic intellectual writing. And yet, we cannot be sanguine about this development. The boom is partly a product of the ease, speed, and sophistication of online publishing and a certain democratization of opportunity, yes. But it is also a by-product of the evisceration of the tenure-track and adjunctification of higher education, which has led many graduate students into journalistic freelancing as an "alt-ac" side gig. Put simply, the "boom" in semipublic writing is directly related to the ongoing "bust" of the academic humanities in the United States: if not as a cause, then as an effect. It depends on the deformation of the profession and also contributes to it. The swelling of the ranks of PhD-holding editors means that their field-specific interests drive both the content they solicit and the writers to whom they turn. As more and more PhD students leave (or are pushed out of) academe, editors need not turn to professional academics for semipublic content. At the same time, salaried academics remain a knowledgeable source of content who are often willing to write for free. This is both the condition of their desirability to some small venues, and another way in which the inequities of academe continue to impact the world beyond it.

Are we seeing an amplification of academic writing, or its displacement?[48] Do we have a newly empowered cohort of public intellectuals among us, or a voluble precariat that has nothing to lose but its think pieces, offered up into the virtual void? Will publishing in journalistic outlets or literary venues help our graduate students succeed on the academic job market? Does public writing make up for locations in private institutions—or for that matter for the enclosure of academic scholarship behind journal paywalls?

What would Said say about all this?

In his 1999 presidential address to the Modern Language Association, Said called for a renewal of "the heroic ideal in humanism"—for a culture of bold non-conformism, risk-taking, and effort. Something should be at stake, he wrote, every time we pick up pen and paper. Down with "inconsequential word-spinning" in the face of the very real jobs crisis. Amid all the talk of "the decline of literacy" and "death of literature," what, he asked, were we going to do?[49] Who were we going to be? A few years later, in the aftermath of September 11 and faced with the devastation of the Iraq War, Said implored his colleagues to cultivate a humanistic spirit of intellectual generosity and hospitality and to renew the "rational interpretive skills" at the heart of "worldly secular rational discourse."[50]

Today's public intellectuals—our semipublic academic writers—do not lack for audience, or purpose, or rational interpretive skills, or political commitment. What they lack is the opportunity for professionalization, sustained and generous employment, and affirmation from institutions worthy of their lives and labors. What we need to build—even if we've never before had it—is a profession grounded in solidarity and driven by shared stakes. We need to be the kind of profession that can come together in acts of celebration and mourning, that acknowledges the contributions of seminal theorists in our fields and creates space for their students to speak, that fights scholasticide both locally and globally, and that continues to inspire new generations to take up the mantle of commitment to something other than professional advancement.

We need to be the kind of profession that's willing to undo itself, in other words. Committed, as Said was, to the promise of resistance and critique.

CHAPTER 7

A Desire Called the Post-Anglophone

Or, On Not Being Jhumpa Lahiri

[My Institutional Position]

In spring 2005, when I was a college sophomore, I took a class on diasporic Indian women's fiction in English—the only course on Indian literature I've ever taken, though by now I've taught a few. Writing this, it strikes me anew that many of us only every take one class in the fields that go on to be "ours," and that the bulk of our education into said fields then happens when we are at the head of the seminar table. You can't major in English taking ten classes in Asian American or postcolonial literature, never mind that in most departments such classes aren't offered every semester anyway.

The class was taught by a charismatic, tenured professor of literature and cultural studies who was neither Indian nor a woman. We read writers like Monica Ali, Bapsi Sidhwa, Sunetra Gupta, Shani Mootoo, Meera Syal—and the one and only Jhumpa Lahiri. I recall that we derived our definition of the Indian diaspora as an extraterritorial, rhizomatic map of communities dispersed across the world from Sandhya Shukla's *India Abroad*. I also remember being thrilled that Shukla wrote about the "immigrant-centered, middlebrow"[1] ethnic magazine *India Currents*, founded in 1987 in San Jose, California, where I grew up, and for which I had been writing a bimonthly column for some years. I was chuffed by the realization that I was contributing to the production of an archive that could serve in books and classrooms as an object of critical consideration.

But as the weeks passed, I began to feel uncomfortable with what I experienced as the course's disciplining effects. I felt assailed by notions of "Indian-ness" that flew against my own vexed and evolving conceptions. I reacted possessively to some of the course texts and wanted to run as far away as possible from others. In part, I was not sure what I was doing in the class. As one of two Indian American students, was I the subject of knowledge, or its object? Was I there to learn about "myself," or to "give an account of myself"?[2] Nothing precluded my professor's teaching the class, of course, but what exactly was he trying to tell us Indian students about "our" literature?

I particularly chafed against my non-Indian classmates' exuberant reception of Lahiri's *The Namesake* and what I heard as the professor's praise of its anthropological rendering of the second-generation Indian American experience. Ironically, I was less concerned about the text's possible inaccuracies than with the eerie accuracy of descriptions such as Indian mothers serving an American pizza dinner "once a week as a treat."[3] My final paper took on Lahiri's novel's politics of assimilation and didn't mince words. It was titled "Diaspora Is Bunk."

Fast forward to August 2022. I returned to the in-person classroom for the first time since March 2020 to teach a course called "The World and South Asia," on South Asian Anglophone literature. A syllabus for that course follows. Three-quarters of the way through the semester—after units on colonialism, the postcolonial, language, subjectivity, and sonic imaginaries—we began a unit on diaspora. My students were almost exclusively self-identified South Asians (eighteen out of nineteen, to be precise), with roots in and routes through countries including Bangladesh, Oman, India, Pakistan, the Philippines, and the United States. For them, I particularly wanted the diaspora unit to land.

Alongside work by Trinidad-born Nobel laureate V. S. Naipaul and Pakistani American playwright Ayad Akhtar, I assigned "Hell-Heaven," a short story from Lahiri's 2008 collection *Unaccustomed Earth*. "Hell-Heaven" is the story of a lonely young Bengali immigrant housewife, Aparna, and her daughter, Usha, who together befriend a Bengali MIT graduate student, Pranab. The story is retrospectively narrated by an adult

Usha, who recalls both her mother's unrequited love for Pranab and the uncertain trajectory of the bond they all shared.

Because of the ongoing pandemic, every session of our class was recorded on Zoom. Watching the video footage months later, I see that "Hell-Heaven" inspired our class to have an engaged conversation about migration narratives, the nature of kith and kin, the meaning of home, the significance of the child's perspective, the figure of Pranab's white girlfriend, Deborah, what it means to be "a child of America," Aparna and Usha's mother-daughter relationship, the distinction between "life" and "living," and the contradiction signaled by the story's title.

To my chagrin, I also hear myself, with just five minutes left to go in class, asking an ill-advised question rooted in my own ambivalence about teaching Lahiri: "Is this an overfamiliar narrative?"

"Yeah," one student pipes up. "It feels exactly like every other Lahiri I've ever read [laughter from the class], like *The Namesake*, and a lot of stories from *Interpreter of Maladies* . . . an MIT/Harvard grad student who falls in love with someone who's white [laughter from the class] . . . like oh my god, that's crazy . . . [more laughter from the class]. I do think there's [sic] small differences, like in this case there's the mother-daughter relationship which I think is interesting . . . but the idea of East and West . . . that's what Lahiri does. I think it's kind of played out."

I had both wittingly and unwittingly set up this response. Now I scrambled, with only four minutes remaining, to contextualize my question and reaffirm the story's significance, adding a too-quick note that "actually Lahiri has changed now—it's really interesting—she's remade herself as an Italian writer."

Why had I impugned the "overfamiliar," casting doubt on the value of Lahiri's story in the eleventh hour of our fifty-minute session? What did my primarily South Asian students recognize and find humorous in their classmate's dismissal of "what Lahiri does"? And why did I represent her turn to Italian as a salutary, even reparative move?

I will have more to say about the specific challenge and opportunity of teaching South Asian literature to South Asian students in the afterword. In this chapter, I unpack the discourse underlying my blurted-out question, with emphasis on the light that Lahiri's "post-Anglophone" forays into Italian might cast on the "played-out" narratives of US ethnic assimilation and postcolonial hybridity.

Because I can't un-ask what I asked my students—that's teaching for you. But this, at least, I can ask of myself.

———⦅⦆———

[Syllabus]

The World and South Asia
English 222 | Rice University
Fall 2022

What does it mean to write "South Asia" in English, and what is the relationship between South Asian literature and the literature of the Anglophone World? The South Asian subcontinent includes eight or ten independent nation-states, depending on how you draw the map, which comprise nearly a quarter of the world's population. These nations have different, historically specific relationships to the English language and literature; Nepal, for instance, unlike India and Pakistan, was never a British colony or protectorate.

Taking inspiration from the Kathmandu-founded, Colombo-based journal *Himal Southasian*'s "Right-Side-Up-Map of South Asia," which challenges dominant modes of visualizing the region, this introductory course invites students to reconceive South Asia and its nations through English literature, on one hand, and to reconceive the literary through engagement with South Asian cultural production, on the other. Key topics of discussion will include colonialism, anticolonial movements, and political violence; the nation, diaspora, and the concept of the global; postcolonial language politics and English's relationship to South Asian vernaculars; sexuality, subjectivity, and sound cultures.

South Asian literature in English both reflects India's political, economic, and military dominance in the region and contests it through the production of a dynamic, regional imaginary. We will therefore strive to decenter Indian English literatures, even as we attend to their particular significance in World Literary formations. Texts will include major 20th- and 21st-century works of Indian, Pakistani, Bangladeshi, Sri Lankan, and South Asian diasporic fiction, nonfiction, drama, and poetry in English.

COURSE SCHEDULE:

Mon, Aug 22: Introductions

UNIT 1: Southasia: Nation, Region, World

Wed, Aug 24: Ragini Tharoor Srinivasan, "South Asia," from *Handbook of Anglophone World Literatures* (2020)

Fri, Aug 26: Rabindranath Tagore, "Visva Sahitya," trans. by Rijula Das and Makarand Paranjape (1907)

—. Select poems from *Gitanjali* (1913, trans. by the author from Bengali)

UNIT 2: Colonialism: The British Raj and the Anti-Colonial Imaginary

Mon, Aug 29: Thomas Babington Macaulay, "Minute on Indian Education" (1835)

M. K. Gandhi, from *Hind Swaraj, or Indian Home Rule* (1909)

Wed, Aug 31: Mulk Raj Anand, *Untouchable* (1935), pgs. 9–53

Fri, Sept 2: Mulk Raj Anand, *Untouchable* (1935), pgs. 53–100

Wed, Sept 7: Mulk Raj Anand, *Untouchable* (1935), pgs. 100–157

B. R. Ambedkar, "Gandhism" (1945)

UNIT 3: The Postcolonial: Partition of India and Pakistan (1947), Bangladesh Independence (1971), National Allegory

Mon, Sept 12: Aanchal Malhotra, from *Remnants of Partition: 21 Objects from a Continent Divided* (2019)

Paul Reyes, "Aanchal Malhotra: A Human History of Partition" (2020)

Explore: "The Museum of Material Memory"; "Remnants of a Separation"

Wed, Sept 14: Saadat Hasan Manto, "Toba Tek Singh," trans. by Tahira Naqvi (1955)

Fri, Sept 16:   *Asynchronous Class*: Archiving South Asia

Mon, Sept 19:   Tahmima Anam, *A Golden Age* (2007), pgs. 3–93

Wed, Sept 21:   Tahmima Anam, *A Golden Age* (2007), pgs. 97–202

Fri, Sept 23:   Tahmima Anam, *A Golden Age* (2007), pgs. 205–274

UNIT 4: Language: English, the Vernacular, and the Postcolonial Language Debate

Mon, Sept 26:   Chinua Achebe, "English and the African Writer" (1965)

Ngũgĩ wa Thiong'o, "On Writing in Gikuyu" (1985)

Wed, Sept 28:   Salman Rushdie, "Good Advice Is Rarer Than Rubies" (1987)

—. "Damme, this is the Oriental Scene for You!" (1997)

Fri, Sept 30:   K. Srilata, "Three Poems" (2018)

Mon, Oct 3:   Vikram Chandra, "The Cult of Authenticity" (2000)

Wed, Oct 5:   Amit Majmudar, "To the Hyphenated Poets" (2016)

UNIT 5: Sound: Music, Accent, Body

Fri, Oct 7:   Agha Shahid Ali, "Beyond English" (2002)

Wed, Oct 12:   Sujata Bhatt, "Search for My Tongue" (1988)

Fri, Oct 14:   Nabeel Zuberi, "Listening While Muslim" (2017)

Discussion of class-sourced playlist

UNIT 6: Subjectivity: Sexuality, the Subaltern, and Other "I's"

Mon, Oct 17:   Divya Victor, "Cicadas in the Mouth" (2014)

Wed, Oct 19:   Ismat Chughtai, "Lihaaf," trans. by Tahira Naqvi and Sayeda S. Hameed (1942)

Fri, Oct 21:   Shruti Swamy, "Earthly Pleasures," from *A House is a Body* (2020)

Mon, Oct 24:   Gayathri Prabhu, *if I had to tell it again* (2017), pgs. 1–71

Wed, Oct 26: Gayathri Prabhu, *if I had to tell it again* (2017), pgs. 72–131

Fri, Oct 28: Gayathri Prabhu, *if I had to tell it again* (2017), pgs. 132–185

UNIT 7: Diaspora: Transnational Imaginaries, Historical Derangement, Hyphenated Identity

Mon, Oct 31: V. S. Naipaul, *An Area of Darkness: A Discovery of India* (1964), Prelude and Part I

Wed, Nov 2: V. S. Naipaul, *An Area of Darkness: A Discovery of India* (1964), Part 2

Fri, Nov 4: V. S. Naipaul, *An Area of Darkness: A Discovery of India* (1964), Part 3

Mon, Nov 7: Jhumpa Lahiri, "Hell-Heaven" (2004)

Wed, Nov 9: Ayad Akhtar, *Disgraced: A Play* (2012), Scenes 1 and 2

Fri, Nov 11: Ayad Akhtar, *Disgraced: A Play* (2012), Scenes 3 and 4

UNIT 8: New India: Globalization, Neoliberalism, and Return Narratives in the Asian Century

Mon, Nov 14: Sarnath Banerjee, *The Harappa Files* (2011)

Wed, Nov 16: Akash Kapur, "How India Became America" (2012)

Anand Giridharadas, "Dreams," from *India Calling: An Intimate Portrait of a Nation's Remaking* (2011)

Fri, Nov 18: Snigdha Poonam, "The Click-Baiter," *Dreamers: How Young Indians are Changing the World* (2018)

Mon, Nov 21: Sonali Gulati, "Nalini by Day, Nancy by Night" (2005)

UNIT 9: Literature and/as Labor: War, Terror, and the Violence of Capital

Mon, Nov 28: Jean Arasanayagam, "I Am an Innocent Man" (1993)

Wed, Nov 30: Deepak Unnikrishnan, excerpts from *Temporary People* (2017)

[Accented Reading]

> I am not rooted in this language.
> —JHUMPA LAHIRI

Jhumpa Lahiri was born in London in 1967. Her family moved to the United States when she was three, and she grew up in Rhode Island, speaking Bengali at home and English at school. She holds an MFA and PhD from Boston University, was a professor at Princeton University from 2015 to 2022, and joined Barnard College of Columbia University in 2023, as Director of Creative Writing.

In 2000, Lahiri's debut short story collection, *The Interpreter of Maladies*, won the Pulitzer Prize, consigning her to perpetual literary stardom.[4] I use the verb "consign" and the noun "stardom" deliberately. The same thing happened to Arundhati Roy when her debut novel, *The God of Small Things*, won the Booker Prize in 1997.[5] Roy experienced her instantaneous consecration as the newly nuclear India's shining literary star as such a violent and intolerable form of interpellation that she did not write another work of fiction for twenty years.[6]

Lahiri, in contrast, kept writing fiction. What's more, she dared to keep writing fiction about the Indian American experience, which remained the subject of her next three books: the 2003 novel, *The Namesake*; the 2008 collection, *Unaccustomed Earth*; and the 2013 novel, *The Lowland*. Together with her debut, these works have cast such a long shadow that every Indian American woman writer in the twenty-first century has had to withstand the comparison to Lahiri, even those writing nonfiction and speculative poetry, like Minal Hajratwala, and graphic memoirs, like Mira Jacob.[7] Interviews with Indian women writers from the early 2000s are replete with accounts of their having been measured in terms of the Pulitzer-winner—"everyone was looking for the next Jhumpa Lahiri"—in ways that sometimes helped and sometimes hindered their own publication efforts. Likewise, all aspiring scholars of South Asian American literature in the twenty-first century have to reckon with Lahiri's oeuvre. Thus, my own preemptive disavowal, recounted in the preface: "Before beginning graduate school, I promised myself that I would never write about Jhumpa Lahiri."

Poor Jhumpa Lahiri! For years now she has appeared as a demon to be ritually slayed by each successive Indian American writer seeking to write in their own—and not her—name. Each must pen a version of Vauhini Vara's 2023 essay, appositely titled "Jhumpa Lahiri and Me."[8] Few writers' names signify as potently as Lahiri's does, in and beyond the community of Indian writers. Fewer still have had such staying power. In 2004, David Carr observed that any author "would gladly saw off their (nonwriting) hand to be the next Jhumpa Lahiri."[9] In 2018, Amit Chaudhuri began *The Origins of Dislike* by enlisting Lahiri's name in service of his own writing philosophy: "The writer's job is not to be Jhumpa Lahiri (I use the name as a shorthand for our obsession with certain forms of acquisition: for instance, awards and column inches in the *New Yorker*)."[10] In 2020, reviewers were still using Lahiri's work from two decades prior as the standard against which to judge the "atmospheric detail" of Megha Majumdar's debut novel, *A Burning*.[11] To adapt novelist Sanjena Sathian's lament from a 2021 essay on "the shadow of Lahirism," "Lahiri is not done haunting [us]."[12]

What is it about Lahiri in particular? It is not simply her attention to the Indian immigrant or ethnic American experience. Bharati Mukherjee, discussed in chapter 1, is considered the Indian American literary pioneer. And it is not her success as such; there is no comparable cult of "Kiran Desai," who won the Booker Prize in 2006. It is the convergence of the two: Lahiri is the paradigmatic example of a "self-ethnicizing" writer who was rewarded by the market for responding to the coercive mimetic imperative—or so the story goes.

This convergence and Lahiri's resulting iconicity are distinctly gendered. On the one hand, Lahiri is singular. On the other hand, publishers could not have gone looking for "the next Lahiri" unless they believed that what Lahiri did was modular, reproducible, and replaceable, or perhaps even the slightly fraudulent work of a "confidence artist," as Vanita Reddy observes.[13] By way of contrast, consider the previous chapters' discussions of the shadow that Salman Rushdie has cast over the postcolonial literary field since the early 1980s. Writers may seek to emulate Rushdie's example at the level of form (to be "Rushdiean"), or else repudiate it entirely (to reject the "huge baggy monster" of *Midnight's Children*), but nobody can be the "next Rushdie"—except an anti-Rushdie like Chetan Bhagat.

Was Lahiri read unfairly, ungenerously? Her early fictions enticed those who sought a thick description of the Indian American community—whether because of anthropological interest or the desire for recognition. At the same time, they frustrated those Indian readers (and writers) who feared being typecast by her texts and pinned like ethnographic specimens on the literary butterfly board. Reading Lahiri's first three books, many readers came to expect that her work be legibly multicultural. Inevitably, other readers found that same content stale. This dynamic was at play even in reviews of *The Lowland*, her most explicitly political novel, on the Naxalite movement and its afterlives. Some praised Lahiri's "lovely fragrant" words that "bridge[d] two cultures"; others decried her "cheaply microwaved otherness. . . . a parody of contemporary transnational literature at best."[14] More than one reviewer singled out this particular sentence in the 340-page novel: "Once more the leaves of the trees lost their chlorophyll, replaced by the shades he had left behind: vivid hues of cayenne and turmeric and ginger pounded fresh every morning in the kitchen, to season the food his mother prepared." Some praised the "surreal perceptions of an immigrant"; others sneered at Lahiri's attempt to become a "mistress of spices."[15]

That's where the story might have ended—with Lahiri signifying powerfully and disappointing mightily and overdetermining all Indian American literary production—if it wasn't for the fact that she herself decided to slough off the straitjacket of "imposed identity."[16] In 2012, she moved her family to Rome and began writing exclusively in Italian, a language in which, by her own description, she is "not rooted."[17] The move raised eyebrows. As Lahiri told a reviewer in 2017, she felt the "heavy burden" of the Indian community's expectations and received numerous anxious queries in the vein of "But won't you be writing about me, my family, my experiences anymore?"[18] Well, no, Lahiri responded: "I would rather find another job."[19]

Lahiri's move away from English stemmed from a desire for "metamorphosis" and "transformation."[20] Theorizing this move then became the new subject of her writing. Fittingly, her first book in Italian was also her first memoir, *In Altre Parole*, which was translated into English by Ann Goldstein and published as *In Other Words* in a bilingual edition in 2016. *In Other Words* is what Alice Kaplan terms a "language memoir": a work that dramatizes the motivations, loves, fears, and "emotional tenor" underlying language learning, as well as "how new selves, new families emerge in a second language . . . as a mirror of the first one."[21] Lahiri describes it as "a travel book," "book of memory," and "book of love," as well as "an indigenous book, born and raised here in Italy."[22] In Italian, she found the liberation of being a true "foreigner,"[23] while previously she was stuck playing the part of the American ethnic subject.

Lahiri has since written four other books in Italian: *Il vestito dei libri* (an essay translated into English as *The Clothing of Books* by her husband, Alberto Vourvoulias-Bush), *Dove mi trovo* (a novel, which Lahiri herself translated into English as *Whereabouts*), *Il quadrino di Nerina* (a book of poetry, not yet translated into English at the time of this writing), and *Racconti Romani* (translated by Lahiri with Todd Portnowitz as *Roman Stories*). *Nerina* is Lahiri's first book of poetry, a form she says she would never have attempted if not for "the intimate exposure to the Italian language that only translation can provide."[24] Indeed, translation has become fundamental to Lahiri's account of her identity and vocation, both in the present and retrospectively. She has gone from expressing a desire to be "two" writers ("It is not possible to become another writer, but it might be possible to become two")[25] to a desire to be something other than a writer: namely, a translator. Between 2017 and 2021, Lahiri translated three books by Domenico Starnone from Italian into English. She also compiled, edited, and cotranslated *The Penguin Book of Italian Short Stories*. In 2021, Lahiri began collaborating with classicist Yelena Baraz to produce a new translation of Ovid's *Metamorphoses*, from Latin into English.

Translation, Lahiri writes, is the highest, most intimate form of reading and writing praxis. She makes this argument in 2022's *Translating Myself and Others*, a book of essays written in English and Italian (the latter are translated either by Lahiri alone or in collaboration). In this collection, Lahiri recasts her earlier ethnic Anglophone fiction as itself an act of translation by a child of immigrants whose characters talked "in Bengali in my head" and then needed to be translated "falsely but necessarily, into English speakers." She writes: "I have been thinking about translation for my entire conscious life"; "I was a translator before I was a writer, not the other way around"; "I have always been a translator. To be a writer-translator is to value both being and becoming."[26]

With these declarations, Lahiri seems to have responded definitively to Chaudhuri's goad, quoted earlier, not only that the writer's job is "not to be Jhumpa Lahiri," but that even "Jhumpa Lahiri doesn't think that it's her job to be Jhumpa Lahiri, but to work out what her writing is about."[27] In fact, Lahiri's turn to metacritical self-assessment is a deeply ironic move, given her own stated rejection of authorial intervention: "A reader's relationship is with the book, with the words, not with the person who created it. I don't want the author to explain anything to me or to interfere."[28] She has often said that she writes for herself, not her audience; however, since her Italian turn, she is increasingly engaged with and directly responsive to the critical discourse on her work.[29]

Perhaps the writer who is now engaging critics and explaining Lahiri's past and present work to readers is not Lahiri the author, but Lahiri the translator—who both is and isn't the Lahiri we once knew. By that same token, if this new Lahiri's project is "to work out what her writing is about," what work remains for the critic? How do we read Lahiri's own account of her oeuvre in relation to the extant discourse on it? When a writer tells us that they want to be another writer, that they wish to forget their own language, do we take them at their word? Or, through the distancing labors of critical interpretation, should we try to return the object to itself? In whose voice is Lahiri speaking when she speaks and writes in Italian? What are the politics of her linguistic turn? And what are its implications for the future teaching of Lahiri as an Asian American writer or in the context of the postcolonial?

If these questions sound familiar, they should. I have been arguing in this book that Indian English literature becomes ethnic, postcolonial, and Anglophone by and through the writer's resistance to the burden of representation: Mukherjee's resistance to the ethnic, Chaudhuri's resistance to the postcolonial, and Bhagat's resistance to elite Indian Anglophonism. In this chapter, the writer's resistance takes on each of these forms and one more, as Lahiri's "post-Anglophone"[30] turn to Italian opens up yet another point of entry into our understanding of the ideological construction of the Indian English writer. Like Mukherjee, Bhagat, and Chaudhuri, Lahiri invites critics into a hermeneutic circle in which our readings of her work have always already been cued by her assessments of it, both retrospective and anticipatory. Her post-Anglophonism is a project of self-erasure and self-formation, negation and affirmation. It is at once anti-identitarian and profoundly identitarian.

In what follows, I continue to strive for a form of critical practice that is invested not only in the identities and locations of writers, but also in the scholar-critic's own desires and dislocations, a form of critical practice that listens closely to the way the writer's words echo in our own readings and writings. Rather than bridle at the demand that Indian American women writers must be like Lahiri or that Indian American critics must have something to say about Lahiri, my accented reading attends to the fact that even Jhumpa Lahiri doesn't exactly want to be Jhumpa Lahiri—or at least not in the way she once was. By considering Lahiri's own theory of translation and linguistic experimentation alongside the critical discourse on her work, we can derive a counterepistemology of the Indian English writer: one who relinquished her ties to India, the English language, and even "being Jhumpa Lahiri"—and paradoxically renewed her claim on all three.

Act I: Who Jhumpa Lahiri Was

I asked the students in my fall 2022 South Asian literature class about Lahiri's "overfamiliarity" because that's what I was thinking when the tables were turned and I was in their place. When I was assigned *The Namesake* in college, it got under my skin in the way that many novels do: not because of the novel itself, but because of what I feared it represented (and to whom), because of its exuberant reception, because of its place in the world republic of letters—and most of all because of its status in our classroom. When I became the professor who assigned Lahiri's work, I wanted my students to know that I knew what she might negatively represent to them: namely, "model minority" mythology, ethnic assimilationist imperatives, and diasporic identity crisis. All three were invoked by my student when he joked that Lahiri's books are always about Ivy League graduate students (model minorities) falling in love with white people (assimilating), which feels crazy (identity crisis).

Long before Lahiri turned her writerly identity into the subject of her writing, the question of her identity vexed critics. Ethnic or postcolonial? Anthropological or allegorical? Particular or universal? In their introduction to *Naming Jhumpa Lahiri*, Lavina Dhingra and Floyd Cheung even question the "Indianness" of her authorship: "Is she a Bengali, Indian, Asian American, American, or a post-colonial writer? Is she simply a writer? Does what we name her matter?"[31]

Lahiri is both ethnic and postcolonial, critics typically conclude; her work makes clear that "the postcolonial is always already within the South Asian American."[32] Likewise, Lahiri's ethnic fiction is read as both anthropological and allegorical: as attending with a participant-observer's precision to one specific community ("mainly professional, middle-class, and upper-middle-class Bengali immigrants and their children living along the Boston-New York corridor")[33] and as reaching for broader meaning, whether regarding Asian Americans, migrants, diasporic subjects, or human beings. Min Hyoung Song finds a way through this seeming contradiction by drawing a critical distinction between allegoresis and allegory. On the one hand, Song observes, Lahiri chooses "to write about her own ethnic group, therefore fulfilling marketplace demands that she do exactly this"; on the other hand, she "foils the process by which her fiction can be read as ethnographic fact by inviting readers to read the literalness of her work and thus to consider how allegory as genre can block pervasive and routine forms of allegoresis."[34] In other words: Lahiri confirms and flouts readers' expectations of the text in one move, by employing what Song terms "allegory against allegory."[35]

Song's reading points us to the key question posed by both mainstream reviewers and academic critics of Lahiri's early work: namely, how to assess its simultaneously "particular" and "universal" qualities. Susan Koshy observes that critics often fail to recognize Lahiri's "minority cosmopolitanism" because of their inability to conceptualize ethnic particularity as anything other than an obstacle to the universal. They credit Lahiri with "her ability to render ethnicity transposable,"[36] resulting in what Reddy also describes as the "standardized popular reading of Lahiri's fiction as emblematic of 'universal' themes of human experience."[37] Lahiri's fiction is applauded for not being *too* ethnic (so ethnic as to impede recognition), while preserving its legibility and audibility *as* ethnic (so as to fulfill the publishing industry's demand for multicultural content). When the Anglo-American reviewer credits Lahiri with rendering "her" particular, ethnic, limited experience of minoritarian "difference" legible to a broad readership, what they really reveal, in other words, are dominant ideologies of national belonging and the racialized, gendered terms in which they conceive of the universal.

By contrast, Koshy argues that Lahiri refashions "the diasporic citizen" as a nonidentitarian representation of "a condition under globalization that affects the long-settled and the migrant"; in this way, she enables readers "to imagine an impossible hospitality from the position of the other who cannot feel at home."[38] The operative word here is "condition," in contrast to identity. For Koshy, Lahiri's subject is not identity at all, but rather "the field in which identities are redefined and communities transformed."[39] Crystal Parikh, like Song, reads Lahiri allegorically, noting that the stories in *Unaccustomed Earth* "provide allegories of the variable and unstable experiences of [embodied] vulnerability and desire."[40] Reddy reframes the particular-universal binary, observing how the writer's "ethnic" beauty shores up her "global" appeal.[41]

Song, Koshy, Parikh, and Reddy, along with Asha Nadkarni and Kalyan Nadiminti, are US-based academic scholar-critics who have found in Lahiri a more nuanced, even radical politics belied by popular characterizations of her work as "immigrant fiction," a category she herself rejects.[42] For Song, the potential of an Asian American writer like Lahiri inheres in her ability to thematize racial difference, as opposed to ethnic resemblance.[43] Koshy argues that *Interpreter of Maladies* rejects "a claim to national membership" in the United States and revels in the exilic contours of diasporic subjectivity: the experience of "not being at home in the world,"[44] or what James Clifford terms "'not here' to stay."[45] Reddy, too, finds in Lahiri's debut collection a critique of "national attachments" that reveals the failures of "neoliberal modes of transnational belonging."[46] (By contrast, consider the title of the *New York Times*' review of *Interpreter of Maladies*: "Liking America, but Longing for India.")[47]

Moreover, Lahiri is understood to have waged this critique by deforming the private sphere of reproductive family values on which the exclusionary official-national public sphere of the United States relies.[48] *Unaccustomed Earth*, Koshy argues in this vein, offers a "devastating" "feminist" critique of how the immigrant family serves as a "vehicle for the reproduction of human capital and cultural identity."[49] In stories about intergenerational dynamics, career choices, unrequited love, adultery, and dud marriages (like "Hell-Heaven," discussed at the top of this chapter), the "emotional infrastructure" of the family is disturbed, inheritance is "deranged,"[50] and its conscription into the neoliberal projects of the nation-state is revealed. Similarly, Nadiminti reads in *The Lowland* a significant "disavowal of reproductive labor" that disrupts the "sanctioned narrative of American family values" through the character Gauri's disavowal of caregiving responsibilities to her daughter and rejection of joyless domesticity.[51] In the process, Nadiminti argues, Lahiri's novel debunks the model minority narrative and its fantasy of nuclear family formation.[52]

Contra Nadiminti's reading of *The Lowland*, which focuses on Gauri, Nadkarni focuses on the character of Gauri's husband, Subhash, whose deceased brother Udayan was a Naxalite. Reading the novel's move from depicting Udayan's revolutionary activism in India to detailing Subhash's academic research in the United States, Nadkarni is wary of "the postcolonial being domesticated within the Asian American."[53] I note this not to adjudicate between Nadiminti's and Nadkarni's readings, but in order to underscore that *The Lowland* contains within it both a political refusal of the domestic and the domestication of the political—and that this contradiction is at the heart of Lahiri's work.

Feminist literary theorists have long argued that the domestic is a profoundly political sphere; in this spirit, Lahiri uses the domestic to "relocate" rather than "avoid" the political.[54] The "unlikely radicalism"[55] of her texts inheres in the smoldering suffering of a mother like Aparna, doused in kerosene, as she contemplates suicide, before returning to the house to cook dinner for her remote husband and unknowing child. Here, by way of an extended example, is how Lahiri writes just that scene in "Hell-Heaven." It is recounted from daughter Usha's perspective, years later, at the close of the story:

> [My mother] had gone through the house, gathering up all the safety pins that lurked in drawers and tins, and adding them to the few fastened to her bracelets. When she'd found enough, she pinned them to her sari one by one, attaching the front piece to the layer of material underneath, so that no one would be able to pull the garment off her body. Then she took a can of lighter fluid and a box of kitchen matches and stepped outside, into our chilly back yard, which was full of leaves needing to be raked. Over her sari she was wearing a kneelength lilac trenchcoat, and to any neighbor she must have looked as though she'd simply stepped out for some fresh air. She opened up the coat and removed the tip from the can of lighter fluid and doused herself, then buttoned and belted the coat. She walked over to the garbage barrel behind our house and disposed of the fluid, then returned to the middle of the yard with the box of matches in her coat pocket. For nearly an hour she stood there, looking at our house, trying to work up the courage to strike a match. It was not I who saved her, or my father, but our next-door neighbor, Mrs. Holcomb, with whom my mother had never been particularly friendly. She came out to rake the leaves in her yard, calling out to my mother and remarking how beautiful the sunset was. "I see you've been admiring it for a while now," she said. My mother agreed, and then she went back into the house. By the time my father and I came home in the early evening, she was in the kitchen boiling rice for our dinner, as if it were any other day.[56]

This passage is an exemplary instance of what critics often describe as the "still-life-like quality"[57] of Lahiri's fiction: how she defamiliarizes the ordinary by "employing restricted or shifting focalization to plumb the teeming constraints and pressures that lurk beneath its surface."[58] Beneath the trenchcoat, a woman's sari doused in lighter fluid. Inside her pocket, a box of matches. Covering the yard, unraked leaves. Within a pot of rice, near suicide. Alongside death, just "any other day."

Like many of Lahiri's self-contained characters who do not explicitly voice their pain or ambivalent struggles, Aparna does not declare her love for Pranab, or her devastation over his love for Deborah. The child Usha does not condemn Pranab for his disregard of her mother's feelings, or give details of her own later heartbreak. More than once, this restrained style has opened Lahiri to criticism. For example, Urmila Seshagiri reads the "hallmark restraint" and "totalizing clarity" of her early fiction as lacking "self-reflexive artistry."[59] Other have found her characters strangely "bereft,"[60] her style "glacial, impersonal,"[61] and her narration "cold, almost clinical."[62] Her characters, one reviewer charges, are not adequately "torn between two cultures."[63] Considering these assessments of Lahiri's style in the context of "Hell-Heaven," it strikes me that, yes, there is not a lot of "confession" or "self-display"[64] in the passage I've just quoted, or anywhere in the story.

But lacking "self-reflexive artistry"? Aparna very nearly lights herself on fire.

Act II: Who Jhumpa Lahiri Became

I will return to the image of Aparna—a woman and mother on the verge of self-annihilation—for what it suggests about Lahiri's own writerly project, inhabitance of liminal spaces, and experiments with self-deformation and reformation. In this section, I unpack a series of binaries that structure how critics have thus far assessed the turn in Lahiri's literary career since 2012, which my section titles refer to as "act one" and "act two": English/Italian; fiction/nonfiction; realism/modernism; immigrant/emigrant; identitarian/nonidentitarian; and expert/amateur. These are the pairs of terms through which one might conceivably teach Lahiri's metamorphosis to students, and they put pressure on the assumptions revealed by my own pedagogical misfire ("Is this overfamiliar?"). I will draw attention to how each binary functions discursively, drawing from both Lahiri's own writing and the extant criticism, in order to lay bare the mutual implication and instability of its terms. I then turn in the next section to the desire for the post-Anglophone that underlies each assessment of her turn. The next time I teach Lahiri, I will present both phases of her writing differently, and I proceed in that heuristic spirit.

FIRST, ENGLISH/ITALIAN

Here's one way to tell Lahiri's story: Just over a decade into her literary career, she stopped writing in one language, English, and started writing in another, Italian. But this was not actually Lahiri's first linguistic transformation. It was a restaging of the move she made as a child from her first language, Bengali, into her second, English. In her first act, Lahiri lived between the Bengali of her home and the English of school and street. Her identity was "divided"; she felt herself to be "incomplete" and "deficient." She writes: "As a girl in America, I tried to speak Bengali perfectly, without a foreign accent, to satisfy my parents, and above all to feel that I was completely their daughter. But it was impossible. On the other hand, I wanted to be considered an American, yet, despite the fact that I speak English perfectly, that was impossible, too. I was suspended rather than rooted." From the vantage of the future, Lahiri's linguistic childhood emerges as a rehearsal of the adult's eventual turn toward Italian: a language that she can also never "completely" possess and in which she will never be "rooted," either.[65] So the story is better expressed like this: Just over a decade into her literary career, Lahiri began to read and write in Italian. In so doing, she added a third language to what had previously been a bilingual project of interpretation and translation between Bengali and English. Equally, she replaced one overdetermining binary (Bengali-English) with another (English-Italian). In her own words, she is not rooted in any of these languages.

SECOND, FICTION/NONFICTION

When Lahiri first switched from English to Italian, she went from primarily writing ethnographic fiction (two books of short stories and two novels) to the writing of self-reflexive nonfictional memoirs and essays. When she then started writing fiction in Italian, it was largely episodic and abstract, devoid of the characterization, texture, and even proper names of her early work.

Her first book-length work of Italian fiction was *Whereabouts*, which unfolds through forty-six brief chapters narrated by an unnamed middle-aged woman writer as an effort to keep "track" of herself as she "perfects" the condition of solitude. As the title suggests, *Whereabouts* is about place: where we are at home and not; what it feels like to be placeless and "surrounded by things that don't belong" to us. Even places that the narrator calls her own sometimes keep her "at arm's length." When others enter her space, they might "contaminate" it; sharing space with others, she feels "trapped." By that same token, she is fascinated by how others take up space—how another woman, for example, "manages to fully inhabit and possess" a certain room in a museum.[66]

Whereabouts dramatizes how we watch each other, as if we were people "on television." The novella achieves this with little dialogue and minimal plot through abstract sketches of "intersecting" lives: of the narrator's parents, whose words from years ago nip irritatingly at her "heels"; her neighbor, with whom she might have "shared a life"; strangers, with whom she feels a "tacit bond"; and friends whose "successful" lives with "husband, kids, constant plans, a country house" represent to her the path not taken. The major action of *Whereabouts* takes place at its close, as the narrator is about to take up a fellowship in another city. She decides to "remove every trace of [herself]" from the city in which she has lived. Preparing for her departure, she enacts the kind of demolition that Lahiri herself enacted when she moved to Rome to begin a new life in a new language and become another writer: "I tell myself: A new sky awaits me, even though it's the same as this one. . . . I might have said no, I might have just stayed put. But something's telling me to push past the barrier of my life."[67]

As the narrator journeys away from herself, she sees another woman dressed like her, offering a vision of her unlived life. "I'm me," she thinks, "and also someone else. . . . I'm leaving and also staying."[68] The narrator of *Whereabouts* is not Lahiri. But words that Lahiri has used to describe herself apply equally to the narrator. "On the one hand, I want desperately to belong," she reflects. "On the other, I refuse . . ." "Who am I?" she asks. "I write not only to avoid the question, but also to seek the answer."[69]

Are "fiction" and "nonfiction" adequate terms with which to capture Lahiri's writing's play with truth and the real, authorial distance and intimacy, the revelation of the self and the investigation of the other? In *In Other Words*, Lahiri retrospectively characterizes her Anglophone fiction as "realistic," but she does this in order to distinguish it from a lesser-category she rejects and has long been accused of inhabiting: the autobiographical. At the same time, she writes: "Unlike my other books, [the memoir] is rooted in my real, lived experiences."[70] The further Lahiri moves away from "her" languages (English and Bengali) and "her" Indian American experiences, the more conventionally autobiographical she becomes.

THIRD, REALISM/MODERNISM

Which brings us to the question of realism. For some critics, Lahiri's rebirth in Italian marks "the birth of a modernist," who has gone from producing "patient, polished," and "lucid realism" to one who now revels in abstraction, aesthetic play, "rule-breaking," and "reinvention" in the spirit of Pablo Picasso and Virginia Woolf.[71] Comparing Lahiri's Anglophone fiction to the Italian fiction included in *In Other Words*, Seshagiri writes: "For the first time in her literary career, Lahiri offers us defamiliarizing, ambiguous fiction stripped of realism's reassurances." In Italian, Lahiri's writing is "urgent," "ecstatic," and "disjointed"; it revels in "separation" and "confusion." As we saw in chapter 5's discussion of Chaudhuri, "realism" and "modernism" are often code words for claims about political efficacy, aesthetic value, the literariness of the literary, and a text's global or universal—as opposed to ethnic or national—appeal. In this light, Seshagiri's laudatory observations of Lahiri's turn may be symptomatic of the broader devaluation of both ethnic fiction and realism.

By that same token, a lack of grounding in the real can be an accusation of inauthenticity. Sathian reads Lahiri's Italian writing as lacking "a sense of place."[72] Tim Parks writes that *In Other Words* has none of "the color and drama" of Italy. Eileen Battersby finds it entirely devoid of "the clamour of Italian life."[73] This is also how some critics are reading *Roman Stories*: as not realist enough. Revisiting Lahiri's Anglophone fiction in light of her Italian stories, Aditya Gandhi laments that "at least [the early work] contained real-seeming characters in real-seeming places."[74] The question, it seems to me, is not whether Lahiri is a realist or a modernist, but why the supposed deficiency of her Indian English fiction (its hyperreal "PBS-quality cultural instruction")[75] is now being held up as desirable corrective to the abstractions of her Italian prose—and by whom.

FOURTH, IMMIGRANT/EMIGRANT

Lahiri is, by her own description, an American. In the first act of her writing life, she felt called as a child of Indian immigrants to "restore a lost country" to her parents who were "in mourning"[76] for India and Bengali. In her second act, she emigrated from the United States to Italy. Rather than a rejection of her parents' journey and attachments, this move was a considered reenactment of her parents' story. Consider how Lahiri described her parents' immigrant experience just before making her own move to Rome:

> [Unlike "the Jews during World War II, the Irish, even the Puritans," my parents] didn't have to come here for their very existence, their survival. They were here for the sake of greater opportunities. . . . And yet it was tough, because they had taken such a huge step and left so much behind. The way my parents explain it to me is that they have spent their immigrant lives feeling as if they are on a river with a foot in two different boats. Each boat wants to pull them in a separate direction, and my parents are always torn between the two. They are always hovering, literally straddling two worlds, and I have always thought of that idea, that metaphor, for how they feel, how they live. . . . I think being an immigrant must teach you so much about the world and about human beings, things you can't understand if you are born and raised and live your whole life in one place. It must be an amazing experience in many ways, but it has a price.[77]

These are almost exactly the same terms Lahiri will later use to describe her relocation. Like her parents, she moves volitionally: not for existential survival, but for greater (artistic) opportunities. Her turn to Italian is "a choice . . . a risk," "an act of demolition, a new beginning." *In Other Words* dramatizes the experience of language learning as one of being pulled in "separate directions" and "straddling two worlds." Studying a new language is like having to cross a lake: "To know a new language, to immerse yourself, you have to leave the shore. Without a life vest." Equally, it is like being in the middle of a bridge: "It might collapse at any moment. . . . English flows under my feet"; "I could survive . . . in English. I wouldn't drown. And yet, because I don't want any contact with the water, I build bridges." In relation to her parents' "hovering," Lahiri likens language learning to lingering before a locked gate: "I am on the threshold, I can see inside, but the gate won't open."[78]

This is her parent's "amazing experience" of immigration to the United States—repeated with a difference. Lahiri's transformation is a deliberate response to her mother's "refusal to change" in the United States. At the same time, moving to Italy allows Lahiri "to know my characters better, my parents." When Lahiri eventually returns to the United States, as a reverse migrant, she understands anew her parents' yearning for their language. She misses Italian deeply and mourns the loss of the Roman soundscape.[79] Moving to Italy takes Lahiri further away from her parents, in one sense; at the same time, it brings her closer to them than ever before.

THE FIFTH BINARY: IDENTITARIAN/NON-IDENTITARIAN

So in which phase of her writing life has Lahiri been most concerned with questions of "identity": in the realistic ethnic fictions about Bengali American immigrants and their children, or in the language memoir and essays rooted in her own experience? Is Lahiri more profoundly a writer of the self when she is detailing characters who she and her family resemble, or when she is exploring the process of becoming other to herself and her family? Is Lahiri an Indian English writer when she is "[restoring] a lost country to my parents"[80] or when she is enmeshed in a subject (here, the pursuit of Italian) that entirely "arises from *me*"?[81]

If we take Lahiri at her word, her refashioning of herself as a linguistic pioneer is clearly in the spirit of—or an act of fulfillment of—her own parents' journey. And yet, one frequent characterization of Lahiri's Italian phase is that it marks her turn *away* from identity, specifically her identity as a postcolonial Indian writer. Reviewing *Whereabouts*, Ben Moser observes that Lahiri had the classic immigrant child's experience of shuttling between her parent's language and English, and that this shuttling is central to her work. But then, contra his own observation, he writes this: "Yet she does not dwell on what one might call the postcolonial or political aspects of her own biography. Neither is she encumbered by the pieties that often surround writing on translation."[82]

Three p's are being dismissed here: postcolonial, political, and pieties. "She does not dwell on the postcolonial" is offered as praise: Lahiri has transcended what we are to understand as hackneyed postcolonial pieties concerning the afterlives of colonialism, the fetters of history and nation, the politics of language, the trap of hybrid subjectivity, and the demands of community and identity. In her essay on Lahiri's modernist turn, Seshagiri performs almost the same move as Moser: "[Lahiri] is no Caliban: her crisis of language lacks the plangent note of postcolonial discontent." She adds that notwithstanding Lahiri's in-depth recounting of her "bilingual childhood," her "aesthetic ambitions—as ever—stand apart from the historical particulars of Indian identity." Likewise, Parks approvingly remarks that Lahiri has "concerned herself not to be pigeonholed as a postcolonial author."[83]

In the preceding chapters, we have encountered numerous repudiations of identity and diminishments of the postcolonial—not only from outside detractors, but also as a ritual rhetorical gesture within the field itself. Some scholars chafe against the term "postcolonial" because it is an analytic we are expected to embody given our particular embodiments. Some lament that the prefix "post-" has led to misunderstandings of the field's relationship to transnational and transhistorical colonialisms. Postcolonialists are in part embattled about the field's identity, I have argued, and the postcolonial is perpetually being rebranded, because we are embattled about identity in general.

For literature scholars, the key terrain on which the drama of identitarian assignment and refusal plays out is that of language, which is why I am interested in the critical response to Lahiri's linguistic turn. When Moser offers Lahiri the backhanded compliment of not dwelling on the postcolonial and the "apparatus of inherited expression," and when Seshagiri notes that her "ambitions—as ever—stand apart from the historical particulars of Indian identity," they are essentially saying that Lahiri is not or is no longer giving in to a crass politics of identity. In writing in Italian, she has supposedly freed herself from who she is, was, might have been, and appears to be.

But what kind of freedom is freedom from the postcolonial? What kind of freedom is freedom from inheritance, and from English? Have we so thoroughly metabolized the critique of identity politics that we are most eager to celebrate a writer's self-annihilation, just so long as it is the ethnic and postcolonial laid out on the pyre? When does the rejection of the coercive mimetic imperative become as knee jerk and routinized as participation in it? Are we not yet tired of the imperative of *not* appearing as ourselves, just because of the inverse imperative that we do so? What would it mean to do justice to the apparatuses of earned and inherited expression, and attend to the dynamics of their intermingling?

In this section thus far, each binary structuring our apprehension of the two acts of Lahiri's writing life has emerged as unstable. The title given to Moser's review—"Jhumpa Lahiri leaves her comfort zone"—is therefore a particularly ironic way of describing her 2012 turn. Lahiri's work has always been about discomfort, unbelonging, "geographical, cultural and linguistic displacement," and the experience of being unmoored. She has often said that she has no home to which to return: "I am exiled even from the definition of exile."[84] Likewise, her characters are "not at home even at home."[85] Lahiri's mother tongue is "paradoxically, a foreign language" to her; her characters, too, speak a "monolingualism of the other."[86]

Long before she began writing in Italian, Lahiri's fictions were preoccupied with the otherness of the self. For example, in "Mrs. Sen's," from *The Interpreter of Maladies*, the child Eliot carefully observes his new babysitter, for whom the story is named. He's never seen anyone like her—from her "shimmering white sari" to her chappals, which he sees as "flip-flops"—and yet the result of her unusual aspect is to make his *own* mother appear "odd." Mrs. Sen, meanwhile, is grappling with the distance between her alienating life in the United States and her family in India's misconceptions about it: "They think I live the life of a queen, Eliot."[87]

By way of another example, Gogol of *The Namesake* is an exemplary "ABCD": American Born Confused Desi. He struggles with his name, his parents, his Indianness, and his identity. Growing up, he feels at a "remove" even from his own birthday parties, and he attempts to establish "distance from his origins."[88] At the same time, he is aware that his parents are trying hard to bridge that same distance. As a young man, Gogol has a series of white American girlfriends before he ultimately marries another Bengali, Moushumi. It is an ill-fated marriage, because of both Gogol's own confusion and Moushumi's "rejection of identity." Moushumi immerses herself in French; she takes "refuge" in a language and culture that is not her own, along with an extramarital lover.[89]

None of these characters is Lahiri. And all of these characters are Lahiri. Gogol is Lahiri, whose kindergarten teacher could not pronounce her given name, Nilanjana.[90] Moushumi, who "wants a release from expectation," is Lahiri, too.[91] Subhash from *The Lowland*, who studies how aquatic ecosystems metabolize pollution and foreign substances, is Lahiri, who is fascinated with the transformative potential of that which is "outside of us."[92] Usha from "Hell-Heaven" is the child Lahiri, who expresses herself most fully in English, although her parents speak to her in Bengali. And Gauri in *The Lowland*—who "remained, in spite of her Western clothes, her Western academic interests, a woman who spoke English with a foreign accent, whose physical appearance and complexion were unchangeable and, against the backdrop of most of America, still unconventional"—is the adult Lahiri, who, in spite of her Italian writing and interests, retains her Indian American's English accent, and whose physical appearance and complexion are unchangeable and, against the Italian backdrop, still unconventional.[93]

Like the author herself, Lahiri's characters have always been consumed by the challenge of self-making. Some, like Gogol, cannot "reinvent [themselves] fully";[94] those who come closest often pay a price. Lahiri's turn to Italian can thus be viewed not only as a reenactment of her parents' journey but also as the fulfillment of a narrative she has been writing since the late 1990s. "I've been telling stories all along about characters who change country, who transform their reality," she writes.[95]

Back to Moser. If Lahiri has left anyone's comfort zone, it is plainly not hers, but the critic's.

CUE OUR SIXTH BINARY: EXPERT/AMATEUR

These are the terms in which Lahiri at first describes her transformation: "I renounce expertise to challenge myself. I trade certainty for uncertainty." By embracing a condition of "useful" ignorance in Italian—ignorance that makes her experience of reading and writing more intense—Lahiri becomes an "author" who doesn't "feel authoritative." By trading her credentialed and internationally lauded expertise in English for an amateur, autodidactic adventure in Italian, she learns anew how "to write." Whereas her English prose bears the burden of her mastery, Lahiri's Italian is free to be imperfect, awkward, and peculiar. In short, Italian allows Lahiri to struggle and feel alive. By contrast, her English, condemned to the inertia of perfection, "no longer appeals."[96]

Over the past decade, the concept of amateurism has gained traction in three different but cross-cutting conversations in the humanities: on postcritique, the postcolonial, and interdisciplinarity.[97] Numerous scholars are currently working to cultivate humility as a critical disposition, to unlearn mastery, and to acknowledge the foundational nature of nonknowledge. This is perhaps why critics have generally accepted Lahiri's account of her Italian writing as an exercise in unskilling and "experiment with weakness."[98] In *In Other Words*, she asks questions that are at the heart of these specific debates on the value of humanistic scholarship and creative writing: "Can I call myself an author if I don't feel authoritative?"; "Why does poverty satisfy me?"[99] Reading such questions, Seshagiri concurs that Lahiri has "sacrifice[d] the serene, authoritative perfection of her English." For Rebecca Walkowitz, her "knowledgeable not-knowing—refusing to be the master of words—is a precondition of civic hospitality."[100]

And yet, Lahiri's amateur Italian is compelling to scholar-critics precisely because she is no amateur. The fascination of her first Italian book, *In Other Words*, is the opportunity to read "bad writing" by a master writer, and to revel in the knower's knowing engagement with not knowing.[101] To this end, I read Lahiri's memoir as a form of "method writing"—to riff off Lucas Thompson's "method reading," discussed in chapter 3—in which Lahiri appears to be trading the visible "protection" of English for "exposure" in Italian, but all the while retains her bodyguards just out of sight.[102] Despite her profession of being "alone" on the page,[103] Lahiri has financial resources, contacts, translators, editors, and a publishing apparatus that only a handful of writers in the world could match. Is it "poverty" we are encountering here, then, or a kind of luxury linguistic tourism? Unskilling or reskilling? While the collaborative nature of Lahiri's Italian writing notably complicates the conventional story of autonomous, individual authorial mastery, in my view it more powerfully lays bare the extent to which Lahiri's "amateurism" is a direct product of what her expertise affords her, and not a repudiation of that expertise at all. (Just as, to return to the preceding chapter, Said's success as an amateur intellectual depended on his professional location.)

This, then, is the second irony: What may have begun as an experiment in amateurism has clearly evolved into a performance of the acquisition of mastery. Lahiri's Italian books don't go on reveling in not knowing; they unfold a process of coming-to-know. In order to write through ignorance, Lahiri has to learn Italian. In learning Italian—in penetrating the language's "closed spaces . . . secrets . . . the unknown"[104]—she loses the specific affordances of what she does not know. It becomes clear that what Lahiri most desires from Italian—intimacy and proximity—is an eventuality she fears and defers, yet cannot, ultimately, avoid. In *In Other Words*, Lahiri states emphatically that if she should ever master Italian, its appeal would be gone: "If it were possible to bridge the distance between me and Italian, I would stop writing in that language."[105] When she first attempts to translate her Italian short stories into English, the latter cannibalizes the former.[106] But by the time she writes *Translating Myself and Others* and *Roman Stories*, Lahiri has become an expert writer and translator in Italian; knowing Italian has even improved her English. Moving fluidly between the two languages, Lahiri acknowledges a mutually strengthening relationship between them (which is maybe why her next project is a translation from Latin). The journey into nonknowledge has reconfigured the knower.

Desire for the Post-Anglophone: Lahiri's and Ours

The previous section considered how Lahiri's turn from English to Italian has been described by critics and reviewers in terms of major transformations at the level of genre, form, style, and theme—even though the turn has conserved and renewed her long-standing literary and political projects. Similarly, the rubric of the post-Anglophone appears to mark the transcendence of the Anglophone paradigm, even as it performs a familiar post-postcolonial critical move. What I am calling the desire for the post-Anglophone, then, is yet another manifestation of the postidentitarian desire I've been discussing throughout this book: the desire to get away from India; the desire to transcend the postcolonial; and the desire to "forget" English.[107] As a critical move, it has followed remarkably swiftly on the heels of the emergence of the Anglophone, which is itself a fairly recent renomination of the postcolonial and an acknowledgment that English is a social and cultural system, in addition to a language.

As a literary category, the post-Anglophone participates in the broader "postmonolingual" and "postlingual turns." For Christopher Cannon and Susan Koshy, the task of the postmonolingual is to rethink the relationship between colonialism and monolingualism, on the one hand, and historical and cultural variants of monolingualism, on the other.[108] For yasser elharity and Walkowitz, the postlingual marks a new orientation in literary studies (drawing on "old" insights from across disciplines) in which languages can no longer be uncritically conceived of as native or foreign, or "additive or countable," but rather as all "additional" languages to each of their readers, speakers, and writers, no matter their relative fluencies and literacies, and "additional" in relation to all other languages, including themselves.[109] Scholars working under both rubrics are responding to long-standing anxieties in postcolonial literary studies about the possession and mastery of languages, their singularity and autonomy, and the inevitability (and menace) of their syncretic mixing.

Thus, Walkowitz reads Lahiri's move into Italian as part of a postlingual turn by migrant writers toward "unpossessing" language; it is "a decision to choose not-knowing rather than have not-knowing thrust upon her." According to Walkowitz, this project contests "the monolingualism and racism of national literatures" differently than did the postcolonial project of "possessing the dominant language"[110] in order to transform it, à la Rushdie's famous chutnification of English. Instead, a writer like Lahiri is transforming what it means for a text to be Anglophone, on the one hand, while emphasizing translation, collaboration, and the partial ownership of languages, on the other. Lahiri's Italian texts enlist "attenuated or collective narration to impede our encounter with native voice or source languages" and in the process expose readers "to other languages."[111]

Walkowitz's argument is explicitly post-postcolonial. She describes Lahiri as a "first-generation migrant" who is "not clearing the space for the right to use a colonial language." She also clubs her with other contemporary writers who are "children of globalization rather than colonization."[112] This is a version of the same move that critics have made with respect to Chetan Bhagat's "global" New Indian English, in contradistinction to the "postcolonial" English of Rushdie and Roy, as discussed in chapter 3. But let's consider the following. Lahiri moved to the United States at age three and considers herself to be an American. As an adult, she migrated to Italy to divest herself of English, which she learned in the United States, not India, which means she encountered the language as a national tongue, not strictly as a colonial bequest. She is motived by the desire to possess another language, Italian, which itself has an indisputably classical and colonial history.[113] To put that differently, Lahiri is only a migrant writer—and only a *postcolonial* writer—now that she possesses Italian, and her project is precisely to clear the space for that right.

To be clear: Walkowitz made these particular arguments relatively early in Lahiri's journey into Italian, and she is right to stress the writer's initial efforts to learn a language she might never possess. As discussed in the preceding section, the appeal of writing in Italian for Lahiri was at first that she could not become an Italian writer. By that same token, I read Lahiri's assignment to the categories of the post-Anglophone, post-monolingual, and postlingual as revealing anew the dominant codes through which we have learned to apprehend what is native and foreign, what is a mother tongue and what is someone else's tongue entirely. As Sohomjit Ray observes, the critical response to Lahiri's turn has thus far been focused almost entirely on her "departure from the monolingual paradigm"; each critic begins from the assumption that "monolingualism is the norm."[114] What if, Ray invites us to ask, we were reading with the bilingual or multilingual writer and reader in mind? What if we acknowledged that the Indian American experience in Lahiri's fiction was already multilingual, even in English? How might we center a reader and writer not steeped in the "monolingual expectations" of Anglophone criticism?[115] When we argue that Lahiri can never possess Italian, what are we assuming about her relationship to her other languages? Might it make sense to think of Lahiri not as possessing this or that language, but as a writer multiply *possessed*?

Before Lahiri, the most famous postcolonial departure from English was Ngũgĩ wa Thiong'o's dramatic turn to writing in Gĩkũyũ.[116] Since the 1980s, this has been the key plot-point in a redemptive story about the postcolonial subject who was at first condemned to speak and write in the colonial language, experienced "self-alienation in self-hearing,"[117] and then said goodbye to English.

Both Ngũgĩ and Lahiri transform English into one of many possible "target" languages for their texts, and not their "source."[118] But that's where the similarities end. Ngũgĩ divests himself of English, a dominant, colonially imposed language, whereas Lahiri pursues Italian, a colonial language she does not yet have. Ngũgĩ's aim, as initially expressed, is the revitalization of a national literature. Lahiri's aim is the renewal of the self. Ngũgĩ's choice is binary: between mother tongue and imperial imposition. Lahiri chooses Italian in order to reconstitute the linguistic binarism of her childhood (Bengali-English) in triangular form (Bengali-English-Italian). Ngũgĩ writes in an African language so as to be able to apprehend African lifeworlds. Lahiri rarely writes about Italy or Italians, some critics observe with "disappointment."[119] Ngũgĩ seeks authenticity. Lahiri craves estrangement. Ngũgĩ's act is a political effort to contest the hegemony of English. Lahiri, in her own description, is playing a privileged "creative game."[120]

Certainly, Lahiri is inviting us to tell another story from Ngũgĩ's, which is why she is being read as a post-postcolonial, post-Anglophone writer. But is hers a story of *unpossession* as such? To put that question in the terms of my section title: What does Lahiri desire from Italian, and what do we critics desire from Lahiri's Italian turn in turn?

The stated reason that Lahiri pursues Italian is "to feel free." She wants a language that is hers alone: one that she can wield as an achieved outcome of *her* passion, desire, and effort—not an overdetermined language that is hers by an accident of birth. And yet, languages are never simply ours, nor can we ever totally possess them, as Lahiri herself knows: "No words are 'my words.'"[121] Even mother tongues alienate. Can you find freedom in using a language that is not itself free? When you know a language, do you also know, in Frantz Fanon's words, "the world expressed and implied by this language"?[122] If a language is not one that you grew up with, if it is not the language of your community, what do you know, by knowing it, of the people to whom it also belongs? "What does it mean, in the end, to belong to a language?"[123] What don't you know when you don't know a language, when it's assumed to be yours?

Some years ago, I was with my then-toddler at a playground in Chicago. A Bulgarian nanny pushing her half-Spanish, half-Italian charge on the next swing watched us, frowning. After a while, she clucked disdainfully and criticized my speaking to my child in English. "You are doing the wrong thing," she scolded, reading my brown skin against my "white" voice.

I stammered a response, flustered by the exposure of my loss. What could I say that would be adequate to my history, which wasn't mine alone? What could I say about the apparatus of English education in the British Raj, and the injunction of colonial mimicry, and the constitution of a class of Indians "more British than the Brits," and my parents' emigration from India after 1965, and my being a second-generation ethnic subject in a country full of paranoid monolinguals, and not choosing *not* to learn "my" language, but having more than one language I hadn't learned?

I immediately recognized the accusation as one that has repeated many times in ethnic and postcolonial writing. In *On Not Speaking Chinese*, Ien Ang, whose ostensible roots in China are complicated by her routes through Indonesia, the Netherlands, and Australia, observes that subjects like her are often "found wanting" in diaspora. She gives the example of how a "self-assured, Dutch, white, middle-class, Marxist leftist" called her "a fake Chinese" when he found out she didn't speak the language.[124] In "Where have all the natives gone?" Rey Chow recounts a similar scene in which an "American Marxist" questions the political identity of a job candidate from China. "An ethnic specimen that was not pure was not of use to him," Chow writes, in words anticipating her later theorization of coercive mimeticism.[125]

The Dutchman's and American's slurs also recall the iconic scene of postcolonial languaging in Hanif Kureishi's *The Buddha of Suburbia*, in which mixed-race Karim, who was raised in South London, is asked to play the part of Mowgli in *The Jungle Book*. Shadwell, the British director, tries to speak to Karim in what he assumes is "[his] own language." Shadwell then reacts with disgust when he learns that Karim not only cannot speak "his own language," but has never been to India. "What a breed of people two hundred years of imperialism has given birth to," Shadwell says to Karim. "Everyone looks at you, I'm sure, and thinks: an Indian boy, how exotic, how interesting, what stories of aunties and elephants we'll hear now from him. And you're from Orpington."[126]

This is what the Bulgarian nanny thought she saw in me: a fake Indian from the American equivalent of Orpington. My not speaking to my child in what she assumed was my language (Malayalam, Tamil, Hindi—all mine and not), like Ang's not speaking Chinese, is "an existential condition which goes beyond the particularities of an arbitrary personal history. It is a condition that has been hegemonically constructed as a lack, a sign of loss of authenticity."[127] The irony, of course, is that there is no such "authenticity" to be named or retrieved outside of that which has been interpellated as such—more often than not *in English*, the very language through which "cultural tradition and originality are ascribed to the colonized."[128]

I offer this reflection for how it speaks to both the overdetermined context in which Lahiri "chooses" Italian and the shared history that conditions readings of her writing in both English and Italian. This history is personal, linguistic, literary, social, and transnational. It lays bare "the emotional violence" of the demand of "authentic cultural identity."[129] It also subtends my accented reading of the critical discourse on Lahiri's work.

In *In Other Words*, Lahiri is obsessed with the pursuit of her love object, Italian. She seeks to make it her own. By the time *Translating Myself and Others* is published, she calls herself "a burglar" who is covetous of an Italian that she now recognizes as "not mine," "not my language."[130] Walkowitz proposes that Italian cannot be Lahiri's, and Lahiri cannot become an Italian writer, because of racializing assumptions about what an Italian should look like, because she "lacks the immersion of many years," and because of "assumptions about how and why women acquire new languages."[131] The elephant in the room—or, in this case, the missing word on the page—is that Lahiri cannot become an Italian writer, because she is already an *Indian* one. She is not a post-Anglophone migrant unpossessing Italian. She is an Indian American writer grappling with the historically specific "diasporic reterritorialization of postcoloniality into ethnicity,"[132] who both possesses and does not possess English and Bengali, who desires Italian, and who is bringing with her into Italian her Indian American readership, readers who read her as an Indian American, and her Indian English accent.

I say this in a critical spirit inflected by my own inhabitance of an Indian American position I "cannot not want"[133] and, like Lahiri, cannot escape. And I say this because, once again, such contradiction is at the heart of Lahiri's work. In Lahiri, we find the tantalizing possibility of linguistic possession and the impossibility of its consummation. We experience simultaneously her desperate longing and refusal to belong.[134] Lahiri's early work gives the lie "to the entrepreneurial myth of self-invention and freedom."[135] At the same time, she maintains, "we can refute our origins."[136] She seeks "detachment" through "immersion."[137] "Identity" as much as "anonymity."[138]

Put simply: Lahiri cannot be an Italian writer because she is an Indian writer. But it is equally true that Lahiri could only become an Italian writer because of her writing in Indian English.

Coda: On Sounding Like Jhumpa Lahiri

I was editing the penultimate draft of this book when *Roman Stories* came out. I bought it, of course, and went to hear Lahiri read from it, all the while cursing the slow pace of academic publishing and myself for writing about living writers, especially productive ones. Was *Roman Stories* going to undo my chapter's claims? I hoped not. Lahiri's Italian novella *Whereabouts* had already confirmed the argument that I was trying to make: In endeavoring to prove that "the writer's job is not to be Jhumpa Lahiri," Lahiri had powerfully returned to her earliest concerns—proving, once again, that "it is only through the far distance that the object comes back to itself."[139]

Roman Stories is a book about migrants, foreigners, travelers in, and returnees to Rome. The characters are variously rooted and unmoored, white collar and working class. Some have "a strategic relationship" with Rome, having acquired the city as a new "[point] of reference" in middle age. For others, being Roman is an accident of birth. Some feel "married" to Rome; others experience the city as a stage of racism and hostility.[140] All of the stories are concerned with questions of proximity and distance, authenticity and impersonation, the apprehension of otherness, and the daily practice of distinguishing natives from strangers.

Lahiri's early fiction was criticized for focusing primarily on the experiences of privileged migrants like the Indian Americans among whom she grew up. In *Roman Stories*, professional-class cocktail party stories are interspersed with narratives about domestic workers and labor migrants, working far from home and alienated from their surrounds. No matter their class positions, all of Lahiri's migrant characters are subject to violence to varying degrees, from feelings of estrangement and experiences of petty bigotry, to housing discrimination, targeted harassment campaigns, and outright physical assault.

In "The Reentry," a lifelong Roman introduces a friend to a trattoria favored by locals, "Even though my city is your city by now." When the nonnative friend is then subject to racist epithets, she realizes that Rome is the only place she "really feel[s] at home" and yet "her relationship with the city is actually quite tenuous." In "Well-Lit House," a migrant observing a local at a bar apprehends his own comparative distance from his surrounds: "it dawned on me that my whole life I'd felt like an intruder or someone passing through."[141]

Story after story poses questions that we are now primed to hear as Lahiri's kinds of questions: Who can be at home in Rome? To whom does Rome belong? Who has the right to tell a "Roman story"? What does a Roman storyteller sound like?

For the most part, *Roman Stories* centers the experiences of foreigners. But Lahiri also writes from the perspective of Italians, Romans, natives, and locals who feel menaced by the arrival of migrants from elsewhere. More than once, this menace is described in linguistic terms. In "The Steps," a widow "feels assaulted, too, by the things people write with their spray cans on the walls that flank the steps. What does that strange, contorted language, cryptic and hideous, mean? . . . she feels insulted. It's a bit like when she hears foreigners talking on the street . . . who work at the market stalls. . . . The incomprehensible writing strikes her as an affront even though it's silent." Similarly, in "The Delivery," a young Italian man who is an accomplice to an assault on a migrant woman describes feeling displaced by people who "have their own little grocery stores" and "put signs in their windows that my family can't read."[142]

In *Vernacular English*, Akshya Saxena observes that English has tremendous symbolic power in India not because of how many people speak or read it but because they have material, corporeal, sonic, and visual relationships to English *despite not being able to speak or read it*. English is "largely unintelligible" to many Indians who confront it on signs, on billboards, on official documents, and in the media, and it becomes "meaningful precisely by not being read." English is experienced as "an acousmatic sound."[143]

Lahiri's stories remind us that even regional, minority, and nondominant (as opposed to global) languages have symbolic resonance for those who do not speak or read them. The sounds and sights of the inscrutable language of the other signify powerfully as *other*—precisely because one is unable to decipher them. (So powerfully in fact as to have led to "globalized theory"—but that is a subject for another book.)[144]

My point is that this is how all languages confront us: sometimes as a locked door; sometimes as an open window; always as something more and other than a linguistic or literary medium. And also, that this is simply the latest version of the old story that Lahiri has been writing all along. Her parents' story: of immigrants whose children speak a foreign "language so well you wouldn't even think they were ours." And her own story: about the desire for metamorphosis by people "who insist on making new lives for themselves"—like the narrator of "Dante Alighieri," who leaves behind her parents, country, childhood, and past, moves to Rome, learns a new language, and becomes convinced that she's "reversed [her] real roots, the original ones."[145]

This narrator is not Lahiri, of course, but—like Gogol and Moushumi, like Gauri and Subhash, like Usha and Aparna, like the narrator of *Whereabouts*—she also profoundly is.

Can you reverse your roots? Can you remake yourself? Can you transcend the accident of birth? Do you have to set yourself on fire? Has Jhumpa Lahiri become an Italian writer?

A few weeks before I finished the final draft of this book, I met a friend who is an avid reader of contemporary fiction. I mentioned that I was writing about Lahiri, and the conversation turned to *Roman Stories*, which he had just read. Well, actually he had listened to it on audio book. "They're stories about Indians," he noted matter-of-factly. "Indians in Rome."

At no point are any of the characters in *Roman Stories* identified as "Indian."

Aha! I thought: Of course, Lahiri is still being overdetermined by readers' expectations of her Indian identity. Even she couldn't help returning to her old concerns. I felt oddly satisfied. At the same time, I was dismayed on Lahiri's behalf. Indians, still? As if she hadn't been writing about everyone all along. As if all of Lahiri's characters could only ever be Indians.

And then I remembered exactly what my friend had said, and on a hunch, I downloaded the English-language audio book of *Roman Stories*. It is narrated by five voice-artists, who, taken together, have lived in Britain, Italy, India, Nigeria, Pakistan, Singapore, and the United States, and speak various languages including Igbo, Italian, Greek, Hindi, and Urdu.[146] They are a cosmopolitan bunch; they speak in what we might call a global English accent.

I clicked on the recording of "The Delivery," in which a working-class woman from somewhere else is shot by a young thug with an air pistol who tells her to wash her "dirty legs." The first half of the story is narrated by the victim, the foreign woman; the second half is narrated by one of the assailants, presumably a young Italian man. I listened. "*I like this pol-ka-dot skirt.*" The Indian English accent, with the pronounced emphasis on the "l" in the middle of the word, was unmistakable. "*I like this pol-ka-dot skirt.*" I fast-forwarded to the second half of the story: "*She was short and wore a polka-dot skirt.*" A male voice spoke in what I heard as an American accent; "polka" here was "poke-a" as opposed to "pol-ka." Two different polka-dot skirts.

I listened to the rest of the audio book, taking notes without cross-referencing each voice to its artist. I heard one woman as "American"; one as "Indian"; couldn't identify the next woman's voice; one sounded "robotic"; another I heard as "African"; the next man (or was it the same man?) sounded "slightly British"; "could be Indian, unclear," I wrote.

One reviewer of the audio book puts it like this: "The mix of voices—Indian subcontinent, mid-American, British-African, Italian-American—highlights the theme of displacement."[147] To me, it highlighted my position of audition, the voice I was listening for.

Which is fitting, when it comes to Jhumpa Lahiri. Fitting that her Roman stories sound Indian, even though they're not. Fitting that all the Indian stories sound like hers, even when they aren't. I will have to assign both her English and Italian fictions to my students next time, along with the audio book, and then ask them which sounds the most "Indian," the most "Italian," the most like "Lahiri"—or not.

I wonder what they will say. We have always wanted Jhumpa Lahiri—and she has tried so hard—to sound like someone else.

Afterword

Writing these words feels like preparing a lecture for the last day of class. I'm torn between competing imperatives: to summarize and retread ground we've covered; but also, to broaden the scope of discussion. I will attempt a little of both at the risk of achieving neither; I will push on until the bell rings in hopes of ending on the right note.

The preceding chapters tell two stories. The first: the story of the overdetermined scholar-teacher, presented in terms of my own journey as an Indian American professor of Indian English literature, via specific institutional scenes that unfold over two decades. The second: the story of the overdetermined writer of Indian English literature, who variously resists the burdens of English, India, the ethnic, the postcolonial, and the Anglophone. In telling these stories together, I have sought to dismantle the hoary divisions between academic writer and writer of literature, between scholar and object, between the critical impulse and the creative drive. I have offered accented readings that are not an expert's definitive explanation of what any text does or says, but rather invested, co-creative engagements with texts by which I have been hailed and their writers, who I have interpellated in turn.

Throughout, I have treated the classroom as the critical node at which these stories and subject positions meet. I have tried to account honestly for my pedagogical missteps, successes, anxieties, and goals, insofar as their excavation might be useful for others seeking to theorize literature from the classroom in years to come. I have been tempted at times to revise the past: to go back into my 2018 "Literatures of Return" syllabus, for instance, and add in the more robust section on Palestine that appears in the latest version of the class. I'd like to revise the 2022 syllabus for "The World and South Asia," too, and bring it up to date. But if I had written different syllabi back then, this would have been a different book.

That's what's so dynamic and generative about teaching, and what I have tried to capture in these pages. An unmotivated reading of a text, written in the homogeneous, empty time of objective criticism, never changes. In contrast, every iteration of a syllabus can be better than the previous one; each is a fresh argument constructed in relation to new texts, contexts, and knowledges. Every class begins on Day 1—which is another way of saying that every class is an opportunity to learn again what you might otherwise risk thinking you already know.

A new semester starts next week. I will be teaching updated versions of "Literatures of Return" and "The World and South Asia," and whatever I offer my students will be thrice-overdetermined. Globally: as the interminable assault on Gaza and the ambivalent status of a once-Rising China powerfully inflect how my students and I grapple with the politics, narrative forms, and (im)possibility of return, and the changing status of South Asia on the world stage. Domestically: as the 2024 US election, and in particular the candidacy of Kamala Harris, resets the terms of the national conversation on immigration, higher education, Asian American communities, and American identity, broadly defined. Professionally: as my colleagues and I continue to grapple with myriad pressures on the humanities, from problems of enrollment and funding, to questions of free speech and academic freedom, to challenges posed by new digital tools, Artificial Intelligence, and online media.

It is a deeply contradictory moment—which is the nature of the contemporary, perhaps. A postpandemic moment in which everyone keeps getting COVID. An era of escalating climate change in which catastrophe is being normalized, instead of addressed. In India, commentators celebrated the lifting of "the suffocating shadow of authoritarianism" after the BJP's electoral losses, but Narendra Modi is still the prime minister.[1] Harris's presidential run has sparked a resurgence of the language of "freedom," "hope," and "joy" in mainstream political discourse, but the defeat of affirmative action and *Roe v. Wade*, the rollback of the advances of the pandemic-era welfare state, mounting economic inequality, and ongoing militarism and imperial violence belie the vibes and rhetorical promise of those words. At my own institution, the School of Humanities just completed a record hiring cycle, and we are launching numerous, innovative interdisciplinary initiatives. But behind closed office doors, some faculty worry that our students are not reading and writing with the sophistication, nuance, and rigor we expect.

As I prepare to meet these challenges, I am also keenly aware that many students who enroll in my particular classes are looking for something other than an education in close reading and literary analysis. They want to know what to do with and how to think about their *identities*. Since moving to Rice, I get emails each semester that say as much:

> Hello Professor Srinivasan . . . My name is . . . I am majoring in . . . I am of south asian ancestry . . . I am Indian and . . . I was really hoping to take a class about my culture to learn more about it.

> Good afternoon Dr. Srinivasan . . . My name is . . . I am very interested in taking the class . . . I grew up in Alabama where diversity was scarce . . . the bulk of my knowledge regarding my culture and its history has been taught to me by my parents.

> Dear Professor . . . My name is . . . As an Asian American whose parents immigrated from India . . . I would love to learn more about my background in an actual classroom setting.

This book has offered an extended response to such declarations of biography, history, interest, hope, and desire. However inadequate representation is as a corrective for injustice, however naïve the politics of recognition may be, and however available identity is for cooptation and perversion, students in US academe often enter the ethnic or postcolonial literature classroom in the hope of engaging literatures by writers, and about communities, they "resemble." For many of them, it's their first opportunity to do so. Or else, they arrive with the expectation of acquiring a new perspective on material they already "know" but seek to know anew. Just as we cannot remain tethered to colonial imaginaries of native informancy, or in the thrall of coercive mimetic performances of ethnic subjectivity, neither can we be dismissive of the multifold attachments that draw students into our classrooms, and that they bring to the table in turn.

In my experience, South Asian American students arrive at university after years of erasure and exclusion from primary and secondary school curricula (except for that world history unit on Harappa and Mohenjo-Daro). They have been interpellated as "model minorities" without regard for social context or history. They have negotiated, often unhappily, the liberal multicultural politics of inclusion on offer in contemporary American film and media.[2] In this context, there is no escaping the "ethnographic and ideological" claims that they will make on texts they recognize, and that we, in teaching said texts, are making on our students in turn.[3] There is no escaping the gaze of the student who takes a class to learn about "their culture"—or, equally, to resist from an "insider" perspective the course's presentation of certain authors and texts.

We can try, of course, to deconstruct the student's possessive "my"—to unschool them in conventional ideas about cultural essences, origins to be pursued, and traditions to be retrieved. That's the approach my college professor took in the 2005 course I described in chapter 7. Or we can develop pedagogical strategies that make space for student contributions of lived experiences, without trafficking in the currency of intimacies and uncritical anecdotes. We can acknowledge the inevitable burden of representation borne by students hailed by the course texts, without demanding that they then serve as informants for their peers. We can critique literature's purchase on the "real," while continuing to think through our desires for it. And we can take up "the invitation of the postcolonial text to think as other, to submit to the difference of the other's ideational world,"[4] while remaining alive to the ways in which we as readers and writers, teachers and students, are also always others to ourselves.

As practitioners of identity studies have long recognized, the "act of knowing [is] related to the power of self-definition," and ethnic and postcolonial studies present "a fundamental challenge to hegemonic knowledge and history."[5] Mounting this challenge is no less our task now in the 2020s than it was in the 1960s or 1990s. I have made a case for the affordances of identity in literary studies, because uncritically rejecting identity risks participating in bad faith critiques of "identity politics" that are being weaponized against the humanities at large, in particular through attacks on Critical Race Theory and DEI. We must be careful not to be conscripted into this delegitimizing project. For example, we cannot allow the demands of the area (e.g., India, South Asia, Asia; or for that matter, the Transnational, Global, or World) to trump or be used against those of the ethnic and postcolonial. We cannot allow the non-West to be represented as a safe site of comparative study elsewhere, while the minoritized and marginalized in the United States are denied their own literatures and histories. By that same token, the ethnic and postcolonial literature classroom remains a key space in which American students learn to engage with the world—a fact and opportunity with existential implications.

In fall 2022, I taught South Asian Anglophone literature to a class of majority South Asian students for the first time. I was nervous. Before the semester started, I shared my worries with a senior colleague at another university: What if the students deemed my knowledge of the material wanting, given their own relationships to it? What if they challenged me in class, saying, *no, that isn't how it is; that's not how you say the word in Urdu; that's not how you'd translate it from Gujarati; what do* you *know?—that's where* I'm *from.*

My colleague laughed. She said that in many years of teaching South Asian literature and film to South Asian students in the United States, she'd never had an experience like that. Just wait, she said. They will want to know what you think—about South Asia, about Partition, about contemporary Indian politics—precisely because many of them have never had a critical lens with which to think it.

Sure enough, before the end of our first week, an Indian American student who had grown up in Dallas showed up at my office hours. She wanted to talk about a passage from an essay that I'd given them as part of our general introduction to "South Asian Anglophone World Literature":

> The irony is that even as "South Asia" is definitionally a regional formation, the inevitably partial nature of its deployment returns us to the primacy of the nation form.... In India, the 2014 and 2019 electoral triumphs of the Hindu-nationalist Bharatiya Janata Party and its chauvinistic leader Narendra Modi indicate the nation's increasing unwillingness to think and act in pluralistic, never mind regional, terms (for over two decades, one of the BJP's slogans has been "Hindi, Hindu, Hindustan," a call which deliberately flies in the face of the nation's incredible linguistic, religious, and ethnic diversity).[6]

There's nothing remarkable about this passage (which is why I reproduce it here). Yet it gave my student pause by offering as *unremarkable*—as a given, widely shared perspective—its assessment of both Modi's divisive politics and India's diversity. The student's parents were staunch Modi supporters, she told me, who had always taught her that "if Pakistan is for Muslims, India should be for Hindus." Now, all of a sudden, she wasn't sure.

It was just what my senior colleague had told me to expect. A frank—and, on my part, carefully considered—discussion ensued that would extend throughout the semester: about the necessity of distinguishing between Hinduism as a religion and Hindutva as a political ideology; about the fascist roots of the BJP and the RSS; about the ongoing curtailment of civil rights and free speech in India, even as it touts its status as the world's largest democracy; about escalating violence against Muslims, Dalits, queer, and other minority subjects in India; about the violence of Hindu majoritarianism as expressed, for example, in the Citizenship Amendment Act and the revocation of the autonomy of Jammu and Kashmir.

I never asked my student if our class had satisfied her desire to unlearn what she had learned. But I hoped, cliché though it is, that it had opened her mind. The South Asia that we read together was pluralistic, syncretic, and inclusive, represented by writers from Bangladesh, India, Pakistan, Sri Lanka, Trinidad, the United Kingdom, and the United States; by and about Christian, Hindu, Muslim, Sikh, and nonreligious subjects; by and about nonbinary and nonconforming artists, laborers, and writers; and written in or translated from languages including Bengali, English, Gujarati, Hindi, Tamil, and Urdu. Students from multiple religious, ethnic, linguistic, class, and caste backgrounds spoke about the texts from their "situated"—which is to say partial and valid—vantages as "Indians."[7] Together, we wrote a "Journal on Contemporary Journalism" that kept us tethered to South Asian literature's "real-life referents":[8] from the victims of devasting floods in Pakistan, to Rohingya refugees persecuted in Myanmar and seeking safety in Bangladesh, to Kashmiri activists demonstrating for civil liberties and human rights.

Surely, it would be impossible for any student to leave "The World and South Asia" and then embrace the ethnocentric, nativist ideology of "Hindi, Hindu, Hindustan" that characterizes Modi's India. Surely, it will be impossible for any student to leave "Literatures of Return" this semester without understanding that there are radical asymmetries and inequities in the histories, contexts, and possibilities for migration around the world, and that sometimes "you can never go home again" means that you need to give up the dangerous idea that you (but not your neighbor) have a special right of return.[9]

Surely.

In teaching, as in life, there are no guarantees. As an educator, you can strive to cultivate a rigorous, ethical, and generative "structure of interresponding" with your students, but you can never fully determine how they respond.[10] In Gayatri Chakravorty Spivak's words, "whatever you do, even if it looks like your plan succeeded completely, in the end, something (else) will have happened."[11]

So, next Tuesday at 9:25 a.m., I will greet a group of students who have decided to study ethnic, postcolonial, and Anglophone literature in an English department in a US university in 2024. I will try to help them understand why. I will train them to read for their own accented positions of reception as much as for the content of the texts. I will do my best to ready them for a lifetime of journeys with literature that hails and repels them—and, sometimes, both at once.

I have no illusion that my teaching will stop any wars or save any lives or overturn any fascist laws. Nevertheless, I hope that this book's sustained consideration of classes I have taken and taught over a period of twenty years communicates in no uncertain terms that teaching matters. That ideas linger. That traces surface. That books follow and find even their most resistant readers. And that, slowly but surely, they do their work in the world.

Acknowledgments

In 2006, I walked into Robyn Wiegman's office and proposed that I would write an honors thesis on Edward Said's Reith Lectures. Robyn humored me for a beat, then handed me Rey Chow's *The Protestant Ethnic*. I have been responding to Rey's work ever since, and to Robyn's, as this book attests. I'm quite sure both Robyn and Rey are fed up with my interpellating them like this, but it's just taken me two decades to finish writing my undergraduate thesis, that's all. The power of the word.

At Berkeley, Colleen Lye asked the questions I needed to be asked and pushed me to do my best work. I would not have become an academic without her generosity, guidance, and standards, and I will forever be grateful. Also at Berkeley: Pheng Cheah, Lawrence Cohen, Gautam Premnath, Juana María Rodríguez, Trinh T. Minh-ha, and especially Shannon Jackson planted seeds of this work. They said words that I'm still working with, thinking about, turning around.

R. Radhakrishnan and Asha Radhakrishnan encouraged my voice and its particular accents before anyone else in this business. John L. Jackson Jr. set the example and the bar I'm reaching for. Michael Allan, Mohan Ambikaipaker, Ulka Anjaria, Sneha Annavarapu, Anjali Arondekar, Tina Chen, Leo Ching, J. Daniel Elam, Mark Greif, Priya Joshi, Rochona Majumdar, Saikat Majumdar, B. Venkat Mani, Sharon Marcus, Cheryl Naruse, Aarthi Vadde, E. Dawson Varughese, and Rebecca Walkowitz gave vital encouragement and inspiration, even if they didn't know that's what they were doing.

Most of this book was drafted between 2020 and 2024, but some sentences go back as far as 2012. In the years since, I have had the tremendous good fortune of an extended network of friends who gave feedback on many parts of this book. As I reread these chapters today, I can hear their voices in my own, proving once again that accent is a biography of thought: that how our ideas ultimately sound is a product of where they came from, in conversation with whom. (All errors are mine, of course.) There are not enough ways to express my gratitude. But briefly:

The Accent Research Collaborative, team-TWA: Pooja Rangan, Akshya Saxena, and Pavitra Sundar. Our collaboration was foundational for this work. Thinking together with an accent gave me the vocabulary and tools with which to express what I'd long been trying to say.

Nasia Anam, Monika Bhagat-Kennedy, Roanne Kantor, Kalyan Nadiminti, and Akshya Saxena engaged drafts of this material with deep insight before I knew it was a book. Stephanie Brown, Marcia Klotz, Leerom Medovoi, and Scott Selisker also responded critically to early chapter drafts, and much here is indebted to their sharp readings. Christopher Fan, Paul Nadal, and Sunny Xiang: dissertation workshop dream team. I wouldn't be in this profession without them, and this wouldn't have become a book.

Other friends have been critical, too. Reid Gómez taught me that every word is a story and, in the process, opened up a key to this book. Chi Rainer Bornfree's preternatural listening opened another key, and without them I might never have learned how to write a book.

Thanks to my colleagues and friends at the University of Nevada, Reno, who gave me the best-ever introduction to professional life: especially Daniel Morse, Meredith Oda, and Jared Stanley. To all those at the University of Arizona who encouraged my research, and for the felicitous course assignments that made it possible for me to first live much of what I've written here. Thanks to my colleagues at Rice University, especially Lisa Balabanlilar, Rosemary Hennessy, Betty Joseph, Alden Sajor Marte-Wood, Alexander Regier, and Dean Kathleen Canning for their support of this book in its final stages, and to Rice's Office of Research and the School of Humanities. My gratitude to engaged audiences at ACLA 2018, ASAP/13, and multiple years' worth of MLA conferences, for asking probing questions that I'm still trying to answer. My hearty thanks—and apologies!—to all those whose words I recount in the "institutional situations" that precede each chapter. Thanks to the Max Planck Institute for Mathematics in Bonn, Germany. And to the Rhine River.

Elizabeth Ault, Leah Pennywark, and Erica Wetter were immensely encouraging as I moved toward publication. Philip Leventhal, Emily Simon, Robert Demke, Michael Haskell, Zachary Friedman, and the rest of the terrific team at Columbia University Press brought this book over the finish line. My deepest appreciation to Philip and the anonymous reviewers for their illuminating feedback and heartening faith in this project. And to Paula Durbin-Westby for the thoughtful and precise index.

I wouldn't have had the time and space to write this book without the commitment and labor of family, friends, and communities on three continents and in seven states who cared for me but even more importantly cared for my children: especially Terrell Allen, Marc Levin, Sharanya Rao, Ananth Tharoor Srinivasan, Raj Srinivasan, Shobha Tharoor Srinivasan, and Smita Tharoor.

Mrinalini and Shai, I hope you read this one day and that it sounds familiar, like a story you've heard before in a voice that you recognize, and that it makes you feel at home.

Every word of this book is indebted to Brandon Levin: to his deeply grounding influence and unflagging support of all I do. And every word is dedicated to my grandparents and my parents, with gratitude for the accident of my birth—and all the other overdeterminations.

Notes

Preface

1. Christopher Lee, *The Semblance of Identity: Aesthetic Mediation in Asian American Literature* (Stanford University Press, 2012).
2. Rey Chow, *The Protestant Ethnic and the Spirit of Capitalism* (Columbia University Press, 2002), 107.
3. Jennifer Nash, *Black Feminism Reimagined: After Intersectionality* (Duke University Press, 2019), 4, 97.
4. Ragini Tharoor Srinivasan, "Lahiri, High and Low," *Public Books*, January 20, 2014, www.publicbooks.org/lahiri-high-and-low/.
5. Louis Althusser, "Ideology and Ideological State Apparatuses (Notes Toward an Investigation)" (1969), in *Lenin and Philosophy and Other Essays* (NLB, 1971).
6. In the United States, identitarian correspondence is never posted as a requirement in job ads; such specification would in almost all cases be illegal.
7. Nasia Anam, "Introduction: Forms of the Global Anglophone," *Post45: Contemporaries*, February 22, 2019, https://post45.org/2019/02/introduction-forms-of-the-global-anglophone/.
8. Sanjay Krishnan, "The Place of India in Postcolonial Studies: Chatterjee, Chakrabarty, Spivak," *New Literary History* 40, no. 2 (2009): 265–280.
9. Tilottama Rajan, "On (Not) Being Postcolonial," *Postcolonial Text* 2, no. 1 (2006).
10. Sangeeta Ray tells a version of this story: "It was the mid-eighties and I had just arrived via a Pan Am flight to the Midwest. I did not know much

theory, but I did know, like most good postcolonial subjects, a lot of British literature. In college in Calcutta, I thoroughly traversed the discipline from Beowulf to Virginia Woolf. Repeating a Master's degree in the US seemed trivial at best. So to theory I gravitated, attempting to master dense literary criticism as philosophy and vice versa." Ray, *Gayatri Chakravorty Spivak: In Other Words* (Wiley-Blackwell, 2009), 2.

11. Gauri Viswanathan, *Masks of Conquest: Literary Study and British Rule in India* (Columbia University Press, 1989).
12. Arnab Chakladar, "Language, Nation, and the Question of 'Indian Literature,'" *Postcolonial Text* 6, no. 4 (2011): 4.
13. Akshya Saxena, *Vernacular English: Reading the Anglophone in Postcolonial India* (Princeton University Press, 2022), 1.
14. Gayatri Chakravorty Spivak, "French Feminism in an International Frame," *Yale French Studies* 62 (1981): 155.
15. R. Radhakrishnan, *Diasporic Mediations: Between Home and Location* (University of Minnesota Press, 1996), xv. See Chakladar, "Language, Nation," for an account of how this interpellation was facilitated by the rise of the Indian English novel in the 1980s.
16. Robert J. C. Young, *Colonial Desire: Hybridity in Theory, Culture, and Race* (Routledge, 1995), 163.
17. Amit Chaudhuri, *Finding the Raga: An Improvisation on Indian Music* (New York Review Books, 2021), 7.

Introduction. Identity and Other Open Secrets

1. J. Daniel Elam, "The Form of Global Anglophone Literature is Grenfell Tower," *Post45: Contemporaries*, February 22, 2019, https://post45.org/2019/02/the-form-of-global-anglophone-literature-is-grenfell-tower/.
2. Sara Ahmed, *On Being Included: Racism and Diversity in Institutional Life* (Duke University Press, 2012); Roderick Ferguson, *The Reorder of Things: The University and Its Pedagogies of Difference* (University of Minnesota Press, 2012); Jodi Melamed, *Represent and Destroy: Rationalizing Violence in the New Racial Capitalism* (University of Minnesota Press, 2011).
3. Rey Chow, "Where Have All the Natives Gone?," in *Writing Diaspora: Tactics of Intervention in Contemporary Cultural Studies* (Indiana University Press, 1993).
4. Gayatri Chakravorty Spivak, *A Critique of Postcolonial Reason: Toward a History of the Vanishing Present* (Harvard University Press, 1999); Rey Chow, *The Protestant Ethnic and the Spirit of Capitalism* (Columbia University Press, 2002).
5. Gayatri Chakravorty Spivak, "French Feminism in an International Frame," *Yale French Studies* 62 (1981): 155.

6. Chow, *Protestant Ethnic*, 124.
7. Stephen Greenblatt, "Racial Memory and Literary History," *PMLA* 116, no. 1 (January 2001): 57.
8. Tilottama Rajan, "On (Not) Being Postcolonial," *Postcolonial Text* 2, no. 1 (2006).
9. Stacy M. Hartman and Bianca C. Williams observe that "derogatory and offensive" terms like "mesearch" are frequently "weaponized against scholars of color and queer scholars doing work with and for their communities. This is especially important in the humanities and humanistic social sciences, where narrative and lived experience are often essential data and useful case studies for understanding structures, systems, and other phenomena." Hartman and Williams, "The Future of Doctoral Education: Four Provocations for a More Just and Sustainable Academy," *Los Angeles Review of Books* (May 29, 2023), https://lareviewofbooks.org/article/the-future-of-doctoral-education-four-provocations-for-a-more-just-and-sustainable-academy/.
10. Louis Althusser, "Contradiction and Overdetermination," in *Notes for an Investigation*, trans. Ben Brewster (Penguin, 1962); Sigmund Freud, *The Interpretation of Dreams* (Macmillan, 1913, 1899). See also Gayatri Chakravorty Spivak, "The Rani of Sirmur: An Essay in Reading the Archives," *History and Theory* 24, no. 3 (1985): 247–272. Spivak discusses Freud's understanding of overdetermination as both "many determinations" (*mehrfach determiniert*) and the state of being "determined otherwise" (*anders determiniert*) in the context of Freud's own institutional position (257).
11. Deepika Bahri, *Native Intelligence: Aesthetics, Politics, and Postcolonial Literature* (University of Minnesota Press, 2003).
12. Claudia Rankine, *Just Us: An American Conversation* (Graywolf, 2020), 50.
13. I will qualify this "we" as it shifts at different points in the discussion. As for the "you" who is reading, you are my colleague, my teacher, and my student. You are a reader of Indian, Asian American, ethnic, postcolonial, and Anglophone literature—or not. You have read these authors and theorists—or not. You are Indian. You are not Indian. You don't know if you are Indian. You are my friend who "crushes identity like a jelly bean." You, too, are overdetermined.
14. Chow, *Protestant Ethnic*, 17, 16.
15. For a comparative case, see the Winter 1996 Bulletin of the Association of Concerned Africa Scholars on "The Ghettoization Debate: Africa, Africans, and African Studies."
16. Beth Loffreda and Claudia Rankine, introduction to *The Racial Imaginary: Writers on Race in the Life of the Mind*, ed. Claudia Rankine, Beth Loffreda, and Max King Cap (Fence, 2015), 17.
17. Erica L. Green, "When It Doesn't Help to Speak the Language: The Fulbright-Hays Fellowship," *New York Times*, March 15, 2023, www.nytimes.com/2023

/03/15/us/politics/fulbright-fellowship-language-education-department.html; Eugenia Zuroski, "Holding Patterns: On Academic Knowledge and Labor," *Medium*, April 5, 2018, https://medium.com/@zugenia/holding-patterns-on-academic-knowledge-and-labor-3e5a6000ecbf.

18. This discrimination takes numerous, subtle forms; anecdotes abound, passed through the whisper network. A scholar born and raised in India, who received their PhD in English from an Ivy League institution in 2017, describes having been "pushed out of the room" of modernist studies in graduate school because they were not white. A professor of feminist and Latinx cultural studies at my graduate institution shared that, in her experience, the only work considered to be "Critical Theory" was routed through the Frankfurt School; the work of scholars in feminist, postcolonial, and ethnic studies was deemed either not "critical" enough or not "theoretical" enough. A postdoctoral fellow in an English department at a Canadian research university recounted a conversation at a hiring meeting in which a colleague said that the English department didn't need to hire a Black Shakespearean, because they already had an African Americanist. At a regional conference in Asian studies in 2023, two scholars of Asian descent described having been hired as Asian Americanists, even though neither of their dissertations was on Asian American literature. And so on.
19. Lorgia García Peña (September 7, 2020, 9:19pm), https://twitter.com/lorgia_pena/status/1303050341169197056?s=20.
20. Viet Thanh Nguyen, "Dislocation is My Location," *PMLA* 133, no. 2 (2018): 429.
21. Keguro Macharia, "Belated: Interruption," *GLQ: A Journal of Lesbian and Gay Studies* 26, no. 3 (2020): 570.
22. Chow, *Protestant Ethnic*, 146.
23. Nancy Leong, *Identity Capitalists: The Powerful Insiders Who Exploit Diversity to Maintain Inequality* (Stanford University Press, 2021).
24. Lorgia García Peña, *Community as Rebellion: A Syllabus for Surviving Academia as a Woman of Color* (Haymarket, 2022); Patricia A. Matthew, Editor, *Written/Unwritten: Diversity and the Hidden Truths of Tenure* (University of North Carolina Press, 2016); Victoria Reyes, *Academic Outsider: Stories of Exclusion and Hope* (Stanford University Press, 2022). The abuse in question is particularly targeted toward Black, Latinx, first-generation, working-class, female-identified, queer, trans, disabled, neurodivergent, fat, caregiving, precariously employed, or otherwise marginalized and structurally disadvantaged academics. But the relatively privileged are interpellated as diversity hires as well. Douglas Ishi, "The Diversity Requirement; or, the Ambivalent Contingency of the Asian American Student Teacher," *American Literature* 94, no. 4 (December 2022): 733–761.
25. Rajan, "On (Not) Being Postcolonial."

26. Mohan Ambikaipaker, "Everyday Political Whiteness and Diversity University," *Kalfou* 6, no. 2 (Fall 2019): 275.
27. Ambikaipaker, "Everyday Political Whiteness," 275–276.
28. In the absence of such an account, the only self-described "honest" discussions on offer are op-eds about "diversity hiring" that assume that the only reasons why identitarian issues might factor into hiring are universities' attempts to correct for "demographic mismatch" between faculty and students or "to remedy past and present societal injustices." Matt Burgess, "It's Time to Stop the Double Talk Around Diversity Hiring," *Chronicle of Higher Education* (June 5, 2024), www.chronicle.com/article/its-time-to-stop-the-double-talk-around-diversity-hiring.
29. Christopher Lee, *The Semblance of Identity: Aesthetic Mediation in Asian American Literature* (Stanford University Press, 2012), 8.
30. Colleen Lye, "Reading for Asian American Literature," in *A Companion to American Literary Studies*, ed. Caroline F. Levander and Robert S. Levine (Blackwell, 2011), 484.
31. Robyn Wiegman, "Feminism, Institutionalism, and the Idiom of Failure," *differences: a journal of feminist cultural studies* 11, no. 3 (1999/2000): 130.
32. Rajan, "On (Not) Being Postcolonial."
33. Loffreda and Rankine, introduction, 16.
34. Susan Koshy, "The Fiction of Asian American Literature," *Yale Journal of Criticism* 9, no. 2 (1996): 315–346.
35. Gayatri Chakravorty Spivak, *A Critique of Postcolonial Reason: Toward a History of the Vanishing Present* (Harvard University Press, 1999), 267.
36. Lee, *Semblance of Identity*, 151.
37. R. Radhakrishnan, *Diasporic Mediations: Between Home and Location* (University of Minnesota Press, 1996), xxiv.
38. Keguro Macharia, "On Quitting," *New Inquiry*, September 19, 2018, https://thenewinquiry.com/on-quitting/.
39. Macharia, "Belated," 563.
40. Lye, "Reading," 484.
41. Pooja Rangan, Akshya Saxena, Ragini Tharoor Srinivasan, and Pavitra Sundar, eds., *Thinking with an Accent: Toward a New Object, Method, and Practice* (University of California Press, 2023).
42. Gayle Rubin, "The Traffic in Women: Notes on the 'Political Economy' of Sex," in *Toward an Anthropology of Women*, ed. Rayna R. Reiter (Monthly Review Press, 1975), 204.
43. Chaudhuri, "*I* am Ramu," nplusonemag.com, August 22, 2017, www.nplusonemag.com/online-only/online-only/i-am-ramu/.
44. Graham Huggan, *The Postcolonial Exotic: Marketing the Margins* (Routledge, 2001); Sarah Brouillette, *Postcolonial Writers in the Global Literary Marketplace*

(Palgrave Macmillan, 2007); Paul Crosthwaite, *The Market Logics of Contemporary Fiction* (Cambridge University Press, 2019).

45. James F. English, *The Economy Of Prestige: Prizes, Awards, and the Circulation of Cultural Value* (Harvard University Press, 2008); Mark McGurl, *The Program Era: Postwar Fiction and the Rise of Creative Writing* (Harvard University Press, 2009); Peter Kalliney, *The Commonwealth of Letters: British Literary Culture and the Emergence of Postcolonial Aesthetics* (Oxford University Press, 2013); Kalyan Nadiminti, "The Global Program Era: Contemporary International Fiction in the American Creative Economy," *Novel: A Forum on Fiction* 51, no. 3 (2018): 375–398; Asha Rogers, *State Sponsored Literature: Britain and Cultural Diversity After 1945* (Oxford University Press, 2020); Richard Jean So, *Redlining Culture: A Data History of Racial Inequality and Postwar Fiction* (Columbia University Press, 2020); Alexander Manshel, *Writing Backwards: Historical Fiction and the Contemporary Canon* (Columbia University Press, 2023); Dan Sinykin, *Big Fiction: How Conglomeration Changed the Publishing Industry and American Literature* (Columbia University Press, 2023). See also the *Public Books* series on "Hacking the Culture Industries": www.publicbooks.org/tag/hacking-the-culture-industries/ and "Post45 x Journal of Cultural Analytics," ed. Richard Jean So (2021): https://post45.org/sections/issue/p45-ca/.

46. Donna Haraway, "Situated Knowledges: The Science Question in Feminism and the Privilege of Partial Perspective," *Feminist Studies* 14, no. 3 (1988): 581.

47. Gayatri Chakravorty Spivak, *Death of a Discipline: 20th Anniversary Edition* (Columbia University Press, 2023), xviii.

48. Gayatri Chakravorty Spivak, *Readings* (Seagull, 2014), 161–162.

49. Robyn Wiegman, *Object Lessons* (Duke University Press, 2012).

50. For an account of the "name change debate" and her own "losing" position within it, see Robyn Wiegman, "Loss, Hope: The University in Ruins, Again," *Feminist Studies* 48, no. 3 (2022): 628.

51. Koshy, "The Fiction of Asian American Literature"; Lye, "Reading," 484; Kandice Chuh, *Imagine Otherwise: On Asian Americanist Critique* (Duke University Press, 2003), 33.

52. Lee, *Semblance of Identity*, 8.

53. Edward Said, *Reflections on Exile, and Other Essays* (Harvard University Press, 2000), 567. See also Jacqueline Rose and Edward W. Said, "Returning to Ourselves," *Jewish Quarterly* (1997/1998): 11.

54. Bulan Lahiri, "In Conversation: Speaking to Spivak," *The Hindu*, February 5, 2011, www.thehindu.com/books/In-Conversation-Speaking-to-Spivak/article15130635.ece.

55. Spivak, *Critique of Postcolonial Reason*, 267.

56. Sangeeta Ray, "Imagining Otherwise: Comparative South Asian Literature and the MLA," *Comparative Literature Studies* 50, no. 2 (2013): 237.
57. R. Radhakrishnan, "The Future of South Asian Studies," *South Asian Review* 38, no. 3 (2017): 25.
58. Olúfémi Táíwò, *Elite Capture: How the Powerful Took Over Identity Politics* (Haymarket, 2022).
59. Keeanga-Yamahtta Taylor, "The Defeat of Identity Politics," *New Yorker* (September 21, 2022), www.newyorker.com/books/under-review/the-defeat-of-identity-politics.
60. Melamed, *Represent and Destroy*, 93, 109.
61. Yascha Mounk, *The Identity Trap: A Story of Ideas and Power in Our Time* (Penguin, 2023).
62. Gayatri Chakravorty Spivak and Robert J. C. Young, "Neocolonialism and the Secret Agent of Knowledge," *Oxford Literary Review* 13, nos. 1/2 (1991): 235.
63. Edward W. Said, "Identity, Authority, and Freedom: The Potentate and the Traveler," *boundary 2* 21, no. 3 (1994 [1991]): 16.
64. Frank Chin, "Come All Ye Asian American Writers of the Real and the Fake," in *A Companion to Asian American Studies*, ed. Kent A. Ono (Blackwell, 2005), 133–156.
65. Mark Chiang, *The Cultural Capital of Asian American Studies: Autonomy and Representation in the University* (New York University Press, 2009), 159.
66. Vikram Chandra, "The Cult of Authenticity," *Boston Review* (2000).
67. Timothy Yu, "Chinese Silence No. 36," from *100 Chinese Silences* (Les Figues, 2016), 54.
68. Ada Limón, "The Contract Says: We'd Like the Conversation to be Bilingual," in *The Carrying* (Milkweed, 2018).
69. Kiese Laymon, *How to Slowly Kill Yourself and Others in America* (Scribner, 2020), 102.
70. Mrinalini Chakravorty, *In Stereotype: South Asia in the Global Literary Imaginary* (Columbia University Press, 2014); Swati Rana, *Race Characters: Ethnic Literature and the Figure of the American Dream* (UNC Press, 2020).
71. Jay Caspian Kang, "The Many Lives of Steven Yeun," *New York Times Magazine*, February 3, 2021, www.nytimes.com/2021/02/03/magazine/steven-yeun.html.
72. Anne Helen Petersen, "These Writers Are Launching a New Wave of Native American Literature," *Buzz Feed*, February 22, 2018, www.buzzfeednews.com/article/annehelenpetersen/dont-f-with-tommy-and-terese#.fxMyKAPBO.
73. Ruth Ozeki, foreword to John Okada's *No-No Boy* (University of Washington Press, 2014), ix.
74. Kang, "Lives of Steven Yeun."

75. Isabella Hammad, "Recognizing the Stranger," *Paris Review*, October 27, 2023, www.theparisreview.org/blog/2023/10/27/recognizing-the-stranger/, my emphasis.
76. Ozeki, foreword, ix–x.
77. Manshel, *Writing Backwards*.
78. Julie Beth Napolin, *The Fact of Resonance: Modernist Acoustics and Narrative Form* (Fordham University Press, 2020).
79. David Palumbo-Liu, "Assumed Identities," *New Literary History* 31, no. 4 (2000): 765–780.
80. Jhumpa Lahiri, *The Clothing of Books*, trans. Alberto Vourvoulias-Bush (Vintage, 2015), 8, 49.
81. Napolin, *Fact of Resonance*, 71. See also Nguyen, "Dislocation," 428.
82. Napolin, *Fact of Resonance*, 72.
83. Michael Warner, "Uncritical Reading," *Polemic* (2012): 20.
84. Radhakrishnan, *Diasporic Mediations*, 114–115.
85. Lee, *Semblance of Identity*, 151–153.
86. Spivak, *Readings*, 79, my emphasis.
87. Spivak, *Readings*, 84.
88. Jane Hu, "Orientalism, Redux," *Victorian Studies* 62, no. 3 (2020): 460–473.
89. Manu Samriti Chander, *Brown Romantics: Poetry and Nationalism in the Global Nineteenth Century* (Bucknell University Press, 2017), 106.
90. Elaine Castillo, *How to Read Now* (Atlantic, 2022), 63.
91. Eugenia Zuroski, "The Tree at the End of the World," *Post45: Contemporaries*, October 13, 2020, https://post45.org/2020/10/the-tree-at-the-end-of-the-world/.
92. Sarah Chihaya, "Slips and Slides," *PMLA* 133, no. 2 (2018): 368.
93. For a related move in a different field, see Jules Gill-Peterson, "Feeling Like a Bad Trans Object," *Post45: Contemporaries*, December 9, 2019, https://post45.org/2019/12/feeling-like-a-bad-trans-object/.
94. Min Hyoung Song, *The Children of 1965: On Writing, and Not Writing, as an Asian American* (Duke University Press, 2013), 24–25.
95. Loffreda and Rankine, introduction, 15, 16.
96. Ignacio Sánchez Prado, "Commodifying Mexico: On *American Dirt* and the Cultural Politics of a Manufactured Bestseller," *American Literary History* 33, no. 2 (2021): 371–393.
97. Napolin, *Fact of Resonance*, 77.
98. Anita Starosta, "Accented Criticism: Translation and Global Humanities," *boundary 2* 40, no. 3 (2013): 178, 176.
99. Jess Shollenberger, "'Ruthless Personalizers': Queer Theory and the Uses of the Personal," *M/m* 8, no. 1 (October 5, 2023): https://modernismmodernity .org/forums/posts/shollenberger-ruthless-personalizers-queer-theory-uses

-personal; see also Abigail De Kosnik, "Personal Theory: Humanities Scholarship in a New Media Moment," *Digital Media: Technological and Social Challenges of the Interactive World* (Scarecrow, 2011).
100. Rosina Lippi-Green, *English with an Accent: Language, Ideology, and Discrimination in the United States* (Routledge, 1997).
101. Jhumpa Lahiri, *In Other Words* (Knopf, 2017), 135–137.
102. Li-Young Lee, *The Winged Seed: A Remembrance* (Simon and Schuster, 1995), 76.
103. Rey Chow, *Not Like a Native Speaker: On Languaging as a Postcolonial Experience* (Columbia University Press, 2014), 8. See also Pavitra Sundar, *Listening with a Feminist Ear: Soundwork in Bombay Cinema* (University of Michigan Press, 2023).
104. Jonathan Rosa, *Looking Like a Language, Sounding Like a Race: Raciolinguistic Ideologies and the Learning of Latinidad* (Oxford University Press, 2019).
105. Divya Victor, *Semblance: Two Essays* (Sputnik and Fizzle, 2016), 24.
106. Napolin, *Fact of Resonance*, 90.
107. Gloria Anzaldúa, *Borderlands/La Frontera: The New Mestiza* (Aunt Lute, 1987); Maxine Hong Kingston, *The Woman Warrior: Memoirs of a Girlhood Among Ghosts* (Knopf, 1976).
108. Lawrence Abu Hamdan, "Aural Contract: Forensic Listening and the Reorganization of the Speaking Subject," in *Forensis: The Architecture of Public Truth* (Sternberg Press and Forensic Architecture, 2014), 72.
109. Akshya Saxena, "Stereo Accent: Reading, Writing, and Xenophilic Attunement," in *Thinking with an Accent: Toward a New Object, Method, and Practice* (University of California Press, 2023), 226.
110. Ragini Tharoor Srinivasan, "Is There a Call Center Literature?," in *Thinking with an Accent: Toward a New Object, Method, and Practice* (University of California Press, 2023), 115.
111. Saxena, "Stereo Accent," 226.
112. Srinivasan, "Is There a Call Center Literature?," 129.
113. Franco Moretti "Conjectures on World Literature," *New Left Review* 1 (2000), 54–68; Stephen Best and Sharon Marcus, "Surface Reading: An Introduction," *Representations* 108, no. 1 (2009): 1–21; Heather Love, "Close but Not Deep: Literary Ethics and the Descriptive Turn," *New Literary History* 41 (2010): 371–391.
114. Juliana Spahr, *Everybody's Autonomy: Connective Reading and Collective Identity* (University of Alabama Press, 2001), 11.
115. Barbara Johnson, *The Critical Difference: Essays in the Contemporary Rhetoric of Reading* (Johns Hopkins University Press, 1980), 3.
116. Loffreda and Rankine, introduction, 18.

117. In developing this approach, I take inspiration from precedents including Chow, "Where Have All the Natives Gone?"; Reginald Jackson, "Solidarity's Indiscipline: Regarding Miyoshi's Pedagogical Legacy," *boundary2* 47, no. 3 (2019); and Rukmini Bhaya Nair, *Lying on the Postcolonial Couch: The Idea of Indifference* (University of Minnesota Press, 2002).

118. Cf. Anne Anlin Cheng, *The Melancholy of Race: Psychoanalysis, Assimilation, and Hidden Grief* (Oxford University Press, 2000); Antonio Viego, *Dead Subjects: Toward a Politics of Loss in Latino Studies* (Duke University Press, 2007).

119. Akshya Saxena, *Vernacular English: Reading the Anglophone in Postcolonial India* (Princeton University Press, 2022), 68, 83, 67.

120. Hamid Dabashi, *On Edward Said: Remembrance of Things Past* (Haymarket, 2020), 11.

121. Robyn Wiegman, "Love and Repudiation in the Feminist Canon," *Feminist Formations* 32, no. 1 (2020): 5.

122. These institutions are Duke University in Durham, North Carolina, where I earned my BA (2007); University of Nevada, Reno, where I held my first job as Assistant Professor of English (2016–2017); University of Arizona, Tucson, where I held my second job as Assistant Professor of English and Social, Cultural, and Critical Theory (2017–2022); and Rice University in Houston, Texas, where I am currently Assistant Professor of English. In addition, I recount some stories from when I was at the University of California, Berkeley, where I earned my PhD (2016). Some readers might advocate anonymizing these institutions in order to create a composite representation that speaks to broadly shared institutional dynamics across US academe. Given the general mystification of higher education in public discourse that obscures important differences between private and public institutions, as well as universities in different regions serving diverse student populations, and given that my own history of institutional affiliations is easily discoverable online, I choose not to anonymize the sites from which my experiences are drawn.

123. Adrianna Kezar, Tom DePaola, and Daniel T. Scott, *The Gig Academy: Mapping Labor in the Neoliberal University* (Johns Hopkins University Press, 2019). See also the *Post45: Contemporaries* cluster "Dark Academia," ed. Olivia Stowell and Mitch Therieau, https://post45.org/sections/contemporaries-essays/dark-academia/.

124. Christopher J. Newfield, "Research for All," *MLA Newsletter* (Spring 2022), https://president.mla.hcommons.org/2022/05/12/research-for-all/.

125. Rebecca Roach, ed., "Contemporary Literature from the Classroom," *Post45: Contemporaries*, May 15, 2024, https://post45.org/sections/contemporaries-essays/contemporary-literature-from-the-classroom/.

126. Rachel Sagner Buurma and Laura Heffernan, *The Teaching Archive: A New History for Literary Study* (University of Chicago Press, 2021), 4.

1. What Was Multiethnic Literature?
Or, Bharati Mukherjee Doesn't Have an Indian Accent

1. Pooja Rangan, Akshya Saxena, Ragini Tharoor Srinivasan, and Pavitra Sundar, eds., *Thinking With an Accent: Toward a New Object, Method, and Practice* (University of California Press, 2023).
2. Rosina Lippi-Green, *English with an Accent: Language, Ideology, and Discrimination in the United States* (Routledge, 2012).
3. Mark McGurl, *The Program Era: Postwar Fiction and the Rise of Creative Writing* (Harvard University Press, 2009).
4. William Grimes, "Bharati Mukherjee, Writer of Immigrant Life, Dies at 76," *New York Times*, February 1, 2017.
5. "An interview with Bharati Mukherjee by Geoff Hancock," in *Conversations with Bharati Mukherjee*, ed. Bradley C. Edwards (University Press of Mississippi, 2009), 16.
6. She cited Timothy Brennan's reading of Mukherjee as a "Third World cosmopolitan." See Brennan, *Salman Rushdie and the Third World* (St. Martin's, 1989), 34; cf. Susan Koshy, "Minority Cosmopolitanism," *PMLA* 126, no. 3 (2011): 592–609.
7. Bharati Mukherjee, preface to *Darkness and Other Stories* (Penguin, 1985), 3.
8. Bharati Mukherjee, "A Four-Hundred-Year-Old-Woman," in *Critical Fictions: The Politics of Imaginative Writing*, ed. Philomena Mariani (Bay, 1991), 33–38.
9. Swati Rana, *Race Characters: Ethnic Literature and the Figure of the American Dream* (University of North Carolina Press, 2020).
10. Bharati Mukherjee, "Two Ways to Belong in America," *New York Times*, September 22, 1996; and "American Dreamer," *Mother Jones*, January-February 1997.
11. Natasha Lavigilante, "Globalization and Change in India: The Rise of an 'Indian Dream' in *Miss New India*: An Interview with Bharati Mukherjee," *MELUS: Multi-Ethnic Literature of the United States* 39, no. 3 (2014): 185.
12. Meenakshi Mukherjee, "The Anxiety of Indianness: Our Novels in English," *Economic and Political Weekly* 28, no. 48 (November 27, 1993): 2610.
13. Bharati Mukherjee is widely recognized as an "Indian American" literary pioneer (along with her contemporary Meena Alexander), whose writing paved the way for mainstays in the field like Chitra Banerjee Divakaruni, Jhumpa Lahiri, Akhil Sharma, Thrity Umrigar, and Abraham Verghese, as

well as a younger crop of writers including Tania James, Karan Mahajan, Sanjena Sathian, Shruti Swamy, and Vauhini Vara. Hers is often the South Asian American example in the Asian American literature class. At the same time, she has been clubbed with other "postcolonial writers" like Attia Hosain, Anita Desai, Bapsi Sidhwa, and Salman Rushdie. See Ulka Anjaria, ed., *A History of the Indian Novel in English* (Cambridge University Press, 2015), 221.
14. Kenneth W. Warren, *What Was African American Literature?* (Harvard University Press, 2011), 9, 18, 80.
15. Homi Bhabha, "Of Mimicry and Man," in *The Location of Culture* (Routledge, 1994), 127.
16. Gayatri Chakravorty Spivak, *Outside in the Teaching Machine* (Routledge, 1993), 55.
17. Warren, *What Was African American Literature?*, 17.
18. Warren, *What Was African American Literature?*, 107.
19. See, for example, Jodi Melamed, *Represent and Destroy: Rationalizing Violence in the New Racial Capitalism* (University of Minnesota Press, 2011). Melamed critiques "liberal-multicultural uses of multicultural literature," arguing that they contribute to what has effectively been an institutionalized "strategy for racial abandonment" (97).
20. Rey Chow, *The Protestant Ethnic and the Spirit of Capitalism* (Columbia University Press, 2002), 30, 146.
21. See in particular MELUS: The Society for the Study of Multi-Ethnic Literature of the United States and its journal, *MELUS*, published continuously since 1974.
22. Caroline Rody, *The Interethnic Imagination: Roots and Passages in Contemporary Asian American Fiction* (Oxford University Press, 2009), 4.
23. Sara Marcus makes the same argument with respect to the "multiracial," identifying "a strain of American studies and Americanist literary studies that has long aspired to being 'multiracial' in the same sense that many have aspired to actualize America itself as a 'multiracial' project . . . a foolhardy ambition at best, perhaps, and certainly a violent and dangerous one at worst, which may be why it sounds woefully dated as I invoke it here." See Marcus, *Political Disappointment: A Cultural History from Reconstruction to the AIDS Crisis* (Harvard University Press, 2023), 13.
24. Sara Ahmed, *On Being Included: Racism and Diversity in Institutional Life* (Duke University Press, 2012).
25. Rody, *The Interethnic Imagination*, 4.
26. Bharati Mukherjee, *The Tiger's Daughter* (Boston: Houghton Mifflin, 1971).
27. Min Hyoung Song, *The Children of 1965: On Writing, and Not Writing, as an Asian American* (Duke University Press, 2013). See also Christopher T. Fan,

Asian American Fiction After 1965: Transnational Fantasies of Economic Mobility (Columbia University Press, 2024).

28. Rody, *Interethnic Imagination*, 9, 20–21.
29. Angela Reyes, "The Voicing of Asian American Figures," in *Raciolinguistics: How Language Shapes Our Ideas About Race*, ed. H. Samy Alim, John R. Rickford, and Arnetha F. Ball (Oxford University Press, 2016), 314.
30. Keeanga-Yamahtta Taylor, "The End of Black Politics," *New York Times*, June 13, 2020.
31. Here, and in my earlier characterization of the classroom as time machine, I am making a double gesture: toward the literary past that the classroom renders present, and toward the production of a contemporary that will one day be recollected as another future's past. This latter move requires taking a real leap of faith. As Rebecca Roach writes, "contemporary literature in the classroom is always out of date, precariously framed by an institutional commitment to predictable futures." See Roach, "Contemporary Literature from the Classroom," *Post45: Contemporaries*, May 15, 2024, https://post45.org/sections/contemporaries-essays/contemporary-literature-from-the-classroom/.
32. Elizabeth A. Harris, "Books on Race Filled Best-Seller Lists Last Year. Publishers Took Notice." *New York Times*, September 15, 2021; and "In Backlash to Racial Reckoning, Conservative Publishers See Gold," *New York Times*, August 15, 2021.
33. Jonathan Raban, "Savage Boulevards, Easy Streets," *New York Times*, June 19, 1988.
34. Rody, *Interethnic Imagination*, 29.
35. Ruth Maxey, *Understanding Bharati Mukherjee* (University of South Carolina Press, 2019), 53.
36. Susan Koshy, "*Jasmine* by Bharati Mukherjee," in *A Resource Guide to Asian American Literature* (Modern Language Association, 2001), 122.
37. McGurl, *The Program Era*, 372.
38. Maxey, *Understanding Bharati Mukherjee*, 74, 62.
39. Bharati Mukherjee, *The Middleman, and Other Stories* (Grove, 1988), 26, 29.
40. Lavina Dhingra and Floyd Cheung, *Naming Jhumpa Lahiri: Canons and Controversies* (Lexington, 2012), xii.
41. Susan Koshy, *Sexual Naturalization: Asian Americans and Miscegenation* (Stanford University Press, 2004).
42. Mukherjee, *Middleman*, 138, 128, 138.
43. Mukherjee, *Middleman*, 138.
44. Maxey, *Understanding Bharati Mukherjee*, 53.
45. Lauren Berlant, *Cruel Optimism* (Duke University Press, 2011).
46. Ruth Maxey, "Bharati Mukherjee and the Politics of the Anthology," *Cambridge Quarterly* 48.1 (2019), 46, 48.

47. Koshy, *Sexual Naturalization*, 133.
48. erin Khuê Ninh, "Gold-Digger: Reading the Marital and National Romance in Bharati Mukherjee's *Jasmine*," *MELUS* 38, no. 3 (2013): 146.
49. Inderpal Grewal, *Transnational America: Feminisms, Diasporas, Neoliberalisms* (Duke University Press, 2005), 38–39.
50. Bharati Mukherjee, "American Dreamer," *Mother Jones* 22, no. 1 (1997): 32–35.
51. Grewal, *Transnational America*, 38–39.
52. Koshy, *Sexual Naturalization*, 138.
53. Julie Beth Napolin, *The Fact of Resonance: Modernist Acoustics and Narrative Form* (Fordham University Press, 2020), 3.
54. See Maxey, "Politics of the Anthology," 43.
55. Tom McEnany, "This American Voice: The Odd Timbre of a New Standard in Public Radio," in *The Oxford Handbook of Voice Studies*, ed. Nina Sun Eidsheim and Katherine Meizel (Oxford University Press, 2018).
56. Jennifer Lynn Stoever, *The Sonic Color Line: Race and the Cultural Politics of Listening* (New York University Press, 2016), 7.
57. James Baldwin, "If Black English Isn't a Language, then Tell Me, What Is?," *The Black Scholar* 27, no. 1 (1997): 5–6.
58. John Baugh, "Linguistic Profiling," in *Black Linguistics* (Routledge, 2002).
59. H. Samy Alim and Geneva Smitherman. *Articulate while Black: Barack Obama, Language, and Race in the US* (Oxford University Press, 2012).
60. Zora Neale Hurston, "Story in Harlem Slang," in *Zora Neale Hurston: Novels and Stories* (Library of America, 1995), 1001–1010.
61. Brooks E. Hefner, *The Word on the Streets: The American Language of Vernacular Modernism* (University of Virginia Press, 2017), 188.
62. Michael Denning, *Mechanic Accents: Dime Novels and Working-Class Culture in America* (Verso, 1998), 83.
63. Steven Connor, *Dumbstruck: A Cultural History of Ventriloquism* (Oxford University Press, 2000), 7, emphasis mine.
64. Anne Karpf, *The Human Voice* (Bloomsbury, 2011), 33.
65. Dominic Pettman, *Sonic Intimacy: Voice, Species, Technics (Or, How to Listen to the World)* (Stanford University Press, 2017), 5.
66. Shilpa Davé, *Indian Accents: Brown Voice and Racial Performance in American Television and Film* (University of Illinois Press, 2013).
67. Davé, *Indian Accents*, 54.
68. Ali M. Latifi, "What South Asian Americans Lost When We Canceled Apu," *Zocalo Public Square*, June 8, 2022, www.zocalopublicsquare.org/2022/06/08/south-asian-americans-the-simpsons-apu/ideas/essay/; Jason Zinoman, "Aakash Singh and His Case for Bringing Back Apu," *New York Times*, March 4, 2022, www.nytimes.com/2022/03/04/arts/television/akaash-singh-apu-the-simpsons.html.

69. Dolores Inés Casillas, Juan Sebastian Ferrada, and Sara Veronica Hinojos, "The Accent on Modern Family: Listening to Representations of the Latina Vocal Body," *Aztlan: A Journal of Chicano Studies* 43, no. 1 (2018), 61–88.
70. Reyes, "Voicing of Asian American Figures."
71. Micah Stack, "The G.R.I.E.F.," *Oxford American*, July 23, 2015, https://oxfordamerican.org/magazine/issue-89-summer-2015/the-g-r-i-e-f.
72. Zadie Smith, "Fascinated to Presume: In Defense of Fiction," *New York Review of Books* 24 (2019).
73. Susan Sniader Lanser, *Fictions of Authority: Women Writers and Narrative Voice* (Cornell University Press, 1992), 4.
74. Gérard Genette, *Narrative Discourse: An Essay in Method* (Cornell University Press, 1980), 213.
75. Gayatri Chakravorty Spivak, "Can the Subaltern Speak? [1999]," in *Can the Subaltern Speak? Reflections on the History of an Idea*, ed. Rosalind C. Morris (Columbia University Press, 2010), 27.
76. Nancy Chen, "'Speaking Nearby': A Conversation with Trinh T. Minh-ha," *Visual Anthropology Review* 8, no. 1 (Spring 1992): 87.
77. Amitava Kumar, *Passport Photos* (University of California Press, 2000), 4.
78. Maxey, *Understanding Bharati Mukherjee*, 54.
79. McGurl, *The Program Era*, 382.
80. Mukherjee, *Middleman*, 79, quoted in Leslie Bow, *Partly Colored: Asian Americans and Racial Anomaly in the Segregated South* (New York University Press, 2010), 160.
81. Rody, *Interethnic Imagination*, 29.
82. Myriam Gurba, "Pendeja, You Ain't Steinbeck: My Bronca with Fake-Ass Social Justice Literature," *Tropics of Meta* (December 12, 2019); Ignacio M. Sánchez Prado, "Commodifying Mexico: On *American Dirt* and the Cultural Politics of a Manufactured Bestseller," *American Literary History* 33, no. 2 (2021): 371–393; Elaine Castillo, *How to Read Now* (Atlantic, 2022); Pamela Paul, "The Long Shadow of *American Dirt*," *New York Times* (January 26, 2023).
83. Mel Watkins, *On the Real Side: A History of African American Comedy* (Lawrence Hill, 1999). Watkins coins the term "racial ventriloquy" in chapter 7 on radio broadcasts and early television.
84. Rody, *Interethnic Imagination*, 29.
85. Connor, *Dumbstruck*, 14.
86. Denning, *Mechanic Accents*, 83. The larger work is a Marxist theorization of the dime novel; in the passage where he makes this distinction, he is drawing on Valentin Voloshinov's theorization of the "multiaccentual" sign in order to argue that the ambiguous "class accents" of the dime novel are active both in the text's production and "in the way readers accent their readings."

87. Denning, *Mechanic Accents*, 83.
88. Helen Davies, *Gender and Ventriloquism in Victorian and Neo-Victorian Fiction: Passionate Puppets* (Palgrave Macmillan, 2012), 6.
89. Davies, 18.
90. Tina Chen and S. X. Goudie, "Holders of the World: an Interview with Bharati Mukherjee," in *Conversations with Bharati Mukherjee*, ed. Bradley C. Edwards (University Press of Mississippi, 2009), 80.
91. Mukherjee, *Middleman*, 43, 45, 46, 52, 49.
92. Lippi-Green, *English with an Accent*, 46.
93. Mukherjee, *Middleman*, 46.
94. Mukherjee, *Middleman*, 47.
95. George P. Krapp, *The English Language in America* (Modern Language Association of America, 1925). Krapp coined the term "eye dialect" "to describe the phenomenon of unconventional spelling used to reproduce colloquial usage."
96. David Finbar Brett, "Eye Dialect: Translating the Untranslatable," *Annali della Facoltà di Lingue e Letterature Straniere di Sassari* 6 (2009): 49.
97. Rey Chow, *Not Like a Native Speaker: On Languaging as a Postcolonial Experience* (Columbia University Press, 2014), 3.
98. Chow, *Not Like a Native Speaker*, 3.
99. Mukherjee, *Middleman*, 52, 53.
100. Bharati Mukherjee, *Jasmine* (Grove, 1989), 112.
101. Mukherjee, *Middleman*, 121.
102. Rody, *Interethnic Imagination*, 40.
103. Maxey, *Understanding Bharati Mukherjee*, 57.
104. See Mary Bucholtz, *White Kids: Language, Race, and Styles of Youth Identity* (Cambridge University Press, 2011); Dan Sinykin, "White Voice," *nplusonemag.com*, no. 35 (Fall 2019); Doreen St. Félix, "Twisted Power of White Voice," *NewYorker.com*, August 13, 2018.
105. Mukherjee, *Middleman*, 138.
106. Lawrence Abu Hamdan, "Aural Contract: Forensic Listening and the Reorganization of the Speaking Subject," in *Forensis: The Architecture of Public Truth* (Sternberg Press and Forensic Architecture, 2014), 72.
107. Abu Hamdan, "Aural Contract," 72.
108. Zadie Smith, "Speaking in Tongues," *New York Review of Books*, February 26, 2009, www.nybooks.com/articles/2009/02/26/speaking-in-tongues-2/.
109. Bharati Mukherjee, "Preface," *Darkness and Other Stories* (Penguin, 1985), 3.
110. Lavigilante, "Globalization," 179–180.
111. For analysis of a related story, see Pooja Rangan, "Auditing the Call Centre Voice: Accented Speech and Listening in Sonali Gulati's *Nalini by Day, Nancy by Night*" (2005), in *Vocal Projections*, ed. Annabelle Honess Roe and Maria Pramaggiore (Bloomsbury Academic, 2019), 29–44.

112. Lavigilante, "Globalization," 183.
113. Bharati Mukherjee, *Miss New India* (Houghton Mifflin Harcourt, 2011), 97, 216, 306.
114. Mukherjee, *Miss New India*, 135, 165, 88–91, 241–242.
115. Lavigilante, "Globalization," 191, 182.
116. Grewal, *Transnational America*, 70.
117. Lavigilante, "Globalization," 182, 179.
118. Ragini Tharoor Srinivasan, "Call Center Agents and Expatriate Writers: Twin Subjects of New Indian Capital," *ARIEL: A Review of International English Literature* 49, no. 4 (2018): 77–107.
119. A. Aneesh, *Neutral Accent: How Language, Labor, and Life Become Global* (Duke University Press, 2015), 61–62, 68.
120. Kiran Mirchandani, *Phone Clones: Authenticity Work in the Transnational Service Economy* (Cornell University Press, 2012), 1, 3.
121. A. Aneesh, *Virtual Migration: The Programming of Globalization* (Duke University Press, 2006), 93.
122. Vineeta Chand, "[V]at Is Going On? Local and Global Ideologies about Indian English," *Language in Society* 38 (2009): 393–419.

2/Recess 1. You Wouldn't Say That to Gayatri Spivak

1. Sangeeta Ray, *Gayatri Chakravorty Spivak: In Other Words* (Wiley-Blackwell, 2009), 3.
2. Rey Chow, "The Resistance of Theory; or, The Worth of Agony," in *Just Being Difficult? Academic Writing in the Public Arena*, ed. Jonathan Culler and Kevin Lamb (Stanford University Press, 2003), 104.
3. Liam O'Loughlin, "'Listening to Three Stacks, Reading Gaya Spivak': Das Racist and the Postcolonial-Studies Generation," Modern Language Association (January 10, 2016). The name "Gaya Spivak" is lyrical grist for the mill in raps songs, like "Ek Shaneesh" by the alternative hip hop group Das Racist, "Spivak" rhymed with "believe that," dropped alongside references to Outkast, V. S. Naipaul, Andy Warhol, and Nancy Reagan. Spivak's name is also in the lyrics to the 1999 song "Hot Topic" by Le Tigre, alongside references to Angela Davis, Nina Simone, Gertrude Stein, Yoko Ono, and Urvashi Vaid; the song was used in a Kohl's commercial in 2016.
4. Yan Hairong, "Position Without Identity: An Interview with Gayatri Chakravorty Spivak," *positions* 15, no. 2 (2007): 442.
5. "Can the Subaltern Speak?" was first delivered as a speech, "Power and Desire," in 1983. It was published in 1985 as "Can the Subaltern Speak?: Speculations

on Widow Sacrifice" in the short-lived journal *Wedge*. A longer version appeared in the much-cited 1988 volume *Marxism and the Interpretation of Culture*, edited by Lawrence Grossberg and Cary Nelson. In 1999, the essay was republished in the "History" chapter of *A Critique of Postcolonial Reason*.

6. Ray, *Gayatri Chakravorty Spivak*; Graham Riach, *An Analysis of Gayatri Chakravorty Spivak's "Can the Subaltern Speak?"* (Routledge, 2017); Stephen Morton, *Gayatri Spivak: Ethics, Subalternity and the Critique of Postcolonial Reason* (Polity, 2007); Rosalind C. Morris, ed., *Can the Subaltern Speak?: Reflections on the history of an idea* (Columbia University Press, 2010).

7. Jeffrey J. Williams, "Name Recognition," *Minnesota Review* 52, no. 1 (2001): 202.

8. Sharon O'Dair, "Stars, Tenure, and the Death," in *Day Late, Dollar Short: The Next Generation and the New Academy*, ed. Peter C. Hermann (SUNY Press, 2000), 45–62; Ann Pellegrini, "Star Gazing," *Minnesota Review* 52, no. 1 (2001); Bruce Robbins, "Celeb-Reliance: Intellectuals, Celebrity, and Upward Mobility," *Postmodern Culture* 9, no. 2 (1999); David R. Shumway, "The Star System in Literary Studies," *PMLA* 112, no. 1 (1997): 85–100.

9. Williams, "Name Recognition," 187, 193, 189.

10. Here is Jenny Sharpe's story of interpellation: "I first met Spivak in Austin, Texas, a little more than twenty years ago. As an entering freshman at the University of Texas, I was instructed to take a class with a new English professor, who, like me, was from India. I, resenting the assumption behind the recommendation, avoided studying with Spivak. But her reputation as a Marxist feminist-deconstructionist (as she was known at the time) soon caught up with me." Sharpe and Gayatri Chakravorty Spivak, "A Conversation with Gayatri Chakravorty Spivak: Politics and the Imagination," *Signs: Journal of Women in Culture and Society* 28, no. 2 (2002): 609.

11. Nasia Anam, "Introduction: Forms of the Global Anglophone," *Post45: Contemporaries*, February 22, 2019, https://post45.org/sections/contemporaries-essays/global-anglophone/.

12. Gayatri Chakravorty Spivak, *A Critique of Postcolonial Reason: Toward a History of the Vanishing Present* (Harvard University Press, 1999), 267. Spivak has referred more than once to the "accidents" of birth and history that have overdetermined her own trajectory. She most famously uses the language of "accident" in "Can the Subaltern Speak?":

> I turn to Indian material because, in the absence of advanced disciplinary training, that accident of birth and education has provided me with a sense of the *historical* canvas, a hold on some of the pertinent languages that are useful tools for a *bricoleur*, especially when armed

with the Marxist skepticism of concrete experience as the final arbiter and a critique of disciplinary formations.

In a characteristic critique of this disclaimer, Hamid Dabashi terms it a "dubious" effort by Spivak to address what he calls "the untenable ground of her hermeneutics" as an "amateur commentator on a legal text uprooted from its historical context"—by which he is referring to Hindu law pertaining to sati. See Dabashi, *Post-Orientalism: Knowledge and Power in Time of Terror* (Routledge, 2009), 132.

Spivak also uses the term "accident" in an interview with Robert J. C. Young, in narrating how she came to her work:

> At first I felt that I couldn't just be an expert on French feminism. . . . And then I began to see that it was necessary in order to study British literature to consider the cultural self-representation of the British. In order to see this, since Literature was one of the instruments of cultural self-representation, I came face to face with the representation of the colonies hidden in the nooks and crannies of the work—and doing this I felt that it was not just enough to look at its representation in Metropolitan literature. . . . It happens that I am bilingual in my mother tongue and English and equally proficient in both; so that accident allowed me to investigate a bit more the Bengali area.

See Spivak and Young, "Neocolonialism and the Secret Agent of Knowledge," *Oxford Literary Review* 13, nos. 1/2 (1991): 229.

For a third instance of Spivak's usage of the term "accident," see Hairong, "Position Without Identity," 442.

13. Ragini Tharoor Srinivasan, "Introduction: South Asia from *Postcolonial* to World *Anglophone*," *Interventions* 20, no. 3 (2018): 309–316.
14. Tilottama Rajan, "On (Not) Being Postcolonial," *Postcolonial Text* 2, no. 1 (2006).
15. Spivak has reflected on such instances: "I was asked to write a catalog essay for an exhibition on the Hindu great goddess at the Smithsonian for which I had *no* qualification—I'm not an art historian—I'm a British literature modernist and French and German comparativist, and completely irreligious, I realized that I was being called because I'm hyphenated, and so I totally let myself go. It is a very crazy piece as to what a hyphenated American can do if she relies on nothing but the fact that she is hyphenated." See Hairong, "Position Without Identity," 442.
16. Ray, *Gayatri Chakravorty Spivak*, 5–6. For a comparative case in which a black, South African professor is wrongly interpellated on his street in

Ithaca, New York, and provides his own cutting, accented response, see Grant Farred, *Martin Heidegger Saved My Life* (University of Minnesota Press, 2015).

17. Gayatri Chakravorty Spivak, *Readings* (Seagull, 2014), 143.
18. Ilan Kapoor, "Spivak, Politics of Pronunciation, and the Search for a Just Democracy," *AlJazeera*, June 7, 2024, www.aljazeera.com/opinions/2024/6/7/spivak-politics-of-pronunciation-and-the-search-for-a-just-democracy.
19. Abhinay Lakshman, "JNU Student Did Not Identify Himself as Dalit: Gayatri Chakravorty Spivak on Row After Seminar," *The Hindu*, May 25, 2024, www.thehindu.com/news/national/gayatri-spivak-on-jnu-row/article68212572.ece.
20. Lara Choksey, "Introduction," in *Readings*, by Gayatri Chakravorty Spivak (Seagull, 2014), ix.
21. Spivak, *Readings*, 87.
22. Martin Jay, "The Academic Woman as Performance Artist," *Salmagundi* 98/99 (1993): 32.
23. Jay, "The Academic Woman," 33, 29.
24. Pellegrini, "Star Gazing," 214.
25. See Hairong, "Position Without Identity," 443–444. Spivak is quoted thus: "People say it was Edward Said and myself and Homi Bhabha . . . we are generally put together as the founders of postcolonialism. I certainly know that two or three things that I wrote at the beginning of the eighties have been vastly reprinted as postcolonial texts, but I didn't really know that I was doing anything postcolonial and I don't believe that when Said was writing *Orientalism* he thought that he was doing something postcolonial, but that is quite often the case, that people who write at the beginning don't . . . because neither Homi nor I were thinking much about the postcolonial in a broad way, the South Asian model, which is a rich field, began to take hold."
26. Ragini Tharoor Srinivasan, "Call Center Agents and Expatriate Writers: Twin Subjects of New Indian Capital," *ARIEL: A Review of International English Literature* 49, no. 4 (2018): 77–107.
27. Terry Eagleton, "In the Gaudy Supermarket," *London Review of Books* 21, no. 10 (May 1999), www.lrb.co.uk/the-paper/v21/n10/terry-eagleton/in-the-gaudy-supermarket.
28. Dinitia Smith, "Creating a Stir Wherever She Goes," *New York Times*, February 9, 2002, www.nytimes.com/2002/02/09/arts/creating-a-stir-wherever-she-goes.html.
29. Jonathan Culler and Kevin Lamb, ed., *Just Being Difficult? Academic Writing in the Public Arena* (Stanford University Press, 2003).

30. See Martha Nussbaum's infamous critique of Butler: "The Professor of Parody," *The New Republic* (February 22, 1999), https://newrepublic.com/article/150687/professor-parody.
31. For an extended discussion of this question, see Ragini Tharoor Srinivasan, "'Can the Subaltern Speak' to My Students?," *Feminist Formations* 32, no. 1 (2020): 58–74.
32. Donna Landry and Gerald MacLean, "Introduction: Reading Spivak," in *The Spivak Reader: Selected Works of Gayatri Chakravorty Spivak* (Routledge, 1996), 3.
33. Judith Butler, "Letters: Exacting Solidarities," *London Review of Books* 21, no. 13 (July 1999), www.lrb.co.uk/the-paper/v21/n13/letters.
34. Hairong, "Position Without Identity," 444.
35. Sharpe, "A Conversation," 622.
36. Spivak, *Readings*, 6.
37. Beth Loffreda and Claudia Rankine, introduction to *The Racial Imaginary: Writers on Race in the Life of the Mind*, ed. Claudia Rankine, Beth Loffreda, and Max King Cap (Fence, 2015), 18.
38. Gayatri Chakravorty Spivak, *Death of a Discipline: 20th Anniversary Edition* (Columbia University Press, 2023), 5–6.
39. Kartik Maini, "Gayatri Chakravorty Spivak on the Art of Translation and Its Inextricable Relationship with Culture," *Firstpost*, March 1, 2018, www.firstpost.com/living/gayatri-chakravorty-spivak-on-the-art-of-translation-and-its-inextricable-relationship-with-culture-4370989.html.
40. Sharpe, "A Conversation," 621.
41. Spivak, *Death of a Discipline*, xv.
42. Alex Sachare, "Spivak Named University Professor," *Columbia College Today*, May/June 2007, www.college.columbia.edu/cct_archive/may_jun07/quads3.html.
43. Spivak, *Readings*, 165.
44. Spivak, *Readings*, 73.
45. Gayatri Chakravorty Spivak, "Translating in a World of Languages," *Profession* (2010): 36.
46. Spivak, *Death of a Discipline*, 8, ix.
47. Colleen Lye, "Identity Politics, Criticism, and Self-Criticism," *South Atlantic Quarterly* 119, no. 4 (October 2020): 702.
48. Fredric Jameson, Special Session on "*The Political Unconscious*—Forty Years On," Modern Language Association Annual Convention (2021), www.youtube.com/watch?v=tEq3GyDYmOk.
49. Sharpe, "A Conversation," 621.
50. Spivak, *Death of a Discipline*, 6.

3. When the Anglophone Reads "Like Hindi": Or, On Not Teaching Chetan Bhagat

1. Robert McCrum, "Chetan Bhagat: The Paperback King of India," *The Observer*, January 23, 2010.
2. Rashmi Sadana, "Writing in English," in *The Cambridge Companion to Modern Indian Culture*, ed. Vasudha Dalmia and Rashmi Sadana (Cambridge University Press, 2012), 137.
3. Manisha Basu, *The Rhetoric of Hindu India: Language and Urban Nationalism* (Cambridge University Press, 2017), 184.
4. Aravind Adiga, *The White Tiger* (Free Press, 2008), 3.
5. The populist, authoritarian, Hindu majoritarian "New Indian politics" that characterizes the Modi years has been contested by numerous popular protest movements. For essays on an array of figures of "the people of India," including the political activist, the agricultural laborer, and the mob, see Ravinder Kaur and Nayanika Mathur, *The People of India: New Indian Politics in the 21st Century* (Penguin Viking, 2022).
6. "Read the Full Transcript of Indian Prime Minister Narendra Modi's Independence Day Speech," *Time*, August 15, 2017, https://time.com/4901564/narendra-modi-india-70-independence-day-speech/. The "New India Pledge" is available from www.mygov.in/newindia/index.html.
7. The idea of a "New India" has been reanimated since at least the mid-nineteenth century, at colonial, anticolonial, postcolonial, and global inflection points. See Ravinder Kaur, *Brand New Nation: Capitalist Dreams and Nationalist Designs in Twenty-First-Century India* (Stanford University Press, 2020).
8. Like English, Hindi is not one language but many, spoken across at least eleven states in India, and variously mixed with languages including Punjabi, Urdu, Nepali, Bhojpuri, and Sanskrit, and inflected by numerous dialects. Hindi is deeply contested and politicized. Alok Rai makes a case for Hindi as a kind of pharmakon in contemporary India, a "disease" and "cure" (3). Rai argues that if Hindi is not "properly understood [and] deployed" the "field of vernacular mobilization in the heartland" will be left clear for the likes of the BJP (13). Rai, *Hindi Nationalism* (Orient Longman, 2001). Relatedly, Rashmi Sadana observes that Hindi contains "democratic energies of the people, and yet . . . has been hijacked by those who want to preserve a Sanskritized Hindi, or Manak or Standard Hindi." Sadana, "Managing Hindi: How We Live Multilingually and What This Says About Our Language and Literature," *Caravan*, April 1, 2012, 62–71.
9. See Prashant Agrawal, "Why Narendra Modi Will Deliver his UN Speech in Hindi," *Quartz* India, September 27, 2014, http://qz.com/272169/why-narendra

-modi-will-deliver-his-un-speech-in-hindi/; and R. Jagannathan, "Behind Pankaj Mishra's Rants: A Pathology of Hindu-Phobia and Self-Hate," *Firstpost .com*, October 26, 2014, www.firstpost.com/india/behind-pankaj-mishras-rants-a-pathology-of-hindu-phobia-and-self-hate-1772105.html.
10. E. Dawson Varughese, *Reading New India: Post-Millennial Indian Fiction in English* (Bloomsbury Academic, 2013), 152.
11. Samanth Subramanian, "India After English?," *New York Review of Books*, June 9, 2014.
12. Ulka Anjaria, "Introduction: Literary Pasts, Presents, and Futures," in *A History of the Indian Novel in English* (Cambridge University Press, 2015), 12.
13. Ulka Anjaria, *Reading India Now: Contemporary Formations in Literature and Popular Culture* (Temple University Press, 2019), 35.
14. Quoted in Basu, *Rhetoric of Hindu India*, 192.
15. Chetan Bhagat, "Skills to Succeed in a Global World," episode from *Chetan Bhagat: Podcast* (December 28, 2022).
16. The operative phrase is "within English itself." For a related discussion of the "multilingual Anglophone" that unfolds through comparisons between English and other Indian languages, see Bhavya Tiwari, "The Multilingual Anglophone: World Literature and Post-Millennial Literature in Postcolonial India," *Interventions* 23, no. 4 (2021): 621–635.
17. Rebecca Walkowitz, *Born Translated: The Contemporary Novel in an Age of World Literature* (Columbia University Press, 2015).
18. See, for example, Rita Felski, "After Suspicion," *Profession* (2009): 28–35; Heather Love, "Truth and Consequences: On Paranoid Reading and Reparative Reading," *Criticism* 52, no. 2 (2010): 235–241; Frida Beckman and Charlie Black, "We Have Been Paranoid Too Long to Stop Now," in *New Directions in Philosophy and Literature* (Edinburgh University Press, 2019), 410–428.
19. Tobias Skiveren, "Postcritique and the Problem of the Lay Reader," *New Literary History* 53 (2022): 162–163.
20. Roanne L. Kantor, "Futures Past: South Asian Literature 'Post-Boom,'" *Interventions* 20, no. 3 (2018): 345–353.
21. Gayatri Chakravorty Spivak, *Death of a Discipline* (Columbia University Press, 2023 [2003]), 10.
22. Spivak, *Death of a Discipline*, 9.
23. Rey Chow, *The Age of the World Target: Self-Referentiality in War, Theory, and Comparative Work* (Duke University Press, 2006), 73.
24. Mrinal Pande, *The Other Country: Dispatches from the Mofussil* (Penguin, 2011), xi–xiii.
25. Bhimraj Muthu, "The Class and Caste Capital Behind Correct English: A Dalit Scholar Writes," *The News Minute*, May 24, 2024, www.thenewsminute

.com/news/the-class-and-caste-capital-behind-correct-english-a-dalit-scholar-writes.
26. Gayatri Chakravorty Spivak, *Readings* (Seagull, 2014), 71.
27. Donald Greenlees, "An Investment Banker Finds Fame off the Books," *New York Times*, March 26, 2008.
28. Priya Joshi, "Chetan Bhagat: Remaking the Novel in India," in *A History of the Indian Novel in English*, ed. Ulka Anjaria (Cambridge University Press, 2015), 311.
29. Basu, *Rhetoric of Hindu India*, 168.
30. On the global distribution and prestige of Bollywood as a complementary sector of cultural production, see Priya Joshi, *Bollywood's India: A Public Fantasy* (Columbia University Press, 2015); and Ulka Anjaria, *Understanding Bollywood: The Grammar of Hindi Cinema* (Routledge, 2021).
31. Chetan Bhagat, *What Young India Wants: Selected Non-Fiction* (Rupa, 2014), xix.
32. *Cyrus Says* (podcast), Episode 375: Chetan Bhagat (May 20, 2019) [6:22–6:40].
33. Saikat Majumdar, "Introduction to Focus: Little India—the Provincial Life of Cosmopolitanism," *American Book Review* 36, no. 6 (September/October 2015). Bhagat endorsed Modi on April 21, 2014, on Facebook, with a selfie and the hashtag #namo.
34. Bhagat, *What Young India Wants*, xxiv. See also *Cyrus Says* (podcast), Episode 375: Chetan Bhagat (May 20, 2019).
35. Basu, *Rhetoric of Hindu India*, 179.
36. Quoted in Pallavi Rao, "The Five-Point Indian: Caste, Masculinity, and English Language in the Paratexts of Chetan Bhagat," *Journal of Communication Inquiry* 42, no. 1 (2018): 92.
37. Rashmi Sadana, *English Heart, Hindi Heartland: The Political Life of Literature in India* (University of California Press, 2012), 176.
38. Mrinalini Chakravorty, *In Stereotype: South Asia in the Global Literary Imagination* (Columbia University Press, 2014), 190.
39. Basu, *Rhetoric of Hindu India*, 170, xii.
40. Sadana, "Writing," 138
41. Ulka Anjaria, "Chetan Bhagat and the New Provincialism," *American Book Review* 36, no. 6 (2015): 6–22.
42. Joshi, "Chetan Bhagat," 318.
43. Basu, *Rhetoric of Hindu India*, 167.
44. Suman Gupta, "Indian 'Commercial Fiction' in English, the Publishing Industry and Youth Culture," *Economic and Political Weekly* (2012): 46–53.
45. Joshi, "Chetan Bhagat," 310.
46. Bhagat, *What Young India Wants*, 115–116.

47. Mathangi Krishnamurthy, "Furtive Tongues: Language Politics in the Indian Call Centre," in *Chutnefying English: The Phenomenon of Hinglish*, ed. Rita Kothari and Rupert Snell (Penguin, 2011).
48. Sadana, *English Heart*, 179.
49. Ulka Anjaria and Jonathan Shapiro Anjaria, "The Fractured Spaces of Entrepreneurialism in Post-Liberalization India," in *Enterprise Culture in Neoliberal India: Studies in Youth, Class, Work and Media*, ed. Nandini Gooptu (Routledge, 2013).
50. Quoted in Randeep Ramesh, "Author's Mass-Market Success Upsets Indian Literati," *Guardian*, October 8, 2008.
51. A group photograph of Indian English expatriate writers was published with the caption "Salman Rushdie and Friends" in *A History of Indian Literature in English* (2003), edited by A. K. Mehrotra. The photo, by Max Vadukul, was first published in the *New Yorker's* June 23/30, 1997, issue with the caption "A Gathering of India's Leading Novelists."
52. Chetan Bhagat, *Half Girlfriend* (Rupa, 2014), vii–viii.
53. Quoted in Divashri Sinha, "Chetanic Verses," *Times of India*, January 1, 2012, http://timesofindia.indiatimes.com/life-style/books/features/Chetanic-Verses/articleshow/10539267.cms.
54. After the publication of *Midnight's Children*, Bill Buford invited Rushdie to give a reading at a space above a hairdresser's salon. "I didn't know who was going to show up," Rushdie recalled. "The room was packed, absolutely bursting at the seams, and a large percentage were Indian readers. I was unbelievably moved. A rather well-dressed middle-aged lady in a fancy sari stood up at the end of the reading, in this sort of Q. & A. bit, and she said, 'I want to thank you, Mr. Rushdie, because you have told my story.' It still almost makes me cry." Bhagat's young woman may not have raised her hand to speak to Rushdie, but the "middle-aged lady in a fancy sari" *did*, with intimacy and familiarity. See David Remnick, "The Defiance of Salman Rushdie," *New Yorker* (February 6 and 13, 2023).
55. Quoted in Sinha, "Chetanic Verses," 2012.
56. In March 2023, Bhagat's books were available on Amazon India for an average of 140 rupees each ($1.66).
57. Basu, *Rhetoric of Hindu India*, 191–192.
58. Homi Bhabha, *The Location of Culture* (Routledge, 1994), 102.
59. David Damrosch, *What Is World Literature?* (Princeton University Press, 2003).
60. Graham Huggan, *The Postcolonial Exotic: Marketing the Margins* (Routledge, 2001).
61. Ulka Anjaria, "Great Aspirations," *Public Books*, July 31, 2017, www.publicbooks.org/great-aspirations/.

62. Anjaria, "Introduction," 12.
63. Sadana, "Writing," 138.
64. Gupta, "Indian 'Commercial Fiction,'" 50.
65. Sadana, *English Heart*, 176.
66. Joshi, "Chetan Bhagat," 318.
67. Joshi, "Chetan Bhagat," 319.
68. Nandini Gooptu, "Introduction," in *Enterprise Culture in Neoliberal India: Studies in Youth, Class, Work and Media*, ed. Nandini Gooptu (Routledge, 2013), 1.
69. Belinda Edmondson, *Caribbean Middlebrow: Leisure Culture and the Middle Class* (Cornell University Press, 2009), 10.
70. Chetan Bhagat, *One Night @ the Call Center* (Rupa, 2005), 6, 8.
71. Chetan Bhagat, *The 3 Mistakes of My Life* (Rupa, 2008), xi, 8.
72. Bhagat, *3 Mistakes*, xvii.
73. Bhagat, *Half Girlfriend*, 2.
74. Bhagat, *One Night @ the Call Center*, 14.
75. Bhagat, *Half Girlfriend*, 2, 13, 8, my emphasis.
76. Bhagat, *Half Girlfriend*, 128–129, 149.
77. Bhagat, *What Young India Wants*, 117.
78. Chetan Bhagat, *One Indian Girl* (Rupa, 2016), 32.
79. Bhagat, *One Night @ the Call Center*, 45.
80. Akshya Saxena, "South Asian Accents: *Bhashas*, Bodies, Borders," *South Asian Review* 45.3-4 (2024): 524-531.
81. Joshi, "Chetan Bhagat," 315.
82. Bhagat, *3 Mistakes*, 64.
83. Sadana, "Writing," 139.
84. Dohra Ahmad, *Rotten English: A Literary Anthology* (W. W. Norton, 2007); Evelyn Nien-Ming Ch'ien, *Weird English* (Harvard University Press, 2005).
85. Urvashi Butalia, "Panel Discussion II: Is Hinglish a Unifying Force?," in *Chutnefying English: The Phenomenon of Hinglish*, ed. Rita Kothari and Rupert Snell (Penguin, 2011), 201–202.
86. Janice A. Radway, *Reading the Romance: Women, Patriarchy, and Popular Literature* (University of North Carolina Press, 1984, 1991), 7.
87. Aatish Taseer, "How English Ruined Indian Literature," *New York Times*, March 19, 2015.
88. Vikram Chandra, "The Cult of Authenticity," *Boston Review* (2000).
89. Chakravorty, *In Stereotype*; see also Liam Connell, "E-Terror: Computer Viruses, Class and Transnationalism in *Transmission* and *One Night @ the Call Center*," *Journal of Postcolonial Writing* 46, nos. 3–4 (2010): 279–290.
90. Sadana, *English Heart*, 175–176.

91. Gupta, "Indian 'Commercial Fiction,'" 48–50.
92. Deepika Bahri, *Native Intelligence: Aesthetics, Politics, and Postcolonial Literature* (University of Minnesota Press, 2003).
93. *Cyrus Says* (podcast), Episode 559: Chetan Bhagat Returns (September 7, 2020), [39:20–50].
94. Chetan Bhagat's Twitter account (November 20, 2021 at 12:09 pm), https://twitter.com/chetan_bhagat/status/1462015127268388865?s=20
95. Here's an example from Twitter, where Bhagat has over 12.5 million followers. On November 20, 2021, Bhagat tweeted the following: "Upbringing in English speaking home, reading a few books, watching a few esoteric films or shows—this is enough for some to believe they are superior than other Indians. They also believe they can judge other writers. No accomplishments of their own—yet better than others!"
96. Sara Ahmed, "Willful Parts: Problem Characters or the Problem of Character," *New Literary History* 42, no. 2 (2011): 231.
97. Kinohi Nishikawa, "Merely Reading." *PMLA* 130, no. 3 (2015): 698.
98. Ahmed, "Willful Parts," 231.
99. Alejandro Zambra, *Not to Read*, trans. Megan McDowell (Fitzcarraldo, 2018), 81; and Amy Hungerford, *Making Literature Now* (Stanford University Press, 2016).
100. Ted Underwood, "A Genealogy of Distant Reading," *Digital Humanities Quarterly* 11, no. 2 (2017).
101. Sheila Liming, "In Praise of Not Reading," *The Point*, April 4, 2017, https://thepointmag.com/criticism/in-praise-of-not-not-reading/
102. Hungerford, *Making Literature*, 94.
103. Ragini Tharoor Srinivasan, "Is There a Call Center Literature?," in *Thinking with an Accent: Toward a New Object, Method, and Practice* (University of California Press, 2023), 129.
104. Lucas Thompson, "Method Reading," *New Literary History* 50 (2019): 295.
105. Thompson, "Method Reading," 297.
106. Radway, *Reading*, 5.
107. Ulka Anjaria and Jonathan Shapiro Anjaria, "*Mazaa:* Rethinking Fun, Pleasure and Play in South Asia," *South Asia: Journal of South Asian Studies* 43, no. 2 (2020): 232–242.
108. Anjaria and Shapiro Anjaria, 203.
109. Anjaria, *Reading India Now*, 31.
110. Anjaria, *Reading India Now*, 50.
111. Michael Warner, "Uncritical Reading," *Polemic* (2012): 32.
112. Nan Z. Da, "Other People's Books." *New Literary History* 51, no. 3 (2020): 477.

113. Toral Gajarawala, "Caste, Complicity, and the Contemporary," *A History of the Indian Novel in English*, ed. Ulka Anjaria (Cambridge University Press, 2015), 373–374.
114. At the time, the Popular Fiction list consisted of Lewis Carroll's *Through the Looking Glass* (1871), Agatha Christie's *The Murder of Roger Ackroyd* (1926), the Sri Lankan-Canadian Shyam Selvadurai's *Funny Boy* (1994), and Durgabai Vyam and Shubhash Vyam's graphic novel *Bhimayana: Experiences of Untouchability* (2011). The proposed revision involved a reconception of "the popular" itself; it was not just a matter of updating the list.
115. Riya Sharma, "Chetan Bhagat—Too Trashy for DU Syllabus, or an 'Easy Read' for an Elective?," *The Times of India*, April 25, 2017, https://timesofindia.indiatimes.com/city/delhi/chetan-bhagat-too-trashy-for-du-syllabus-or-an-easy-read-for-an-elective/articleshow/58347021.cms.
116. Quoted in Sharma.
117. Heena Kausar, "Chetan Bhagat's *Five Point Someone* in Delhi University English Literature Syllabus," *Hindustan Times*, April 25, 2017, www.hindustantimes.com/delhi/chetan-bhagat-s-five-point-someone-in-delhi-university-english-literature-syllabus/story-JVRGnIQX5C7oGkaLnfysIN.html.
118. Quoted in Saket Suman, "Chetan Bhagat's Inclusion in DU Syllabus Was Arbitrary: Stakeholders," *The Week*, September 25, 2017, www.theweek.in/news/india/chetan-bhagats-inclusion-in-du-syllabus-was-arbitrary-stakeholders.html.
119. Huggan, *Postcolonial Exotic*, 81.
120. Huggan, *Postcolonial Exotic*, 81.
121. Kantor, "Futures Past," 5.
122. Salman Rushdie, "Damme, This Is the Oriental Scene for You!" *New Yorker*, June 23 and 30, 1997, 50–61.
123. Bhagat, *What Young India Wants*, 117–118.
124. Spivak, *Death of a Discipline*, 10.
125. Ragini Tharoor Srinivasan, "Introduction: South Asia from Postcolonial to World Anglophone," *Interventions* 20, no. 3 (2018): 309–316; Tobias Warner, *The Tongue-Tied Imagination: Decolonizing Literary Modernity in Senegal* (Fordham University Press, 2019).
126. Akshya Saxena, *Vernacular English: Reading the Anglophone in Postcolonial India* (Princeton University Press, 2022), 124.
127. Saxena, *Vernacular English*, 6–8.
128. Saxena, *Vernacular English*, 15.
129. Bhagat, "Skills."
130. Sadana, "Managing Hindi," 71.
131. Saxena, *Vernacular English*, 6.

132. Diasporic Indians and students from India in these classrooms will experience studying Bhagat in the United States differently, whether because of existing relationships to the figure of "the Bhagat reader" (e.g., identification or repudiation) or because of the overdetermined position into which they are hailed when an "Indian" text is taught.

4/Recess 2. The Ambivalence of Homi Bhabha's Discourse

1. J. Daniel Elam and Ragini Tharoor Srinivasan, "Introduction to 1990 at 30," *Post45: Contemporaries* (May 19, 2020), https://post45.org/2020/05/introduction-to-1990-at-30/#footnote_1_11678.
2. Sangeeta Ray, "I mean seriously cannot get behind the Bhabha essay alongside the others. Just not at par!," Twitter (now X), May 20, 2020, https://twitter.com/tallsasian/status/1262882746793328646?s=20.
3. Homi Bhabha, "The Commitment to Theory," *New Formations* 5, no. 1 (1988): 5–23.
4. Paul Reitter and Chad Wellmon, *Permanent Crisis: The Humanities in a Disenchanted Age* (University of Chicago Press, 2021). See also Abigail Boggs and Nick Mitchell, "Critical University Studies and the Crisis Consensus," *Feminist Studies* 44, no. 2 (2018): 432–463.
5. Robert J. C. Young, *Colonial Desire: Hybridity in Theory, Culture, and Race* (Routledge, 1995), 163.
6. Homi Bhabha, "Of Mimicry and Man: The Ambivalence of Colonial Discourse," *October* 28 (1984): 125–133; reprinted in Bhabha, *The Location of Culture* (Routledge, 1994).
7. Pooja Rangan, Akshya Saxena, Ragini Tharoor Srinivasan, and Pavitra Sundar, "Introduction: Thinking with an Accent," in *Thinking with an Accent: Toward a New Object, Method, and Practice* (University of California Press, 2023), 3, 2.
8. John Guillory, "The Sokal Affair and the History of Criticism," *Critical Inquiry* 28, no. 2 (2002): 470–508.
9. Toril Moi, *Revolution of the Ordinary: Literary Studies After Wittgenstein, Austin, and Cavell* (University of Chicago Press, 2017), 163.
10. Gayatri Chakravorty Spivak and Robert J. C. Young, "Neocolonialism and the Secret Agent of Knowledge," *Oxford Literary Review* 13, nos. 1/2 (1991): 238.
11. Moi, *Revolution*, 165. Bhabha himself notes, "That a book should be impaired by a lack of clarity, so that people cannot respond to it and meditate on it and use it, must be a major indictment of anybody who wants to do serious

work." W. J. T. Mitchell and Homi Bhabha, "Translator Translated," *Artforum* 33 (1995): 81.
12. Moi, *Revolution*, 165.
13. Bhabha, "Translator Translated," 81–82.
14. Homi Bhabha, "DissemiNation: Time, Narrative, and the Margins of the Modern Nation," in *Nation and Narration*, ed. Homi Bhabha (Routledge, 1990), 297.
15. Homi Bhabha, "Introduction: Narrating the Nation," in *Nation and Narration*, ed. Homi Bhabha (Routledge, 1990), 2–3.
16. Bhabha, "DissemiNation," 292, 300.
17. Bhabha, "DissemiNation," 308, 309.
18. Bhabha, "Introduction," 6.
19. Bhabha, "DissemiNation," 302.
20. Robert J. C. Young, "The Dislocations of Cultural Translation," *PMLA* 132, no. 1 (2017): 186.
21. Kavita Daiya, "The World After Empire; or, Whither Postcoloniality," *PMLA* 132, no. 1 (2017): 153.
22. Arjun Appadurai, "Patriotism and Its Futures," *Public Culture*, no. 5 (1993): 412.
23. Neil Larsen, *Determinations: Essays on Theory, Narrative and Nation in the Americas* (Verso, 2001), 42–43.
24. Lauren Berlant, *The Queen of America Goes to Washington City: Essays on Sex and Citizenship* (Duke University Press, 1997); Benedict Anderson, *The Spectre of Comparisons: Nationalism, Southeast Asia, and the World* (Verso, 1998); Pheng Cheah, *Spectral Nationality: Passages of Freedom from Kant to Postcolonial Literatures of Liberation* (Columbia University Press, 2003); Manisha Basu, *The Rhetoric of Hindu India: Language and Urban Nationalism* (Cambridge University Press, 2016).
25. This is a charge that has been leveled at postcolonial theory writ large: "The obligatory subversiveness of postcolonial literature is seriously limited by the notion of 'textual politics' favoured by postcolonial literary theory. In a move which effectively replaces politics with textuality, such theory delivers a world where power is exclusively an operation of discourse, and resistance a literary contest of representation." See Leela Gandhi, *Postcolonial Theory: A Critical Introduction* (Columbia University Press, 1998), 156.
26. For instance, in comparison to Said, Joseph Massad describes Bhabha as "committed to depoliticizing deeply political questions." See Massad, "The Intellectual Life of Edward Said," *Journal of Palestine Studies* 33, no. 3 (2004): 15.
27. Writing in July 2024, the statistician-turned-political-commentator Nate Silver described Karl Rove's Iraq War–era discourse on the creation of reality as a species of "postmodern relativism." See Silver, "Blaming the Media

Is What Got Democrats Into This Mess," *Silver Bulletin* (July 8, 2024), www.natesilver.net/p/blaming-the-media-is-what-got-democrats. See also Ava Kofman, "Bruno Latour, the Post-Truth Philosopher, Mounts a Defense of Science," *New York Times*, October 25, 2018, www.nytimes.com/2018/10/25/magazine/bruno-latour-post-truth-philosopher-science.html.

28. Jeffrey J. Kripal, *The Superhumanities: Historical Precedents, Moral Objections, New Realities* (University of Chicago Press, 2022), 78.
29. Merve Emre, "Has Academia Ruined Literary Criticism?" *New Yorker*, January 16, 2023, www.newyorker.com/magazine/2023/01/23/has-academia-ruined-literary-criticism-professing-criticism-john-guillory.
30. Sarah Brouillette, "Reading After the University," *Public Books*, November 23, 2022, www.publicbooks.org/reading-after-the-university-english-departments/.
31. Jennifer Schuessler, "What Is Literary Criticism For?" *New York Times*, February 3, 2023, www.nytimes.com/2023/02/03/arts/john-guillory-literary-criticism.html.
32. Nicholas Dames, "A Profession! What Has Become of Literary Studies?," *The Nation*, February 21, 2023, www.thenation.com/article/culture/john-guillory-professing-criticism/. See also Eric Hayot, "The Sky Is Falling," *Profession*, May 2018, https://profession.mla.org/the-sky-is-falling/.
33. Patricia Yaeger, "The End of Postcolonial Theory?: A Roundtable with Sunil Agnani, Fernando Coronil, Gaurav Desai, Mamadou Diouf, Simon Gikandi, Susie Tharu, and Jennifer Wenzel," *PMLA* 122, no. 3 (2007): 633–651; Dipesh Chakrabarty, "Postcolonial Studies and Climate Change," *New Literary History* 43, no. 1 (2012): 1–18; Robert Stam and Ella Shohat, "Whence and Whither Postcolonial Theory?" *New Literary History* 43, no. 2 (2012): 371–390; Robert J. C. Young, "Postcolonial Remains," *New Literary History* 43, no. 1 (2012): 19–42; and Daiya, "World After Empire," 149–155.
34. Jesse Aleman, "The End of English," *PMLA* 136, no. 3 (2021): 470–474.
35. Sara Marcus, *Political Disappointment: A Cultural History from Reconstruction to the AIDS Crisis* (Harvard University Press, 2023), 1.
36. Marcus, 16, 23, 14, 13, 1.
37. Nathan Heller, "The End of the English Major," *New Yorker*, March 6, 2023, www.newyorker.com/magazine/2023/03/06/the-end-of-the-english-major.
38. I am referring to academic and critical secondary discourse. There is also a robust *public* discourse on the work of canonical theorists. The question of whether one can understand Judith Butler's theorization of gender, for example, through Saba Mahmood's reading of Butler is different from whether or not one can or should apprehend Butler's work through popular cultural criticism. See Mahmood, *The Politics of Piety: The Islamic Revival and*

the Feminist Subject (Princeton University Press, 2005); cf. Molly Fischer, "Think Gender Is Performative? You Have Judith Butler to Thank for That," *The Cut*, June 13, 2016, www.thecut.com/2016/06/judith-butler-c-v-r.html.

39. David Attwell, "Interview with Homi Bhabha," *Current Writing: Text and Reception in Southern Africa* 5, no. 2 (1993): 112.
40. Boggs and Mitchell, "Critical University Studies," 444.
41. Andrew H. Miller, "Implicative Criticism, or The Display of Thinking," *New Literary History* 44, no. 3 (2013): 345–360.
42. Dinitia Smith, "When Ideas Get Lost in Bad Writing; Attacks on Scholars Include a Barbed Contest with 'Prizes,'" *New York Times*, February 27, 1999, www.nytimes.com/1999/02/27/arts/when-ideas-get-lost-bad-writing-attacks-scholars-include-barbed-contest-with.html.
43. Sara Marcus, "Novels of Democratic Exhaustion," *American Literary History* 35, no. 1 (2023): 364.

5. Fictions of Divergence: Or, Amit Chaudhuri Doesn't Write the Postcolonial

1. Amit Chaudhuri, *Calcutta: Two Years in the City* (Vintage, 2013), 44–45.
2. Marketing text for Amit Chaudhuri, *Finding the Raga: An Improvisation on Indian Music* (New York Review Books, 2021), www.nyrb.com/products/finding-the-raga?variant=32752895950985.
3. Chaudhuri, *Calcutta*, 247. He writes about the same compulsion in *Origins of Dislike*, in reflecting on his years as Professor of Contemporary Literature at the University of East Anglia: "About that institution, I feel as I had about England when I was a student: that I happened to be in it at a certain point of time, and that I have been there for longer than I thought I would be. I always expected—and expect—to go back one day to where I came from." See Amit Chaudhuri, *The Origins of Dislike* (Oxford University Press, 2018), 80.
4. Dirk Wiemann, "Writing Home: Into the Interior with Amit Chaudhuri," *Genres of Modernity: Contemporary Indian Novels in English* (Rodopi, 2008), 213.
5. Vikram Chandra, "The Cult of Authenticity," *Boston Review* (2000), www.bostonreview.net/articles/vikram-chandra-the-cult-of-authenticity/.
6. I offer a close reading of this photograph in "Call Center Agents and Expatriate Writers: Twin Subjects of New Indian Capital," *ARIEL: A Review of International English Literature* 49, no. 4 (2018): 77–107.
7. Amit Chaudhuri, "The Construction of the Indian Novel in English," in *The Vintage Book of Modern Indian Literature*, ed. Amit Chaudhuri (Vintage, 2001), xxiii.

8. Amit Chaudhuri, *Friend of My Youth* (New York Review Books, 2019), 65.
9. Amit Chaudhuri, "Modernity and the Vernacular," Chaudhuri, *Vintage Book of Modern Indian Literature*.
10. Francesca Orsini, "India in the Mirror of World Fiction," *New Left Review* 13 (2002): 76.
11. See Literary Activism, www.literaryactivism.com/; see also Ragini Tharoor Srinivasan, "What Literature Does," *boundary2online* (2018), www.boundary2.org/2018/10/ragini-tharoor-srinivasan-what-literature-does-review-of-amit-chaudhuri-ed-literary-activism/.
12. Sanjay Krishnan, "The Place of India in Postcolonial Studies: Chatterjee, Chakrabarty, Spivak," *New Literary History* 40, no. 2 (2009): 265.
13. Robyn Wiegman, *Object Lessons* (Duke University Press, 2012), 336.
14. This is Nasia Anam's phrase from an unpublished argument regarding texts that are "ready to read."
15. Chaudhuri, *Origins of Dislike*, 1.
16. Chaudhuri, *Origins of Dislike*, 5.
17. Chaudhuri sometimes compares himself directly to these interlocutors, as in this note on Marcel Proust: "I speak of this background not to aggrandize myself (though the charge of self-aggrandizement may be inescapable), but to put on record the fact that the mention of Proust was unusual once, and to address, today, what it means to the literary history of a writer like myself." Chaudhuri, 288.
18. Chaudhuri, 288.
19. Richard Jean So, *Redlining Culture: A Data History of Racial Inequality and Postwar Fiction* (Columbia University Press, 2021).
20. John Guillory, "Monuments and Documents: Panofsky on the Object of Study in the Humanities," *History of Humanities* 1, no. 1 (2016): 22.
21. Edward W. Said, "The Text, the World, the Critic," *Bulletin of the Midwest Modern Language Association* 8, no. 2 (1975): 8–9, 1–23.
22. Anu Shukla, "Such Stuff as Amit Chaudhuri's Song Is Made On," in *The Novels of Amit Chaudhuri: An Exploration in the Alternative Tradition* (Sarup and Sons, 2004).
23. Saikat Majumdar, "Dallying with Dailiness: Amit Chaudhuri's Flaneur Fictions," *Studies in the Novel* (2007): 448–464.
24. Saikat Majumdar, *Prose of the World: Modernism and the Banality of Empire* (Columbia University Press, 2013), 160.
25. Majumdar, *Prose of the World*, 135, 148.
26. Chaudhuri, *Finding the Raga*, 11.
27. Chaudhuri, *Calcutta*, 79.
28. Ulka Anjaria, *Reading India Now: Contemporary Formations in Literature and Popular Culture* (Temple University Press, 2019).

29. Veena Das, *Textures of the Ordinary: Doing Anthropology After Wittgenstein* (Fordham University Press, 2020).
30. Fredric Jameson, "Third-World Literature in the Era of Multinational Capitalism," *Social Text* 15 (1986): 65–88.
31. Majumdar, *Prose*, 137.
32. Pardis Dabashi, "Introduction to 'Cultures of Argument': The Loose Garments of Argument," *PMLA* 135, no. 5 (2020): 946–955.
33. Wai Chee Dimock, "A Literary Scramble for Africa," *The Chronicle of Higher Education*, February 17, 2015, www.chronicle.com/blogs/conversation/a-literary-scramble-for-africa.
34. Ulka Anjaria, *Realism in the Twentieth-Century Indian Novel: Colonial Difference and Literary Form* (Cambridge University Press, 2012).
35. The dominance of caste Hindu Bengalis among Indian English literary writers and Anglo-American academic critics is well observed, and includes many discussed in this book (Bharati Mukherjee, Amit Chaudhuri, Jhumpa Lahiri, and Gayatri Chakravorty Spivak).
36. Anand Giridharadas, *India Calling: An Intimate Portrait of a Nation's Remaking* (Henry Holt, 2011), 40.
37. Raka Ray and Seemin Qayum, *Cultures of Servitude: Modernity, Domesticity, and Class in India* (Stanford University Press, 2009), 146.
38. When the character of the servant does take center stage, it is in texts like Aravind Adiga's 2008 *The White Tiger*, which indigenizes Richard Wright's *Native Son* in a hyperbolically allegorical tale of "entrepreneurial" murder. Despite its own compromised caste politics, *The White Tiger* pierced the heart of the hypocrisy underlying the premise of India's global rise by refusing to take India's conventional divisions of labor for granted and by dramatizing the threat of New India's rise through the murder plot. See Snehal Shingavi, "Capitalism, Caste, and Con-Games in Aravind Adiga's *The White Tiger*," *Postcolonial Text* 9, no. 3 (2014).
39. Gayatri Chakravorty Spivak, *Readings* (Seagull, 2014), 7.
40. Akshya Saxena, "South Asian Accents: *Bhashas*, Bodies, Borders," *South Asian Review* 45, nos. 3–4 (2024): 524–531.
41. Isabel Huacuja Alonso and Hoda Bandeh-Ahmadi, "Who Is a South Asianist: A Conversation on Positionality," *Who Is the Asianist?: The Politics of Representation in Asian Studies*, ed. Marvin D. Sterling, Nitasha Tamar Sharma, and Will Bridges (Association of Asian Studies, 2022), 36.
42. Amitava Kumar, ed., *The Humour and the Pity: Essays on V. S. Naipaul* (Buffalo, 2002).
43. Amit Chaudhuri, *A Strange and Sublime Address*, in *Freedom Song: Three Novels* (Knopf, 1999 [1991]), 15–17.
44. Chaudhuri, *A Strange and Sublime Address*, 79.

45. Amit Chaudhuri, *Afternoon Raag*, in *Freedom Song: Three Novels* (Knopf, 1999 [1993]), 163.
46. Chaudhuri, *Afternoon Raag*, 169–170.
47. Amit Chaudhuri, *A New World* (Knopf, 2000), 18–19.
48. Chaudhuri, *A New World*, 143, 184, 31.
49. Chaudhuri, *A New World*, 184.
50. Ray and Qayum, *Cultures of Servitude*, 10.
51. Bruce Robbins, *The Servant's Hand: English Fiction from Below* (Duke University Press, 1993), x, 3.
52. Suketu Mehta, *Maximum City: Bombay Lost and Found* (Vintage, 2004), 29.
53. Saikat Majumdar, "What Does Untouchability Mean During India's Covid Crisis?" *Literary Hub*, May 21, 2021, https://lithub.com/what-does-untouchable-mean-during-indias-covid-crisis/.
54. Chaudhuri, *Calcutta*, 262, 266.
55. Chaudhuri, *Calcutta*, 261. See also Ray and Qayum, *Cultures of Servitude*, 27.
56. Chaudhuri, *Calcutta*, 261.
57. Bruce Robbins, *The Beneficiary* (Duke University Press, 2017).
58. Chaudhuri, *Calcutta*, 262, 284.
59. Namwali Serpell, "The Banality of Empathy," *New York Review of Books*, March 2, 2019, www.nybooks.com/online/2019/03/02/the-banality-of-empathy/.
60. Majumdar, *Prose*, 157.
61. Reviewing *Calcutta*, Simon During calls Chaudhuri a "literary intellectual," who has a "particular literary sensibility" and whose "literary apprehension" of his experience of his "literary life" provides material for his "literary writing." During also notes that *Calcutta* evidences a "literary ethic" in sync with Calcutta's "literary ethos." All this "literariness" serves as a shorthand for "moral nonchalance." See During, "Calcutta's Via Negativa," *Public Books*, August 6, 2013, www.publicbooks.org/calcuttas-via-negativa/.
62. Majumdar, *Prose*, 159.
63. Chaudhuri, *The Origins of Dislike*, 292.
64. Paul Crosthwaite, *The Market Logics of Contemporary Fiction* (Cambridge University Press, 2019).
65. Amit Chaudhuri, "Prelude to an Autobiography: A Fragment," in *Real Time: Stories and a Reminiscence* (Picador, 2002), 73.
66. Chaudhuri, *Friend*, 42–43.
67. Chaudhuri, *Friend*, 67.
68. Chaudhuri, *Friend*, 117.
69. Spivak, *Readings*, 147.
70. Chaudhuri, *Finding the Raga*, 33.
71. Spivak, *Readings*, 145.

72. Chaudhuri, "*I Am Ramu*," nplusonemag.com, August 22, 2017. www.nplusonemag.com/online-only/online-only/i-am-ramu/. See also Chaudhuri, *Origins of Dislike*, 292.
73. Michel Foucault, *This Is Not a Pipe*, trans. James Harkness (University of California Press, 1982), 36, 47.
74. Foucault, *This Is Not a Pipe*, 49.
75. Elif Shafak, *How to Stay Sane in an Age of Division* (Profile, 2020), 34–35.
76. Chaudhuri, *Calcutta*, 247.
77. Rukmini Bhaya Nair, "Book Review: Amit Chaudhuri's *A New World*," *India Today*, March 6, 2000, www.indiatoday.in/magazine/society-and-the-arts/books/story/20000306-book-review-amit-chaudhuris-a-new-world-777176-2000-03-05.
78. Richard Eder, "A Life Like Old Postcards," *New York Times*, October 22, 2000, https://archive.nytimes.com/www.nytimes.com/books/00/10/22/reviews/001022.22ederlt.html.
79. Chaudhuri, *New World*, 50–51, 60, 29.
80. Chaudhuri, *Calcutta*, 13, 217, 216.
81. Chaudhuri, *Calcutta*, 22, 30.
82. Chaudhuri, *Calcutta*, 30–31.
83. Snigdha Poonam, *Dreamers: How Young Indians are Changing the World* (Harvard University Press, 2018).
84. Giridharadas, *India Calling*, 86.
85. Chaudhuri, *Origins of Dislike*, 289.
86. Chaudhuri, *Finding the Raga*, 42.
87. Spivak, *Readings*, 165.
88. These others include the cast of minor characters and domestic workers I've written about in this chapter. More recently, in his 2022 novella, *Sojourn*, set in Berlin, Chaudhuri's narrator and his housekeeper Gerta have numerous exchanges in which Gerta speaks to the narrator in German, and he relates his own uncomprehending, nonsensical responses (e.g., she makes a note about dishwashing soap, and he feels "reassured: happy she was happy"). See Amit Chaudhuri, *Sojourn* (New York Review Books, 2022), 63.
89. Chaudhuri, *Real Time*, 47.
90. Chaudhuri, *Origins of Dislike*, 3, 288, 4, 291.
91. Chaudhuri, *Origins of Dislike*, 5.
92. In the 2020s, "Creative and Critical" was consolidated in both the Indian and US university contexts as an institutional formation, a genre, and a hiring category. See Ragini Tharoor Srinivasan, "Memoir, Autofiction, and the New Indian Humanities," in *The Oxford Handbook of Modern Indian Literatures*, ed. Ulka Anjaria and Anjali Nerlekar (Oxford University Press,

2024), 257–272; and "Creative Critical," a special issue of *Minnesota Review*, ed. Ranjan Ghosh, no. 99 (2022).
93. Saikat Majumdar, "How to Build a Creative Writing Programme as Part of Academic Courses at an Indian University," *Scroll.in*, September 6, 2020, https://scroll.in/article/972281/how-to-build-a-creative-writing-programme-as-part-of-academic-courses-at-an-indian-university.
94. Alfred Kazin, quoted in Mark McGurl, "The Program Era: Pluralisms of Postwar American Fiction," *Critical Inquiry* 32, no. 1 (2005): 102–103.
95. Chaudhuri, *Friend*, 4, 16, 117.
96. Eric Hayot, *The Elements of Academic Style: Writing for the Humanities* (Columbia University Press, 2014), 1.
97. Chaudhuri, *Friend*, 68.
98. Chaudhuri, *Finding the Raga*, 114.

6/Recess 3. The Idea of Edward Said

1. Sina Rahmani, "Review of *Edward Said: The Last Interview*, and *Selves and Others: A Portrait of Edward Said*, and *The Battle of Algiers*," *Comparative Studies of South Asia, Africa and the Middle East* 25, no. 2 (2005): 512–514.
2. Keith Lawrence, "News Tip: Edward Said Set Intellectual Example, Duke Professor Says," *Duke Today*, September 26, 2003, https://today.duke.edu/2003/09/saidtip926.html.
3. Hamid Dabashi, *On Edward Said: Remembrance of Things Past* (Haymarket, 2020), 10.
4. Prakash Deer, Gyan Prakash, and Ella Shohat, "Introduction to Edward Said: A Memorial Issue," *Social Text* 87, 24, no. 2 (2006): 1–9.
5. Kenzaburo Oe, "The Art of Fiction, No. 195, interviewed by Sarah Fay," *Paris Review* 183 (Winter 2007), www.theparisreview.org/interviews/5816/the-art-of-fiction-no-195-kenzaburo-oe.
6. Edward W. Said, *Culture and Imperialism* (Vintage, 1993), 71, xxv, xii, 14.
7. Dipesh Chakrabarty, *Provincializing Europe: Postcolonial Thought and Historical Difference* (Princeton University Press, 2000), 27.
8. Edward W. Said, "Opponents, Audiences, Constituencies, and Community," *Critical Inquiry* 9, no. 1 (1982): 1.
9. Abigail Boggs and Nick Mitchell, "Critical University Studies and the Crisis Consensus," *Feminist Studies* 44, no. 2 (2018): 432–463.
10. Katie Kadue, "The End of the Star System," *Chronicle of Higher Education*, January 3, 2023, www.chronicle.com/article/the-end-of-the-star-system.
11. Edward W. Said, *Representations of the Intellectual* (Random House, 1994), 92.

12. John Guillory, "We Cannot All Be Edward Said," *Chronicle of Higher Education* (February 13, 2023), www.chronicle.com/article/we-cannot-all-be-edward-said.
13. R. Radhakrishnan, *A Said Dictionary* (Wiley-Blackwell, 2012), xii.
14. Ella Shohat, "In Memory of Edward Said: The Bulletproof Intellectual," *University of Toronto Quarterly* 83, no. 1 (Winter 2014).
15. Said, *Representations*, 24.
16. Radhakrishnan, *Said Dictionary*, xiv.
17. Said, *Representations*, 64.
18. David Graeber, *Bullshit Jobs: A Theory* (Simon and Schuster, 2018).
19. Said, "Opponents," 5.
20. Hussein Ibish, "Nationalism, Secularism, Postcoloniality: An Interview with Edward Said," *Cultural Dynamics* 14, no. 1 (2002): 98.
21. Ibish, "Nationalism," 97–98.
22. Rey Chow, *The Age of the World Target: Self-Referentiality in War, Theory, and Comparative Work* (Duke University Press, 2006), 42.
23. Ibish, "Nationalism," 98.
24. Pankaj Mishra, "The Reorientations of Edward Said," *New Yorker*, April 26 and May 3, 2021, www.newyorker.com/magazine/2021/04/26/the-reorientations-of-edward-said.
25. Homi Bhabha, "Untimely Ends," *Artforum*, February 2004, 19. For an analysis of this species of critique, see Joseph Massad, "The Intellectual Life of Edward Said," *Journal of Palestine Studies* 33, no. 3 (2004): 7–22.
26. Natasha Lennard, "Columbia Task Force for Dealing with Campus Protests Declares That Anti-Zionism Is Antisemitism," *The Intercept*, June 17, 2024, https://theintercept.com/2024/06/17/israel-columbia-antisemitism-task-force-zionism/.
27. Edward Said, *The Question of Palestine* (Vintage, 1979); see also Rashid Khalidi, *The Hundred Years' War on Palestine: A History of Settler Colonialism and Resistance, 1917–2017* (Henry Holt, 2020).
28. Radhakrishnan, *Said Dictionary*, xi.
29. Said, *Representations*, 31.
30. Said, "Opponents," 12, 19.
31. Radhakrishnan, *Said Dictionary*, xi.
32. Said, *Representations*, 76, my emphasis.
33. Edward W. Said, "Identity, Authority, and Freedom: The Potentate and the Traveler," *boundary 2* 21, no. 3 (1994): 14.
34. Jhumpa Lahiri, *In Other Words*, trans. Ann Goldstein (Penguin Random House, 2016), 173.
35. Said, *Representations*, 31.

36. Some critics charge that Said neglected gender and sexuality because he was not comfortable with these topics: "as a man-educated man, it was a matter of not being correctly positioned, of lacking entitlement." See Elleke Boehmer, "Edward Said and (the Postcolonial Occlusion of) Gender," in *Edward Said and the Literary, Social, and Political World*, ed. Ranjan Ghosh (Routledge, 2009), 130.
37. Said, *Representations*, 10.
38. Jacqueline Rose and Edward W. Said, "Returning to Ourselves," *Jewish Quarterly* (1997/1998): 11.
39. Said, *Representations*, 57, 59, 39.
40. Said, *Representations*, 66, 73.
41. Massad, "The Intellectual Life," 17.
42. Said, *Representations*, 66–69.
43. Lili Loofbourow and Phillip Maciak, "Introduction: The Time of the Semipublic Intellectual," *PMLA* 130, no. 2 (2015): 445.
44. Sharon Marcus, "How to Talk About Books You *Have* Read," *PMLA* 130, no. 2 (2015): 476–477.
45. Edward W. Said, "Response to 'Edward Said's *Culture and Imperialism*: A Symposium," *Social Text* 40 (1994): 24.
46. Ragini Tharoor Srinivasan, "It's All Very Suggestive, but It Isn't Scholarship," in *The Critic as Amateur*, ed. Saikat Majumdar and Aarthi Vadde (Bloomsbury, 2019).
47. Loofbourow and Maciak, "Introduction," 441.
48. For a related discussion, see Claire Bishop's essay on the professionalization of fine art through PhD programs and the rise of research-based art. Bishop, "Information Overload," *ArtForum* (April 2023), www.artforum.com/features/claire-bishop-on-the-superabundance-of-research-based-art-252571/.
49. Edward W. Said, "Presidential Address 1999: Humanism and Heroism," *PMLA* 115, no. 3 (2000): 290, 287.
50. Edward Said, "A Window on the World," *Guardian*, August 1, 2003, www.theguardian.com/books/2003/aug/02/alqaida.highereducation.

7. A Desire Called the Post-Anglophone: Or, On Not Being Jhumpa Lahiri

1. Sandhya Shukla, *India Abroad: Diasporic Cultures of Postwar America and England* (Princeton University Press, 2003), 133.
2. Judith Butler, *Giving an Account of Oneself* (Fordham University Press, 2005).

3. Jhumpa Lahiri, *The Namesake* (Houghton Mifflin, 2003), 65.
4. Jhumpa Lahiri, *The Interpreter of Maladies* (Houghton Mifflin, 1999).
5. Arundhati Roy, *The God of Small Things* (Random House, 1997); and Roy, *The Ministry of Utmost Happiness* (Penguin, 2017).
6. Roy and Lahiri are both beautiful women, whose images were used to build "Brand India" and the brand of a multicultural United States, respectively. Both were conscripted into the "preexisting symbolic domain of Indian women in beauty pageants" alongside the five Indian women who won the Miss World and Miss Universe beauty pageants between 1994 and 2000. See Vanita Reddy, *Fashioning Diaspora* (Temple University Press, 2016), 95.
7. Amy S. Choi, "Mira Jacob on Arranged Marriage, Jewish In-Laws, and Tabla," *The Mashup Americans* (undated), www.mashupamericans.com/relationships/mira-jacob-arranged-marriage-jewish-laws-beauty-loss/; Minal Hajratwala, "On Being Discovered," *Color Lines* (2006), www.thefreelibrary.com/On+being+discovered%3A+as+a+writer%2C+I+found+it+carries+risks.-a0155406203.
8. Vauhini Vara, "Jhumpa Lahiri and Me," *New York Times*, September 18, 2023, www.nytimes.com/2023/09/18/books/review/jhumpa-lahiri-and-me.html.
9. David Carr, "New Yorker Fiction, by the Numbers; A Princeton Student Does the Math on a Magazine's Choices," *New York Times*, June 1, 2004, www.nytimes.com/2004/06/01/books/new-yorker-fiction-numbers-princeton-student-does-math-magazine-s-choices.html. See also "Ira Trivedi: You Could Say I'd Want to Be the Next Jhumpa Lahiri," *Telegraph*, September 27, 2009, www.telegraphindia.com/7-days/you-could-say-i-d-want-to-be-the-next-jhumpa-lahiri/cid/590178.
10. Amit Chaudhuri, *The Origins of Dislike* (Oxford University Press, 2018), 5.
11. Chloe Schama, "23 Best Books to Read this Summer," *Vogue*, April 23, 2020, www.vogue.com/article/the-best-books-for-summer.
12. Sanjena Sathian, "Good Immigrant Novels: Jhumpa Lahiri and the Aesthetics of Respectability," *The Drift*, May 6, 2021, www.thedriftmag.com/good-immigrant-novels.
13. Reddy, *Fashioning Diaspora*, 96.
14. Ragini Tharoor Srinivasan, "Lahiri, High and Low," *Public Books*, January 20, 2014, www.publicbooks.org/lahiri-high-and-low/.
15. Chitra Banerjee Divakaruni, *The Mistress of Spices* (Doubleday, 1997). Divakaruni is part of a trio of famous Indian American (and, more specifically, Bengali) women writers, along with Bharati Mukherjee and Lahiri. Having written over two dozen books, Divakaruni is the most prolific and popular of the three. She is also the most critically overlooked despite having won

numerous awards. See Amritjit Singh, Robin E. Field, and Samina Najmi, eds., *Critical Perspectives on Chitra Banerjee Divakaruni: Feminism and Diaspora* (Lexington, 2022).

16. Jhumpa Lahiri, *The Clothing of Books* (Vintage, 2015), 8, 49.
17. Jhumpa Lahiri, *In Other Words*, trans. Ann Goldstein (Knopf, 2016), 111.
18. Francesca Pellas, "'What Am I Trying to Leave Behind?': An Interview with Jhumpa Lahiri," *Literary Hub*, August 31, 2017, https://lithub.com/what-am-i-trying-to-leave-behind-an-interview-with-jhumpa-lahiri/.
19. Quoted in Pellas, "What Am I Trying to Leave Behind?"
20. Pellas, "What Am I Trying to Leave Behind?"
21. Alice Kaplan, "On Language Memoir," in *Displacements: Cultural Identities in Question*, ed. Angelika Bammer (Indiana University Press, 1994), 59–60.
22. Lahiri, *In Other Words*, 213, 229.
23. Megan O'Grady, "Jhumpa Lahiri in Rome: The Pulitzer Prize–Winner Talks About Her New Novel and New Ideas," *Vogue*, September 25, 2013.
24. Jhumpa Lahiri, *Translating Myself and Others* (Princeton University Press, 2022), 8.
25. Lahiri, *In Other Words*, 173.
26. Lahiri, *Translating Myself*, 2, 8.
27. Chaudhuri, *Origins of Dislike*, 5.
28. "Jhumpa Lahiri: By the Book," *New York Times*, September 5, 2013, www.nytimes.com/2013/09/08/books/review/jhumpa-lahiri-by-the-book.html.
29. Tim Parks reads the questions posed by the narrator of *Whereabouts* as a sign that Lahiri is now "teasing us" critics. See Parks, "Vaporous Shapes," *London Review of Books*, July 1, 2021, www.lrb.co.uk/the-paper/v43/n13/tim-parks/vaporous-shapes.
30. Rebecca Walkowitz, "Less Than One Language: Typographic Multilingualism and Post-Anglophone Fiction," *SubStance* 50, no. 1 (2021).
31. Lavina Dhingra and Floyd Cheung, "Introduction," in *Naming Jhumpa Lahiri: Canons and Controversies*, ed. Dhingra and Cheung (Lexington, 2012), xiii.
32. Asha Nadkarni, "The South Asian American Challenge," in *The Cambridge History of Asian American Literature*, ed. Rajini Srikanth and Min Hyoung Song (Cambridge University Press, 2015), 365.
33. Min Hyoung Song, *The Children of 1965: On Writing, and Not Writing, as an Asian American* (Duke University Press, 2013), 23–24.
34. Song, *The Children of 1965*, 159.
35. Song, *The Children of 1965*, 152, 156.

36. Susan Koshy, "Minority Cosmopolitanism," *PMLA* 126, no. 3 (2011): 595.
37. Reddy, *Fashioning Diaspora*, 91.
38. Koshy, "Minority Cosmopolitanism," 594.
39. Koshy, "Minority Cosmopolitanism," 607. Cf. Susan Koshy, "Neoliberal Family Matters," *American Literary History* 25, no. 12 (2013): 353. In her 2013 essay, Koshy argues that kinship for Lahiri is "an activity rather than biology."
40. Crystal Parikh, "Being Well: The Right to Health in Asian American Literature," *Amerasia* 39, no. 1 (2013): 41.
41. Reddy, *Fashioning Diaspora*, 95.
42. "Lahiri: By the Book."
43. Song, *Children of 1965*. See chapter 3, "Not Ethnic Literature."
44. Koshy, "Minority Cosmopolitanism," 608.
45. James Clifford, "Diasporas," *Cultural Anthropology* 9, no. 3 (1994): 311.
46. Reddy, *Fashioning Diaspora*, 31.
47. Michiko Kakutani, "Liking America, but Longing for India," *New York Times*, August 6, 1999, www.nytimes.com/1999/08/06/books/books-of-the-times-liking-america-but-longing-for-india.html.
48. Lauren Berlant, *The Queen of America Goes to Washington City: Essays on Sex and Citizenship* (Duke University Press, 1997).
49. Koshy, "Neoliberal Family," 355.
50. Koshy, 351, 371. Koshy calls this style "filial gothic" (355). Cf. Mary Jacobus, *On Belonging and Not Belonging* (Princeton University Press, 2022).
51. Kalyan Nadiminti, "'A Betrayal of Everything': The Law of the Family in Jhumpa Lahiri's *The Lowland*," *Journal of Asian American Studies* 21, no. 2 (2018): 240.
52. Nadiminti, "'A Betrayal of Everything,'" 240.
53. Nadkarni, "South Asian American," 366.
54. Koshy, "Neoliberal Family," 354. Cf. Nadkarni, who argues that Lahiri's work is political not only because of the critique it offers of nation and family, but because it represents "the experiences [of] privileged migrants," which may then be understand in relation to the experiences of undocumented migrant workers, and in this way contribute to a broader understanding of the diversification and fracturing of the South Asian American diaspora post-1965.
55. Koshy, "Neoliberal Family," 355.
56. Jhumpa Lahiri, *Unaccustomed Earth* (Vintage, 2008), 83.
57. Parikh, "Being Well," 41.
58. Koshy, "Neoliberal Family," 353.
59. Urmila Seshagiri, "Jhumpa Lahiri's Modernist Turn," *Public Books*, February 15, 2016, www.publicbooks.org/jhumpa-lahiris-modernist-turn/.

60. Siddhartha Deb, "Sins of the Brothers," *New York Times*, September 27, 2013, www.nytimes.com/2013/09/29/books/review/jhumpa-lahiris-lowland.html.
61. Manasi Subramanian, "Review of *The Lowland*," *Asian Review of Books*, September 8, 2013, http://asianreviewofbooks.com/content/archived-article/?articleID=1578.
62. Ellah Allfrey, "With Controlled, Clinical Prose Lahiri Explores Love and Sacrifice," *NPR*, September 23, 2013, www.npr.org/2013/09/23/223425487/with-controlled-clinical-prose-lahiri-explores-love-and-sacrifice.
63. Fran Hawthorne, "After Her Pulitzer-Winning Debut, Jhumpa Lahiri's Latest Fiction Is a Bit of a Detour," *The National*, August 22, 2013.
64. Rey Chow, *The Protestant Ethnic and the Spirit of Capitalism* (Columbia University Press, 2002), 126.
65. Lahiri, *In Other Words*, 111.
66. Jhumpa Lahiri, *Whereabouts* (Alfred A. Knopf, 2021), 77, 27, 102, 8, 42, 59, 31.
67. Lahiri, *Whereabouts*, 20, 64, 39, 85, 5, 54, 35, 142, 132–33.
68. Lahiri, *Whereabouts*, 151.
69. Lahiri, *Clothing of Books*, 64, 51.
70. Lahiri, *In Other Words*, 219, 213.
71. Seshagiri, "Modernist Turn"; Koshy, "Neoliberal Family," 353.
72. Sathian, "Good Immigrant Novels."
73. Tim Parks, "L'Avventura," New York Review of Books, March 24, 2016, https://www.nybooks.com/articles/2016/03/24/jhumpa-lahiri-lavventura/; Eileen Battersby, "Embracing a Passionate Culture," *Irish Times*, February 20, 2016, www.irishtimes.com/culture/books/in-other-words-by-jhumpa-lahiri-review-embracing-a-passionate-culture-1.2538577.
74. Aditya Gandhi, "Lahiri's Metamorphoses," *Public Books*, June 18, 2024, www.publicbooks.org/lahiris-metamorphoses/.
75. Sathian, "Good Immigrant Novels."
76. Lahiri, *In Other Words*, 221, 127.
77. "A Conversation with Jhumpa Lahiri," www.york.cuny.edu/enrollment-mngmt-office/first-year-experience-fye/orientation-and-transition/freshman-reader-program/the-namesake-spring-2012a/outcasts-united-synopsis.
78. Lahiri, *In Other Words*, 35, xiii, 207, 5, 97–99, 23.
79. Lahiri, 223, 169, 127.
80. Lahiri, 221.
81. Quoted in Seshagiri, "Modernist Turn," my emphasis.
82. Benjamin Moser, "Jhumpa Lahiri Leaves Her Comfort Zone," *New York Times*, May 17, 2022, www.nytimes.com/2022/05/17/books/review/translating-myself-and-others-jhumpa-lahiri.html.
83. Parks, "L'Avventura."

84. Parks, "Vaporous Shapes"; Lahiri, *In Other Words*, 133.
85. Koshy, "Minority Cosmopolitanism," 601.
86. Lahiri, *In Other Words*, 21; Jacques Derrida, *Monolingualism of the Other: Or, The Prosthesis of Origin* (Stanford University Press, 1998).
87. Lahiri, *Interpreter*, 112, 125.
88. Lahiri, *Namesake*, 220, 281.
89. Song, *Children of 1965*, 173.
90. Dhingra and Cheung, *Naming Jhumpa Lahiri*, vii.
91. Song, *Children of 1965*, 173.
92. Lahiri, *In Other Words*, 43.
93. Lahiri, *Lowland*, 286.
94. Lahiri, *Namesake*, 287.
95. Lahiri, *Translating Myself*, 21.
96. Lahiri, *In Other Words*, 37, 43, 37, 83, 37, 213, 117.
97. On amateurism and postcritique, see Rita Felski, *The Limits of Critique* (University of Chicago Press, 2015); Saikat Majumdar and Aarthi Vadde, eds., *The Critic as Amateur* (Bloomsbury Academic, 2019); Tobias Skiveren, "Postcritique and the Problem of the Lay Reader," *New Literary History* 53 (2022): 161–180; and the PMLA dossier on "The Cultures of Argument" (2020), edited by Pardis Dabashi. On amateurism and the postcolonial, see J. Daniel Elam, *World Literature for the Wretched of the Earth: Anticolonial Aesthetics, Postcolonial Politics* (Fordham University Press, 2020); Saikat Majumdar, *The Amateur: Literary Self-Making and the Humanities in the Post-Colony* (Bloomsbury Academic, 2024); and Julietta Singh, *Unthinking Mastery: Dehumanism and Decolonial Entanglements* (Duke University Press, 2017). On amateurism and interdisciplinarity, see Ragini Tharoor Srinivasan, "'It's All Very Suggestive, but It Isn't Scholarship,'" in *The Critic as Amateur*, ed. Majumdar and Vadde (Bloomsbury Academic, 2019), 63–84.
98. Lahiri, *Translating Myself*, 18.
99. Lahiri, *In Other Words*, 83, 85.
100. Rebecca Walkowitz, "On Not Knowing: Lahiri, Tawada, Ishiguro," *New Literary History* 51, no. 2 (2020): 335.
101. Tessa Hadley, "A Pulitzer Winner Gives Up Writing and Speaking in English," *Guardian* (January 30, 2016), www.theguardian.com/books/2016/jan/30/in-other-words-jhumpa-lahiri-review-learning-italian.
102. Lahiri, *In Other Words*, 173.
103. Lahiri, *In Other Words*, 63; Lahiri, *Translating Myself*, 14.
104. Lahiri, *Translating Myself*, 16.
105. Lahiri, *In Other Words*, 95.
106. Lahiri, 117. The verbs she uses are "devouring" and "dismantling."

107. Aamir Mufti, *Forget English! Orientalisms and World Literature* (Harvard University Press, 2018).
108. Christopher Cannon and Susan Koshy, "Introduction to 'Monolingualism and its Discontents,'" *PMLA* 137, no. 5 (2022): 771–778; Yasemin Yildiz, *Beyond the Mother Tongue: The Postmonolingual Condition* (Fordham University Press, 2012).
109. yasser elhariry and Rebecca Walkowitz, "The Postlingual Turn," *SubStance* 50, no. 1 (2021): 3–9. Cf. Akshya Saxena, "Spoken Wor(l)ds: Anglophony, Poetry, Translation," *Wasafiri* 37, no. 3 (2022): 85.
110. Walkowitz, "On Not Knowing," 329, 323.
111. Walkowitz, "Less Than One Language," 96–97.
112. Walkowitz, "On Not Knowing," 324, 323.
113. As Hadley stresses, Italian "isn't really abstract, or a new beginning: it bristles with its own history and particular cultural meanings." Italy is one of Europe's key imperial languages. Like English, French, German, Portuguese, and Spanish, it cannot be divorced from the history of global colonialism. Neither, for that matter, can Italian or moving to Italy be disarticulated from the politics of Catholicism, the ideological foundations of "the West," or contemporary refugee crises. See Hadley, "Pulitzer Winner."
114. Sohomjit Ray, "Translation, Poetics of Instability, and the Postmonolingual Condition in Jhumpa Lahiri's *In Other Words*," *MFS: Modern Fiction Studies* 68, no. 3 (Fall 2022): 546.
115. Ray, "Translation, Poetics," 547.
116. Ngũgĩ wa Thiong'o, *Decolonising the Mind: The Politics of Language in African Literature* (Heinemann, 1981).
117. Julie Beth Napolin, *The Fact of Resonance: Modernist Acoustics and Narrative Form* (Fordham University Press, 2020), 71.
118. Walkowitz, "On Not Knowing," 326.
119. Sathian, "Good Immigrant Novels."
120. Lahiri, *Translating Myself*, 18.
121. Lahiri, *Translating Myself*, 11, 53.
122. Frantz Fanon, *Black Skins, White Masks*, trans. Richard Philcox (Grove, 1952, 2008), 2.
123. Lahiri, *Translating Myself*, 22.
124. Ien Ang, *On Not Speaking Chinese: Living Between Asia and the West* (Routledge, 2001), 30.
125. Rey Chow, *Writing Diaspora: Tactics of Intervention in Contemporary Cultural Studies* (Indiana University Press, 1993), 28.
126. Hanif Kureishi, *The Buddha of Suburbia* (Penguin, 1990), 141.
127. Ang, *On Not Speaking Chinese*, 30.

128. Mufti, *Forget English!*, 14.
129. Koshy, "Neoliberal Family," 371.
130. Lahiri, *Translating Myself*, 15, 22.
131. Walkowitz, "On Not Knowing," 327–328.
132. R. Radhakrishnan, *Diasporic Mediations: Between Home and Location* (University of Minnesota Press, 1996), xxiv.
133. Gayatri Chakravorty Spivak and Robert J. C. Young, "Neocolonialism and the Secret Agent of Knowledge," *Oxford Literary Review* 13, nos. 1/2 (1991): 248.
134. Lahiri, *Clothing of Books*, 64.
135. Koshy, "Neoliberal Family," 371.
136. Lahiri, *Translating Myself*, 21.
137. Lahiri, *In Other Words*, 183.
138. Lahiri, *Clothing of Books*, 5.
139. Napolin, *Fact of Resonance*, 100.
140. Jhumpa Lahiri, *Roman Stories*, trans. Jhumpa Lahiri and Todd Portnowitz (Knopf, 2023), 34, 203.
141. Lahiri, *Roman Stories*, 16, 22, 75.
142. Lahiri, *Roman Stories*, 90, 133.
143. Akshya Saxena, *Vernacular English: Reading the Anglophone in Postcolonial India* (Princeton University Press, 2022), 53, 148, 116.
144. Rey Chow, "How (the) Inscrutable Chinese Led to Globalized Theory," *PMLA* 116, no. 1 (2001): 69–74.
145. Lahiri, *Roman Stories*, 71, 187, 191.
146. The narrators are Carlotta Brentan, Cassandra Campbell, Ari Fliakos, Deepti Gupta, and Michael Obiora.
147. "Review: Roman Stories," *AudioFile*, October 2023, www.audiofilemagazine.com/reviews/read/239594/roman-stories-by-jhumpa-lahiri-todd-portnowitz-trans-read-by-deepti-gupta-carlotta-brentan/.

Afterword

1. Pratap Bhanu Mehta, "Suffocating Shadow Has Lifted, Balance Restored," *Indian Express*, June 5, 2024, https://indianexpress.com/article/opinion/columns/2024-lok-sabha-election-results-narendra-modi-9371534/.
2. South Asian American Digital Archive, *Our Stories: An Introduction to South Asian America* (SAADA, 2021).
3. Deepika Bahri, *Native Intelligence: Aesthetics, Politics, and Postcolonial Literature* (University of Minnesota, 2003), 5.
4. Elleke Boehmer and Rosinka Chaudhuri, eds., *The Indian Postcolonial: A Critical Reader* (Routledge, 2011), 191.

5. Chandra Talpade Mohanty, "On Race and Voice: Challenges for Liberal Education in the 1990s," in *Between Borders: Pedagogy and the Politics of Cultural Studies*, ed. Henry A. Giroux and Peter McLaren (Routledge, 1994), 147–154, 145–166.
6. Ragini Tharoor Srinivasan, "South Asia," in *Handbook of Anglophone World Literatures*, ed. Stefan Helgesson, Birgit Neumann, and Gabriele Rippl (DeGruyter, 2020), 471–488, 473.
7. Donna Haraway, "Situated Knowledges: The Science Question in Feminism and the Privilege of Partial Perspective," *Feminist Studies* 14, no. 3 (1988): 575–599.
8. Iyko Day, "Lost in Transnation: Uncovering Asian Canada," *Amerasia* 33, no. 2 (2007): 73.
9. Ghassan Kanafani, *Palestine's Children: Returning to Haifa and Other Stories* (Lynne Rienner, 2020); Daniel Boyarin, *The No-State Solution: A Jewish Manifesto* (Yale University Press, 2023); Fady Joudah, *[...]* (Milkweed, 2024).
10. Gayatri Chakravorty Spivak, *Readings* (Seagull, 2014), 83.
11. Spivak, *Readings*, 80.

Bibliography

Abu Hamdan, Lawrence. "Aural Contract: Forensic Listening and the Reorganization of the Speaking Subject." In *Forensis: The Architecture of Public Truth*, 65–82. Sternberg Press and Forensic Architecture, 2014.

Adiga, Aravind. *The White Tiger*. Free Press, 2008.

Agrawal, Prashant. "Why Narendra Modi Will Deliver His UN Speech in Hindi." *Quartz India*, September 27, 2014. http://qz.com/272169/why-narendra-modi-will-deliver-his-un-speech-in-hindi/.

Ahmad, Dohra, ed. *Rotten English: A Literary Anthology*. Norton, 2007.

Ahmed, Sara. *On Being Included: Racism and Diversity in Institutional Life*. Duke University Press, 2012.

———. "Willful Parts: Problem Characters or the Problem of Character." *New Literary History* 42, no. 2 (2011): 231–253.

Aleman, Jesse. "The End of English." *PMLA* 136, no. 3 (2021): 470–474.

Alim, H. Samy, and Geneva Smitherman. *Articulate While Black: Barack Obama, Language, and Race in the US*. Oxford University Press, 2012.

Allfrey, Ellah. "With Controlled, Clinical Prose Lahiri Explores Love and Sacrifice." NPR, September 23, 2013. www.npr.org/2013/09/23/223425487/with-controlled-clinical-prose-lahiri-explores-love-and-sacrifice.

Alonso, Isabel Huacuja, and Hoda Bandeh-Ahmadi. "Who Is a South Asianist: A Conversation on Positionality." In *Who Is the Asianist? The Politics of Representation in Asian Studies*, edited by Marvin D. Sterling, Nitasha Tamar Sharma, and Will Bridges, 36. Association of Asian Studies, 2022.

Althusser, Louis. "Contradiction and Overdetermination." In *Notes for an Investigation*, translated by Ben Brewster. Penguin, 1962.

———. "Ideology and Ideological State Apparatuses (Notes Toward an Investigation)" (1969). In *Lenin and Philosophy and Other Essays*. NLB, 1971.
Ambikaipaker, Mohan. "Everyday Political Whiteness and Diversity University." *Kalfou* 6, no. 2 (Fall 2019): 268–279.
Anam, Nasia. "Introduction: Forms of the Global Anglophone." *Post45: Contemporaries*, February 22, 2019. https://post45.org/sections/contemporaries-essays/global-anglophone/.
Anderson, Benedict. *The Spectre of Comparisons: Nationalism, Southeast Asia, and the World*. Verso, 1998.
Aneesh, A. *Neutral Accent: How Language, Labor, and Life Become Global*. Duke University Press, 2015.
———. *Virtual Migration: The Programming of Globalization*. Duke University Press, 2006.
Ang, Ien. *On Not Speaking Chinese: Living Between Asia and the West*. Routledge, 2001.
Anjaria, Ulka. "Chetan Bhagat and the New Provincialism." *American Book Review* 36, no. 6 (2015): 6–22.
———. "Great Aspirations." *Public Books*, July 31, 2017. www.publicbooks.org/great-aspirations/.
———, ed. *A History of the Indian Novel in English*. Cambridge University Press, 2015.
———. "Introduction: Literary Pasts, Presents, and Futures." In *A History of the Indian Novel in English*, edited by Ulka Anjaria, 1–30. Cambridge University Press, 2015.
———. *Reading India Now: Contemporary Formations in Literature and Popular Culture*. Temple University Press, 2019.
———. *Realism in the Twentieth-Century Indian Novel: Colonial Difference and Literary Form*. Cambridge University Press, 2012.
———. *Understanding Bollywood: The Grammar of Hindi Cinema*. Routledge, 2021.
Anjaria, Ulka, and Jonathan Shapiro Anjaria. "The Fractured Spaces of Entrepreneurialism in Post-Liberalization India." In *Enterprise Culture in Neoliberal India: Studies in Youth, Class, Work and Media*, edited by Nandini Gooptu, 190–205. Routledge, 2013.
———. "*Mazaa*: Rethinking Fun, Pleasure and Play in South Asia." *South Asia: Journal of South Asian Studies* 43, no. 2 (2020): 232–242.
Anzaldúa, Gloria. *Borderlands/La Frontera: The New Mestiza*. Aunt Lute, 1987.
Appadurai, Arjun. "Patriotism and Its Futures." *Public Culture* 5 (1993): 411–429.
Association of Concerned African Scholars. "The Ghettoization Debate: Africa, Africans and African Studies." *Bulletin*, no. 46 (Winter 1996).
Attwell, David. "Interview with Homi Bhabha." *Current Writing: Text and Reception in Southern Africa* 5, no. 2 (1993): 100–113.

Bahri, Deepika. *Native Intelligence: Aesthetics, Politics, and Postcolonial Literature.* University of Minnesota Press, 2003.

Baldwin, James. "If Black English Isn't a Language, Then Tell Me, What Is?" *The Black Scholar* 27, no. 1 (1997): 5–6.

Basu, Manisha. *The Rhetoric of Hindu India: Language and Urban Nationalism.* Cambridge University Press, 2017.

Battersby, Eileen. "Embracing a Passionate Culture." *Irish Times,* February 20, 2016. www.irishtimes.com/culture/books/in-other-words-by-jhumpa-lahiri-review-embracing-a-passionate-culture-1.2538577.

Baugh, John. "Linguistic Profiling." In *Black Linguistics,* 167–180. Routledge, 2002.

Beckman, Frida, and Charlie Black. "We Have Been Paranoid Too Long to Stop Now." In *New Directions in Philosophy and Literature,* 410–428. Edinburgh University Press, 2019.

Berlant, Lauren. *Cruel Optimism.* Duke University Press, 2011.

———. *The Queen of America Goes to Washington City: Essays on Sex and Citizenship.* Duke University Press, 1997.

Best, Stephen, and Sharon Marcus. "Surface Reading: An Introduction." *Representations* 108, no. 1 (2009): 1–21.

Bhabha, Homi. "DissemiNation: Time, Narrative, and the Margins of the Modern Nation." In *Nation and Narration,* edited by Homi Bhabha, 291–322. Routledge, 1990.

———. "Introduction: Narrating the Nation." In *Nation and Narration,* edited by Homi Bhabha, 1–7. Routledge, 1990.

———. *The Location of Culture.* Routledge, 1994.

———. "Of Mimicry and Man: The Ambivalence of Colonial Discourse." *October* 28 (1984): 125–133.

———. "Untimely Ends." *Artforum,* February 2004.

Bhagat, Chetan. *The 3 Mistakes of My Life.* Rupa, 2008.

———. *Half Girlfriend.* Rupa, 2014.

———. *One Indian Girl.* Rupa, 2016.

———. *One Night @ the Call Center.* Rupa, 2005.

———. "Skills to Succeed in a Global World." *Chetan Bhagat: Podcast,* December 28, 2022.

———. *What Young India Wants: Selected Non-Fiction.* Rupa, 2014.

Bhagat, Chetan (@chetan_bhagat). Twitter, November 6, 2019, 11:33 am. https://twitter.com/chetan_bhagat/status/1192027290336518144?s=20&t=KhBNdXhi77KzrfXNs6G7mg.

———. Twitter, November 20, 2021, 12:09 pm. https://twitter.com/chetan_bhagat/status/1462015127268388865?s=20.

Bhaya Nair, Rukmini. "Book Review: Amit Chaudhuri's *A New World.*" *India Today,* March 6, 2000. www.indiatoday.in/magazine/society-and-the-arts/books

/story/20000306-book-review-amit-chaudhuris-a-new-world-777176-2000-03-05.

Bishop, Claire. "Information Overload." *ArtForum*, April 2023. www.artforum.com/features/claire-bishop-on-the-superabundance-of-research-based-art-252571/.

Boehmer, Elleke. "Edward Said and (the Postcolonial Occlusion of) Gender." In *Edward Said and the Literary, Social, and Political World*, edited by Ranjan Ghosh, 148–60. Routledge, 2009.

Boehmer, Elleke, and Rosinka Chaudhuri, eds. *The Indian Postcolonial: A Critical Reader*. Routledge, 2011.

Boggs, Abigail, and Nick Mitchell. "Critical University Studies and the Crisis Consensus." *Feminist Studies* 44, no. 2 (2018): 432–463.

Bow, Leslie. *Partly Colored: Asian Americans and Racial Anomaly in the Segregated South*. New York University Press, 2010.

Boyarin, Daniel. *The No-State Solution: A Jewish Manifesto*. Yale University Press, 2023.

Brennan, Timothy. *Salman Rushdie and the Third World*. St. Martin's, 1989.

Brett, David Finbar. "Eye Dialect: Translating the Untranslatable." *Annali della Facoltà di Lingue e Letterature Straniere di Sassari* 6 (2009): 49–62.

Brouillette, Sarah. *Postcolonial Writers in the Global Literary Marketplace*. Palgrave Macmillan, 2007.

———. "Reading After the University." *Public Books*, November 23, 2022. www.publicbooks.org/reading-after-the-university-english-departments/.

Bucholtz, Mary. *White Kids: Language, Race, and Styles of Youth Identity*. Cambridge University Press, 2011.

Burgess, Matt. "It's Time to Stop the Double Talk Around Diversity Hiring." *Chronicle of Higher Education*, June 5, 2024. www.chronicle.com/article/its-time-to-stop-the-double-talk-around-diversity-hiring.

Butalia, Urvashi. "Panel Discussion II: Is Hinglish a Unifying Force?" In *Chutnefying English: The Phenomenon of Hinglish*, edited by Rita Kothari and Rupert Snell, 199–207. Penguin, 2011.

Butler, Judith. *Giving an Account of Oneself*. Fordham University Press, 2005.

———. "Letters: Exacting Solidarities." *London Review of Books* 21, no. 13 (July 1999). www.lrb.co.uk/the-paper/v21/n13/letters.

Buurma, Rachel Sagner, and Laura Heffernan. *The Teaching Archive: A New History for Literary Study*. University of Chicago Press, 2021.

Cannon, Christopher, and Susan Koshy. "Introduction to 'Monolingualism and Its Discontents.'" *PMLA* 137, no. 5 (2022): 771–778.

Carr, David. "New Yorker Fiction, by the Numbers; A Princeton Student Does the Math on a Magazine's Choices." *New York Times*, June 1, 2004. www.nytimes.com/2004/06/01/books/new-yorker-fiction-numbers-princeton-student-does-math-magazine-s-choices.html.

Casillas, Dolores Inés, Juan Sebastian Ferrada, and Sara Veronica Hinojos. "The Accent on *Modern Family*: Listening to Representations of the Latina Vocal Body." *Aztlan: A Journal of Chicano Studies* 43, no. 1 (2018): 61–88.

Castillo, Elaine. *How to Read Now*. Atlantic, 2022.

Chakladar, Arnab. "Language, Nation, and the Question of 'Indian Literature.'" *Postcolonial Text* 6, no. 4 (2011).

Chakrabarty, Dipesh. "Postcolonial Studies and Climate Change." *New Literary History* 43, no. 1 (2012): 1–18.

———. *Provincializing Europe: Postcolonial Thought and Historical Difference*. Princeton University Press, 2000.

Chakravorty, Mrinalini. *In Stereotype: South Asia in the Global Literary Imaginary*. Columbia University Press, 2014.

Chand, Vineeta. "[V]at Is Going On? Local and Global Ideologies About Indian English." *Language in Society* 38 (2009): 393–419.

Chander, Manu Samriti. *Brown Romantics: Poetry and Nationalism in the Global Nineteenth Century*. Bucknell University Press, 2017.

Chandra, Vikram. "The Cult of Authenticity." *Boston Review*, 2000. www.bostonreview.net/articles/vikram-chandra-the-cult-of-authenticity/.

Chaudhuri, Amit. "Afternoon Raag." In *Freedom Song: Three Novels*. Knopf, 1999 [1993].

———. *Calcutta: Two Years in the City*. Vintage, 2013.

———. *Finding the Raga: An Improvisation on Indian Music*. New York Review Books, 2021.

———. *Friend of My Youth*. New York Review Books, 2019.

———. *I Am Ramu*. nplusonemag.com, August 22, 2017. www.nplusonemag.com/online-only/online-only/i-am-ramu/.

———. *A New World*. Knopf, 2000.

———. *The Origins of Dislike*. Oxford University Press, 2018.

———. *Real Time: Stories and a Reminiscence*. Picador, 2002.

———. *Sojourn*. New York Review Books, 2022.

———. "A Strange and Sublime Address." In *Freedom Song: Three Novels*. Knopf, 1999 [1991].

———, ed. *The Vintage Book of Modern Indian Literature*. Vintage, 2001.

Cheah, Pheng. *Spectral Nationality: Passages of Freedom from Kant to Postcolonial Literatures of Liberation*. Columbia University Press, 2003.

Chen, Nancy. "'Speaking Nearby': A Conversation with Trinh T. Minh-ha." *Visual Anthropology Review* 8, no. 1 (Spring 1992): 82–91.

Chen, Tina, and S. X. Goudie. "Holders of the World: An Interview with Bharati Mukherjee." In *Conversations with Bharati Mukherjee*, edited by Bradley C. Edwards, 76–100. University Press of Mississippi, 2009.

Cheng, Anne Anlin. *The Melancholy of Race: Psychoanalysis, Assimilation, and Hidden Grief.* Oxford University Press, 2000.

Chiang, Mark. *The Cultural Capital of Asian American Studies: Autonomy and Representation in the University.* New York University Press, 2009.

Ch'ien, Evelyn Nien-Ming. *Weird English.* Harvard University Press, 2005.

Chihaya, Sarah. "Slips and Slides." *PMLA* 133, no. 2 (2018): 364–370.

Chin, Frank. "Come All Ye Asian American Writers of the Real and the Fake." In *A Companion to Asian American Studies*, edited by Kent A. Ono, 133–156. Blackwell, 2005.

Choi, Amy S. "Mira Jacob on Arranged Marriage, Jewish In-Laws, and Tabla." *The Mashup Americans*, undated. www.mashupamericans.com/relationships/mira-jacob-arranged-marriage-jewish-laws-beauty-loss/.

Choksey, Lara. "Introduction." In *Readings*, by Gayatri Chakravorty Spivak. Seagull, 2014.

Chow, Rey. *The Age of the World Target: Self-Referentiality in War, Theory, and Comparative Work.* Duke University Press, 2006.

———. "How (the) Inscrutable Chinese Led to Globalized Theory." *PMLA* 116, no. 1 (2001): 69–74.

———. *Not Like a Native Speaker: On Languaging as a Postcolonial Experience.* Columbia University Press, 2014.

———. *The Protestant Ethnic and the Spirit of Capitalism.* Columbia University Press, 2002.

———. "The Resistance of Theory; or, The Worth of Agony." In *Just Being Difficult? Academic Writing in the Public Arena*, edited by Jonathan Culler and Kevin Lamb, 95–105. Stanford University Press, 2003.

———. "Where Have All the Natives Gone?" In *Writing Diaspora: Tactics of Intervention in Contemporary Cultural Studies*, 27–54. Indiana University Press, 1993.

———. *Writing Diaspora: Tactics of Intervention in Contemporary Cultural Studies.* Indiana University Press, 1993.

Chuh, Kandice. *Imagine Otherwise: On Asian Americanist Critique.* Duke University Press, 2003.

Clifford, James. "Diasporas." *Cultural Anthropology* 9, no. 3 (1994): 302–338.

Connell, Liam. "E-Terror: Computer Viruses, Class and Transnationalism in *Transmission* and *One Night @ the Call Center.*" *Journal of Postcolonial Writing* 46, nos. 3–4 (2010): 279–290.

Connor, Steven. *Dumbstruck: A Cultural History of Ventriloquism.* Oxford University Press, 2000.

"A Conversation with Jhumpa Lahiri." www.york.cuny.edu/enrollment-mngmt-office/first-year-experience-fye/orientation-and-transition/freshman-reader

-program/the-namesake-spring-2012a/outcasts-united-synopsis; available from https://archive.ph/OZN8U.

Crosthwaite, Paul. *The Market Logics of Contemporary Fiction*. Cambridge University Press, 2019.

Culler, Jonathan, and Kevin Lamb, eds. *Just Being Difficult? Academic Writing in the Public Arena*. Stanford University Press, 2003.

Cyrus Says, episode 375, "Chetan Bhagat." May 20, 2019. Podcast.

———. episode 559, "Chetan Bhagat Returns." September 7, 2020. Podcast.

Da, Nan Z. "Other People's Books." *New Literary History* 51, no. 3 (2020): 475–500.

Dabashi, Hamid. *On Edward Said: Remembrance of Things Past*. Haymarket, 2020.

———. *Post-Orientalism: Knowledge and Power in Time of Terror*. Routledge, 2009.

Dabashi, Pardis. "Introduction to 'Cultures of Argument': The Loose Garments of Argument." *PMLA* 135, no. 5 (2020): 946–955.

Daiya, Kavita. "The World After Empire; or, Whither Postcoloniality." *PMLA* 132, no. 1 (2017): 149–155.

Dames, Nicholas. "A Profession! What Has Become of Literary Studies?" *The Nation*, February 21, 2023. www.thenation.com/article/culture/john-guillory-professing-criticism/.

Damrosch, David. *What Is World Literature?* Princeton University Press, 2003.

Das, Veena. *Textures of the Ordinary: Doing Anthropology After Wittgenstein*. Fordham University Press, 2020.

Davé, Shilpa. *Indian Accents: Brown Voice and Racial Performance in American Television and Film*. University of Illinois Press, 2013.

Davies, Helen. *Gender and Ventriloquism in Victorian and Neo-Victorian Fiction: Passionate Puppets*. Palgrave Macmillan, 2012.

Day, Iyko. "Lost in Transnation: Uncovering Asian Canada." *Amerasia* 33, no. 2 (2007): 68–86.

De Kosnik, Abigail. "Personal Theory: Humanities Scholarship in a New Media Moment." In *Digital Media: Technological and Social Challenges of the Interactive World*, edited by Megan A. Winget and William Aspray, 137–160. Scarecrow, 2011.

Deb, Siddhartha. "Sins of the Brothers." *New York Times*, September 27, 2013. www.nytimes.com/2013/09/29/books/review/jhumpa-lahiris-lowland.html.

Deer, Prakash, Gyan Prakash, and Ella Shohat. "Introduction to Edward Said: A Memorial Issue." *Social Text* 87, 24, no. 2 (2006): 1–9.

Denning, Michael. *Mechanic Accents: Dime Novels and Working-Class Culture in America*. Verso, 1998.

Derrida, Jacques. *Monolingualism of the Other: Or, The Prosthesis of Origin*. Stanford University Press, 1998.

Dhingra, Lavina, and Floyd Cheung. "Introduction." In *Naming Jhumpa Lahiri: Canons and Controversies*, edited by Lavina Dhingra and Floyd Cheung, xi–xxiv. Lexington, 2012.

Dimock, Wai Chee. "A Literary Scramble for Africa." *The Chronicle of Higher Education*, February 17, 2015. www.chronicle.com/blogs/conversation/a-literary-scramble-for-africa.

Divakaruni, Chitra Banerjee. *The Mistress of Spices*. Doubleday, 1997.

During, Simon. "Calcutta's Via Negativa." *Public Books*, August 6, 2013. www.publicbooks.org/calcuttas-via-negativa/.

Eagleton, Terry. "In the Gaudy Supermarket." *London Review of Books* 21, no. 10 (May 1999). www.lrb.co.uk/the-paper/v21/n10/terry-eagleton/in-the-gaudy-supermarket.

Eder, Richard. "A Life Like Old Postcards." *New York Times*, October 22, 2000. https://archive.nytimes.com/www.nytimes.com/books/00/10/22/reviews/001022.22ederlt.html.

Edmondson, Belinda. *Caribbean Middlebrow: Leisure Culture and the Middle Class*. Cornell University Press, 2009.

Elam, J. Daniel. "The Form of Global Anglophone Literature is Grenfell Tower." *Post45: Contemporaries*, February 22, 2019. https://post45.org/2019/02/the-form-of-global-anglophone-literature-is-grenfell-tower/.

———. *World Literature for the Wretched of the Earth: Anticolonial Aesthetics, Postcolonial Politics*. Fordham University Press, 2020.

Elam, J. Daniel, and Ragini Tharoor Srinivasan. "Introduction to 1990 at 30." *Post45: Contemporaries*, May 19, 2020. https://post45.org/2020/05/introduction-to-1990-at-30/#footnote_1_11678.

elhariry, yasser, and Rebecca Walkowitz. "The Postlingual Turn." *SubStance* 50, no. 1 (2021): 3–9.

Emre, Merve. "Has Academia Ruined Literary Criticism." *New Yorker*, January 16, 2023. www.newyorker.com/magazine/2023/01/23/has-academia-ruined-literary-criticism-professing-criticism-john-guillory.

English, James F. *The Economy Of Prestige: Prizes, Awards, and the Circulation of Cultural Value*. Harvard University Press, 2008.

Fan, Christopher T. *Asian American Fiction After 1965: Transnational Fantasies of Economic Mobility*. Columbia University Press, 2024.

Fanon, Frantz. *Black Skins, White Masks*. Translated by Richard Philcox. Grove, 1952, 2008.

Farred, Grant. *Martin Heidegger Saved My Life*. University of Minnesota Press, 2015.

Felski, Rita. "After Suspicion." *Profession* (2009): 28–35.

———. *The Limits of Critique*. University of Chicago Press, 2015.

Ferguson, Roderick. *The Reorder of Things: The University and its Pedagogies of Difference*. University of Minnesota Press, 2012.

Fischer, Molly. "Think Gender Is Performative? You Have Judith Butler to Thank for That." *The Cut*, June 13, 2016. www.thecut.com/2016/06/judith-butler-c-v-r.html.

Foucault, Michel. *This Is Not a Pipe*. Translated by James Harkness. University of California Press, 1982.

Freud, Sigmund. *The Interpretation of Dreams*. Macmillan, 1913, 1899.

Gajarawala, Toral. "Caste, Complicity, and the Contemporary." In *A History of the Indian Novel in English*, edited by Ulka Anjaria, 373–388. Cambridge University Press, 2015.

Gandhi, Aditya. "Lahiri's Metamorphoses." *Public Books*, June 18, 2024. www.publicbooks.org/lahiris-metamorphoses/.

Gandhi, Leela. *Postcolonial Theory: A Critical Introduction*. Columbia University Press, 1998.

Garcia Pena, Lorgia. *Community as Rebellion: A Syllabus for Surviving Academia as a Woman of Color*. Haymarket, 2022.

Garcia Pena, Lorgia (@lorgia_pena). Twitter, September 7, 2020, 2:19pm, https://twitter.com/lorgiapena/status/1303050341169197056?s=20.

Genette, Gerard. *Narrative Discourse: An Essay in Method*. Cornell University Press, 1980.

Ghosh, Ranjan. "Introduction to the Special Focus Section 'Creative Critical': To Be or Not to Be." *Minnesota Review* 99 (2022): 77–79.

Gill-Peterson, Jules. "Feeling Like a Bad Trans Object." *Post45: Contemporaries*, December 9, 2019. https://post45.org/2019/12/feeling-like-a-bad-trans-object/.

Giridharadas, Anand. *India Calling: An Intimate Portrait of a Nation's Remaking*. Henry Holt, 2011.

Gooptu, Nandini. "Introduction." In *Enterprise Culture in Neoliberal India: Studies in Youth, Class, Work and Media*, edited by Nandini Gooptu, 1–24. Routledge, 2013.

Graeber, David. *Bullshit Jobs: A Theory*. Simon and Schuster, 2018.

Green, Erica L. "When It Doesn't Help to Speak the Language: The Fulbright-Hays Fellowship." *New York Times*, March 15, 2023. www.nytimes.com/2023/03/15/us/politics/fulbright-fellowship-language-education-department.html.

Greenblatt, Stephen. "Racial Memory and Literary History." *PMLA* 116, no. 1 (January 2001): 48–63.

Greenlees, Donald. "An Investment Banker Finds Fame off the Books." *New York Times*, March 26, 2008. www.nytimes.com/2008/03/26/books/26bhagat.html.

Grewal, Inderpal. *Transnational America: Feminisms, Diasporas, Neoliberalisms*. Duke University Press, 2005.

Grimes, William. "Bharati Mukherjee, Writer of Immigrant Life, Dies at 76." *New York Times*, February 1, 2017. www.nytimes.com/2017/02/01/books/bharati-mukherjee-dead-author-jasmine.html.

Guillory, John. "Monuments and Documents: Panofsky on the Object of Study in the Humanities." *History of Humanities* 1, no. 1 (2016): 9–30.

———. "The Sokal Affair and the History of Criticism." *Critical Inquiry* 28, no. 2 (2002): 470–508.

———. "We Cannot All Be Edward Said." *The Chronicle of Higher Education*, February 13, 2023. www.chronicle.com/article/we-cannot-all-be-edward-said.

Gupta, Suman. "Indian 'Commercial Fiction' in English, the Publishing Industry and Youth Culture." *Economic and Political Weekly* (2012): 46–53.

Gurba, Myriam. "Pendeja, You Ain't Steinbeck: My Bronca with Fake-Ass Social Justice Literature." *Tropics of Meta*, December 12, 2019. https://tropicsofmeta.com/2019/12/12/pendeja-you-aint-steinbeck-my-bronca-with-fake-ass-social-justice-literature/.

Hadley, Tessa. "A Pulitzer Winner Gives Up Writing and Speaking in English." *Guardian*, January 30, 2016. www.theguardian.com/books/2016/jan/30/in-other-words-jhumpa-lahiri-review-learning-italian.

Hairong, Yan. "Position Without Identity: An Interview with Gayatri Chakravorty Spivak." *positions* 15, no. 2 (2007): 429–448.

Hajratwala, Minal. "On Being Discovered." *Color Lines*, 2006. www.thefreelibrary.com/On+being+discovered%3A+as+a+writer%2C+I+found+it+carries+risks.-a0155406203.

Hammad, Isabella. "Recognizing the Stranger." *Paris Review*, October 27, 2023. www.theparisreview.org/blog/2023/10/27/recognizing-the-stranger/.

Haraway, Donna. "Situated Knowledges: The Science Question in Feminism and the Privilege of Partial Perspective." *Feminist Studies* 14, no. 3 (1988): 575–599.

Harris, Elizabeth A. "Books on Race Filled Best-Seller Lists Last Year. Publishers Took Notice." *New York Times*, September 15, 2021. www.nytimes.com/2021/09/15/books/new-books-race-racism-antiracism.html.

———. "In Backlash to Racial Reckoning, Conservative Publishers See Gold." *New York Times*, August 15, 2021. www.nytimes.com/2021/08/15/books/race-antiracism-publishing.html.

Hartman, Stacy M., and Bianca C. Williams. "The Future of Doctoral Education: Four Provocations for a More Just and Sustainable Academy." *Los Angeles Review of Books*, May 29, 2023. https://lareviewofbooks.org/article/the-future-of-doctoral-education-four-provocations-for-a-more-just-and-sustainable-academy/.

Hawthorne, Fran. "After Her Pulitzer-Winning Debut, Jhumpa Lahiri's Latest Fiction Is a Bit of a Detour." *The National*, August 22, 2013. www.thenationalnews

.com/arts-culture/books/after-her-pulitzer-winning-debut-jhumpa-lahiri-s-latest-fiction-is-a-bit-of-a-detour-1.468647.

Hayot, Eric. *The Elements of Academic Style: Writing for the Humanities.* Columbia University Press, 2014.

———. "The Sky Is Falling." *Profession*, May 2018. https://profession.mla.org/the-sky-is-falling/.

Hefner, Brooks E. *The Word on the Streets: The American Language of Vernacular Modernism.* University of Virginia Press, 2017.

Heller, Nathan. "The End of the English Major." *New Yorker*, March 6, 2023. www.newyorker.com/magazine/2023/03/06/the-end-of-the-english-major.

Hu, Jane. "Orientalism, Redux." *Victorian Studies* 62, no. 3 (2020): 460–473.

Huggan, Graham. *The Postcolonial Exotic: Marketing the Margins.* Routledge, 2001.

Hungerford, Amy. *Making Literature Now.* Stanford University Press, 2016.

Ibish, Hussein. "Nationalism, Secularism, Postcoloniality: An Interview with Edward Said." *Cultural Dynamics* 14, no. 1 (2002): 97–105.

"I'm Not the Best Writer, but the Bestselling One: Chetan Bhagat." *Firstpost*, October 19, 2014. www.firstpost.com/living/im-not-the-best-writer-but-the-bestselling-one-chetan-bhagat-1763475.html.

"An Interview with Bharati Mukherjee by Geoff Hancock." In *Conversations with Bharati Mukherjee*, edited by Bradley C. Edwards, 10–24. University Press of Mississippi, 2009.

"Ira Trivedi: You Could Say I'd Want to Be the Next Jhumpa Lahiri." *Telegraph*, September 27, 2009. www.telegraphindia.com/7-days/you-could-say-i-d-want-to-be-the-next-jhumpa-lahiri/cid/590178.

Ishi, Douglas. "The Diversity Requirement; or, the Ambivalent Contingency of the Asian American Student Teacher." *American Literature* 94, no. 4 (December 2022): 733–761.

Jackson, Reginald. "Solidarity's Indiscipline: Regarding Miyoshi's Pedagogical Legacy." *boundary 2* 47, no. 3 (2019): 65–88.

Jacobus, Mary. *On Belonging and Not Belonging.* Princeton University Press, 2022.

Jagannathan, R. "Behind Pankaj Mishra's Rants: A Pathology of Hindu-Phobia and Self-Hate." *Firstpost*, October 26, 2014. www.firstpost.com/india/behind-pankaj-mishras-rants-a-pathology-of-hindu-phobia-and-self-hate-1772105.html.

Jameson, Fredric. Special Session on "The Political Unconscious—Forty Years On." *Modern Language Association Annual Convention* (2021). www.youtube.com/watch?v=tEq3GyDYmOk.

———. "Third-World Literature in the Era of Multinational Capitalism." *Social Text* 15 (1986): 65–88.

Jay, Martin. "The Academic Woman as Performance Artist." *Salmagundi* 98/99 (1993): 28–34.

"Jhumpa Lahiri: By the Book." *New York Times,* September 5, 2013. www.nytimes.com/2013/09/08/books/review/jhumpa-lahiri-by-the-book.html.

Johnson, Barbara. *The Critical Difference: Essays in the Contemporary Rhetoric of Reading.* Johns Hopkins University Press, 1980.

Joshi, Priya. *Bollywood's India: A Public Fantasy.* Columbia University Press, 2015.

———. "Chetan Bhagat: Remaking the Novel in India." In *A History of the Indian Novel in English,* edited by Ulka Anjaria, 310–323. Cambridge University Press, 2015.

Joudah, Fady. *[…]* (Milkweed Editions, 2024).

Kadue, Katie. "The End of the Star System." *Chronicle of Higher Education,* January 3, 2023. www.chronicle.com/article/the-end-of-the-star-system.

Kakutani, Michiko. "Liking America, but Longing for India." *New York Times,* August 6, 1999. www.nytimes.com/1999/08/06/books/books-of-the-times-liking-america-but-longing-for-india.html.

Kalliney, Peter. *The Commonwealth of Letters: British Literary Culture and the Emergence of Postcolonial Aesthetics.* Oxford University Press, 2013.

Kanafani, Ghassan. *Palestine's Children: Returning to Haifa and Other Stories.* Lynne Rienner, 2020.

Kang, Jay Caspian. "The Many Lives of Steven Yeun." *New York Times Magazine,* February 3, 2021. www.nytimes.com/2021/02/03/magazine/steven-yeun.html.

Kantor, Roanne L. "Futures Past: South Asian Literature 'Post-Boom.'" *Interventions* 20, no. 3 (2018): 345–353.

Kaplan, Alice. "On Language Memoir." In *Displacements: Cultural Identities in Question,* edited by Angelika Bammer, 59–70. Indiana University Press, 1994.

Kapoor, Ilan. "Spivak, Politics of Pronunciation, and the Search for a Just Democracy." *Al Jazeera,* June 7, 2024. www.aljazeera.com/opinions/2024/6/7/spivak-politics-of-pronunciation-and-the-search-for-a-just-democracy.

Karpf, Anne. *The Human Voice.* Bloomsbury, 2011.

Kaur, Ravinder. *Brand New Nation: Capitalist Dreams and Nationalist Designs in Twenty-First-Century India.* Stanford University Press, 2020.

Kaur, Ravinder, and Nayanika Mathur. *The People of India: New Indian Politics in the 21st Century.* Penguin Viking, 2022.

Kausar, Heena. "Chetan Bhagat's *Five Point Someone* in Delhi University English Literature Syllabus." *Hindustan Times,* April 25, 2017. www.hindustantimes.com/delhi/chetan-bhagat-s-five-point-someone-in-delhi-university-english-literature-syllabus/story-JVRGnIQX5C7oGkaLnfysIN.html.

Kezar, Adrianna, Tom DePaola, and Daniel T. Scott. *The Gig Academy: Mapping Labor in the Neoliberal University.* Johns Hopkins University Press, 2019.

Khalidi, Rashid. *The Hundred Years' War on Palestine: A History of Settler Colonialism and Resistance, 1917–2017.* Henry Holt, 2020.

Kingston, Maxine Hong. *The Woman Warrior: Memoirs of a Girlhood Among Ghosts.* Knopf, 1976.

Kofman, Ava. "Bruno Latour, the Post-Truth Philosopher, Mounts a Defense of Science." *New York Times,* October 25, 2018. www.nytimes.com/2018/10/25/magazine/bruno-latour-post-truth-philosopher-science.html.

Koshy, Susan. "The Fiction of Asian American Literature." *Yale Journal of Criticism* 9, no. 2 (1996): 315–346.

———. "Jasmine by Bharati Mukherjee." In *A Resource Guide to Asian American Literature,* edited by Sau-ling Cynthia Wong and Stephen H. Sumida, 121–129. Modern Language Association, 2001.

———. "Minority Cosmopolitanism." *PMLA* 126, no. 3 (2011): 592–609.

———. "Neoliberal Family Matters." *American Literary History* 25, no. 12 (2013): 344–380.

———. *Sexual Naturalization: Asian Americans and Miscegenation.* Stanford University Press, 2004.

Krapp, George P. *The English Language in America.* Modern Language Association of America, 1925.

Krishnamurthy, Mathangi. "Furtive Tongues: Language Politics in the Indian Call Centre." In *Chutnefying English: The Phenomenon of Hinglish,* edited by Rita Kothari and Rupert Snell, 82–97. Penguin, 2011.

Krishnan, Sanjay. "The Place of India in Postcolonial Studies: Chatterjee, Chakrabarty, Spivak." *New Literary History* 40, no. 2 (2009): 265–280.

Kumar, Amitava, ed. *The Humour and the Pity: Essays on V. S. Naipaul.* Buffalo, 2002.

———. *Passport Photos.* University of California Press, 2000.

Kureishi, Hanif. *The Buddha of Suburbia.* Penguin, 1990.

Lahiri, Bulan. "In Conversation: Speaking to Spivak." *The Hindu,* February 5, 2011. www.thehindu.com/books/In-Conversation-Speaking-to-Spivak/article15130635.ece.

Lahiri, Jhumpa. *The Clothing of Books.* Translated by Alberto Vourvoulias-Bush. Vintage, 2015.

———. *In Other Words.* Translated by Ann Goldstein. Penguin Random House, 2016.

———. *The Interpreter of Maladies.* Houghton Mifflin, 1999.

———. *The Namesake.* Houghton Mifflin, 2003.

———. *Roman Stories.* Translated by Jhumpa Lahiri and Todd Portnowitz. Knopf, 2023.

———. *Translating Myself and Others.* Princeton University Press, 2022.

———. *Whereabouts.* Alfred A. Knopf, 2021.

Lakshman, Abhinay. "JNU Student Did Not Identify Himself as Dalit: Gayatri Chakravorty Spivak on Row After Seminar." *The Hindu*, May 25, 2024. www.thehindu.com/news/national/gayatri-spivak-on-jnu-row/article68212572.ece.

Landry, Donna, and Gerald MacLean. "Introduction: Reading Spivak." In *The Spivak Reader: Selected Works of Gayatri Chakravorty Spivak*. Routledge, 1996.

Lanser, Susan Sniader. *Fictions of Authority: Women Writers and Narrative Voice*. Cornell University Press, 1992.

Larsen, Neil. *Determinations: Essays on Theory, Narrative and Nation in the Americas*. Verso, 2001.

Latifi, Ali M. "What South Asian Americans Lost When We Canceled Apu." *Zocalo Public Square*, June 8, 2022. www.zocalopublicsquare.org/2022/06/08/south-asian-americans-the-simpsons-apu/ideas/essay/.

Lavigilante, Natasha. "Globalization and Change in India: The Rise of an 'Indian Dream' in *Miss New India*: An Interview with Bharati Mukherjee." *MELUS: Multi-Ethnic Literature of the United States* 39, no. 3 (2014): 178–194.

Lawrence, Keith. "News Tip: Edward Said Set Intellectual Example, Duke Professor Says." *Duke Today*, September 26, 2003. https://today.duke.edu/2003/09/saidtip926.html.

Laymon, Kiese. *How to Slowly Kill Yourselves and Others in America*. Scribner, 2020.

Lee, Christopher. *The Semblance of Identity: Aesthetic Mediation in Asian American Literature*. Stanford University Press, 2012.

Lee, Li-Young. *The Winged Seed: A Remembrance*. Simon & Schuster, 1995.

Lennard, Natasha. "Columbia Task Force for Dealing with Campus Protests Declares That Anti-Zionism Is Antisemitism." *The Intercept*, June 17, 2024. https://theintercept.com/2024/06/17/israel-columbia-antisemitism-task-force-zionism/.

Leong, Nancy. *Identity Capitalists: The Powerful Insiders Who Exploit Diversity to Maintain Inequality*. Stanford University Press, 2021.

Liming, Sheila. "In Praise of Not Reading." *The Point*, April 4, 2017. https://thepointmag.com/criticism/in-praise-of-not-not-reading/.

Limón, Ada. "The Contract Says: We'd Like the Conversation to be Bilingual." In *The Carrying*. Milkweed, 2018.

Lippi-Green, Rosina. *English with an Accent: Language, Ideology, and Discrimination in the United States*. Routledge, 1997.

Loffreda, Beth, and Claudia Rankine. "Introduction." In *The Racial Imaginary: Writers on Race in the Life of the Mind*, edited by Claudia Rankine, Beth Loffreda, and Max King Cap. Fence, 2015.

Loofbourow, Lili, and Phillip Maciak. "Introduction: The Time of the Semipublic Intellectual." *PMLA* 130, no. 2 (2015): 439–445.

Love, Heather. "Close but Not Deep: Literary Ethics and the Descriptive Turn." *New Literary History* 41 (2010): 371–391.

———. "Truth and Consequences: On Paranoid Reading and Reparative Reading." *Criticism* 52, no. 2 (2010): 235–241.
Lye, Colleen. "Identity Politics, Criticism, and Self-Criticism." *South Atlantic Quarterly* 119, no. 4 (October 2020): 701–714.
———. "Reading for Asian American Literature." In *A Companion to American Literary Studies*, edited by Caroline F. Levander and Robert S. Levine, 483–499. Blackwell, 2011.
Macharia, Keguro. "Belated: Interruption." *GLQ: A Journal of Lesbian and Gay Studies* 26, no. 3 (2020): 561–573.
———. "On Quitting." *The New Inquiry* (September 19, 2018). https://thenewinquiry.com/on-quitting/.
Mahmood, Saba. *The Politics of Piety: The Islamic Revival and the Feminist Subject*. Princeton University Press, 2005.
Maini, Kartik. "Gayatri Chakravorty Spivak on the Art of Translation and Its Inextricable Relationship with Culture." *Firstpost*, March 1, 2018. www.firstpost.com/living/gayatri-chakravorty-spivak-on-the-art-of-translation-and-its-inextricable-relationship-with-culture-4370989.html.
Majumdar, Saikat. *The Amateur: Literary Self-Making and the Humanities in the Post-Colony*. Bloomsbury Academic, 2024.
———. "Dallying with Dailiness: Amit Chaudhuri's Flaneur Fictions." *Studies in the Novel* (2007): 448–464.
———. "How to Build a Creative Writing Programme as Part of Academic Courses at an Indian University." *Scroll.in*, September 6, 2020. https://scroll.in/article/972281/how-to-build-a-creative-writing-programme-as-part-of-academic-courses-at-an-indian-university.
———. "Introduction to Focus: Little India—the Provincial Life of Cosmopolitanism." *American Book Review* 36, no. 6 (September/October 2015): 3–4.
———. *Prose of the World: Modernism and the Banality of Empire*. Columbia University Press, 2013.
———. "What Does Untouchability Mean During India's Covid Crisis?" *Literary Hub*, May 21, 2021. https://lithub.com/what-does-untouchable-mean-during-indias-covid-crisis/.
Majumdar, Saikat, and Aarthi Vadde, eds. *The Critic as Amateur*. Bloomsbury Academic, 2019.
Manshel, Alexander. *Writing Backwards: Historical Fiction and the Contemporary Canon*. Columbia University Press, 2023.
Marcus, Sara. "Novels of Democratic Exhaustion." *American Literary History* 35, no. 1 (2023): 364–373.
———. *Political Disappointment: A Cultural History from Reconstruction to the AIDS Crisis*. Harvard University Press, 2023.

Marcus, Sharon. "How to Talk About Books You Have Read." *PMLA* 130, no. 2 (2015): 474–480.

Massad, Joseph. "The Intellectual Life of Edward Said." *Journal of Palestine Studies* 33, no. 3 (2004): 7–22.

Matthew, Patricia A., ed. *Written/Unwritten: Diversity and the Hidden Truths of Tenure*. University of North Carolina Press, 2016.

Maxey, Ruth. "Bharati Mukherjee and the Politics of the Anthology." *Cambridge Quarterly* 48, no. 1 (2019): 33–49.

———. *Understanding Bharati Mukherjee*. University of South Carolina Press, 2019.

McCrum, Robert. "Chetan Bhagat: The Paperback King of India." *The Observer*, January 23, 2010. www.theguardian.com/books/2010/jan/24/chetan-bhagat-robert-mccrum.

McEnany, Tom. "This American Voice: The Odd Timbre of a New Standard in Public Radio." In *The Oxford Handbook of Voice Studies*, edited by Nina Sun Eidsheim and Katherine Meizel. Oxford University Press, 2018.

McGurl, Mark. "The Program Era: Pluralisms of Postwar American Fiction." *Critical Inquiry* 32, no. 1 (2005): 102–129.

———. *The Program Era: Postwar Fiction and the Rise of Creative Writing*. Harvard University Press, 2009.

Mehta, Pratap Bhanu. "Suffocating Shadow Has Lifted, Balance Restored." *The Indian Express*, June 5, 2024. https://indianexpress.com/article/opinion/columns/2024-lok-sabha-election-results-narendra-modi-9371534/.

Mehta, Suketu. *Maximum City: Bombay Lost and Found*. Vintage, 2004.

Melamed, Jodi. *Represent and Destroy: Rationalizing Violence in the New Racial Capitalism*. University of Minnesota Press, 2011.

Miller, Andrew H. "Implicative Criticism, or The Display of Thinking." *New Literary History* 44, no. 3 (2013): 345–360.

Mirchandani, Kiran. *Phone Clones: Authenticity Work in the Transnational Service Economy*. Cornell University Press, 2012.

Mishra, Pankaj. "The Reorientations of Edward Said." *New Yorker*, April 26 and May 3, 2021. www.newyorker.com/magazine/2021/04/26/the-reorientations-of-edward-said.

Mitchell, W. J. T., and Homi Bhabha. "Translator Translated." *Artforum* 33 (1995): 80–83, 110, 113.

Mohanty, Chandra Talpade. "On Race and Voice: Challenges for Liberal Education in the 1990s." In *Between Borders: Pedagogy and the Politics of Cultural Studies*, edited by Henry A. Giroux and Peter McLaren, 145–166. Routledge, 1994.

Moi, Toril. *Revolution of the Ordinary: Literary Studies After Wittgenstein, Austin, and Cavell*. University of Chicago Press, 2017.

Moretti, Franco. "Conjectures on World Literature." *New Left Review* 1 (2000): 54–68.

Morris, Rosalind C., ed. *Can the Subaltern Speak? Reflections on the History of an Idea*. Columbia University Press, 2010.

Morton, Stephen. *Gayatri Spivak: Ethics, Subalternity and the Critique of Postcolonial Reason*. Polity, 2007.

Moser, Benjamin. "Jhumpa Lahiri Leaves Her Comfort Zone." *New York Times*, May 17, 2022. www.nytimes.com/2022/05/17/books/review/translating-myself-and-others-jhumpa-lahiri.html.

Mounk, Yascha. *The Identity Trap: A Story of Ideas and Power in Our Time*. Penguin, 2023.

Mufti, Aamir. *Forget English! Orientalisms and World Literature*. Harvard University Press, 2018.

Mukherjee, Bharati. "American Dreamer." *Mother Jones* 22, no. 1 (1997): 32–35.

——. "A Four-Hundred-Year-Old-Woman." In *Critical Fictions: The Politics of Imaginative Writing*, edited by Philomena Mariani, 33–38. Bay, 1991.

——. *Jasmine*. Grove, 1989.

——. *The Middleman, and Other Stories*. Grove, 1988.

——. *Miss New India*. Houghton Mifflin Harcourt, 2011.

——. "Preface." In *Darkness and Other Stories*, Penguin, 1985.

——. *The Tiger's Daughter*. Boston: Houghton Mifflin, 1971.

——. "Two Ways to Belong in America." *New York Times*, September 22, 1996.

Mukherjee, Meenakshi. "The Anxiety of Indianness: Our Novels in English." *Economic and Political Weekly* 28, no. 48 (November 27, 1993): 2607–2611.

Muthu, Bhimraj. "The Class and Caste Capital Behind Correct English: A Dalit Scholar Writes." *The News Minute*, May 24, 2024. www.thenewsminute.com/news/the-class-and-caste-capital-behind-correct-english-a-dalit-scholar-writes.

Nadiminti, Kalyan. "'A Betrayal of Everything': The Law of the Family in Jhumpa Lahiri's *The Lowland*." *Journal of Asian American Studies* 21, no. 2 (2018): 239–262.

——. "The Global Program Era: Contemporary International Fiction in the American Creative Economy." *Novel: A Forum on Fiction* 51, no. 3 (2018): 375–398.

Nadkarni, Asha. "The South Asian American Challenge." In *The Cambridge History of Asian American Literature*, edited by Rajini Srikanth and Min Hyoung Song, 355–370. Cambridge University Press, 2013.

Nair, Rukmini Bhaya. *Lying on the Postcolonial Couch: The Idea of Indifference*. University of Minnesota Press, 2002.

Napolin, Julie Beth. *The Fact of Resonance: Modernist Acoustics and Narrative Form*. Fordham University Press, 2020.

Nash, Jennifer. *Black Feminism Reimagined: After Intersectionality*. Duke University Press, 2019.

Newfield, Christopher J. "Research for All." *MLA Newsletter*, Spring 2022. https://president.mla.hcommons.org/2022/05/12/research-for-all/.

Ngũgĩ wa Thiong'o. *Decolonising the Mind: The Politics of Language in African Literature*. Heinemann, 1981.

Nguyen, Viet Thanh. "Dislocation Is My Location." *PMLA* 133, no. 2 (2018): 428–436.

Ninh, erin Khuê. "Gold-Digger: Reading the Marital and National Romance in Bharati Mukherjee's *Jasmine*." *MELUS* 38, no. 3 (2013): 146–159.

Nishikawa, Kinohi. "Merely Reading." *PMLA* 130, no. 3 (2015): 697–703.

Nussbaum, Martha. "The Professor of Parody." *New Republic*, February 22, 1999. https://newrepublic.com/article/150687/professor-parody.

O'Dair, Sharon. "Stars, Tenure, and the Death." In *Day Late, Dollar Short: The Next Generation and the New Academy*, edited by Peter C. Hermann, 45–62. SUNY Press, 2000.

Oe, Kenzaburo. "The Art of Fiction, No. 195." Interview by Sarah Fay. *The Paris Review* 183 (Winter 2007). www.theparisreview.org/interviews/5816/the-art-of-fiction-no-195-kenzaburo-oe.

O'Grady, Megan. "Jhumpa Lahiri in Rome: The Pulitzer Prize–Winner Talks About Her New Novel and New Ideas." *Vogue*, September 25, 2013.

Orsini, Francesca. "India in the Mirror of World Fiction." *New Left Review* 13 (2002): 75–88.

Ozeki, Ruth. "Foreword to John Okada's *No-No Boy*." University of Washington Press, 2014.

Palumbo-Liu, David. "Assumed Identities." *New Literary History* 31, no. 4 (2000): 765–780.

Pande, Mrinal. *The Other Country: Dispatches from the Mofussil*. Penguin, 2011.

Parikh, Crystal. "Being Well: The Right to Health in Asian American Literature." *Amerasia* 39, no. 1 (2013): 33–47.

Parks, Tim. "L'Avventura." *New York Review of Books*, March 24, 2016. www.nybooks.com/articles/2016/03/24/jhumpa-lahiri-lavventura/.

———. "Vaporous Shapes." *London Review of Books*, July 1, 2021. www.lrb.co.uk/the-paper/v43/n13/tim-parks/vaporous-shapes.

Paul, Pamela. "The Long Shadow of *American Dirt*." *New York Times*, January 26, 2023. www.nytimes.com/2023/01/26/opinion/american-dirt-book-publishing.html.

Pellas, Francesca. "'What Am I Trying to Leave Behind?' An Interview with Jhumpa Lahiri." *Literary Hub*, August 31, 2017. https://lithub.com/what-am-i-trying-to-leave-behind-an-interview-with-jhumpa-lahiri/.

Pellegrini, Ann. "Star Gazing." *minnesota review* 52, no. 1 (2001): 209–214.

Petersen, Anne Helen. "These Writers Are Launching a New Wave of Native American Literature." *BuzzFeed*, February 22, 2018. www.buzzfeednews.com/article/annehelenpetersen/dont-f-with-tommy-and-terese#.fxMyKAPBO.

Pettman, Dominic. *Sonic Intimacy: Voice, Species, Technics (Or, How to Listen to the World)*. Stanford University Press, 2017.

Poonam, Snigdha. *Dreamers: How Young Indians Are Changing the World*. Harvard University Press, 2018.

Raban, Jonathan. "Savage Boulevards, Easy Streets." *New York Times*, June 19, 1988. www.nytimes.com/1988/06/19/books/savage-boulevards-easy-streets.html.

Radhakrishnan, R. *Diasporic Mediations: Between Home and Location*. University of Minnesota Press, 1996.

———. "The Future of South Asian Studies." *South Asian Review* 38, no. 3 (2017): 25–31.

———. *A Said Dictionary*. Wiley-Blackwell, 2012.

Radway, Janice A. *Reading the Romance: Women, Patriarchy, and Popular Literature*. University of North Carolina Press, 1984, 1991.

Rahmani, Sina. "Review of Edward Said: The Last Interview, and Selves and Others: A Portrait of Edward Said, and the Battle of Algiers." *Comparative Studies of South Asia, Africa and the Middle East* 25, no. 2 (2005): 512–514.

Rai, Alok. *Hindi Nationalism*. Orient Longman, 2001.

Rajan, Tilottama. "On (Not) Being Postcolonial." *Postcolonial Text* 2, no. 1 (2006).

Ramesh, Randeep. "Author's Mass-Market Success Upsets Indian Literati." *Guardian*, October 8, 2008. www.theguardian.com/world/2008/oct/09/india.

Rana, Swati. *Race Characters: Ethnic Literature and the Figure of the American Dream*. University of North Carolina Press, 2020.

Rangan, Pooja, Akshya Saxena, Ragini Tharoor Srinivasan, and Pavitra Sundar. "Introduction: Thinking with an Accent." In *Thinking with an Accent: Toward a New Object, Method, and Practice*, 1–20. University of California Press, 2023.

———, eds. *Thinking with an Accent: Toward a New Object, Method, and Practice*. University of California Press, 2023.

Rangan, Pooja. "Auditing the Call Centre Voice: Accented Speech and Listening in Sonali Gulati's *Nalini by Day, Nancy by Night* (2005)." In *Vocal Projections*, edited by Annabelle Honess Roe and Maria Pramaggiore, 29–44. Bloomsbury Academic, 2019.

Rankine, Claudia. *Just Us: An American Conversation*. Graywolf, 2020.

Rao, Pallavi. "The Five-Point Indian: Caste, Masculinity, and English Language in the Paratexts of Chetan Bhagat." *Journal of Communication Inquiry* 42, no. 1 (2018): 91–113.

Ray, Raka, and Seemin Qayum. *Cultures of Servitude: Modernity, Domesticity, and Class in India*. Stanford University Press, 2009.

Ray, Sangeeta. *Gayatri Chakravorty Spivak: In Other Words*. Wiley-Blackwell, 2009.

——. "Imagining Otherwise: Comparative South Asian Literature and the MLA." *Comparative Literature Studies* 50, no. 2 (2013): 236–243.

Ray, Sohomjit. "Translation, Poetics of Instability, and the Postmonolingual Condition in Jhumpa Lahiri's *In Other Words*." *MFS: Modern Fiction Studies* 68, no. 3 (Fall 2022): 544–565.

"Read the Full Transcript of Indian Prime Minister Narendra Modi's Independence Day Speech." *Time*, August 15, 2017. https://time.com/4901564/narendra-modi-india-70-independence-day-speech/.

Reddy, Vanita. *Fashioning Diaspora*. Temple University Press, 2016.

Reitter, Paul, and Chad Wellmon. *Permanent Crisis: The Humanities in a Disenchanted Age*. University of Chicago Press, 2021.

Remnick, David. "The Defiance of Salman Rushdie." *New Yorker*, February 6 and 13, 2023. www.newyorker.com/magazine/2023/02/13/salman-rushdie-recovery-victory-city.

"Review: Roman Stories." *AudioFile*, October 2023. www.audiofilemagazine.com/reviews/read/239594/roman-stories-by-jhumpa-lahiri-todd-portnowitz-trans-read-by-deepti-gupta-carlotta-brentan/.

Reyes, Angela. "The Voicing of Asian American Figures." In *Raciolinguistics: How Language Shapes Our Ideas About Race*, edited by H. Samy Alim, John R. Rickford, and Arnetha F. Ball, 309–326. Oxford University Press, 2016.

Reyes, Victoria. *Academic Outsider: Stories of Exclusion and Hope*. Stanford University Press, 2022.

Riach, Graham. *An Analysis of Gayatri Chakravorty Spivak's "Can the Subaltern Speak?"* Routledge, 2017.

Roach, Rebecca, ed. "Contemporary Literature from the Classroom." *Post45: Contemporaries*, May 15, 2024. https://post45.org/sections/contemporaries-essays/contemporary-literature-from-the-classroom/.

Robbins, Bruce. *The Beneficiary*. Duke University Press, 2017.

——. "Celeb-Reliance: Intellectuals, Celebrity, and Upward Mobility." *Postmodern Culture* 9, no. 2 (1999).

——. *The Servant's Hand: English Fiction from Below*. Duke University Press, 1993.

Rody, Caroline. *The Interethnic Imagination: Roots and Passages in Contemporary Asian American Fiction*. Oxford University Press, 2009.

Rogers, Asha. *State Sponsored Literature: Britain and Cultural Diversity After 1945*. Oxford University Press, 2020.

Rosa, Jonathan. *Looking Like a Language, Sounding Like a Race: Raciolinguistic Ideologies and the Learning of Latinidad*. Oxford University Press, 2019.

Rose, Jacqueline, and Edward W. Said. "Returning to Ourselves." *Jewish Quarterly* (1997/1998): 5–11.

Roy, Arundhati. *The God of Small Things*. Random House, 1997.

——. *The Ministry of Utmost Happiness*. Penguin, 2017.

Rubin, Gayle. "The Traffic in Women: Notes on the 'Political Economy' of Sex." In *Toward an Anthropology of Women*, edited by Rayna R. Reiter. Monthly Review Press, 1975.

Rushdie, Salman. "Damme, This Is the Oriental Scene for You!" *New Yorker*, June 23 and 30, 1997, 50–61.

Sachare, Alex. "Spivak Named University Professor." *Columbia College Today* (May/June 2007). www.college.columbia.edu/cct_archive/may_jun07/quads3.html.

Sadana, Rashmi. *English Heart, Hindi Heartland: The Political Life of Literature in India*. University of California Press, 2012.

———. "Managing Hindi: How We Live Multilingually and What This Says About Our Language and Literature." *Caravan*, April 1, 2012, 62–71.

———. "Writing in English." In *The Cambridge Companion to Modern Indian Culture*, edited by Vasudha Dalmia and Rashmi Sadana, 124–141. Cambridge University Press, 2012.

Said, Edward W. *Culture and Imperialism*. Vintage, 1993.

———. "Identity, Authority, and Freedom: The Potentate and the Traveler." *boundary 2* 21, no. 3 (1994 [1991]): 1–18.

———. "Opponents, Audiences, Constituencies, and Community." *Critical Inquiry* 9, no. 1 (1982): 1–26.

———. *Orientalism*. Pantheon, 1978.

———. "Presidential Address 1999: Humanism and Heroism." *PMLA* 115, no. 3 (2000): 285–291.

———. *The Question of Palestine*. Vintage, 1979.

———. *Reflections on Exile and Other Essays*. Harvard University Press, 2000.

———. *Representations of the Intellectual*. Random House, 1994.

———. "Response to 'Edward Said's *Culture and Imperialism*: A Symposium.'" *Social Text* 40 (1994): 1–24.

———. "The Text, the World, the Critic." *Bulletin of the Midwest Modern Language Association* 8, no. 2 (1975): 1–23.

———. "A Window on the World." *Guardian*, August 1, 2003. www.theguardian.com/books/2003/aug/02/alqaida.highereducation.

Sanchez Prado, Ignacio. "Commodifying Mexico: On *American Dirt* and the Cultural Politics of a Manufactured Bestseller." *American Literary History* 33, no. 2 (2021): 371–393.

Sathian, Sanjena. "Good Immigrant Novels: Jhumpa Lahiri and the Aesthetics of Respectability." *The Drift*, May 6, 2021. www.thedriftmag.com/good-immigrant-novels/.

Saxena, Akshya. "South Asian Accents: *Bhashas*, Bodies, Borders." *South Asian Review* (2024): 1–8.

———. "Spoken Wor(l)ds: Anglophony, Poetry, Translation." *Wasafiri* 37, no. 3 (2022): 82–92.

———. "Stereo Accent: Reading, Writing, and Xenophilic Attunement." In *Thinking with an Accent: Toward a New Object, Method, and Practice*, 211-228. University of California Press, 2023.

———. *Vernacular English: Reading the Anglophone in Postcolonial India.* Princeton University Press, 2022.

Schama, Chloe. "23 Best Books to Read This Summer." *Vogue*, April 23, 2020. www.vogue.com/article/the-best-books-for-summer.

Schuessler, Jennifer. "What Is Literary Criticism For?" *New York Times*, February 3, 2023. www.nytimes.com/2023/02/03/arts/john-guillory-literary-criticism.html.

Serpell, Namwali. "The Banality of Empathy." *New York Review of Books*, March 2, 2019. www.nybooks.com/online/2019/03/02/the-banality-of-empathy/.

Seshagiri, Urmila. "Jhumpa Lahiri's Modernist Turn." *Public Books*, February 15, 2016. www.publicbooks.org/jhumpa-lahiris-modernist-turn/.

Shafak, Elif. *How to Stay Sane in an Age of Division*. Profile, 2020.

Sharma, Riya. "Chetan Bhagat—Too Trashy for DU Syllabus, or an 'Easy Read' for an Elective?" *Times of India*, April 25, 2017. https://timesofindia.indiatimes.com/city/delhi/chetan-bhagat-too-trashy-for-du-syllabus-or-an-easy-read-for-an-elective/articleshow/58347021.cms.

Sharpe, Jenny, and Gayatri Chakravorty Spivak. "A Conversation with Gayatri Chakravorty Spivak: Politics and the Imagination." *Signs: Journal of Women in Culture and Society* 28, no. 2 (2002): 609–624.

Shingavi, Snehal. "Capitalism, Caste, and Con-Games in Aravind Adiga's *The White Tiger*." *Postcolonial Text* 9, no. 3 (2014).

Shohat, Ella. "In Memory of Edward Said: The Bulletproof Intellectual." *University of Toronto Quarterly* 83, no. 1 (Winter 2014): 12–20.

Shollenberger, Jess. "'Ruthless Personalizers': Queer Theory and the Uses of the Personal." *M/m* 8, no. 1 (October 5, 2023), https://modernismmodernity.org/forums/posts/shollenberger-ruthless-personalizers-queer-theory-uses-personal.

Shukla, Anu. "Such Stuff as Amit Chaudhuri's Song Is Made On." In *The Novels of Amit Chaudhuri: An Exploration in the Alternative Tradition*, 98–115. Sarup and Sons, 2004.

Shukla, Sandhya. *India Abroad: Diasporic Cultures of Postwar America and England*. Princeton University Press, 2003.

Shumway, David R. "The Star System in Literary Studies." *PMLA* 112, no. 1 (1997): 85–100.

Silver, Nate. "Blaming the Media Is What Got Democrats Into This Mess." *Silver Bulletin*, July 8, 2024. www.natesilver.net/p/blaming-the-media-is-what-got-democrats.

Singh, Amritjit, Robin E. Field, and Samina Najmi, eds. *Critical Perspectives on Chitra Banerjee Divakaruni: Feminism and Diaspora*. Lexington, 2022.

Singh, Julietta. *Unthinking Mastery: Dehumanism and Decolonial Entanglements.* Duke University Press, 2017.

Sinha, Divashri. "Chetanic Verses." *Times of India,* January 1, 2012. http://timesofindia.indiatimes.com/life-style/books/features/Chetanic-Verses/articleshow/10539267.cms.

Sinykin, Dan. *Big Fiction: How Conglomeration Changed the Publishing Industry and American Literature.* Columbia University Press, 2023.

———. "White Voice." *nplusonemag.com* Issue 35 (Fall 2019). https://www.nplusonemag.com/issue-35/essays/white-voice/.

Skiveren, Tobias. "Postcritique and the Problem of the Lay Reader." *New Literary History* 53 (2022): 161–180.

Smith, Dinitia. "Creating a Stir Wherever She Goes." *New York Times,* February 9, 2002. www.nytimes.com/2002/02/09/arts/creating-a-stir-wherever-she-goes.html.

———. "When Ideas Get Lost in Bad Writing; Attacks on Scholars Include a Barbed Contest with 'Prizes.'" *New York Times,* February 27, 1999. www.nytimes.com/1999/02/27/arts/when-ideas-get-lost-bad-writing-attacks-scholars-include-barbed-contest-with.html.

Smith, Zadie. "Fascinated to Presume: In Defense of Fiction." *New York Review of Books,* October 24, 2019. www.nybooks.com/articles/2019/10/24/zadie-smith-in-defense-of-fiction/.

———. "Speaking in Tongues." *New York Review of Books,* February 26, 2009. www.nybooks.com/articles/2009/02/26/speaking-in-tongues-2/.

So, Richard Jean. *Redlining Culture: A Data History of Racial Inequality and Postwar Fiction.* Columbia University Press, 2020.

Song, Min Hyoung. *The Children of 1965: On Writing, and Not Writing, as an Asian American.* Duke University Press, 2013.

South Asian American Digital Archive. *Our Stories: An Introduction to South Asian America.* SAADA, 2021.

Spahr, Juliana. *Everybody's Autonomy: Connective Reading and Collective Identity.* University of Alabama Press, 2001.

Spivak, Gayatri Chakravorty. "Can the Subaltern Speak? [1999]." In *Can the Subaltern Speak? Reflections on the History of an Idea,* edited by Rosalind C. Morris. Columbia University Press, 2010.

———. *A Critique of Postcolonial Reason: Toward a History of the Vanishing Present.* Harvard University Press, 1999.

———. *Death of a Discipline: 20th Anniversary Edition.* Columbia University Press, 2023.

———. "French Feminism in an International Frame." *Yale French Studies* 62 (1981): 184–211.

———. *Outside in the Teaching Machine.* Routledge, 1993.

———. "The Rani of Sirmur: An Essay in Reading the Archives." *History and Theory* 24, no. 3 (1985): 247–272.

———. *Readings*. Seagull, 2014.

———. "Translating in a World of Languages." *Profession* (2010): 35–43.

Spivak, Gayatri Chakravorty, and Robert J. C. Young. "Neocolonialism and the Secret Agent of Knowledge." *Oxford Literary Review* 13, nos. 1/2 (1991): 220–251.

Srinivasan, Ragini Tharoor. "Call Center Agents and Expatriate Writers: Twin Subjects of New Indian Capital." *ARIEL: A Review of International English Literature* 49, no. 4 (2018): 77–107.

———. "'Can the Subaltern Speak' to My Students?" *Feminist Formations* 32, no. 1 (2020): 58–74.

———. "Introduction: South Asia from Postcolonial to World Anglophone." *Interventions* 20, no. 3 (2018): 309–316.

———. "Is There a Call Center Literature?" In *Thinking with an Accent: Toward a New Object, Method, and Practice*, 113–133. University of California Press, 2023.

———. "It's All Very Suggestive, but It Isn't Scholarship." In *The Critic as Amateur*, edited by Saikat Majumdar and Aarthi Vadde, 63–84. Bloomsbury, 2019.

———. "Lahiri, High and Low." *Public Books*, January 20, 2014. www.publicbooks.org/lahiri-high-and-low/.

———. "Memoir, Autofiction, and the New Indian Humanities." In *The Oxford Handbook of Modern Indian Literatures*, edited by Ulka Anjaria and Anjali Nerlekar, 257–272. Oxford University Press, 2024.

———. "South Asia." In *Handbook of Anglophone World Literatures*, edited by Stefan Helgesson, Birgit Neumann, and Gabriele Rippl, 471–488. DeGruyter, 2020.

———. "What Literature Does." *boundary 2 online*, October 2018. www.boundary2.org/2018/10/ragini-tharoor-srinivasan-what-literature-does-review-of-amit-chaudhuri-ed-literary-activism/.

St. Félix, Doreen. "Twisted Power of White Voice." *NewYorker.com*, August 13, 2018. www.newyorker.com/culture/cultural-comment/the-twisted-power-of-white-voice-in-sorry-to-bother-you-and-blackkklansman.

Stack, Micah. "The G.R.I.E.F." *Oxford American*, July 23, 2015. https://oxfordamerican.org/magazine/issue-89-summer-2015/the-g-r-i-e-f.

Stam, Robert, and Ella Shohat. "Whence and Whither Postcolonial Theory?" *New Literary History* 43, no. 2 (2012): 371–390.

Starosta, Anita. "Accented Criticism: Translation and Global Humanities." *boundary 2* 40, no. 3 (2013): 163–179.

Stoever, Jennifer Lynn. *The Sonic Color Line: Race and the Cultural Politics of Listening*. New York University Press, 2016.

Subramanian, Manasi. "Review of The Lowland." *Asian Review of Books*, September 8, 2013. http://asianreviewofbooks.com/content/archived-article/?articleID=1578.

Subramanian, Samanth. "India After English?" *New York Review of Books*, June 9, 2014. www.nybooks.com/online/2014/06/09/india-newspapers-after-english/.

Suman, Saket. "Chetan Bhagat's Inclusion in DU Syllabus Was Arbitrary: Stakeholders." *The Week*, September 25, 2017. www.theweek.in/news/india/chetan-bhagats-inclusion-in-du-syllabus-was-arbitrary-stakeholders.html.

Sundar, Pavitra. *Listening with a Feminist Ear: Soundwork in Bombay Cinema*. University of Michigan Press, 2023.

Táíwò, Olúfémi. *Elite Capture: How the Powerful Took Over Identity Politics*. Haymarket, 2022.

Taseer, Aatish. "How English Ruined Indian Literature." *New York Times*, March 19, 2015. www.nytimes.com/2015/03/22/opinion/sunday/how-english-ruined-indian-literature.html.

Taylor, Keeanga-Yamahtta. "The Defeat of Identity Politics." *New Yorker*, September 21, 2022. www.newyorker.com/books/under-review/the-defeat-of-identity-politics.

———. "The End of Black Politics." *New York Times*, June 13, 2020. www.nytimes.com/2020/06/13/opinion/sunday/black-politicians-george-floyd-protests.html.

Thompson, Lucas. "Method Reading." *New Literary History* 50 (2019): 293–321.

Tiwari, Bhavya. "The Multilingual Anglophone: World Literature and Post-Millennial Literature in Postcolonial India." *Interventions* 23, no. 4 (2021): 621–635.

Underwood, Ted. "A Genealogy of Distant Reading." *DHQ: Digital Humanities Quarterly* 11, no. 2 (2017).

Vara, Vauhini. "Jhumpa Lahiri and Me." *New York Times*, September 18, 2023. www.nytimes.com/2023/09/18/books/review/jhumpa-lahiri-and-me.html.

Varughese, E. Dawson. *Reading New India: Post-Millennial Indian Fiction in English*. London: Bloomsbury Academic, 2013.

Victor, Divya. *Semblance: Two Essays*. Sputnik and Fizzle, 2016.

Viego, Antonio. *Dead Subjects: Toward a Politics of Loss in Latino Studies*. Duke University Press, 2007.

Viswanathan, Gauri. *Masks of Conquest: Literary Study and British Rule in India*. Columbia University Press, 1989.

Walkowitz, Rebecca. *Born Translated: The Contemporary Novel in an Age of World Literature*. Columbia University Press, 2015.

———. "Less Than One Language: Typographic Multilingualism and Post-Anglophone Fiction." *SubStance* 50, no. 1 (2021): 95–115.

———. "On Not Knowing: Lahiri, Tawada, Ishiguro." *New Literary History* 51, no. 2 (2020): 323–346.

Warner, Michael. "Uncritical Reading." *Polemic* (2012): 13–38.

Warner, Tobias. *The Tongue-Tied Imagination: Decolonizing Literary Modernity in Senegal.* Fordham University Press, 2019.

Warren, Kenneth W. *What Was African American Literature?* Harvard University Press, 2011.

Watkins, Mel. *On the Real Side: A History of African American Comedy.* Lawrence Hill, 1999.

Wiegman, Robyn. "Feminism, Institutionalism, and the Idiom of Failure." *differences: A Journal of Feminist Cultural Studies* 11, no. 3 (1999/2000): 107–136.

———. "Loss, Hope: The University in Ruins, Again." *Feminist Studies* 48, no. 3 (2022): 616–637.

———. "Love and Repudiation in the Feminist Canon." *Feminist Formations* 32, no. 1 (2020): 1–14.

———. *Object Lessons.* Duke University Press, 2012.

Wiemann, Dirk. "Writing Home: Into the Interior with Amit Chaudhuri." In *Genres of Modernity: Contemporary Indian Novels in English*, 207–228. Rodopi, 2008.

Williams, Jeffrey J. "Name Recognition." *minnesota review* 52, no. 1 (2001): 185–208.

Yaeger, Patricia. "The End of Postcolonial Theory? A Roundtable with Sunil Agnani, Fernando Coronil, Gaurav Desai, Mamadou Diouf, Simon Gikandi, Susie Tharu, and Jennifer Wenzel." *PMLA* 122, no. 3 (2007): 633–651.

Yildiz, Yasemin. *Beyond the Mother Tongue: The Postmonolingual Condition.* Fordham University Press, 2012.

Young, Robert J. C. *Colonial Desire: Hybridity in Theory, Culture, and Race.* Routledge, 1995.

———. "The Dislocations of Cultural Translation." *PMLA* 132, no. 1 (2017): 186–197.

———. "Postcolonial Remains." *New Literary History* 43, no. 1 (2012): 19–42.

Yu, Timothy. *100 Chinese Silences.* Les Figues, 2016.

Zambra, Alejandro. *Not to Read.* Translated by Megan McDowell. Fitzcarraldo Editions, 2018.

Zuroski, Eugenia. "Holding Patterns: On Academic Knowledge and Labor." *Medium*, April 5, 2018. https://medium.com/@zugenia/holding-patterns-on-academic-knowledge-and-labor-3e5a6000ecbf.

———. "The Tree at the End of the World." *Post45: Contemporaries*, October 13, 2020. https://post45.org/2020/10/the-tree-at-the-end-of-the-world/.

Index

academe: "40-40-20" tenure-track positions, 34–35; "academostar," 32–33, 74, 79–80; adjunctification/casualization of, 35, 127–128, 177–178; Bhagat's relationship to, 99–100; "creative and critical," 163–164, 262n92; dominant culture of argument in, 144; funding cuts for language study, 92; job market/hiring, 8, 34–35, 74–75, 145, 231n28; PhD students pushed out of, 177; political whiteness in, 8–9; professionalism, 174–175, 177–178; research machine, teaching of, 33–36; "Southern Hemisphere languages" devalued in, 93–94; star system, 74–75, 77, 79–80, 121. *See also* humanities

accent: academic, 168; "acoustic" criticism, 25, 28, 53; "American accents," 30–31; aural-textual performance, 58; "bad writing" as, 122–123; "biography of migration," 27, 65; "coloring ear" and eye, 26; English, types of, 32; "eye dialect," 63, 65, 242n95; L1 and L2, 25, 62; "listening ear," 54–56, 65; "literary," 31; "mechanic accents," 103; neutral, 39, 69; as relational, 26–27; as sonic envelope, 27, 56; as "therapeutic," 19, 27

accented reading, 1, 11, 118, 121, 191, 209, 215; as metacritical and metalinguistic, 25, 28, 29, 107, 145; not reading as, 197; toward a method of, 22–29. *See also* reading/reading method; resistance

Achebe, Chinua, 112, 114

address, process of, 11–12

Adiga, Aravind, 90, 97, 260n38

African American literature, 45–50

Afternoon Raag (Chaudhuri), 137, 138, 149–150

Age of the World Target, The (Chow), 171

Akhtar, Ayad, 180, 185

Alexie, Sherman, 18, 20

Alim, H. Samy, 54
All About H. Hatterr (Desani), 112
allegory form, 144–146, 153, 192–193; allegoresis, 192
Alonso, Isabel Huacuja, 148
amateurism, 174–177; expert/amateur binary, 203–205; and semipublic writing, 175–177
Ambikaipaker, Mohan, 8
Ambudkar, Utkarsh, 61
American Comparative Literature Association, 71
American Dirt (Cummins), 24, 59, 60
American Fiction (Jefferson), 18
Anand, Mulk Raj, 112
Anderson, Benedict, 123
Aneesh, A., 69
Ang, Ien, 208–209
Anglophone literatures, non-Western, 1–4, 12, 14, 93; Against English, or, The Anglophone and Its Critics course, 85–89; burden of representation placed on, 104, 114, 159. *See also* Global Anglophone; Indian English literature
Anglophonism, colonial, 85–86
Anjaria, Ulka, 91, 96, 108–110, 143
Anthropocene discourse, 127
"antimiscegenation," 5
Anzaldúa, Gloria, 27
Appadurai, Arjun, 124
Area of Darkness, An: A Discovery of India (Naipaul), 185
Arpaio, Joe, 124
"articulate blackness," 54
artificial intelligence, 36, 125
Ashoka University (Sonipat, India), 164
Asian American literary studies, 2, 14–16, 22, 48. *See also* Indian English literature
Asian Century, 90

assimilation, 20, 28, 180; Americanization novels, 48; Mukherjee's, 43–44, 50, 68
audience/reader: Bhagat's, 107–108; hailing of, 13; identity-inflected reading, 16, 23–24; lay reader, 92–93; "method reading," 107–108, 110; production of through insider-outsider explanation, 54–55; reading "alongside the grain" and "with a loving eye," 110, 143; unintended addressees, 22–23, 28, 108, 110. *See also* accented reading; students
audio books, 213–214
authenticity, 26, 49, 198; "crudeness" as "credibility," 105; "cult of," 17, 148; "emotional violence" of demands for, 209; and reading of demotic non-Western Englishes, 103, 113, 116–117; "real" voice of India, 93
"autobiography," 24
Azaria, Hank, 56

"bad English," 31, 94, 101–102, 111
"bad writing": as accent, 122–123; bad reading required of, 110; "Bad Writing Contest," 121, 122; Bhabha, 32–33, 79, 120, 121, 130, 255–256n11; Bhagat, 95–96, 100, 102, 108–109, 121; Lahiri, 204; Spivak, 79, 121. *See also* writing
Baldwin, James, 54
Bandeh-Ahmadi, Hoda, 148
Banerjee, Sarnath, 97, 185
Bangalore, India, 66–70
Baraz, Yelena, 189
Basu, Manisha, 96
Battersby, Eileen, 198
Baugh, John, 54
Beatty, Paul, 18
Berlant, Lauren, 52

Bhabha, Homi K., 13, 74, 98, 119–130; as "bad writer," 32–33, 79, 120, 121, 130, 255–256n11; difficulty of writing as reflection of thought process, 122–123; and Hindu nationalism, 90–91, 106, 117; iconicity of, 32–33, 121, 246n25; optimism of, 123–124, 129; performative time and nation in writing of, 123–125; on Said, 171; Works: "DissemiNation," 120, 123–125; *The Location of Culture*, 120, 124; *Nation and Narration*, 120, 124–125; "Of Mimicry and Man: The Ambivalence of Colonial Discourse," 120, 121

Bhagat, Chetan, 13, 69, 84–118, 255n132; as Anglophone returnee to India, 31; as "anti-literary," 99–100, 103, 109; authorial persona, 100–101, 104–105; as "bad writer," 95–96, 100, 102, 108–109, 121; characters as stock New Indian types, 99–100; disavowals of, 31, 89; English of said to be "like Hindi," 91–94, 111, 113, 117; essays, 95, 104; fetishization of readership, 103–104; film adaptations of, 95, 96, 112; as foil for Chaudhuri, 154–155; frame stories, 100–101; iconicity of, 92, 131; India-based reviews of, 95–96; Indian audience of, 97–99; as India's "paperback king," 89–90; on not reading, 106–110, 117–118; on not teaching, 110–116; novels as primers for learning English, 99, 101–102; phenomenon of, 95–99; and postcolonial language debate, 115–116; privileged position of, 105–106; proximity in works of, 31–32; on reading, 99–106; scholarly attention to, 96–97; on teaching, 116–118; Works: *Five Point Someone: What Not to Do at IIT*, 89–90, 100, 111, 116; *Half Girlfriend*, 95, 101, 154; *One Arranged Murder*, 116; *One Indian Girl*, 101; *One Night @ the Call Center (ON@CC)*, 89–90, 96, 100, 101; *3 Idiots*, 95, 116; *The 3 Mistakes of My Life*, 100

Bharatiya Janata Party (BJP), 90, 95, 159, 216, 218
Black English, 54
Black Linguistics (Baugh), 54
Black Lives Matter protests, 49
Bloom, Harold, 106
Bollywood films, 95, 116
Borderlands/La Frontera (Anzaldúa), 27
Born Translated: The Contemporary Novel in an Age of World Literature (Walkowitz), 92
Bow, Leslie, 59
Bring Back Apu (Singh), 56–57
Broacha, Cyrus, 104–105
Brouillette, Sarah, 126
Brown, Stephanie, 38
Brown Romantics (Chander), 23
"brown voice," 56–57
Buddha of Suburbia, The (Kureishi), 209
burden of representation, 12; Bhagat's, 107, 117; placed on object, 22; resistance to, 17; for scholars, 1, 5; for students, 20–21, 218; for writers, 1, 5, 20–21, 159, 162, 215. See also interpellation; overdetermination
Butalia, Urvashi, 102
Butler, Judith, 72, 79, 121, 257n38
Buurma, Rachel Sagner, 36

Calcutta (Chaudhuri), 151–152, 158, 261n61
call centers, India, 66–70, 78; English of, 68–69, 99, 113

Cannon, Christopher, 205
canon formation, 2–3, 12, 170; "canon wars" of the 1980s and 1990s, 15, 48, 122, 129; critiques of, 32; and Mukherjee's project, 39, 53, 66; noncanonical objects and fields, 145; and not reading, 107; through teaching, 12, 38–39, 111–112, 114
"Can the Subaltern Speak?" (Spivak), 71, 73, 78, 243–244n5, 244–245n12
capitalism, 79, 147, 152; "identity capitalists," 8–9
Carr, David, 187
caste, 32, 76–77, 146, 260n35
Castillo, Elaine, 23
Ceci n'est pas une pipe (Magritte), 156
Centre for the Creative and the Critical (Ashoka University), 164
Chakravorty, Mrinalini, 18, 96
Chander, Manu Samriti, 23
Chandra, Vikram, 17, 103, 138
Chaudhuri, Amit, 11–13, 89, 131–165; allegory form transcended by, 144–146, 153; alternative imaginary of, 139, 144; autofictional writing, 24, 132, 137, 154–155; Bhagat as foil for, 154–155; "counter-manifesto" to the postcolonial in, 139; critiques of, 142, 162–163; disavowals of, 31, 132, 138, 154–156, 159; domestic servants represented by, 132, 146–153; dominant project produced by, 139–140; and four stages of literary production, 141; on Lahiri, 189; life of as resource for his fiction, 132, 138; "literary activism," 139; as modernist, 132, 139, 142, 144–145, 153, 154; ordinary, avowals of, 138, 143; as own critic, 140–146; presence and absence in, 156–157; return to India, 31, 156–161, 164–165, 258n3; Western writers engaged by, 141, 259n17; writing about writing, 162–164; Works: *Afternoon Raag*, 137, 138, 149–150; "Beyond Translation," 161; *Calcutta*, 151–152, 158, 261n61; *Finding the Raga: An Improvisation on Indian Music*, 137; *Freedom Song*, 137; *Friend of My Youth*, 137, 138, 140, 154–155, 164–165; *The Immortals*, 137, 154; *A New World*, 138, 150, 156–157, 160; *Odysseus Abroad*, 137; *The Origins of Dislike*, 137, 163, 187, 258n3; "Prelude to an Autobiography," 154; *Real Time*, 137; *Sojourn*, 137, 262n88; *A Strange and Sublime Address*, 137, 138, 141, 143–144, 149; *This Is Not Fusion*, 156; *The Vintage Book of Modern Indian Literature* (edited), 114, 139

"Chetan Bhagat and the New Provincialism" (Anjaria), 96
"Chetan Bhagat: Remaking the Novel in India" (Joshi), 96–97
Cheung, Floyd, 191
Chiang, Mark, 17
Chihaya, Sarah, 23
Children of 1965, The (Song), 24, 48
Chin, Frank, 17
China, 90
Cho, Margaret, 57
Choi, Susan, 48
Chow, Rey, x, 3–7, 209; "protesting ethnic subject," 3–4, 7, 46; reactionary gatekeeping anticipated by, 16–17; on "theoretical critical language," 73; Works: *The Age of the World Target*, 171; *The Protestant Ethnic and the Spirit of Capitalism*, ix, xiv, 5, 7; "Where have all the natives gone?," 209
civic hospitality, 205

clarity, accessibility conflated with, 122
Clifford, James, 193
coercive mimeticism, ix, 5–6, 8, 209, 217–218; and Lahiri's writing, 187, 202; and Mukherjee's writing, 31, 60, 66, 69; writers rewarded for rejecting, 18, 202
Coetzee, J. M., 155
colonialism, 44, 146, 201, 205, 271n113; education practices, xiii, 76, 112; English as colonial bequest, 112, 115, 206; settler-colonialism, 171–172
"coloring ear," 26–27
Columbia University, 171
comparative literature, 75, 81–82, 92, 113
contemporaneity, 112–113, 127; "collagist," 109–110
Contours of the Heart: South Asians Map North America, 52
"Contract Says, The: We'd Like the Conversation to Be Bilingual" (Limón), 18
"cosmopolitan" writers, 43–44, 59, 113, 192; anticosmopolitan stances, 98, 106
courses and syllabi, 30; Against English, or, The Anglophone and Its Critics, 85–89; English Literature with an Accent, 37, 39–42, 54–58; Literatures of Return, 133–137, 160–161, 216; The World and South Asia, 182–185, 216. *See also* teaching
COVID pandemic, xi, 34–35, 49, 175, 216
"creative and critical," 163–164, 262n92
"critical intimacy," 13
Critical Race Theory, attacks on, 28, 125, 218
criticism: "accented," 25; "acoustic" criticism, 25, 28, 53; "implicative," 130; "invested," 24–25; as literary genre, 164; sociality of, 29–33. *See also* literary criticism; postpostcolonial criticism; Theory
cultural appropriation, 58–59
culture wars of the 1980s and 1990s, 15, 48, 122, 129
Cummins, Jeanine, 24, 59, 60

Dabashi, Hamid, 32, 167, 245n12
Dabashi, Pardis, 144
Dainik Bhaskar (newspaper), 95
Daiya, Kavita, 124
Dalit Anglophone writers, 32
Dames, Nicholas, 126
Davidar, David, 105, 154
Davies, Helen, 60
defamiliarization, 21, 30, 54–55, 112
deference politics, 15
DEI, attacks on, 28, 125, 218
Deleuze, Gilles, 78, 82
Delhi University (DU), 111–112
Denning, Michael, 60, 103, 241n86
Derrida, Jacques, 73, 79
Desai, Kiran, 187
Desani, G. V., 112
Devi, Mahasweta, 82
Dhingra, Lavina, 191
"dialect," 54–55
dialect accommodation, 145
diaspora, 179–180, 191–193; Bhagat's relationship to, 102, 109; "biography of migration," 27, 65; Mukherjee's relationship to, 43–44, 49, 65, 69; reterritorialization of postcoloniality into ethnicity, 10, 210; subjects "found wanting," 208–209; in US academe, 2, 127, 132. *See also* return
Diaz, Hernan, 164
Dickens, Charles, 23
disappointment, political, 127–128

INDEX [305]

disavowals, 107; bad English as, 31, 94; Bhagat's, 31, 89; Chaudhuri's, 31, 132, 138, 154–156, 159; of identity, 155–156; Lahiri's, 31, 193; of literary Anglophonism, 31; Mukherjee's, 30–31, 38–39, 43–44; of the postcolonial, 132, 138; of public intellectuals, 174

Disgraced: A Play (Akhtar), 185

disidentification, 11–12, 17

"DissemiNation" (Bhabha), 120, 123–125

Divakaruni, Chitra Banerjee, 266–267n15

diversity politics, x, 4, 12, 231n28

"Diversity University" scenario, 8–9

Do I Sound Gay? (Thorpe), 56, 57

domestic servants (kaajer lok), 132, 146–153; dehumanization and depersonalization of, 149–151, 153; in realist novel, 151; as threat in New India, 159

domestic sphere, as political, 193–194

dominant ideologies, 25, 53, 68, 78, 103, 192; "difficult" writing as a mode of disrupting, 122; as white-authored narratives, 59

DuBois, W. E. B., 76

During, Simon, 152–153, 261n61

Eagleton, Terry, 79

Eggers, Dave, 59

Elam, J. Daniel, 119, 124

elhariry, yasser, 205–206

El-Rifae, Yasmin, 19

Emre, Merve, 126

English: as acousmatic sound, 212; "bad," 31, 94, 101–102, 111; of call centers, 68–69, 99, 113; changing status of in India, 101; as colonial bequest, 112, 115, 206; "global," 84, 91, 93, 115, 131, 206, 213; as imperial knowledge project, 82; "like Hindi," 91–94, 111, 113, 117; "postcolonial," 84, 94, 131, 201, 206; as psychically alienating, 85; readers manipulated via, 114; used by writers of caste, 32; use-value of, 85, 104; vernacularization of in India, 2, 93, 99, 113–115

English Heart, Hindi Heartland (Sadana), 96

English literature programs: as conservative, xii–xiii; English literary studies as identity studies, 13–22; expectations of "ethnic" academics, 3–7; identity studies as, 13–22; not theorized under identity studies, 14; "risk of enforced performativity" in, 4; subfields and periods, organization into, 2–3; teaching with an accent, 54–58; Theory enlisted by, 82; white academics, and "antimiscegenation" process, 5; work on minority archives hosted by, 82. *See also* academe; humanities; Indian English literature

Erasure (Everett), 18

"ethnicity, compulsory," 4–5

ethnic literatures, 2, 46–47, 53; reterritorialization of as American, 2–3, 10, 210. *See also* Indian English literature

ethnic-multiethnic distinction, 47

ethnic studies, 6, 48, 230n18

"ethnography of reading," 108

Everett, Percival, 18

exile, 168; "double perspective" of, 173–174

"eye dialect," 63, 65, 242n95

faculty and scholars of color: middle-class and upper-middle-class and caste, 146–147; as "native informants," 3–7; pushed out of areas of interest, 6–8, 230nn18, 24. *See also* scholar, overdetermined
"family photographs," 74–75, 139
Fanon, Frantz, 123, 208
Farred, Grant, 166
feminist theory, 11, 13, 53, 194
Five Point Someone: What Not to Do at IIT (Bhagat), 89–90, 100, 111, 116
Foreign Student, The (Choi), 48
Foucault, Michel, 78, 82, 156
Freud, Sigmund, 229n10
Friend of My Youth (Chaudhuri), 137, 138, 140, 154–155, 164–165

Gajarawala, Toral, 109
Gandhi, Aditya, 198
García Peña, Lorgia, 5
Ghosh, Amitav, 71, 89
Giridharadas, Anand, 147, 185
Global Anglophone, xi, xiv, 3, 32, 206; and New India, 92–93, 98–99, 101, 115; world literature, 92, 98, 113
"global," the, 84, 91, 93, 115, 131, 206. *See also* Indian English literature
God of Small Things, The (Roy), 114, 185
Graeber, David, 170
Great Derangement, The: Climate Change and the Unthinkable (Ghosh), 89
Greenblatt, Stephen, 4
Grewal, Inderpal, 53
"G.R.I.E.F, The" (Stack), 57–58
Guillory, John, 126, 141, 169
Gupta, Suman, 104

Half Girlfriend (Bhagat), 95, 101, 154
Hamid, Mohsin, 103
Hammad, Isabella, 19, 27

Harappa Files, The (Banerjee), 185
Harootunian, Harry, 171
Harris, Kamala, 216
Hartman, Stacy M., 229n9
Hayot, Eric, 165
Heffernan, Laura, 36
"Hell-Heaven" (Lahiri), 180–181, 193–194, 203
hermeneutic circle, 29, 30, 106
Himal Southasian, 182
Hindi language, 91–92, 101, 113–114, 248n7
Hindu nationalism, 90–91, 106, 117, 159
Hinglish-speaking milieu, 114–115
"How India Became America" (Kapur), 185
"How to Tame a Wild Tongue" (Anzaldúa), 27
Hu, Jane, 23
Huggan, Graham, 114
humanities: comparison to mathematics, 128; "crisis consensus," 120, 169, 175; devaluation of in United States, 16, 33, 81, 125, 127, 169; new critical methods needed, 35–36; "permanent crisis" of, 120; primary and secondary texts, 127–128; and semipublic writing, 175–177. *See also* academe
Hungerford, Amy, 106–107
Hurston, Zora Neale, 54–56

iconicity: academic star system, 32–33, 74–75, 77, 79–80, 121; as "adjectified," 33; anxieties produced by, 32–33; of Bhabha, 13, 32–33, 121; of Bhagat, 92, 131; of Lahiri, 187; positioning next to, 32; of Rushdie, 131, 187; of Said, 13, 32–33, 168; of Spivak, 13, 32–33, 243n3, 246n25. *See also* postcolonial studies identification, 26; and accent, 49; with characters or authors, 14, 23, 100; with disidentification, 17; neoliberal and national, 53; overidentification, 132; self-identification, 47; as suspect response, 14; as vehicle of critique, 21

identitarian issues, ix–x; anti-identitarian positions, 169, 190; correspondence of scholar-subject and literary-object, 1, 9, 16, 21; demands of texts and disciplines, 5; embodied in scholars of color, x, xiii, 3, 73, 201; identitarian/nonidentitarian binary, 200–203; imperative to *be*, 10–11; postidentitarian thinking, 10, 16, 19, 24, 205

identity: anchored in processes and relations, 9–10; "assumed," 20; and "autobiography," 24; call of, 8–9, 14, 18, 20–22, 29; hyphenated American, 44, 46, 53, 66, 245n15; "identity capitalism," 8, 9; "imposed," 20, 188; as methodological problem, 22–23; overdetermined scholar as best positioned to assess, 21–22; of postcolonial field, 201; post-identity turn, 14–15; resistance to, 11–12, 15, 17; rhetorical disavowal of, 155–156; singular voice as impossible, 49; of text, 28

identity politics: and Asian American literary studies, 14–15; "bad," 16, 21, 28–29; right-wing weaponization of, 15, 218–219, 229n9

identity studies: English literary studies as, 13–22; objects of, 13–14, 16, 22

Imagined Communities (Anderson), 123

Immigration and Nationality Act of 1965, xiii–xiv, 48

Immortals, The (Chaudhuri), 137, 154

"impersonation," 60–61, 70

India: call centers, 66–70; Chaudhuri's return to, 31, 156–161, 164–165, 258n3; Delhi University (DU), 111–112; Hindi language, 91–92, 101, 113–114, 248n7; Hindu nationalism, 90–91, 106, 117, 159, 216, 218–219, 248n5; market reforms, 143–144; Mukherjee's return to, 43, 66–70; Partition and Emergency, 115, 142; regional languages devalued in, 93–94; "sentimental attachments" to, 43–44; vernacularization of English in, 2, 93, 99, 113, 115. *See also* New India

India Abroad (Shukla), 179

India Calling: An Intimate Portrait of a Nation's Remaking (Giridharadas), 147

India Currents, ix–x, 179–180

Indian English literature: as always ethnic, postcolonial, or Anglophone, 1–2, 11–12; contemporaneity of, 112–113, 127; "expatriate," 44, 69; identities of, 2–3; "New India," 31, 248nn5, 7, 260n38; as object of study, 2, 11; reterritorialization of, 2–3, 10, 66–67, 210; taught to South Asian students, 181; zero-sum game of evaluating, 103. *See also* Anglophone literatures; English literature programs; South Asian studies; specific writers

Indian Institutes of Technology and Management (IIT and IIM), 89, 99–100, 105

informancy, native, 3–7, 78, 104, 218; as career, 19; hailing into, x, xiv, 2, 4–5, 13; protesting-proxy-native-informant, position of, 4, 9; and speaking subaltern, 78, 80; writers interpellated into by market, 18–19. *See also* interpellation

In Other Words (Lahiri), 26, 188, 198, 204, 210
In Other Worlds (Spivak), 79
"intercultural" fictions, 48–49
"interethnic" literature, 47, 48
Interior Chinatown (Yu), 18
interpellation, x, xiv, 1, 5, 186, 244n10; in English, 209; failure to outrun, 4, 8, 29; fugitivity of, 23–24; identitarian, 9, 22, 24, 104, 167; of "model minorities," 218; of Mukherjee, 66–70; resistance to, 9, 17, 80, 167; of writers into identity performances, 18–19, 192, 202. *See also* burden of representation; informancy, native; overdetermination
Interpreter of Maladies (Lahiri), 48, 186, 193, 202
Israel, 171–172
Italian language, 206, 271n113

Jaaware, Aniket, 22–23
Jameson, Fredric, 82, 121, 144, 166
Japanese American literature, 20
Jasmine (Mukherjee), 38, 51, 53, 67
"Jasmine" (Mukherjee), 38, 51–53, 63, 64
Jawaharlal Nehru University (JNU), 76–77, 79, 94
Jay, Martin, 77–80, 122
Jefferson, Cord, 18
Jha, Raj Kamal, 97
"Jhumpa Lahiri and Me" (Vara), 187
Johnson, Barbara, 28
Joshi, Priya, 96–97
journals, semipublic, 176
Joy Luck Club, The (Tan), 18, 21, 156

Kadue, Katie, 169
Kakutani, Michiko, 163
Kang, Jay Caspian, 18–19, 21, 27, 156

Kaplan, Alice, 188
Kapur, Akash, 185
Kaur, Ravinder, 113
Kindley, Evan, 126
Kingston, Maxine Hong, 17, 27, 48
knowledge: "native intelligence," 100, 104; nonknowledge, 101, 204–205; not knowing and unlearning, 29; Orientalist knowledge-power nexus, 168; situated, 13, 29, 122, 126
Kondabolu, Hari, 56–57, 61
Koshy, Susan, 53, 192, 205, 268n39
Krapp, George P., 242n95
Kripal, Jeffrey J., 125–126
Krishnan, Sanjay, 140
Kunzru, Hari, 103
Kureishi, Hanif, 209

Lahiri, Jhumpa, x, xiii, 13, 21, 156, 179–214, 266n6; "act one" and "act two" career trajectory of, 195–205; autobiographical, disavowal of, 198; "being Jhumpa Lahiri," 163, 187, 189–191, 211; Bengali language in childhood, 189, 196; Chaudhuri on, 189; critiques of, 187–190, 198–199; domestic and political in, 183–184; English/Italian binary, 196; expert/amateur binary, 203–205; fiction/nonfiction binary, 196–198; identitarian/nonidentitarian binary, 200–203; as immigrant, 48–49; immigrant/emigrant binary, 199–201; Italian, switch to, 20, 180, 188–189; Italian-language books, 188–189; on language learning, 199–200; metacritical self-assessment, turn to, 189–191; "overfamiliarity" of, 181, 191; "particular" and "universal" qualities, 192–193; possession/unpossession binary,

Lahiri, Jhumpa (*continued*)
206–208, 210; as post-Anglophone
writer, 31, 181, 190, 196, 207–208;
postcolonial, turn away from,
200–201; racial difference thematized
by, 193; realism/modernism binary,
195, 198–199; restrained style, 194; on
sounding like, 210–214; as translator,
189–190, 205, 210; and unskilling,
204; *Works:* "Hell-Heaven," 180–181,
193–194, 203; *Interpreter of Maladies*,
48, 186, 193, 202; *The Lowland*, x,
186, 188, 193–194, 203; "Mrs. Sen's,"
202; *The Namesake*, 180, 186, 191,
202; *In Other Words*, 26, 188, 198, 210;
Roman Stories, 189, 198, 205, 210–214;
Translating Myself and Others, 189,
205, 210; *Unaccustomed Earth*, 180,
186, 192–193; *Whereabouts*, 189, 197,
200–201, 211

language: "additional" languages, 206;
as political instrument, 54; regional,
minority, and nondominant, 212;
"unpossessing," 206–208, 210

language learning, as activism, 81–82

Larsen, Neil, 124–125

Laymon, Kiese, 18

Lee, Chang-rae, 48–49

Lee, Christopher, ix, 10, 14–15

Lee, Li-Young, 26

Leong, Nancy, 8

Liming, Sheila, 107

Limón, Ada, 18

"linguistic profiling," 54

Lippi-Green, Rosina, 37

listening: with "coloring ear," 26–27;
forensic, 39; "listening ear," 54–56, 65

"literary activism," 139

literary criticism: decline, discourse of,
126–127; postcritical turn, 31, 93,
106, 110, 143, 163, 169; public sphere
of, 154; through semipublic writing,
175–177; written by non-academics,
35–36

literary object: Bhagat as, 117;
Chaudhuri as, 145; constructed as
artifact of the real, 118; four stages of
production, 141; justice sought
through, 22; reader framed as, 23. *See
also* objects of study

literary objects, xiii, 2, 3, 9–10, 12, 16,
133, 141; correspondence of with
critical-subject, 21, 29, 164

Location of Culture, The (Bhabha), 120, 124

Loffreda, Beth, 24

Loofbourow, Lili, 175–176

"Loose Ends" (Mukherjee), 61–64

Lowland, The (Lahiri), x, 186, 188,
193–104, 203

Lye, Colleen, 9

Ma, Ling, 23

Macharia, Keguro, 7, 10

Maciak, Phillip, 175–176

Magritte, René, 156

Majumdar, Saikat, 142, 144, 145, 151

Marcus, Sara, 127–128, 176, 238n23

market, 204; interpellation of writers
into identity performances, 18–19,
192, 202; prestige cultures, 12, 163

mass culture debates of 1950s, 103, 108

Maxey, Ruth, 50, 52, 59

Maximum City (Mehta), 151

mazaa, 108, 142

McGurl, Mark, 59

"mechanic accents," 103

Mehta, Suketu, 151

Melamed, Jodi, 15, 238n19

"me-search," 4, 6, 21, 229n9

metacritical analysis, 25, 28, 29, 107,
189–190

Metamorphoses (Ovid), 189

"method reading," 107–108, 110, 204
Middleman and Other Stories, The (Mukherjee), 40, 50–54; American accent in, 64–68; New York as South Asian in, 51; as romance with America, 50–54; as ventriloquism, 58–64; *Stories:* "Fathering," 63–64; "Fighting for the Rebound," 59; "Jasmine," 38, 51–53, 63, 64; "Loose Ends," 61–64; "Orbiting," 51; "A Wife's Story," 51, 65
Midnight's Children (Rushdie), 112, 114, 139, 187
migration, 59, 65, 133; "biography of," 27, 65; "epic narrative" of immigration, 43; "expatriate" Indian English writing, 44, 69; "unhousement" and "rehousement," 68. *See also* diaspora; return
Miller, Andrew H., 130
Miss New India (Mukherjee), 43, 66–70
Mitchell, W. J. T., 122
Modern Family (television show), 57
modernism, 55; and Chaudhuri, 132, 139, 142, 144–145, 153, 154; Lahiri's realism/modernism binary, 195, 198–199
Modern Language Association convention, 6–7, 81
Modi, Narendra, 90–91, 95, 113, 216, 218–219
Moi, Toril, 122
monolingual paradigm, 81, 202, 205–208
Moser, Ben, 200–201
Mother Jones, 51
mother tongue, 202, 207–208; "Mother Tongue Influence," 69
Mukherjee, Bharati, 13, 37–70, 237–238n13; American accent of, 30–31, 64–66; and assimilationist values, 43–44, 50, 68; characters' voices, 53–54; course syllabus, 39–42; disavowals, 30–31, 38–39, 43–44; dominant ideologies reproduced by, 53; "epic narrative" of immigration in works of, 43; gendered and racialized dynamic in, 51–52; as immigrant, 44; as Indian American literary pioneer, 187; interpellation of by call center worker, 66–70; as multiethnic American, 47, 61, 66, 93; nationalism and liberal feminism of, 38, 53, 66; neoliberal, national identification of, 53; and New India, 66–67; as outmoded, 38–39; proximity in works of, 31–32; return to India, 43, 66–70; romance with America, 50–54; "romance with the American language," 50, 53, 60; as U.S. citizen, 31, 44, 50; and ventriloquism, 58–64; *Works: Jasmine*, 38, 51, 53, 63, 67; *Miss New India*, 43, 66–70; *The Tiger's Daughter*, 43. *See also The Middleman and Other Stories* (Mukherjee)
Mukherjee, Meenakshi, 43–44
multiculturalism, 4, 15–16, 20, 46, 81; and Lahiri's work, 188; and Mukherjee's work, 51, 64–65
"multiethnic" as term, 46–48
multiethnic literature, 30–31; as aural-textual performance of accents, 58; ethnic-multiethnic distinction, 47; how of, 49; "interethnic," 47, 48; "multiethnic" not a discipline, 46–47; "post-65," 48–49; "was" and "is" (past and present of), 45–50

Nadiminti, Kalyan, 192
Nadkarni, Asha, 192, 193–194, 268n54

Naipaul, V. S., 149, 180, 185
Namesake, The (Lahiri), 180, 186, 191, 202
Naming Jhumpa Lahiri (Dhingra and Cheung), 191
Napolin, Julie Beth, 20, 21; "acoustic" criticism, 25, 28, 53
Nash, Jennifer, x, xiii
national, logic of, 123–124
National Book Critics Circle Award, 50
Nation and Narration (Bhabha), 120, 124–125
"native intelligence," 100, 104
Nehru, Jawaharlal, 91
neoliberalism, x, 4, 146, 152, 193; entrepreneurial personhood, 100; inclusion, politics of, 8; neoliberal university, 74; New India, 31, 53, 90, 100
neutrality: ideology of, 77–79; neutral accent, 39, 69; rejection of, 24–25
New Criticism, 170
New India, x, 143, 248nn5, 7, 260n38; Anglophone diasporas rejected by, 91; and Bhagat, 90; discourse of weaponized by right, 159; and Global Anglophone, 92–93, 98–99, 101, 115; Mukherjee's engagement with, 66–70; neoliberalism in, 31, 53, 90, 100; as post-Anglophone, 91; as "postexotic," 113; social positions in, 99; two stories of, 159. *See also* India
New World, A (Chaudhuri), 138, 150, 156–157, 160
Ngũgĩ wa Thiong'o, 112, 207–208
Nguyen, Viet Thanh, 6–7, 23–24
Ninh, erin Khuê, 53
Nishikawa, Kinohi, 105
No-No Boy (Okada), 19, 20, 21
Nothing Ever Dies (Nguyen), 23–24

Obama, Barack, 49
Object Lessons (Wiegman), 14
objects of study, 13; identity objects, 14, 22; Indian English literature as, 2, 11. *See also* literary object
Oe, Kenzaburo, 167
Of Grammatology (Derrida), 73, 79
"Of Mimicry and Man: The Ambivalence of Colonial Discourse" (Bhabha), 120, 121
Okada, John, 18, 20, 21, 48
100 Chinese Silences (Yu), 17–18
One Indian Girl (Bhagat), 102
One Night @ the Call Center (ON@CC) (Bhagat), 89–90, 96, 100, 101
On Not Speaking Chinese (Ang), 208–209
opposition, relations of, 154–155
Orange, Tommy, 18–20
"ordinary" culture, 103, 108
Orientalism (Said), 74, 167, 171
Orientalist knowledge-power nexus, 168
Origins of Dislike, The (Chaudhuri), 137, 163, 187, 258n3
Orsini, Francesca, 139
Our Feet Walk the Sky: Women of the South Asian Diaspora, 52
overdetermination, 1, 4, 229n10; "accident-of-birth," 10, 15, 75, 244–245n12; dynamic circuit of, 11; expectations of "ethnic" academics, 3–7. *See also* burden of representation; interpellation; scholar, overdetermined
Ovid, 189
Oxford American, 57
Ozeki, Ruth, 18–20, 21

Pakistan, 180, 182, 213, 220
Palestine, 168, 171, 216
Palumbo-Liu, David, 20

Parikh, Crystal, 192
Parks, Tim, 198, 201
Pellegrini, Ann, 77–78
performance, 77–78
performativity, 27, 123–125; enforced, 4; of literature, 58; resistance to, 123
"personalization," movement of, 25
Philosophy and Literature, 121
Post45 (journal), 35; "1990 at 30," 119, 124
post-Anglophone, 13; desire for, 205–210; Lahiri's writing as, 31, 181, 190, 196, 207–208; New India as, 91; "postmonolingual" and "postlingual turns," 205
postcolonial, the: allegory form, 144–146; Anglophone as renomination of, xi; dominant conception of, 139–140; global turn from, 96; "postcolonial, political, and pieties (three p's)", 201
postcolonial studies, x, xiii; contemporaneity of, 127; iconicity of theorists, 13, 32, 246n25; identity of field, 201; Mukherjee's rejection of, 44; obligatory subversiveness of, 256n25; Palestine ignored by, 172; post-identity turn, ix, 15; renomination of, 127; Said on, 170–171; universality demanded of, 78. *See also* iconicity; post-postcolonial criticism; Theory
postcritical turn, 31, 93, 106, 110, 143, 163, 169. *See also* literary criticism
postcritique, 93, 204
"postlingual" turn, 205–206
"postmonolingual" turn, 205
post-postcolonial criticism: and Bhagat's writing, 94, 109–110, 112–113, 11531; and Chaudhuri's writing, 139–140, 143; and Lahiri's writing, 205–206, 208. *See also* postcolonial studies
postracial discourse, 49
Prado, Ignacio Sánchez, 24–25
"Prelude to an Autobiography" (Chaudhuri), 154
Premnath, Gautam, xiv
prestige culture, 12, 163
Problem with Apu, The (Kondabolu), 56–57, 61
Professing Criticism (Guillory), 126
Program Era, 12, 162, 163–164
The Protestant Ethnic and the Spirit of Capitalism (Chow), ix, xiv, 5, 7
protesting ethnics, 3–7, 9, 46
public intellectuals, 32–33, 167–168, 173; amateur, 173–174; and semipublic writing, 175–177

Qayum, Seemin, 148

Raban, Jonathan, 50, 53, 60
racism, 5, 48, 50, 211; capitalism linked with by Spivak, 79; causal, 23; institutionalized, 8; of national literatures, 206
Radhakrishnan, R., xiv, 15, 21, 172
Rai, Alok, 248n8
Rajan, Tilottama, xi, 4, 5, 10, 75
Rajmohan's Wife (Bankim), 96, 112
Ramesh, Randeep, 96
Rana, Swati, 18, 44
Rangan, Pooja, 26, 37
Rankine, Claudia, 24
Rao, Gorvika, 111
Rao, Raja, 112
Ray, Raka, 148
Ray, Sangeeta, 15, 71–72, 75, 227–228n10
Ray, Sohomjit, 207
reactionary gatekeeping, 16–18

reading/reading method: bad reading required of "bad writing," 38–39; close reading, 38–39; "method reading," 107–108, 110, 204; on not reading, 106–110, 117–118; willful misreadings of Theory, 125. *See also* accented reading; audience/reader

Reddy, Vanita, 187, 192, 193

Reluctant Fundamentalist, The (Hamid), 103

Renan, Ernest, 119

Representations of the Intellectual (Said), 170, 173

research machine, teaching of, 33–36

resistance: to conscription, 78; to identity, 11–12, 15, 17; to interpellation, 9, 17, 80, 167; minority capacity for, 124; to performativity, 123. *See also* accented reading

reterritorialization, 2–3, 10, 66–67, 210

return: competing reals of past and present, 157–158; from (linguistic) distance, 20; as ideological project, 160; impossibility of, 133, 168, 216, 221; to India, Chaudhuri's, 31, 156–161, 164–165; to India, Mukherjee's, 43, 66–70; Literatures of Return course, 133–137, 160–161, 216; as narrative form, 133; of texts to syllabi, 12, 121; and theorization of writing, 164–165. *See also* diaspora

Rhetoric of Hindu India, The (Basu), 96

"Right-Side-Up-Map of South Asia," 182

Roach, Rebecca, 239n31

Robbins, Bruce, 151, 152

Rody, Caroline, 47, 48, 50, 59, 60

Roman Stories (Lahiri), 189, 198, 205, 210–214

Rosa, Jonathan, 26

Roy, Arundhati, 103, 114, 186, 266n6

Rupa Publications, 98, 104

Rushdie, Salman, xiii, 84, 98, 103, 131, 251n54; chutnification of English, 38, 109, 114, 206; iconicity of, 131, 187; Works: *Midnight's Children*, 112, 114, 139, 187

Sachan, Nikhil, 116

Sadana, Rashmi, 96, 116, 248n8

Said, Edward, 13, 15, 74, 166–178; as Arab Palestinian, 168; contradictory position of, 170; death and memorials for, 166–167; and distinction between scholarship and politics, 172–175; as exile, 173–174; gender neglected by, 265n36; iconicity of, 32–33, 168, 246n25; MLA address, 177–178; partisanship attributed to, 169, 171; on postcolonial studies, 170–171; as public intellectual, 32–33, 167–168, 173; as "sacred," 166–167; as secular intellectual, 166, 168; Works: *Orientalism*, 74, 167, 171; *Representations of the Intellectual*, 170, 173

Sathian, Sanjena, 187, 198

Saxena, Akshya, xiii, 26, 37, 115, 212

scholar, overdetermined, 107, 161, 215; as best positioned to assess identity, 21–22; dialogue with other scholars, 145; distance from object compromised, 21; "historical positioning," 5; identity as disciplinary assignment, 10; miseducation of, 8–12; rejection of neutral position, 24–25; as subject, 1, 9, 16, 21; uncriticality expected of, 21–22, 80, 109–110; as "we," 102, 105–106. *See also* faculty and scholars of color

secondary discourse, 128–129, 257n38

self-hearing, 20, 207
self-reflexivity, 7, 9, 13, 114; of Bhagat's texts, 101, 104, 154; of Chaudhuri, 140–141, 152, 154; in Lahiri's work, 195, 196
Selisker, Scott, 37–38
Sellers, Peter, 56
Sellout, The (Beatty), 18
Semblance of Identity, The (Lee), 22
Sen, Amartya, 154
Serpell, Namwali, 152
Seshagiri, Urmila, 194, 198, 201, 205
Seth, Vikram, 105
Severance (Ma), 23
Shafak, Elif, 157
Shakespeare, William, 22–23
Sharpe, Jenny, 244n10
Shohat, Ella, 169
Shollenberger, Jess, 25
Shukla, Sandhya, 179
Simpsons "Apu debate," 56–57, 61
Singh, Aakash, 56–57
Singh, Manmohan, 91, 113
"slang," 54–55
Smith, Zadie, 58
Smitherman, Geneva, 54
So, Richard Jean, 141
sociological turn in literary studies, 12
Sojourn (Chaudhuri), 262n88
Sokal Affair, 122
Song, Min Hyoung, 23, 48, 192, 193
South Asia, pedagogy of in United States, 2; The World and South Asia course, 182–185, 216
South Asian studies, 2, 148. *See also* Indian English literature
Spahr, Juliana, 28
Spivak, Gayatri Chakravorty, 71–83, 221, 229n10, 245n15; as "academostar," 32–33, 74, 79–80, 121; accented self-presentation, 72–73; "accident-of-birth" facility claim, 10, 15, 75, 244–245n12; on authentication, 161; as "bad writer," 79, 121; as challenge, 80–83; "English accent" of, 75–76; hailing of, 74–75; iconicity of, 13, 32–33, 243n3, 246n25; identity game played by, 75–76; inaccessibility attributed to, 78–79; language learning as activism, 81–82; lecture hall as "a text," 77; on marginality, 45; native informant, concept of, 3–4, 7, 16; scholars hailed by "Spivak," 74–75, 80; on "structuralist imperative," 155; on "ventriloquism," 58–59; Works: "Can the Subaltern Speak?," 71, 73, 78, 243–244n5, 244–245n12; *In Other Worlds*, 79
Spivak Reader, The, 79
Sprinker, Michael, 124
Stack, Micah, 57–58
Standard American English, privileging of, 57
Starnone, Domenico, 189
Starosta, Anita, 25
star system, academic, 74–75, 121; "academostar," 32–33, 74, 79–80
Stoever, Jennifer Lynn, 54
"Story in Harlem Slang" (Hurston), 54–56
Strange and Sublime Address, A (Chaudhuri), 137, 138, 141, 143–144, 149
students, xi–xii; burden of representation taught to, 20–21; hailing of by course texts, 218; how not to read Bhagat, 117–118; resistance to conscription, 7; unschooling of, 117, 218. *See also* audience/reader; courses and syllabi; teaching

subaltern, 58–59, 78, 103, 123
Subramanian, Samanth, 91
Summertime (Coetzee), 155
Sundar, Pavitra, 26, 37

Táíwò, Olúfẹ́mi, 15
Tan, Amy, 18, 20, 21, 156
Taseer, Aatish, 103
Taylor, Keeanga-Yamahtta, 15
teaching, 33–34, 215–221; with an accent, 54–58; canon formation through, 12, 38–39, 111–112, 114; classroom as time machine, 48, 239n31; on not teaching Bhagat, 110–116; on teaching Bhagat, 116–118. *See also* courses and syllabi; students
Teaching Archive, The (Buurma and Heffernan), 36
temporalities, 123–124, 128, 133
Theory, 119–120; canon of, 74–75; caricature of, 125–126; "commitment to" in 1990, 120; enlisted by English literature, 82; failure to change the world, 125; paranoid response to, 79–80; and performance, 77–78; post-Theory era, 127; restaging of disruptive event of, 72–73; Said-Bhabha-Spivak as Holy Trinity of, xiv, 93, 120, 168; turn away from, 123; willful misreadings of, 125. *See also* criticism; postcolonial studies
There There (Orange), 19
Thinking with an Accent (Rangan, Saxena, Srinivasan, and Sundar), 26, 37
"Third World literature" debate, 144–145
"Third-World Literature in the Era of Multinational Capitalism" (Jameson), 144

This Is Not Fusion (Chaudhuri), 156
Thompson, Lucas, 107–108, 204
Thorpe, David, 56, 57
3 Idiots (Bhagat), 95, 116
3 Idiots (film), 95, 116
3 Mistakes of My Life, The (Bhagat), 100
Tiger's Daughter, The (Mukherjee), 43
Tomine, Adrian, 48
Translating Myself and Others (Lahiri), 189, 205, 210
Transmission (Kunzru), 103
Trinh T. Minh-ha, 59
Trump, Donald, 124
truth claims, 125–126, 173
Twitter, 32, 120, 162, 175

Unaccustomed Earth (Lahiri), 180, 186, 192–193
uncriticality, 21–22, 80, 109–110, 117–118, 218; postcolonial, 109–110; "ritual gestures" of, 109, 113
United States: "American" ideal of language, 38, 64–65; "American Voices" course, 37–38; devaluation of humanities in, 16, 33, 81, 125, 127; genocide in Gaza backed by, 171; hyphenated American identity, 44, 46, 53, 66, 245n15; as "object of desire," 50; reproductive family values, fantasy of, 193; "Southern Hemisphere languages" devalued in, 93–94; subcategories of the national, 2; "tyranny of the American dream," 51
"Unite the Right" (Charlottesville, Virginia), 124
University of Delhi, xiii
"unpossessing" language, 206–208, 210
UP 65 (Sachan), 116

Vara, Vauhini, 187
ventriloquism, 58–64, 241n83; of American voice, 31; "blackface" and "brownface" ("blackvoice" and "brownvoice"), 60; "impersonation" differentiated from, 60–61, 70; as a process of self-estrangement, 60; of speaking subaltern, 58–59; "white-authored narratives of Black life," 59; of white men by Mukherjee, 63–64. *See also* voice
Vergara, Sofia, 57
Vernacular English (Saxena), 115, 212
vernacularization of English in India, 2, 93, 99, 113–115
Victor, Divya, 278
Victorian studies, 23
Vintage Book of Modern Indian Literature, The (ed. Chaudhuri), 114, 139
Viswanathan, Gauri, 112
voice, 56; "black voice," 60; "brown voice," 56–57, 60; cybernetic voice of Siri, 39; "real" voice of India, 93; "white voice," 39, 54, 66, 208. *See also* ventriloquism
Voloshinov, Valentin, 241n86
Vourvoulias-Bush, Alberto, 189

Walkowitz, Rebecca, 92, 205–207
Wallace, David Foster, 106–107
Warner, Michael, 21
Warren, Kenneth, 45–50, 66
What Is the What (Eggers), 59
"What Was African American Literature?" (Warren), 45–50, 66

"When Deportation Is a Death Sentence" (Stillman)
Whereabouts (Lahiri), 189, 197, 200–201, 211
"Where have all the natives gone?" (Chow), 209
white academics, 8–9, 16–17; latitude given to, 6; and racism, 5, 7
white gaze, imperative of meeting, 19
whiteness, "skin tones" of, 63
White Tiger, The (Adiga), 90, 260n38
Wiegman, Robyn, 10, 14, 22
"Wife's Story, A" (Mukherjee), 51, 65
Williams, Bianca C., 229n9
Williams, Jeffrey J., 74
Williams, Raymond, 103
Woman Warrior, The (Kingston), 27
women's studies, 14
Wood, James, 163
world literature, 92, 98, 113. *See also* Global Anglophone
writers, burden of representation for, 1, 5, 20–21, 159, 162, 215
writing: "difficult," as mode of disrupting dominant ideologies, 122; as learning, 165; "method writing," 204; return and theorization of, 164–165; semipublic, 175–177. *See also* "bad writing"

Young, Robert J. C., 124
Yu, Charles, 18
Yu, Timothy, 17–18

Zambra, Alejandro, 106
Zuroski, Eugenia, 23, 24

GPSR Authorized Representative: Easy Access System Europe, Mustamäe tee 50, 10621 Tallinn, Estonia, gpsr.requests@easproject.com